Fighting for Liberty and Right

Fighting for Liberty and Right

THE CIVIL WAR DIARY OF
WILLIAM BLUFFTON MILLER,
FIRST SERGEANT, COMPANY K,
SEVENTY-FIFTH INDIANA
VOLUNTEER INFANTRY

EDITED BY
JEFFREY L. PATRICK
AND ROBERT J. WILLEY

Voices of the Civil War
Peter S. Carmichael, Series Editor

THE UNIVERSITY OF TENNESSEE PRESS / *Knoxville*

The Voices of the Civil War series makes available a variety of primary source materials that illuminate issues on the battlefield, the homefront, and the western front, as well as other aspects of this historic era. The series contextualizes the personal accounts within the framework of the latest scholarship and expands established knowledge by offering new perspectives, new materials, and new voices.

Unless otherwise noted, all photographs are from the private collection of Robert Willey.

An earlier version of chapter 10 appeared as "'We Have Surely Done a Big Work': The Diary of a Hoosier Soldier on Sherman's 'March to the Sea,'" *Indiana Magazine of History* 94 (Sept. 1998): 214–39, copyright 1998 by the Trustees of Indiana University. It is reproduced with permission of the *Indiana Magazine of History*.

This book is printed on acid-free paper.

LIBRARY OF CONGRESS CATALOGING-IN-PUBLICATION DATA

Miller, William Bluffton, 1839–1918.
    Fighting for liberty and right: the Civil War diary of William Bluffton Miller, first sergeant, Company K, Seventy-Fifth Indiana Volunteer Infantry / edited by Jeffrey L. Patrick and Robert J. Willey.—1st ed.
        p.   cm.—(Voices of the Civil War)
    Includes bibliographical references and index.
    ISBN 1-57233-329-4 (hardcover)
    1. Miller, William Bluffton, 1839–1918—Diaries. 2. United States. Army. Indiana Infantry Regiment, 75th (1861–1865) 3. Soldiers—Indiana—Diaries. 4. Indiana—History—Civil War, 1861–1865—Personal narratives. 5. United States—History—Civil War, 1861–1865—Personal narratives. 6. Indiana—History—Civil War, 1861–1865—Regimental histories. 7. United States—History—Civil War, 1861–1865—Regimental histories.
    I. Patrick, Jeffrey L., 1963– II. Willey, Robert J. III. Title. IV. Voices of the Civil War series.
E506.575th.M55   2004
973.7'472'092—dc22

                    2004022896

CONTENTS

FIGURES

MAPS

FOREWORD

William B. Miller of the Seventy-fifth Indiana Volunteer Infantry discovered how much the Civil War had changed him during an 1863 furlough to his native Bluffton, Indiana. His wife and family were probably the first to notice that he no longer resembled the naïve volunteer who had donned the Union blue in 1862. Miller had returned as a hardened veteran, and with this enhanced status came a great deal of attention both at home and in public. Friends and strangers peppered him with an array of questions about his experiences in the army. Miller responded with captivating stories filled with high drama and adventure, but he inevitably concluded his performances with a serious political statement about the meaning and purpose of the war. Many in the audience were shocked to hear a man who had been a longtime Democrat suddenly embrace the "radical" policies of the Republican Party and the Lincoln administration. Emancipation, conscription, and a hard war against the South were not only necessary measures, Miller argued, but also morally just. In a discussion about the Emancipation Proclamation, a friend asked "how I would like to have a Negro Sit on a Jury for me." Miller bluntly replied that he should "not object on account of color if the man was intelligent." Another man "derisively" shouted at Miller if he "would like to wait at the polls until a big 'Buck Nigger' voted before I could deposite my Ballott." The Hoosier soldier admitted that he did not "favor Negro suffrage but I would much rather wait on the blackest Nigger in America to vote as one of those 'Cannada Vetrians'" who fled the country in order to avoid the draft.

Miller must have been disappointed by his reception in Bluffton. He had looked forward to this furlough as a way to reconnect with his community and enjoy the simple pleasures of home and family. Instead he encountered a strange land filled with familiar people whose opinions resembled those of Confederates. "I find a number of friends who call themselves Democrats who entertain the Same views in regard to the war as the Johnies and they are proud to be called Rebels," a disgusted Miller wrote in his journal. There was a difference, he noted, between Northerners who sympathized with the Confederacy and Southerners who wore the gray: "The Rebs come out manfully and

Sacrifice their lives for their opinions and Show themselves to be men while those I find here only talk and have not got the courage to take sides openly."

Miller's estrangement from his hometown attests to his political radicalization from a conservative war Democrat into a staunch supporter of the Union and the antislavery cause. Many Civil War historians, most notably Gerald Linderman, have brilliantly described how the rank-and-file became alienated from civilians, largely because the latter never gave up their naïve view of war. Along the way, many veterans wondered why they were fighting when so many people back home seemed unsympathetic to the cause or to the plight of the individual soldier. A number of men bitterly denounced their loved ones for failing to understand the reality of army life, for forgetting that soldiers were dying horrible deaths while they enjoyed a comfortable, insulated existence. Not all soldiers, however, responded so negatively to civilian apathy or criticism. Northern dissent against the Lincoln administration actually inspired Miller to elevate the struggle for Union into a crusade for human liberty. His idealism might have been exceptional, as many did not view the Civil War as a morality play between North and South, but his wartime journals remind us that not all soldiers were cynical drones who fought solely because of an apolitical sense of duty to their comrades.

Fighting for Liberty and Right not only chronicles Miller's involvement in some of the most important military campaigns in the Western theater, including Chickamauga and the Atlanta campaign, but also uncovers the personal journey of a man who perceptively grasped that a limited war for Union had moved away from its old, conservative trajectory to a route that inescapably led to the end of human servitude. Only thoughtful people possess such a capacity for intellectual dexterity, and Miller managed to reconstruct himself during the war by critically examining his most basic assumptions about the world—many of them dear and treasured—particularly those ideas dealing with race. War, with all of its attendant horrors and unintended consequences, forced Miller to confront his personal history within the context of the nation's past and his own vision of the future.

The citizens of Bluffton, however, largely had escaped such a life-altering confrontation, which Miller must have realized by the time his furlough ended on December 1, 1863. Just before he headed to the depot for his return trip to the army, he "took a last look" at his old bedroom, wondering to himself if he would ever return to the room "I have occupied almost all my life." He then turned to his mother, and while kissing her farewell, she said, "Will I hate to see you go back again." Miller knew that his determination to stay in the ranks hurt the people he loved the most. The emotional turmoil of this decision, however, did not confuse him or cause self-doubt. He knew that personal sacrifices were necessary. Just one day before his departure, he explained to his diary why he could never give up his place in the ranks of the Seventy-fifth Indiana: "I am Sworn to Serve three years or during the war and I Shall go back to do my duty and Serve my time honorably and faithfully and if permitted to return I can enjoy my home and friends and not be afraid to look any man in the face and tell him I soldiered during the war of the Rebellion in the Union Army and for the Union one and inseperable and that Freedom might live to the Abolition of Slavery and all men regardless of collor may be free."

Peter S. Carmichael
UNIVERSITY OF NORTH CAROLINA
AT GREENSBORO

ACKNOWLEDGMENTS

The editors gratefully acknowledge the following institutions and individuals for their assistance in researching the story of William Bluffton Miller: William Henry Smith Library, Indiana Historical Society; Alan Nolan, Indianapolis; Wells County Public Library, Bluffton, Indiana; National Archives and Records Administration, Washington, D.C.; U.S. Army Military History Institute, Carlisle, Pennsylvania; Craig Dunn, Kokomo, Indiana; Genealogy Division, Indiana State Library; Charleston Public Library, Charleston, Illinois; Craig Leonard, president, and the board of directors, Wells County Historical Society, Bluffton, Indiana.

WILLIAM BLUFFTON MILLER:
A BIOGRAPHICAL SKETCH

Born on June 4, 1839, William Bluffton Miller was celebrated locally as the first white child born in the city of Bluffton, Wells County, Indiana. Although practically nothing is known about his early life, by the age of twenty-one he was living in a fairly affluent home with his father Michael, his mother Louisa, and two sisters. In 1860, Michael Miller, the sheriff of Wells County, claimed to own twenty-four hundred dollars worth of real estate and three hundred dollars in personal wealth. William Bluffton Miller worked with his father as a deputy sheriff but left the family home when he married Melissa Jeannette Karns on June 14, 1860.[1]

After the Confederate attack on Fort Sumter in April 1861, and President Abraham Lincoln's call for volunteers to crush the "rebellion" in the Southern states, Miller chose to remain at home and earn a living as a carpenter. Undoubtedly he felt a strong desire to begin life with his new wife, and he probably felt obligated to help contribute to the support of his parents and siblings. But in the summer of 1862, when Lincoln asked for additional troops to bolster the strength of the Union army, the patriotic William Miller decided to answer the nation's call. He left his wife and six-month-old son and enlisted for three years in Company K, Seventy-fifth Indiana Volunteer Infantry Regiment. The company was made up of many of his friends and acquaintances from the area, and they became, in Miller's words, "fully resolved to do our duty regardless of danger."[2] Miller was described in army records as being five feet ten and a half inches in height, with a fair complexion, blue eyes, and light-colored hair.

Both physical and mental pain visited Miller on many occasions during his army service. In the process of helping to save the Union, Miller, like countless other soldiers, suffered through long marches, gnawing hunger, and intense pain from wounds and disease. He experienced the horrific sights of the battlefield, loneliness, the thrill of victory, and the friendship and camaraderie of fellow soldiers. While far from home, unable to be comforted by his family, he learned of the death of both his mother and his infant son. He received a wound in both legs at the Battle of Chickamauga, Georgia, wounds that in many cases required amputation and discharge from the army. Miller, however, suffered on, spending long days and agonizing nights in hospitals, refusing to be discharged, longing to rejoin his regiment. He accepted an unwanted job as a clerk and a general's orderly during the Atlanta campaign because he could not march and was unable to serve with his company in the field. Finally, he recovered sufficiently to go back to his company, took part in Sherman's March to the Sea and the Carolinas campaign, then suffered further mental anguish when he learned of the death of President Abraham Lincoln by an assassin's bullet.

Miller was mustered out of the army in June 1865, having attained the rank of first sergeant, and returned home to Indiana. He spent the first four years after his discharge as a carpenter in Bluffton, then the remainder of his life as a druggist in Ossian, Anderson, Fort Wayne, and Marion, Indiana, and he fathered three children.[3] In 1915, Miller and his wife moved to Charleston, Illinois, to live with their daughter. He died from a sudden attack of apoplexy at 6:00 p.m. on May 29, 1918, while visiting his son in Fort Wayne, just a few days before his seventy-ninth birthday. His body was taken home to Bluffton, where the town's Grand Army of the Republic post held a memorial service. He was then buried beneath a modest, unassuming headstone in Mound Cemetery in Charleston, where the local newspaper mourned Miller as "a man of sterling worth and character."[4]

Just prior to his enlistment, William Bluffton Miller began keeping a diary in which he faithfully noted his observations, thoughts, and daily activities. He continued to maintain his journal until the end of the war, despite having to perform the often exhausting daily duties required of an enlisted soldier. Surprisingly, he also maintained an extensive personal correspondence with friends and relatives at home, but unfortunately none of these letters survive. By recording his thoughts in a private diary, Miller left behind an impressive record of one common soldier's view of the Civil War.

Like many fighting men on both sides, Miller freely expressed his opinion on a number of issues in the pages of his diary. An intensely patriotic soldier, he was anxious to see the rebellion continue until the Confederates were forced to surrender unconditionally. But Miller also respected his resourceful and hard-fighting foes and regretted making war on Southern women and children. On the other hand, he had little respect or tolerance for those Northern civilians who showed sympathy for the Rebel cause or did not fully support the Union war effort.

Although he initially subscribed to the racist views so pervasive at the time, Miller seemed to change his beliefs about black Americans during the course of his army service. By the end of the war, he was certain that with the death of slavery a great evil had been eradicated. He also acquired a new appreciation for African Americans, especially for the "colored" troops who labored with him to save the Union and make all men free.

When it came to his superiors, Miller believed that there were two distinct classes of officers. He made it clear that an arrogant commander who used his authority to abuse a subordinate was a poor leader and not worthy of respect. On one occasion he nearly came to blows with one of his own officers over just such an issue. On the other hand, Miller consistently praised personable, talented, and "fatherly" superiors, such as Gen. George H. Thomas and Gen. Absalom Baird.

In many ways Miller was a typical soldier in the Union army. He came from a farming background, served as an enlisted man in an infantry regiment (the largest branch of the service on either side), fought in several actions, and endured the usual hardships of soldiering until he was honorably discharged. But William Bluffton Miller was a determined chronicler of life in the Union army. He fastidiously recorded entries in his diary every day for three years and, unlike many soldiers, did not simply record weather conditions or make terse notations of the duties he performed. For the most part, Miller made a conscious effort to explain, in detail, his daily activities, feelings, and concerns and the people and events around him.

In addition, Miller participated in and wrote about some of the Civil War's bloodiest battles and most memorable campaigns, from Chickamauga to Atlanta to the March to the Sea, events that traditionally have received less attention from historians than the fighting in Virginia and Pennsylvania. He was badly wounded in one battle and wrote in detail about his recovery in hospitals and at home. Finally, Miller did not carry a musket in the ranks as an ordinary foot soldier for his entire service but performed several ancillary roles, including hospital steward, baggage guard, and orderly to a general officer.

Fortunately, Miller left behind two valuable legacies for future generations. The first was his diary, which enables us to glimpse the daily trials of an extraordinary soldier during many important events of the Civil War. The second was a reunited nation, the Union Miller held so dear.

EDITORIAL METHOD

Like many soldiers, William Bluffton Miller carried small pocket diaries with him during his Civil War service. At some point after the war, he copied those diaries into a large ledger book. Unfortunately, the original pocket diaries have been lost and only Miller's transcription survives. The consolidated diary, although undated, appears to be from the 1870s or 1880s. As he transcribed his work, it is likely that Miller made minor changes to his entries (see his July 25, 1862, entry, for example), but it does not appear that he made any significant alterations.

After Miller's death, the journal was passed to subsequent generations of the family. In the early 1980s, Miller descendant Irene Szink and her husband Robert gave both the journal and Miller's other Civil War memorabilia to collector Robert Willey. Regretfully, both Irene and Robert Szink are now deceased.

Miller's transcription appears here exactly as written. Spelling and punctuation have been retained from the original document, along with nonstandard capitalization. Brackets indicate words or letters that have been added by the editors. Brackets and a question mark [?] indicate unclear or unreadable words. Words originally underlined in the diary are italicized in the transcription. Due to the large number of lengthy entries, short portions of the diary dealing with mundane matters (primarily notations about writing and receiving letters and visits to friends and comrades) and redundant or repeated words have been omitted. Omitted sections are indicated by ellipses. The original diary is now in the possession of coeditor Robert J. Willey.

CHAPTER 1

A Full-fledged Soldier

By the summer of 1862, President Abraham Lincoln could claim only limited success in his efforts to crush the Confederate States of America and end the American Civil War. Despite significant victories west of the Appalachians at places like Fort Donelson, Pea Ridge, and Shiloh, Union forces had suffered serious losses. In Virginia, an ambitious Federal campaign led by Maj. Gen. George B. McClellan to capture the enemy capital of Richmond had failed. It soon became painfully obvious that Union victory was unlikely without additional manpower.

On July 2, President Lincoln called for three hundred thousand recruits to serve for three years. Five days later, Governor Oliver P. Morton of Indiana issued a proclamation asking every Hoosier man to "come to the rescue of his country." Morton assured his constituents that three hundred thousand soldiers would be "entirely adequate to the crushing out of the rebellion."[1] Building on an impressive patriotic response during the first year of the war, the citizens of Indiana rapidly recruited several new regiments under this call. One of these was the Seventy-fifth Indiana Volunteer Infantry.

Raised in the state's Eleventh Congressional District, the regiment was composed of ten companies from towns and rural areas in the north-central counties of Wabash, Tipton, Clinton, Howard, Hamilton, Huntington, Jay, Madison, Wells, and Blackford. Many of the officers and enlisted men who joined the regiment were already veterans of earlier service in the prewar Regulars or the wartime volunteer army. The majority "left comfortable homes and profitable professions, trades, and lines of business to volunteer their services to the country and flag," according to the regimental history.[2] Another historian noted that the unit was "composed of a very energetic, intelligent and upright class of young men, who went into the army from a pure sense of duty and feelings of patriotism."[3] One these "upright" recruits was William Bluffton Miller, who joined other enlistees from the counties of Wells and Blackford to form Company K.

Assembled at Wabash, Indiana, by August 10, the combined companies received orders a few days later to report to Indianapolis. During their short journey to the state capital, the new recruits were showered with cheers, tears, food, and mementoes given by enthusiastic civilians in the towns through which they passed.

Formally mustered into United States service at Camp Carrington in Indianapolis on August 19, these volunteers officially became the Seventy-fifth Indiana Infantry Regiment. They were issued Springfield rifles and soon had an opportunity to use them, not in battle or training, but in visits to the local photographers to preserve a first wartime image for the folks back home. Many of the new soldiers were seeing a large city for the first time, but they conducted themselves with dignity. One Indianapolis newspaper editor observed that the regiment contained no drunken men, created no uproar in camp, were guilty of no unbecoming conduct, and were courteous and gentlemanly toward civilians. Undoubtedly all the members of the regiment looked forward to an extended period of instruction at Camp Carrington. Unlike many Union recruits who spent weeks or even months in training camps located in "friendly" territory, however, the green Hoosiers of the Seventy-fifth found themselves called upon to leave Indiana immediately to face the enemy. Their training was to begin at the front.

POCKET DIARY.

Three Years or During the War of The Great Rebellion in the United States Kept by W B Miller a member of Company "K" 75th Regt Ind Vols of the Second Brigade Third Division 14th Army Corps

Friday July 25th 1862

To day I Enlisted in United States Service in Town of Bluffton Wells county Indiana in a company being raised by Captain S. R. Karns for three years or during the continuance of the war now rageing between what was known as the Southren or Slave holding States and the Northren or Free States. I was the Seventh name on the Roll and James W Spake and George Hurt enlisted at the same time. I was eating Breakfast when Spake came in and haveing made arrangements the day previus we went to Recruiting office and meeting Hurt on the way solicited him to join us. On returning home on my way to work I found my little famly and that of my Parents in tears and then realized what it was to leave them for the Seat of War. But it was then to[o] late to retrace my Steps if wanted to And being very anxious that the war should not close without doing something to assist in upholding our free Government a[nd] put down resistence to the Laws. I felt it not only honorable to wear the Garb of a Soldier but it was my duty to respond to the call of country and being classed with her defenders.[4] I never regreted in the Three years following that I had enlisted and I had the concelation to know that I did not make the move under excitement but weighed it all and counted the cost before makeing the Step. And I took what followed as a natural consequence and properly belonged to the life of a Soldier and I must bear the cross I had taken up.

Saturday July 26th

This day was Set apart for the Loyal people to hold a Grand War meeting to try to recruit our company to the full number of men required to fill it full. The meeting was held in the Court House in Bluffton and it was crouded to its utmost capacity. Speeches were made by Mr Banta and others and we made Severel additions to our Ranks.[5] . . .

Sunday July 27th

I did not attend Church to day but remained at home untill after dinner and then went out for a walk with Nettin & Rolla around Town.[6]

Monday July 28th

I put in the day soliciting men to join us and we Suceeded in obtaining severel good additions.[7] I tried to work in the Faning mill Shop but could not content my self and gave it up. It seamed that enlisting had taken all the Industry out of me and nothing will do but to get into camp as soon as possible.

Tuesday July 29th

I did not go to the shop to day. The war Fever is to[o] high and I put in the day recruiting and Success seams to "crown our effort" as we got severel to enroll their names. I spent the evening as I did the day and run around town untill about Eight Oclock and then went home.

Wednesday July 30th

I put in to day trying to get Recruits but there was not many in town and I did not get a man to enlist. I was up town untill about Eight Oclock and went home.[8]

Thursday July 31st

This morning I Started with Captain Karns for the country on a Recruiting Tour. We went to Rock Creek Township and was at Uncle Jacob Eversoles and from there to Markle in Huntington county and then to Batys School House in Union Township where there was a war meeting which was addressed by Judge E R Wilson and Dwight Klinck with others.[9] We enlisted only Three men. We went and Stayed all night at Joseph Beatys. The Roads a[re] Tereable bad and we drove Slow.

Friday August 1st

We left Mr Beaties early and we Stoped severel times on the road and at Murray we got one Recruit and then went on to Bluffton where we arrived about Sunset. . . .

Saturday August 2nd

. . . There was severel names added to the muster Roll and generally good men and those who will pass muster into the service.

August 3rd Sunday

This day I spent at home untill after dinner when Nettin and [I] went down to Aunt Affie Bulgers. We returned about dark.

Monday August 4th

This day I worked in the Shop all day. I was out in Town a while this evening. I Sold my Hogs to Ardy Barlow for Seven Dollars And made Some other Arrangements about leaveing home.[10]

Tuesday August 5th

I was in the Shop all day and rented the Stahl house to move into and made arrangements to move my Famly.[11]

Wednesday August 6th

I done some repairing to the House and did not go to the Shop to work.[12]

Thursday August 7th

We moved to day and I was buissy helping to fix up. . . . There was severel Recruits enrolled to day.

Friday August 8th

There was another war meeting to day. The Election of Officers for the Company was held to day. S R Karns was elected Captain & James Starbuck 1st Lieutenant and the contest for 2nd Lieutenant was warm. The Candidates were J V Kennagy Saml Buckmaster Uriah Todd and myself.[13] Haveing passed a resolution that a majority of the Company was required to elect after a number of Ballots it was resolved to postpone the election untill we went to Camp the Boys all went home for the last time as tomorrow we go to camp. . . . This I Suppose will be my last night at home for Some time.

SATURDAY AUG 9TH [WABASH, INDIANA]

This morning we left for "Camp Wabash." The Town was full of the friends of our Boys. We had one hundred and Eight men. We went in wagons to Huntington and thence by Rail Road. Many were the Sad Scenes of parting. Fathers Mothers Brothers Sisters and Husbands & Wives bidding farewell knowing that some of us will never return again. I bid my Wife and little Son Seven months old "good Bye" at home & did not see them any more. Addresses were deliverd by Severel men and responded to in our behalf by others and many were the tears Shed. We Stopped a[t] Markle where a Basket Dinner was prepard for us by the good and patriotic people of that village and vacinity. Some of the Ladies of Bluffton come here with us among them My Sister "Mollie."[14] We made it lively and had amusement on the road. Among other things a chase after a chicken which was captured and taken to camp. We got one Recruit at Markle James Ratcliff. We arrived at Camp about five Oclock and were put into "Seibly Tents" which are round and hold about Twenty men.[15] A heavy rain Storm came up and we had a wet night for an introduction to Camp life. We found Severel Companies in Camp and all others haveing been assigned positions we was made Company "K."

SUNDAY AUGUST 10TH

We were called out by "Revillie" to Roll Call and our Soldier life commences in reality. I was detailed for Camp Guard after visiting the Town of Wabash. We also had an election of Second Lieutenant and by some coniving and unfairness I was beaten by Uriah Todd who was declared elected. I was on Guard all night and it was a very rainy night. Rather a rough introduction I thought. This is the first Sunday in camp.

MONDAY AUG 11TH

Being relieved from Guard about 8 Oclock I went to my Company quarters and not being called for Drill I wrote my first Letter home and also a Letter to Sister Mollie. Nothing to do but cook and eat and I like the change to *"Hard Tack"* & ["]*Sow Belly.*"[16]

TUESDAY AUG 12TH

We were out at the usual hours for company Drill in accordance with Camp Regulations. I was over in town with some of the Boys. It is quite hilly around Wabash and plenty of Stone Sand & Gravell And our Camp is located on the west Side of the River on a hill. We have a nice camp and plenty of Good water supplied by numerous Springs within the Inclosure. A number of citizens come into camp to sell Apples and produce. The Boys make considerable noise and seem to enjoy themselves.

Wednesday Aug 13th

We were called out this morning by the usual way to "Wake up" Soldiers the "Revellie." I was appointed Second Corporal of my company which is not an office of very great responsibility and the same Salery of a "High Private in the rear rank." We had company Drill at the usual hours And also Officers Drill once.

Thursday Aug 14th

We drew our pants and I doned the uniform for the first time. We Also drew one Blanket a piece. Severel of our Boys went home on leave of absence. I Sent Mat Bassett a pipe by Jim Cutter but I concluded I did [not] want anothe[r] experience of parting from friends and famly and did not ask for a furlough but remained in Camp.

Friday Aug 15th

We drilled as usual with Officers drill in the morning. There was a rumor in Camp that we would leave for Indianapolis soon but no positive orders was given. I was in Camp all day.

Saturday Aug 16th

No drill to day it being Saturday. I was over to Town. I bought some flannel Shirts & Some Combs. I put in the most of the day in camp. I did not get any mail.

Monday Aug 18th ["17" in pencil in margin]
[Indianapolis, Indiana]

Although this is the Sabbath we were orderd to Strike Tents to move. We went to the Depot and took the Train via Peru changed car[s] at Peru and Thence by the Peru & Indianapolis Rail Road.[17] We left Wabash at one Oclock we passed Noblesville about 5 pm where we found the Good People out with their Baskets with provission to feed us. We Stoped about an hour and left there feeling that we were very thankfull for the kindness Shown us and we will long remmember with pleasure the nice reception at Noblesville. We Arrived at Indianapolis about one Oclock a.m. and quarterd in the Union Depot. It rained and we had good quarters in comparison to some others. We layed down on the floor and I Slept very well.

TUESDAY AUG 18TH ["MON 18" IN PENCIL IN MARGIN]

We moved out of the depot and marched west and went into Camp in rear or North of [the] Freight House. We put up our Tents and after pre-pareing Camp I went to See the 12th Regt who were under marching orders for Dixey. I met severel Boys in that Regiment I was acquainted with who were from Bluffton and Assian.[18] They left this afternoon on the Jeffersonville Rail Road.[19]

WEDNESDAY AUG 19TH ["TUES 19" IN PENCIL IN MARGIN]

We drew our Arms and Bal[lance] of Uniform and our Muster and pay Rolls were made out preparatory to being Musterd into United States Service and drawing one months pay and Twenty five Dollars Bounty. I can Say to day I am a full fledged Soldier Armed & equiped as the law directs and ready to march to Dixey. Severel of our Boys got a little to[o] much of the "Over Joyfull" and were very noisey and quarrelsom.[20]

THURSDAY AUG 20TH ["WED 20" IN PENCIL IN MARGIN]

To day we drew one months pay and Twenty five dollars Bounty and was musterd into the service for Three years or during the war by Col Carington U.S.A and I was in the city to the Post Office.[21] I Sent Nett Twenty two dollars and my clotheing by Express and wrote a letter home telling them we will leave here in a few days to meet the "Rebs." Our men seam to be anxious to push ahead for the purpose we enlisted. We dont know where we will be sent but await devellopments.

FRIDAY AUG 21ST ["THUR 21" IN PENCIL IN MARGIN]

Orders come to "Strike Tents" and get ready to move. We were marched to the Rail Road and got aboard of a Freight Train on Jeffersonville Road. I was detailed to go with our Company Baggage. We left

Indianapolis about 5 Oclock pm and did not reach Jeffersonvill untill daylight. At all the Towns along our line crouds of citizens were out to see us and bid us a gods Speed to cheer us on our way. Some threw flowers into our cars requesting a corespondence with us. Our Boys are in good cheer and although it is very Sad to See our own beloved State receeding from us and that every mile brings us nearer danger. But on we Speed fully resolved to do our duty regardless of danger.

CHAPTER 2

Kentucky

Confederate generals Braxton Bragg and Edmund Kirby Smith launched a joint invasion of Kentucky in the summer of 1862 in order to threaten Louisville and Cincinnati, recruit Kentuckians sympathetic to the Confederacy, and install a Confederate government in the state. In mid-August, Smith crossed the border, crushed the Union army at Richmond on August 30, and captured the state capital at Frankfort a few days later. In early September, Bragg likewise entered Kentucky, captured the Union garrison at Munfordville on September 17, and approached Louisville and the Ohio River. Union commanders rushed all available troops south to meet the threat, including several recently raised Indiana units. Only two days after being sworn into service, the men of the Seventy-fifth boarded a train for Louisville, where they went into camp on the southern outskirts of the city, prepared to face the advancing Rebels.

The new regiment did not have to wait long for field service. In order to help combat Confederate cavalry raids on Federal supply bases south of Louisville, William Miller and his comrades were sent from Louisville on August 25 to occupy the town of Lebanon and join Brig. Gen. Ebenezer Dumont's Twelfth Division of the Army of the Ohio. Although they eagerly anticipated combat, an opportunity for glory eluded the Hoosiers. Instead, they "were drilled often, guard and picket duty was daily performed, and frequent 'scares' occurred," according to Sgt. David B. Floyd, the regimental historian.[1] Ordered to fall back rapidly to Louisville, the Seventy-fifth served as the rear guard of the Twelfth Division and arrived safely back in the city on September 23. "Though we were not actually attacked," wrote Floyd, "the discipline taught us to be on the alert at all times, and, doubtless enabled us to prevent capture on more occasions than this one."[2] Although disappointed at not having "seen the elephant" (the Civil War euphemism for experiencing battle), the recruits were given valuable time to learn the rudiments of drill and discipline before facing the foe.

The first serious trial for the regiment came a few days later, when they were ordered to march back south toward Elizabethtown in order to escort an army wagon train to Louisville. Though only an eighteen-mile trek, the untried men of the Seventy-fifth were weighed down with unnecessary equipment and plagued by a warm sun and a scarcity of drinking water. Despite the hardships, they successfully returned with the two thousand supply wagons.

Don Carlos Buell, commanding general of the Army of the Ohio, faced a critical command decision by early October 1862. Fortunately for the Union cause, he had secured Louisville, but the Confederate armies of Bragg and Smith were poised near the city, separated but within supporting distance. Buell decided that he would move the majority of his army to face Bragg, but he also sent two divisions to operate against Smith's force and prevent the Rebel armies from uniting. Buell met Bragg on October 8 at the Battle of Perryville, and after a vicious fight, the Confederates withdrew. The Seventy-fifth missed the chance to see action at Perryville, as Dumont's Twelfth Division was directed to move against Smith. Dumont's men drove toward Frankfort and entered the city on October 10, but Smith withdrew without fighting a major battle. The Hoosiers pursued the retreating Confederates for several miles beyond Frankfort, skirmishing and taking some prisoners, then returned to the capital. Bragg joined Smith and marched out of Kentucky and back to Tennessee. The Confederate threat to Kentucky was over, due in part to the efforts of the two-month-old soldiers of the Seventy-fifth Indiana.

Even though the regiment had performed well in its initial test, the behavior of some Union troops tarnished the success. During their stay in Frankfort, the raw and relatively undisciplined volunteers, now in "enemy" territory, saw fit to commit some depredations on the civilian population. In fact, General

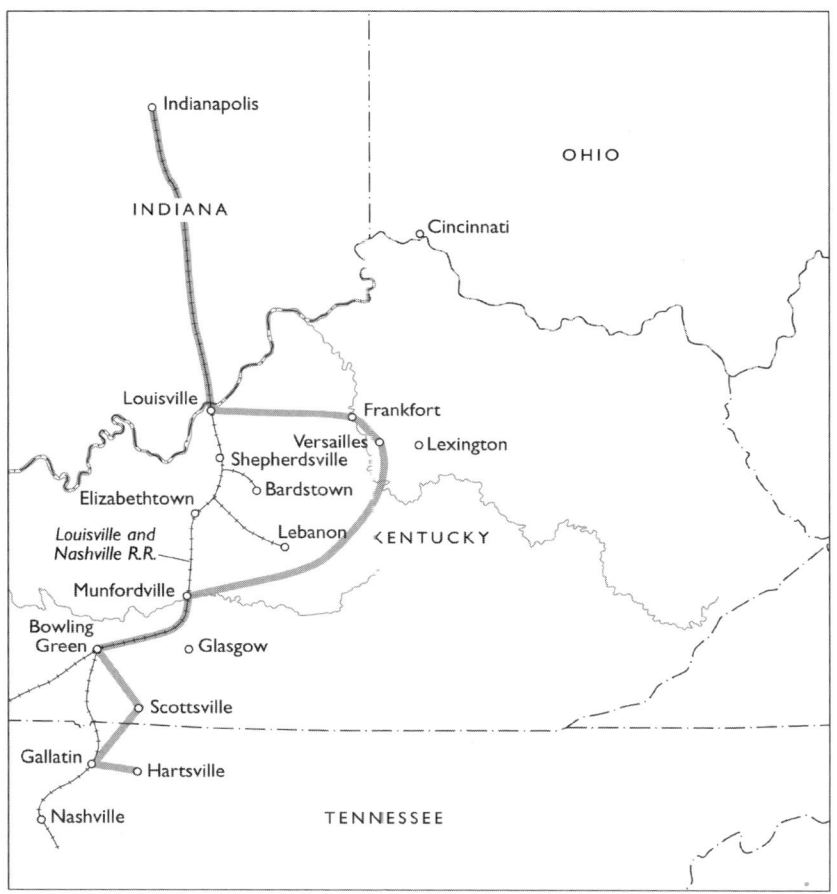

MAP 1. Travels of William Bluffton Miller in Kentucky and Tennessee, 1862.

Dumont was forced to arrest and confine one of his brigade commanders for stealing fine horses and shipping them north. The division commander admitted that lapses in discipline did occur and required punishment, although some crimes were undoubtedly exaggerated.

Any further opportunities for such pillaging were to be severely limited. Following Perryville, Buell did not closely pursue the Confederates, and he was replaced on October 30 by Maj.

Gen. William Starke Rosecrans as commander of the Army of the Ohio (soon renamed the Army of the Cumberland). The new commanding general lost no time in composing a general order to be read before his army, in which he stressed that officers guilty of drunkenness, theft, or misbehavior before the enemy would be dismissed. He exhorted both officers and enlisted men "to aid him in bringing [the army] to a state of discipline at least equal to that of the rebels" and stated that he was determined to exercise his authority to deal with those who would undermine the effectiveness of the army.[3]

In late October, orders came moving the Seventy-fifth to Bowling Green and, after a few days, Scottsville. No event of any great importance occurred in either location, except for the notable arrival of Col. Milton S. Robinson, the regiment's new commanding officer. Although John Pettit had been appointed colonel of the unit back in Indiana, he had opted to remain at home due to feeble health and soon resigned his commission. Instead, Lt. Col. William O'Brien had actually commanded the regiment in the field. Colonel Robinson, who had prior experience in the Forty-seventh Indiana Infantry, was destined to lead the Hoosiers through several difficult campaigns before resigning in 1864. Although he proved to be popular with the men, his appointment stirred conflicting feelings. Years after the war, the unit historian believed that "the officers and enlisted men of the Regiment extended to him many expressions of good will, confidence and affection" when he took command. But another soldier described the opposite reaction, noting the regiment's "fiery indignation" and bitterness at the "outrage" of Robinson's appointment over Lieutenant Colonel O'Brien.[4] One soldier even claimed that all the commissioned officers signed a petition urging O'Brien's appointment and sent it to Indiana governor Oliver Morton, to no avail.[5]

SATURDAY AUG 22ND ["FRI 22" IN PENCIL IN MARGIN]
[LOUISVILLE, KENTUCKY]

We crossed the beautifull Ohio river after daylight on a Ferry Boat. We loaded our Baggage on Government wagons. Our Regiment numbers Ten Hundred and Twenty five men Rank & file. We took up our line of march for Camp Oakland about 5 miles South of Louisville on the Richmond Pike where we arrived about noon and went into camp. Louisville is a nice city of Severel thousand inhabitants nicely located on a level Scope of country.[6] The Soil is Some Sandy. Here we see some of the beauties of war Such as Fortifications Scarcety of fence Rails with large Seige Guns and many other things to remind us that we are actually Soldiers.

SUNDAY AUG 23RD
[LEBANON, KENTUCKY]

I received a Letter from Nett And Soon after we received marching orders and we Struck tents and marched back to the city to Nashville Depot and took the Train for Lebanon Sixty five miles South of Louisville. I was Sick and Captain Karns took me with him to a private house where we Satyed all night. We got to Lebanon about ten Oclock at night. We passed Shepardsville and Severel other towns on our rout. Nothing of importance occured.

MONDAY AUG 24TH

We went into camp near the Depot this morning and put up our Tents. I am Sick and did not go out of Camp untill after noon when I was down in town. This is a small Town & county Seat.[7] The country is hilly. To the South is some large hills that would be called mountains in our county. The Streets are Baracaded in a number of places and our men are buissy fortifying and prepareing for defense. We are under the command of Genl Dumont of our own State of Indiana.[8] He is a small[?] man of very thin visage. Light complexion and has a peculiar way of Squinting one Eye with a nasal tone of voice and a terible man to Swear. But perhaps I may have an opportunity to become better acquainted with him before many days.[9] Now we are in dixey but have not Seen any Rebel Soldiers in Arms yet.

TUESDAY AUG 25TH

I am Still Sick and was excused from duty and drill. We got orders this evening to move our camp but only moved about a half mile south and camped in an old Corn field on a high piece of ground and we have a good Camp Ground.

WEDNESDAY AUG 26TH

I was excused from Drill and duty to day and went to Medical Perveyors in town for medicin. I come back and layed in the Tent the rest of the day. Rebles reported to be at Manchester and threatening to attack our camp but we are well fortified and will give them a warm reception.

THURSDAY AUG 27TH

I was not able for duty to day and remained in the Tent all day. I went to Sleep early and rested very well but I feel very bad. The heat is very oppressive.

FRIDAY AUG 28TH

I was excused from duty to day and went to town and bought some things I needed. I returned this evening and layed down in the Tent.

SATURDAY AUG 29TH

No drill to day but got orders to wash our clotheing. I was not able to wash but remained in the Tent about all day to keep out of the hot sun. This was a very hot day. I wrote to Nett.

SUNDAY AUG 30TH

We had preaching by Rev Boyden of Co "E" and it was close to my tent and I listend to him and could hear all of the Sermon. Mr Boyden is a Methodist and preached in Bluffton Severel years ago. He will probably be commissioned C[h]aplain of the Regiment.

MONDAY AUG 31ST

I was detailed for Picket duty this morning and we went out on the Manchester Pike about a mile and a half. After being at post awhile I was Sent with a detail to arrest an old "*Secesh*."[10] His family was considerably Scared. We took him back to the reserve and surrenderd him to Lieut Todd Officer of the picket. We also arrested Some Turkys that we were afraid would bite us and got and old Lady to cook them for us and we had a Square meal. We had only Nineteen to take to camp. Some Boys from the 98th Illinois got to[o] close to our post and was arrested and kept untill morning. I was Corporal of Second Relief and Stood two hours on and four off. Nothing occured to frighteen us as no Johnies put in an appearence. So ends August the first month and without a fight.

TUESDAY SEPT 1ST

Being relieved from Picket duty this morning and returned to camp takeing our Turkeys and prisoners to camp. I was detailed to guard the prisoners and when we got into the camp we told the 98th Boys to Skip as we did not want to report them to Genl Dumont. Those of us who were on picket last night we did not have to drill and I went down town and loafed around untill evening and returned to camp before Roll Call as I was absent without leave.

WEDNESDAY SEPT 2ND

I was out to drill at all the calls and Dress Parade this eveining.[11] . . . weather very hot.

THURSDAY SEPT 3RD

We done the usual amount of drilling And heavy details were sent onto the fortifications and we lay on our Arms all night expecting an Attack. We are very anxious to try our hand in a fight. I did not Sleep much as the excitement run high. But the night passed and no "Johnies" did not pay us a visit.[12]

FRIDAY SEPT 5TH

We got orders to Strike Tents before Breakfast and get ready to move at a moments warning. We are now prepared to fight or run as the case may be[.] We lay all day in the hot sun in an open field with our Arms in our hands and remained in that position all night. There Seams to be something expected. The Rebs must be in our vacinity and our General does not want to be caught "napping." This is the third night and Second day that we was hardly allowed to put our Arms out of our hands. I am very tiard for want of Sleep and the excitement worries us. What the next few hours may bring fourth I cannot tell[.] Where we may go I cannot surmise but we will await devellopments and "trust in god and keep our powder dry." I did not Sleep much to night.

SATURDAY SEPT 6TH

We are Still under marching orders and under Arms. I was detailed for Picket duty and went out but was orderd to return to camp Shortly and we were put on the Cars and took the Road North to Lebanon Junction where we arrived about midnight and went into a field and layed down on the Ground until morning. I am very tiard from exposure and not haveing my Arms off for so many days and I Slept Soundly.

SUNDAY SEPT 7TH

I was writing a letter to Nett when the "Long Roll" beat to Arms and we rushed into line of Battle on a "double quick" and it made considerable Stir in camp. We Stood in line about an hour and then moved South of our Camp about a half mile and remained there in line Some time. Genl Dumont rode into our quarters and Said there was some Rebel Cavalry made their appeerence on the Shepherdsvill road. That they had burned the Rail Road Bridge across Salt River at Shepherdsville and threatend our Camp but they did not attact us and we returned to our old camp Ground this evening and went into camp.

MONDAY SEPT 8TH

The usual amount of drilling was done to day and we received orders this eveining to be ready to move we were under Arms all night and of course I did not Sleep much. Our men are all aixious to have a little fight to try their hand and we may get all we want Soon.

TUESDAY SEPT 9TH
[SHEPHERDSVILLE, KENTUCKY]

About Nine Oclock am we got on the cars and went to Shepherdsville where we arrived about Noon and camped on the South Bank of Salt

River in a clover field and we have a nice camp and good water. The Town of Shepherdsville is situated on the North Bank of the river right opposite our camp. It is a Small place of only a few houses. The Pioneer Corps are rebuilding the Rail Road Bridge burned by the Rebels recently.[13] It come my turn to cook for the mess and I enterd on that duty to day and it keeps me employed and I like it. J V Kennagy is my assistent and we get things up in *Splendid Style* as we never had any experience in that line before but Such is Soldiering.

WEDNESDAY SEPT 10TH

No excitement in camp to day and nothing but drill going on. We have a nice drill ground. I was out for drill but did not go on Dress Parade. No marching orders.

THURSDAY SEPT 11TH

J V Kennagy is sick and I am "chief cook and Bottle Washer["] and was excused from drill & Dress Parade. Our mess consists of the entire company and they get away with considerable "Grub." I received a Letter from Nett and partly answerd it. How much good it does me to receive a letter from the dear friends left behind. It Shows that we are not forgotten and reminds us of the duty we owe them and [our] country. It is a great solace in Camp life. It encourages us on the march and we hope when the time comes we will not betray the confidence reposed in us.[14] If we are called to Battle we know we will leave some of our comrades on the field. Who it may be we cannot tell but we are ready to meet the "Rebs" any time.

FRIDAY SEPT 12TH

I was not out for drill but done the cooking for the company. . . .

SATURDAY SEPT 13TH

No drill to day and I went with Some of the Boys to the River for a Swim and to wash my clotheing. This is the first time I done my washing. But I Suppose it will not be the last time as we cant always find washerwomen. No moveing orders to day yet.

SUNDAY SEPT 14TH

There was preaching in camp but I put in the day writing Letters. I wrote to Nett & Mollie. I had to do the cooking as my detail was not up. No orders to move yet.

MONDAY SEPT 15TH

I was detailed on Camp Guard this morning and we got orders to move to night and took the Cars for Lebanon Junction where we arrived about midnight and every fellow looked out for quarters for himself. We did not go into camp but layed on our Arms.

TUESDAY SEPT 16TH

We were drawn up in line of Battle to day and thought we were going to get a fight but was disappointed and we got orders to get ready to march with two days rations in our Haversacks at Eight Oclock am to morrow and consequently it required some extra cooking but we were ready and went to bed in good time.[15] I could not go to sleep as I am concerned about what may come on to morrow. We are now in the vacinity of the Army of the Rebel Genl Braxton Bragg who is advanceing and is beseigeing Munfordsville and I think there is where we will go tomorrow. But we will have to wait and see what the next few hours may bring fourth.[16]

WEDNESDAY SEPT 17TH

Four Companies and with them "Co K" was orderd out and got aboard the Train and pulled out for Munfordsvill and passed the "Cumberland Tunnel" and over some very hilly country. On arriveing at Elisabeth Town we were orderd off the Train and got our Dinner. About three or four Oclock a Courier come dashing into town and reported the surrender of Col Wilder and Garrison at Munfordsville.[17] Then we were orderd by Col Knox of the 51st Indiana to load the Train with the Camp and Garrison Equipage and what could not be loaded was distroyed. The cars was all filled and then we got on with the 51st makeing about Twelve hundred men on Top of the Cars and then we pulled out for the north. It commenced to rain and made the Track Slipp[r]y. The conductor told our men to set up the Breaks when we enterd the Tunnel as it was a heavy "down Grade" from there to McColesville. We went through the Tunnel like a Streak and on over the high Trustle work at north end and down the mountains to the valey. It was a very dangerous ride as the Train was heavy loaded and had a car broke down in our mad run we might [have] been precipitated down into the valey hundreds of feet below. But we arrived at Lebanon Junction in the night and our men were ready to move and we had no Shelter from the rain and Slept the best we could. It was a tereble night and one I Shall long remember.

THURSDAY SEPT 18TH

This morning I feel bad from the exposure last night and I am wet through. We were put on the Cars again and returned to Shepherdsville where we camped for the night. Rumors that we will return to Louisville as our Army is returning from Alabama and that the great Battle will be near Louisville. Things look very Gloomy to our Army. Braggs Army is comeing north and Genl Buel following with his disheartend Soldiers and we have nothing but New Soldiers to meet him.[18] It looks as though our Native State of Indiana might be the Battle ground.

FRIDAY SEPT 19TH

I took the Sick men to the Surgeons quarters and missed the first drill but was out [for] the rest of the calls. . . . It seems we run away from the "Johnies" and they have not caught up with us. There are all kinds of rumors in regard to our army. Some that Buels men cannot get through but we will trust to providence and "keep our Powder dry."

SATURDAY SEPT 20TH

This being wash day there was no drilling and I wrote to Uncle Gary.[19] We changed our camp a Short distance east of the old camp. We had inspection of Knapsacks. That was a new feature. The object is to see that they were kept clean and not over loaded and that the clotheing was clean.

SUNDAY SEPT 21ST

I was detailed with some other men to go to the Hospital in Town to make Bunks for the Sick and while there received orders to move. Our

Cavalry had a fight at Lebanon Junction with Braggs Cavalry resulting in the defeat of the "Rebs" and we were held in readiness to help our Cavalry if needed but we did not go. . . . There was preaching in camp but I did not go. I was on Dress Parade but was not present at inspection of Knapsacks.

MONDAY SEPT 22ND
[LOUISVILLE, KENTUCKY]

We got orders to Strike tents and took the Train to Louisville. We marched through the city and perceive quite a difference in our reception before. When we march[ed] through the city before there was no demonstration and all was quiet when the war was not so close but now the city being in danger the citizens are ready to welcome us to defend their property. I did not form a very good opinion of the people. They Should have a little taste of war and I think it would benefit their loyalty. We are camped about two miles from the center of Town and near the Street Car Track to Portland. We have a nice level place to camp and we are happy.

TUESDAY SEPT 23RD

Capt Karns J W Spak[e] James Cutter and myself went up to the city and had some pictures taken. We went to a Boarding House and got our Dinners and when we returned the Regiment had changed camp but we found them. . . . Rumors of the advance of the Rebels and Some expectations of a fight but all passed of[f] quietly. We prepared quarters and have a nice camp. We were called into the Trenc[h]es about 3 Oclock a.m.

WEDNESDAY SEPT 24

Daylight finds us still in the Trenches and we cooked our Breakfast at the Fortifications. I was detailed to work on the Fortifications and worked all day. I was not out for Drill and the day passed quietly except the cannonadeing along our lines. I guess it is only target practice although Rebels are reported in our vacinity. We were called out at three Oclock a.m. and lay in the trenches untill daylight.

Thursday Sept 25th

I went to sick call this morning and got some medicin. I was sick all day and did no[t] do any duty. I was in camp all day.

Friday Sept 26th

I am Still Sick and was excused from duty. The Regiment are on Picket but I am in camp. We got orders to move this evening and marchd through the city and camped cn the South side about Six miles from our old camp. I gave out on the march & R Buckmaster and J W Spake carried my Knapsack and we got to camp after the Regiment got in. We had no Tents but was not uncomfortable. I wrote to Nett and Sent her the Captains Likeness. . . .

Saturday Sept 27th

I am on the sick list yet but I feel better. The Regiment did not get in from Picket untill near noon. It rained Some and I went to see the 101st Indiana and found them under orders to move and their tents all Struck. I found quite a number of men I knew Among the rest Uncle Will Miller. I also met Wash Wandall Shannon Deam and W J McAffee of the 22nd Ind the[y] haveing been with Genl Buels Army. They say he will get through all right. Dick Buckmaster and myself got Breakfast in the city. We returned to camp this evening.

Sunday Sept 28th

. . . There was some cannon fireing to day which seams rather out of place and not very appropriate music for Sunday. There was no fighting but the Rebs keep us Stired up with expectations.

Monday Sept 29th

Our Regiment received orders this evening to be ready to march in the morning with three days cooked rations in our Haversacks. We had no drill to day. I am Sick yet but prepared to march with the rest. The preparations was going on all night and we did not Sleep much as many were the conjectures as to where we are going. Some Say down the Ohio and Some to the interior of Kentucky.

TUESDAY SEPT 30TH

We left camp this morning leaveing our Tents Standing which looks as though we might return but it is hard to tell what may be the result. We marched about Eight miles down the river to a Steam Boat landing where we embarked on [a] Boat and was orderd off about ten Oclock at West Paint where we camped for the night.

WEDNESDAY OCT 1ST

This was our first days march. We Started early and took the road towards Elisabeth Town and traveld about twenty miles. I played out but got into camp about Nine Oclock p.m. I was tiard and Sick and could not eat anything. My feet is also very Sore but I think I will be all right in the morning. I am not accustomed eaven to walking any distance.

THURSDAY OCT 2ND

We understand now that we will meet the wagon Train of Genl Buel which we will guard to Louisville. We Started early and met the wagon train and we went on to Elisabeth Town which is quite a place and I suppose there was considerable buisiness done prior to the war. But all buisiness is Suspended now. We arrived here about noon and after noon Started on the return. As Some of the Train had taken another rout we did not have to guard it. It is raining and we camped about five miles from Elisabeth Town for the night. We have no Tents and Slept in the rain. The country is more level here and the Soil Sandy and we are on a Pike Road. I Stood the march much better to day and come into camp with the Regiment.

FRIDAY OCT 3RD

We resumed our march to day and marched about fourteen miles toward West Point. I am Sick and tiard and road about three miles on our Brigade wagon. But managed to reach camp in good time. I will Sleep well as I am about played out.

SATURDAY OCT 4TH

We passed through west point and Bivuacd about two miles from there for dinner. We are on the Bank of the beautiful Ohio River and we See numerous Steamers at a distance. Then we can look across into gods country and my native State of Indiana. We marched this pm to within about Eight miles of Louisville and camped near the river. One of our Boys captured a "dangerous["] chicken that was brave enough to Show himself and we cooked it in water from the river and we got So much Sand mixed with the chicken we could not eat it So we had our labor for nothing.

SUNDAY OCT 5TH

We resumed the march to day toward Louisville where we arrived about Noon after marching altogether Sixty Eight miles. We returned to our old camp passing a number of old Regiments of Buels men who look hard as they have come from Alabama across the country. They designated us "Band Box Soldiers" and express the opinion that we wont look so nice after awhile. I suppose because our Clotheing and Accouterments are new. We received more[?] [orders] this evening to march to morrow but where time will have to demonstrate. I rested well as I am tiard out.

MONDAY OCT 6TH

We Struck Tents and Started toward Frankford. We had a Turn Pike road and moved rapidly. We passed Shelbyville in the evening and went into camp about a mile South of Town. Shelbyville is quite a nice place of Severel hundred inhabitants.[20] Good water is very Scarce but we have a good camp. We marched about thirty miles which is a big days march for raw Soldiers. We met no Rebels to day but the[y] have possession of Frankford. The country is Some hilly but the soil Seems productive and we passed a number of nice plantations. There is a great many vine yards and in good condition. Fences are Scarce they haveing been distroyed by the Army. I am very tiard and Some what under the weather yet.

TUESDAY OCT 7TH

We resumed the march early with orders to fill our Canteens with water as it would be very Scarce on our rout. We marched all day and Camped early in the evening. . . . The water in our Camp is bad and Scarce. It is hardly fit to use. I feel better to night. I think I will be all right when I become accustomed to the great change of diet and manner of liveing.

But I often think of the comforts of home and loved ones left behind and trust the war will Soon end So we may return to our homes. We now begin to see the effects of the war in the people being destitute of the necissaries of life. When I compare their present Situation with the home in Indiana we left it seams terible.

WEDNESDAY 8TH
[FRANKFORT, KENTUCKY]

We Started on the march about nine Oclock a.m. and did not camp untill about Eight to night. Then we just filed off the road and did not build any fires but lay on our Arms untill twelve Oclock when we formed quietly and Started for Frankford. We expect a little fight and our Cavalry have the advance. We have eight miles yet to the Capitol and we are passing a very rough hilly country. The road is hard and we are tiard but the prospect of the long coveted battle Stimulates us to efforts to keep up with the command and Should our service be needed to be on hands. For myself I would not miss it for any thing and I think I Speak the feeling of the entire Regiment. But we came around the mountain on the North Side of the mountain without meeting with any Johnies at daylight. The Cavalry had run them out of the city. The Rebs was engaged in tearing up the floor of the Bridge across the Kentucky river and our men charged through and they Skedaddled up the hill by the State Prison. There were Blood marks near the Bridge but we seen no dead men. There is lots of Ball marks on the Bridge. The Rebels were pushed so hard that some of them were crouded off the road near the State prison where it looks very dangerous. The Legislature was in cession but they adjourned in a hurry and the members all left during the night.[21] The city of Frankford is Situated on the Kentucky River and it is entirely surrounded by mountains and hills. The road we came in on winds around the mountain on the east side of the city and the natural defences are good and had they not been taken by surprise they might of given us quite a fight. Frankford has Severel thousand inhabitants and Some fine buildings.[22] We marched through the city and crossed the river and up the hills above the State Prison and camp[ed] So that we can look down into the prison yard. We have a splendid camp. It is high and dry and the soil is Sandy.

THURSDAY OCT 9TH

After our capture of the city and got a camp Ground we put up our Tents and made ourselves as comfortable as possible. I was down to the Bridge to look over the Battle ground. I also visited the Cemetry which is very fine. Daniel Boons monument is nice. The cemetry generally is in nice and has not been molested by the Soldiers. We can Sit on the hill and See the prisoners at work in the Penitentiary with their Striped suits on. I believe I prefer Soldiering to wearing that kind of uniform. We rested to day and had no drill.

FRIDAY OCT 10TH

We pulled out this morning to look after the Johnies and went to Versales where they had been but did not wait to receive us. We passed through the town and camped about a mile South of it. I was on Picket to night and it was very windy and disagreeable for that duty. The night passed with out any appearance of the Johnies. Varsalles is a Small town and like all the rest no business of any kind going on.[23] This is a very nice country. The soil is somewhat Sandy.

SATURDAY OCT 11TH

We come off Picket and we pursued the flying Rebels about seven miles South of Versalles but could not pursuade them to meet us. We countermarched and passed through Versalles and camped about three miles north of town. We marched about twenty miles. We have a good camp and plenty of good water. We Slept in an Old Stable which Shelterd us from the rain as we left our Tents Standing at Frankford. But we were not uncomfortable but rested good. Every thing was quiet in and around camp and the Rebs did not disturb us.

SUNDAY OCT 12TH

We resumed the march toward Frankford and arrived there about noon. Some of our Boys captured Some Turkys and Col Miller commanding Brigade Sent details to arrest them. One of them under arrest threw his Turky down and swore he would not cary it to head quarters and I gathered it up and carried it to camp. . . . It seams like comeing home to get into our Old Quarters.

MONDAY OCT 13TH

We remained in our old camp and I wrote home and rested up. After we had retired to our beds to night we were orderd out to prepare two days Rations and be ready to move at a moments warning. Consequently haveing to draw our Rations from the Commissary before we could cook them we put in nearly all night prepareing to march. But we are ready for orders.

TUESDAY OCT 14TH

We got no orders to move as we expected and the usual time for drill found us out for that duty. One wing of the Penitentiary took fire and was distroyed but the rest of the Prison was not damaged. I did not learn how it caught.

WEDNESDAY OCT 15TH

We are Still under marching orders but did not move to day. . . .

THURSDAY OCT 16TH

I was in the Penitentiary and bought Severel Rings from the convicts. . . . We did not move.

FRIDAY OCT 17TH

. . . No marching orders yet. We are Still held in readiness to move but drilled as usual. We are haveing nice weather and good times only it keeps us on Suspense expecting a move.

SATURDAY OCT 18TH

This is wash day and I done mine. We also had to drill as usual. I was taken with Plewracy and was Sick all night. The Regiment was called out about midnight and I could not go. They returned near morning to quarters. The "Rebs" were in the vacinity but did not attack us.

SUNDAY OCT 19TH

We were orderd to load our guns about Noon as the Rebel Cavalry are close to the city and we were not to be taken by surprise. The Sick were musterd by Major McCole and sent to the Hospittal in the city. I did not want to go as I expect to be better soon. We were not attacked an[d] remained in our old camp.

Monday Oct 20th

I am Still Sick and not able for duty. I was excused by the surgeon. I was detailed in place of J V Kernagy to write in the Adjutants office. Kennagy was sent away Sick and I am to keep his place untill he returns to the Regiment. We have no orders to move yet and the "Johnies" keep away far enough to be safe and not molest us for fear of getting hurt.

Tuesday Oct 21st

There seems to be considerable writing to do as the buisiness is behind on account of Kennagys Sickness. I was writing all day copying General orders and makeing up the order file to date. I did not drill any.

Wednesday Oct 22nd

I was drawing off Co As discriptive Rolls to day which kept me to work about all day.[24] I am not well yet and my Eyes are sore. No marching orders yet.

Thursday Oct 23rd

I worked on Co Bs Rolls to day. I was not out on duty or drill. No orders to move.

Friday Oct 24th

I received a Letter from Nett. It was so cold and disagreeable I could not write. I did not drill and put in the day in camp.

Saturday Oct 25th

After makeing out Adjutants Morning Report I did not try to write any more. There is about four inches of Snow on the ground. Our orders come this evening to prepare two days cooked Rations and be ready to move at Six Oclock in the morning to Bowling Green and I presume this is the last night for us in Frankfort for us. It is severel days march from here to our destination. We are under the command of Genl Ward of Kentucky.[25]

Genl Dumont has gone on leave of absence. It will be hard marching but anything for a change. I dont like lying in camp so long.

SUNDAY OCT 26TH

It seams that all our important moves come on Sunday and this was a hard days work. We Struck Tents early and Started following the Kentucky River on the North Side for severel miles. We marched nineteen miles and the Snow made it Slipery[,] and wet our feet[,] and we could not Sit down when we stopped to rest and lots of our Boys gave out. We camped after dark and had to build fires to dry the ground before we could lye down to sleep. If ever I was tiard in my life it is to night. I dont know how I will Stand it through as I am Sick and many such marches will kill a well man. The men are complaining of Genl Ward bitterly for this days march. We are camped on Salt river and five miles from Laurance.

MONDAY OCT 27TH

The 75th being in advance yesterday it took the rear to day and we did not Start untill eight Oclock am. We only marched about twelve miles and camped about Sun Set on a Rebels Plantation about two miles from Johnsonville. I stood it very well to day and I guess I will get through all right.

TUESDAY OCT 28TH

We took the advance to day and our Regiment in advance of Brigade which put us in front. We only marched fourteen miles and camped near Bardstown. We camped about dark. We have a nice camp and good water. This is a little hilly but a nice country.

WEDNESDAY OCT 29TH

We did not get on the road this morning untill about nine Oclock as we had the rear and waited untill the rest of our divission was gone. We passed New Haven and camped about two miles from town. We have a good camp and plenty of water.

THURSDAY OCT 30TH

We were on the move in good time this morning and we had a good road. We camped about dark after marching fourteen miles. Passed no towns. I have noticed so far that there is no school Houses in this state out side of the towns as we have not seen any. I find the people have hardly any education. But few can read and write.

FRIDAY OCT 31ST

This is the Sixth day from Frankfort. We marched Sixteen miles and being in the center we were late getting into camp. Water was very Scarce along the rout but we find plenty here. Thus ends October without a fight but we marched twenty two days in this month and upwards of three hundred miles. We were marching the first and last days.[26] There was nothing of very great importance transpired but we look forward with great expectations for the next.

SATURDAY NOV 1ST

We occupied the center to day and got on the road in good time and camped on Bacon creek eight miles from Munfordsville about Sun Set. This is a nice camp ground and plenty of good water. The country is like the rest of this State very hilly and rocky.[27] It Shows the ravages of the war in the Scarcity of Fences.

SUNDAY NOV 2ND

Did not leave camp untill nine Oclock a.m. and got to Munfordsville at noon and Built fires for dinner near Green River. There is only a few houses here.[28] The Pontoons were thrown into the river so we could cross. We halted only about an hour and Started on. The Banks on the river is very high and Steep and I crossed the river on the Rail Road Bridge which is Said to be over a hundred feet high but it Saved climbing up and down the hills. We passed over the late Battle field but there is nothing to Show there had ever been a battle. The hills have no timber on them. Our line of Fortifications are in good Shape yet as also the Stockade. We marched about nine miles this after noon and camped within three miles of Cave city. We are now in the neighborhood of the

Mamouth Cave. . . . We made seventeen miles and had a good camp.
Water Scarce.

MONDAY NOV 3RD

I started in advance of the Regiment and followed the Rail Road to
Cave city to see the 101st Boys. . . . I Stopped and Seen Uncle Will
Miller untill the Regiment came up and then joined them. . . . It seams
that Genl Bragg is falling back as we advance and if he intends to give
us battle he wants to get us as far from home as possible so in case we
are defeated we cant get away from him. We marched twenty miles and
now have only fourteen miles to Bowling Green and will reach there
to morrow and perhaps rest a few days any way and recruit up and rest.

TUESDAY NOV 4TH
[BOWLING GREEN, KENTUCKY]

We Started early and passed through Bowling Green and went into
camp at Mill Cave about four Miles from town on the Nashville Road.
It was dark when we camped and wood was scarce but plenty of Good
water. The road was very dusty and the day warm and I came into camp
very tiard. The Town of Bowling Green is Small but the natural den-
fences are good and then the Yankees have built Severel Forts on a hill
South of town [which] looks formidable.

WEDNESDAY NOV 5TH

Being at our destination for the present we changed our camp a Short
distance handy to water and pitched our Tents and arranged our quarters. We are near Lost River. It takes its name from the following dis-
cription of it. I[t] comes out of the hills and the Banks are high on boath
Sides and about thirty rods below where it comes out it disappears in
the hills again. The current is Strong and water deep. The Source of
the river has never been discoverd after it disappears. Mill Cave is situated at the lower end or where the river disappears and is a large Cave
and takes its name from there haveing at one time a mill built there. I
was in the cave for some distance and it is a desolate looking place.
Some places we had to crawl on our hands & feet to get between the
Stone. At other times we could Stand up and then it be ten fifteen &

twenty feet high. We had to cary candles as it is very dark. We can hear the wagons rolling along the Pike above us and it Sounds like distant thunder. The water in the River is Soft and the Rock are Sand Stone. The Soil is Sandy and more level. The country has been cleard up and cultivated Some but every thing Shows war now. The fences have all been burned by the two Armies and it makes it look desolate.

THURSDAY NOV 6TH

. . . At four Oclock we were reviewed by Genl Rosencrans & Genl Dumont. This was the first time I ever seen Gen Rosencrans.[29] He is a German and a fine looking millitary man and makes a fine appearance on horseback. We formed in open order and he road down in our front and back in the rear while we Stood at "Parade Rest."[30] We did not get relieve[d] untill nearly dark and did not get supper untill long after dark.

FRIDAY NOV 7TH

We drew Shoes only and had expected other clotheing as campaigning has been hard on our clotheing and Some of us are very needy. We had Battalion drill and Dress Parade only. . . .

SATURDAY NOV 8TH

I wrote a letter to Mollie & Nett and was out for drill and done my washing. Rumors of another move but no orders to day. . . .

SUNDAY NOV 9TH

After Inspection this morning I went to Bowlin Green to see some acquaintances of other Regiments. The 88th Ind come out here and camped close to us. I know Severel of that Regiment who were out in the old 12th Ind. . . .

MONDAY NOV 10TH

A part of our Division moved to day and we have orders to be ready. We drew Pantaloons and Dress Coats. We did not get orders to move and remained in our old camp.

TUESDAY NOV 11TH

We Struck Tents this morning and Started on the road to Scottsville. We marched about thirteen miles and went into camp. We did not put up our Tents and it commenced raining in the night and we had to get up and put in the rest of the night without Sleep. Being tired from marching this is not a pleasent way to rest.

WEDNESDAY NOV 12TH
[SCOTTSVILLE, KENTUCKY]

We were on the road about Six Oclock. It is Still raining and we camped about a mile north of Scottsville in the evening and put up our Tents to protect us from the rain. . . .

THURSDAY NOV 13TH

We did not move to day and the Adjutant come for me to write for him. I was makeing out Receipts for Ordinance Stores turned over to the Colonel by the Captains of the severel companies. It is still raining Some. We are severel miles from the Rail Road and our Supplies come from Bowling Green by wagons and our mail is brought from there also.

FRIDAY NOV 14TH

I was writing for the Adjutant J. C Medsker makeing Discriptive Rolls for "Co C" and copying General orders. . . . We are camped in a grove of timber and have a nice camp and good water.

SATURDAY NOV 15TH

I was in the office Tent all day again. I am getting tiard writing So much. I would rather drill and be out with the company. I wrote another Letter home. I can pass the time pleasently by writing Letters to my friends and it is something to employ the mind. I did not receive any Letters.

SUNDAY NOV 16TH

The rain prevented preaching to day. I made out the company Morning Report and took it to the Adjutant. . . . It rained all night which makes it very disagreeable in camp.

Monday Nov 17th

It is still raining. I done some writing. I also wrote a Letter to "pa." I did not go out for Drill or Dress Parade.

Tuesday Nov 18th

. . . I was in the Adjutants Tent. . . . It seams very Menotinous lying in camp with nothing to change the regular camp duties and continnuos[?] raining. I would prefer being on the march or any thing for a change. We have not heard of a "Johnie" for some time. If they would give us a little "Shakeing up" it would let us know that they are not all dead.

Wednesday 19th

I was engaged as usual on Discriptive Rolls. . . . Still it rains and the mud is getting deep.

Thursday Nov 20th

. . . I was also at work in the adjutants office. I [had] an attack of Jaundice and had to take medicin.

Friday Nov 21st

I done my usual days work and was not out on drill or Dress Parade. No marching orders to day.

Saturday Nov 22nd

We done our[?] washing and I was writing the rest of the day. I was not out on Drill or parade.

Sunday Nov 23rd

Lieut Starbuck and I left camp and went out in [the] country. We were forageing for something to eat but found there was nothing to get. We found Some walnuts & Chestnuts and Percimmons. We found marks of war all around and the people are destitute. Their Stock and produce has all been seized by one or the other Army.

MONDAY NOV 24TH

. . . There are rumors of a move are going about camp. This evening orders came to prepare one days rations and be ready to move in the morning. It seams almost like leaving home to leave our old camp after Staying awhile in one place.

CHAPTER 3

First Blood in Tennessee

In late November, General Dumont was ordered to deploy his division in north-central Tennessee, near Nashville, with a brigade each at the towns of Gallatin, Castalian Springs, and Hartsville, in order to guard the Louisville and Nashville Railroad and the Cumberland River, two vital Union supply routes. With loud cheers, the troops of the Seventy-fifth and the rest of their brigade crossed the Tennessee state line and soon settled into a heavily guarded winter camp at Castalian Springs.

All was quiet until the morning of December 7, when the sound of cannon fire was heard coming from the direction of Hartsville. Gen. John Hunt Morgan's Confederate cavalrymen had launched a devastating surprise attack on the brigade encamped there, destroying the still relatively inexperienced Union regiments. The Seventy-fifth quickly formed into ranks and set off to render what assistance it could. "We went on double-quick the whole way, mostly in line of battle," wrote Sergeant Floyd, "over fences and hills, through ravines and fields. The morning was chilly—a little snow having fallen during the night." Although they moved ten miles in two hours, the Hoosiers arrived too late, only in time to fire at Morgan's rear guard.[1] After sadly burying the dead, the Hoosiers returned to Castalian Springs and began constructing fortifications to defend against Morgan. "We worked like beavers. . . .We determined that there should be no repetition of Hartsville," added Floyd.[2]

After many enjoyed a Christmas dinner of hardtack crackers and salt pork, the regiment was ordered back into Kentucky to operate against the "Christmas Raid" of Morgan's four thousand Rebel horsemen on the Louisville and Nashville Railroad (December 21, 1862–January 2, 1863). Marching through the towns of Scottsville, Glasgow, and Munfordville, the Seventy-fifth assisted in the Union effort to end Morgan's successful

venture before being ordered to return to Tennessee, this time
to the town of Murfreesboro.

In the meantime, Rosecrans went into position facing
Bragg at a point just outside Murfreesboro along the banks of
Stones River. There, on the last day of 1862, Bragg launched a
massive strike against the Army of the Cumberland. After the
loss of a good deal of ground in several hours of savage fighting,
Rosecrans and his Federals managed to stem the Confederate
onslaught by forming a substantial defensive line. After a
respite on New Year's Day, Bragg attempted a far less successful attack on January 2, then withdrew the Army of Tennessee
from the battlefield. The soldiers of the Seventy-fifth joined
their comrades in the Army of the Cumberland just a few days
after the end of the costly Battle of Stones River.

Tuesday Nov 25th

We bid our old camp adieu this morning and Started South. We crossed
the Tennessee line about 2 Oclock p.m. We camped near the Rock
House after marching about twenty miles. We pitched our Tents and
have a nice camp and plenty of good water and are very comfortable.

Wednesday Nov 26th

We were in the rear and did not get Started very early. We reached
Gallatin Tenn about Sunset. We passed through the town and camped
South west of the town. We have a good camp. Gallatin is a Small town
of about one Thousand inhabitants and a county Seat. The country
Generally is level and under good State of cultivation. Considerable
cotton is raised and corn. We are camped near a large cotton factery
and there is a Grist mill and our men are running it grinding Corn.[3]

Thursday Nov 27th

We received orders to pitch our Tents. I have a very bad [case of] Dioreah
caused from the water. I wrote to Nett and we did not drill so we could
rest. My feet is Sore for the first time marching on the Stone Pike. I dont
know how long we will remain here but I dont think it will be a great

while as Rosencrans is pushing Bragg to the wall and they must make a stand soon or give up the Ghost. Our entire Army is in splendid condition and us new soldiers now begin to consider ourselves about as good as the old Regiments. We have put in the time faithfully Since we come out And although we have not done any fighting we are perfectly willing at any time the "Rebbs" will give us an opportunity.[4] But they dont Seam to desire an acquaintance. Some of us went out and got a hog that was cross and we were afraid would bite Some yankee Soldier.[5]

Friday Nov 28th
[Castalian Springs, Tennessee]

I am crippled with something like Rheumatism and can hardly get around. We received marching orders and I was put in an Ambulance by order of the Surgeon and we moved to Castilleon Springs about Eight miles east of Gallatin. This is an out post for guardin[g] our flanks to keep the Rebbs from getting in our rear. We are only a few miles from the Cumberland River. The Rebel Strong hold is at Murfreesboro Thirty miles South of Nashville. Our forces hold Nashville as they did not let go of it during Buels retreat.

Saturday Nov 29th

We put in to day fixing quarters and washing and prepareing for Inspection to morrow. My Rheumetism is better. I cleaned up my gun and accouterments and did not go out on duty. Our camp is in a grove of timber and the springs Supply us plenty of good water.[6] I received a letter from Nett of the 24th.

Sunday Nov 30th

Colonel Miller of [the] 72nd Ind inspected our Regiment this morning. I patched my pants and under clotheing. I find out I am not much of a Tailor but perhaps three years experience in that line may make a difference in my patching. . . .

Monday Dec 1st

We had quite a racket this morning in our mess between the mess and commissioned Officers. We concluded they were imposeing on us. They

have messed off us all the time Since we come into the service. We drew
Rations for twenty men and fed the three officers out of that. They furnished nothing which made it clear gain to them and made our Rations
Short. We concluded it was imposeing on us as they are drawing "Big pay"
and allowed so many rations additional.[7] There had been murmers for
Some time which culminated in an out break this morning and there was
some Sharp words passed and very near resulting in some one getting hurt
but it was fineally quieted by the Officers withdrawing from the mess. I
took rather an active part in the fracas and Ad Haines and Lieut Todd
Stripped to fight but Todd put his coat on and it was well enough for it
would not be pleasent to fight a comrade but I still think we were in the
right as they can buy their Grub better than we could afford to go hungry as we dont draw any more than is necissary to keep us comfortable.[8]

Tuesday Dec 2nd

Our Mess was divided. Some of the "Pets" going with the Officers. I find
in occupations some men will be the tools and court favor with their
superiors. I am working out my own Salvation and "paddling my own
Canoe" and think I will probably get through as well as Some others.
The man who enlisted with me and who promised to stick to me like
a Brother has now gone out of my mess Simply to court favor with company head quarters. But our mess is now composed of Boys that can be
relied on always and we will See who will be on hands in times of emergency. I received Netts letter of Nov 25th after I had went to bed and
read it by fire light.

Wednesday Dec 3rd

I answerd Netts Letter the first thing and then went to writing on Co
Hs Rolls and finished them up. I was not out on duty and I am getting
about disgusted with my detail. I Shall get excused from company duty
or quit the Adjutants office Soon. It is lonesome to be in the Tent alone
all day while the Boys are haveing their fun in camp. No marching
orders to day.

Thursday Dec 4th

I coppied the last Rolls to day and now done with a very tedious task
and I am heartily Glad of it. I wrote home for pass time and did not go

out for drill or Dress Parade. It is quite cold and a heavy frost last night. We have plenty of wood and keep warm.

[No entry Friday]

[*Miller misdated his entries from Friday, December 5, until he apparently discovered his mistake on Friday, December 19.*]

Saturday Dec 5th

. . . I done my washing and put in the rest of the day in Such amusements as I could find to attract attention. Such as pitching Horse Shoes and jumping and playing "Eucher."

Sunday Dec 6

We heard cannonadeing about daylight and we were called out in a hurry and Started on double quick for Heartsville. It is eight miles and we run about all the way.[9] But we were to[o] late to Save the 104th Ills 106th and 108th Ohio and one Section of the 13th Ind Battery with Some of the 2nd Indiana Cavalry who were Surprised and captured by John Morgan.[10] We Skirmished with his rear guard but they had about all crossed the Cumberland River. We formed in line of Battle and went through the woods on double quick untill we got near the Battle field and then marched by the right flank and we soon found Signes of the Battle. We run on to a Dead Johny first. He is the first man I have seen killed in Battle. I thought he was the longest man I ever saw. He was lying on his face with his Arms extended. We see what [in] a few moments can be done when "Greek meets Greek" as the Tents are all burned. The dead and dieing are left on the field and those wounded So they could not get away from their Tents perished in them. It seams Morgan crossed the river during the night and attacked the camp at daylight takeing it by surprise and some of our men were killed in their Bunks. We did not get any Breakfast and we find plenty to eat and we helped our selves. Major Widmer of the 104th Illinois an old School Teacher of mine were among the captured. We buried the dead by diggin large Trenches and wide enough to lay men in Cross wise. Those who had a handkerchif in their pocket it was spread over their face and those who had none the Skirt of their coats were turned up over their face and then the Trench was filled up and no mark of any kind designates the place where "Some bodys darling["] is left to rot. While looking at the dead I thought of the anguish it would bring to a mother a wife or Sister when in looking over the long list of killed they might discover the name of the Son B[r]other or Husband as among the killed. To day I realize war in its worse phaze.[11] We had Seen the camp The march and now the Battlefield. Details gathered up the Arms that lay Scatterd about and loaded them in the wagons. Who can discribe the feelings of a Soldier on going into Battle. I do not fear for myself but dread[?] Seeing others Shot down Who I have been with for six months and for whome I have a feeling of a Brother and we know some of us must die the death of a Soldier. Seeing others go Stimulates me to go and I dont feel like flinching. But [it] is a dreadful ordeal to pass through. After takeing care of the wounded and putting them in Ambulances and gathering up the Camp & Garrison equipage and paying the last Sad writes to the dead we form and with Sorrow turn our faces toward our old camp leaveing the smouldering ruins of the Battle field behind us. Many Sad reflections accompany us on our return and with a determination to be revenged upon the Rebels at some future day we "jog" along. There are only a few houses in Hartsville and the importance of the position of guarding the ford across the river and the troops Stationed here were not cautious enough. If they had not been caught Sleeping they might of defended themselves and averted the disaster. We did not reach our old camp untill about midnight. I am terible tired and worn out. The Snow and Ice made it hard marching.

MONDAY DEC 7TH

To guard against a Surprise we commenced to build fortifications and had no drill. We chopped down timber and built a line around our camp. The lesson at Heartsville will probably teach our officers an important lesson. There Seams to be considerable uneasiness among them and I think we have cause to be wide awake and not let the Johnies get away with us. We also received an order to be ready to move at a moments notice. I dont know whether it is just to keep us energetic or whether it means a move. There certainly will be some thing done before many days as the Rebel Army will not allow us to remain here harrasing them and desolateing their country without some effort to drive us out. I am Satisfied there is some warm work before us and I cant tell what the result may be. . . .

TUESDAY DEC 8TH

We were called out about four Oclock and Stood under Arms untill after day light. I dont like to get out quite so early but I would much rather be called out by our Bugle than to be waked up by the "Rebs" a little later in the day. I want to be ready when they pay us a visit and give them a grand reception ore they will remember for some time to come. We done some work on our line of defence. We had a change in the way of a kettle of old fashioned Hominy made from corn and it was nice. Our line of Fortifications look now as though we would be pretty Safe against Morgan and his raiders.

WEDNESDAY DEC 9TH

We were called into line about one Oclock this a.m and I was detailed to work on our defences untill daylight. There was no "Rebs" put in an appearance. This getting out every night and looseing our rest is not very pleasent but we will have to Stand it. J. S. Wilson and I made some more hominy And I was out on Battallion drill twice.

THURSDAY DEC 10TH

We were in line as usual untill "Roll Call." . . . We were musterd out to discharge our Guns and did not work any so as to clean them up.

FRIDAY DEC 11TH

We did not get out untill Roll Call as I guess the scare is over for the present. The 101st Ind come this evening and I got the Countersign from Col Robinson and went over to see them. I was in their camp untill about ten oclock. I found them well except Uncle Charly is Sick. They are to join our Division and will Stay with us. There is two companies from Wells county viz B & G. Cap Studabaker and Cap Truesdale. There is a number of acquaintances in the two companies. It does me good to meet some one of my old neighbors and to think we all have the one great cause at heart. I meet old "Republicans and Democrats" all Battling for the Union.

Saturday Dec 12th
[Gallatin, Tennessee]

I was put on duty as a Corporal of Camp Guard but soon after "Guard Mounting" I was relieved and orderd to report to the Surgeon Dr Arthur and was detailed to go to Hospital No 5 in Gallatin for duty.[12] I packed my Knapsack and turned over my Gun to the Captain and bid the Boys "Good bye" and got into an Ambulance and Started. I got there about two Oclock pm and reported to Dr Brown Surgeon in charge.[13] He took me into the Presbyterian church to point out my dutys.[14] Here I find about two hundred Sick men. Severel dead men and some dieing. They are lying on the floor with nothing under them but a Single Blanket and their knapsacks for Pillows. Imagine if you can a man to[o] Sick to help himself and no one to help him. Dr Brown Said to me to provide "Bunks" for them and he would furnish me plenty of help. I went to post Quartermaster for Teams. I sent one to the country for Straw and one for Lumber and in a Short time I had men to work makeing Bunks for a Single man and our Straw come in about dark. I visited the Sanatary commission and drew some Small "Ticks" and we worked untill midnight and succeeded in makeing Some of the sick comfortable.[15] It would make the Stoutest heart quail to see the misery and suffering of these men in all Stages of disease coverd with "Gray Backs" lying here and dieing without a kind voice or a helping hand to do little acts of kindness So welcome to a Sick man.[16] If we had more of a Supply we might do more for them but we do the best we can under the circumstances. One of my company John B Dumond I find dead haveing died friday night. The dead were not taken out untill I come and I had them taken to the Basement. I was very Tired and disgusted with this place. I heartily wish my self back to the Regiment.

[No entry Sunday]

Monday Dec 14th
[Gallatin, Tennessee]

I took charge of Ward No 1 and we had nearly the same routine to go through with as yesterday and now we have things in much better Shape. Another Boy by name of Zerse from Indiana has the other ward. I got up at twelve oclock and remained up the rest of the night. We are scarce of

Nurses. Some men we did not have room for were moved to another Hospital. . . . I cant tell how long I may remain here as I will have to stay untill I am relieved. I wrote Cap Karns to Send my mail here.

TUESDAY DEC 15TH

I was on duty untill noon and was relieved as we have succeeded in pro-cureing Sufficient Nurses to keep us on duty only half the night and day. I took a good Sleep and I feel all right for to night. There was three deaths last night but none who I knew. I will not have so much to do now and will not have to nurse any only oversee it. I was out in town awhile.

WEDNESDAY 16TH

I got out at midnight and was on duty the rest of [the] night. . . . I found two Boxes in the Express office for our Boys.[17] I would Sooner do my duty at camp as in the Hospital. There was Some deaths to day and we have a number of cases that cant live long. It is Sad to see men die here So far from home and only us rough Soldier[s] to take care of them. I know Some die here that if they could go home only a Short time would get well. Some lament and grieve to get to go home but there is no opportunity as Genl Rosencrans will not grant any furloughs now.

THURSDAY 17TH

I was up at the usual hour. A Boy by the name of Walton died in my ward to night.[18] It was my duty to take an inventory of his effects and I did so and packed his Knapsack to be sent to his friends. I tried to Send the Express Boxes but did not get an opportunity. I wrote to Waltons friends notifying them of his death and that his Knapsack and cloth-ing was held subject to their orders and would be forwarded on receive-ing a reply. . . . The weather is cold and rainy and very disagreeabel. Of course I have good quarters being in the house all the time but I prefer being with the Boys.

FRIDAY DEC 19TH

I did not get out untill about Six Oclock and Superintended the clean-ing out. . . . There was some excitement caused by Morgan being reported in the neighborhood. I did not go to bed untill Twelve Oclock.

Saturday Dec 20th

One of our Boys "Shinn" died to night. I did not get to bed untill midnight. . . . I was down town to draw Bread. This is the Second man from my company that has died in Gallatin and there are severel others in town Sick. . . .

Sunday Dec 21st

I got up at Six and was on duty all day and I did not go out in town. There was three men died to day. I took a bath and changed clothes. There is no difference between Sunday and any other day here. We have the same dutys to perform as during any other day. Our principle diseases are "Chronic Dioreah" Typhoid & Lung Fever and Some cases of Rheumatism caused from exposure and laying on the Ground. Some have nothing els but "homesickness" and it is the worst disease to manage. They seam to go down in Spite of all medical Treatment and die.

Monday Dec 22nd

I was called out at midnight and found three men in my ward who were about to pay the last debt of Nature and they all died before daylight. . . . I did not get to bed untill twelve Oclock as there was three more men died this afternoon and evening makeing Six "Noble Boys" who have Sacrificed their lives that the "Nation May live." It Seams so terible that men have to suffer and die here with no one to smooth their pillows or speak a kind word to them but their comrads and they are so accustomed to such Scenes that they have not the simpathy of Mothers and Sisters or Wives and dont know how to care for them properly. Then we have none of the comforts of home to give them. All we can do is care for them the best we can. I had a horror for a dead man when I was at home. I could hardly bear the idea of even looking at one let alone touching him. How different now I Sit by their Bunks and see them "breath their last" and then they are removed to the Basement with no one to watch over their Body but left some times two or three days before they are buried. Then they are put into a rough Coffin and hauled to the cemetry and burried by men detailed for that purpose and a little board Set up at their head with the number of the grave put on it and no other mark to tell who he is where he belonged or came from.

Tuesday Dec 23rd

Haveing been two nights in succession I was permitted to sleep and did not get up untill Seven Oclock. . . . I was out in town and went to See some of our Boys in other Hospittals. . . . I found severel of our men in town. I did not get to bed untill twelve Oclock. . . .

Wednesday Dec 24th

We had a general clean out to day for Inspection. I did not go to bed untill twelve Oclock. We did not have a "Christmas Tree" and I guess "Santa Claus" has forgotten us a way out here in "Dixey" as I dont see any Signs of his comeing. I was wondering if nex[t] Christmas will find us Still in the Army or what will another year bring to our country. Will it then be all peace and harmony or will the two Sections be engaged and the Severel Armies be Situated as they are now. I think not although this year has but one Short week I dont believe it will pass before a great Battle will take place. Troops are now moveing to the front.

Thursday Dec 25th

I cant Say that we have a merry Christmas as the same routine is before us. I wanted to go out to see the Boys but could not get a pass as our men are moveing and I suppose my Regiment is either on the march or will be Soon. We had no change of any kind not eaven in "Grub" as we had "Hard Tack & Sow Belly." Some Sick men came in from camp and reported the 75th on the move and it Seams to be a general move and now we may expect lively times soon. Rosencrans or Bragg must give back and I dont think either will give without a fight. I dont know which way our Boys are going.

Friday Dec 26th

This was a rainey day and our Boys left their camp about day light. I received Two letters from Nett and also Two pairs of Socks and a pair of wollen mittens by mail from her. All of which demonstrates that although we are many miles from home and exposed to all kinds of hardships that our comfort is first in the minds of the dear ones left at home. It is a great Satisfaction to know that we are even thought of and such little tokens of comfort cheer us on to duty and makes us feel proud of our friends and know they appretiate our wants and if it were possible would contribute much more to sustain us. Then it seams that us soldiers can much better appretiate the comforts of home when peace Shall reign all over our Land and our Glorious Republic Shall be again united under the "dear old flag" and we shall be permitted to return to our fire Sides. But how many of us will be permitted to return. There are thousands no[w] sleeping in unknown Graves and many more yet will have to die martyrs to perpetuate the best Government in the world. I feel lonesom to know that our Boys here left and I [am] not with them.

Saturday Dec 27th

Rumor is afloat that the Rebel John Morgan burned Beacon Creek Bridge and Severd communication with Louisville our base of supplies. I heard cannonadeing in the direction of Nashville. I dont know what it means unless the "Ball" has oppend up. I learned that my Regiment has gone back into Kentucky after Morgan. Well the time Still draws near when a decisive Battle must be fought and I would not be surprised if the fireing we heard to day is the commencement. Our Army is in splendid condition and will do good work. But if we are defeated then we will have to fall back again. An old Seargent by name of Ashley called me to his Bunk and requested me to write a Letter to his famly "Saying I am going to die Soon and want to advise my wife how to manage after I am gone.["] I tried to diseuade him but he insisted on me writeing. I got a large Sheet of paper and he Sat on his bunk and told me what to Say. I worded it in his own language as near as possible. He Spoke of severel of his children and advised his wife what to do untill the Sheet was nearly full. He is a Baptist minister and Seams very intelligent and in his Sound mind. After I finished he made me promise that I would Send it to his wife at Ladoga Indiana. I tried to reason with him and get him to relinquish the notion but he Said he would be a dead man within Twenty four hours. He lamented that he had to die so far from home but had no regrets that he was a Soldier and was Solaced with the consciousness of thinking he had done only his duty in enlisting. After he talked to me he laid down [and] he was reconciled and rested easy. He is a man between forty & fifty years of age. Small in Stature but does not appear to be dangerously Sick.

Sunday Dec 28th

I was over to the Depot for news and there [are] all kinds of rumors. One that Rosencrans is driveing the Rebels towards Stone River and that they are opposeing every Step. My Old Friend and fellow Soldier Mr Ashley died to day and I complied with his request of yesterday and Sent his "Last Will & Testament" to his wife with a Short Letter telling when he died and that I held his Knapsack subject to her orders.[19] This seams a Strange presentiment of approaching death. When I wrote his Letter I did not think him dangerously Sick and supposed he was perhaps a little homesick. He was undoubtedly in his right mind. His age and his asking me to write for him caused me to take an interest in him and he was a very pleasent and kind old gentleman. But it appears he had a presentment that he was going to die within the next twenty four hours and his predictions prove to true. I can account for it. He died appearently easy and when I closed his eyes he look[ed] as though he only Slept. Sad will be the hearts of the wife and children when they receive the word that they will never see the face of the Husband & Father and think he is another Sacrifice to the cause of Liberty & Right. But one great consolation they have is he died doing his duty that they may inherit the rights of a free people.

Monday Dec 29th

We had a Scrubbing frollic and cleaned out the Room and it is as neat as a pin. . . . I was out to get the news and our camps and Town is full of rumors that our Army is gradually advanceing and we can hear the cannon but we cant get any thing reliable. But I believe there is [a] grand move on hands.

Tuesday Dec 30th

Some others and myself was out in the country to get some chickens and any thing els that sick men can eat but the Chickens have all Strayed off since the "Yanks" come in. I went to a house in the south part of Town to a "Negro Dance" and they seamed to enjoy themselves. But it did not interest me and I did not Stay long. It smelt rather strong of "Nigger."

WEDNESDAY DEC 31ST

I was out to day for some thing to eat but had no better success than yesterday. The cannonadeing commenced early this morning and continued all day. I am satisfied there is a Battle going on in the front between the two Armies and I wait anxiously for the result as every thing depends on our success. If we are defeated we loose our hold and it would be a great disaster and hard telling where it would end. I hope Genl Rosencrans will succeed in teaching Bragg and his minions a good lesson and drive them from their Strong hold at Stone River. The Battle rages fiercely in the front and now we almost hold our breath. The cannonadeing is terific. It is misting rain and is quite cold and will be terible for wounded me[n] who will have to lay on the Battle field all night. We contemplated giveing our Sick men a treat but with two days hunting did not succeed in getting much of a variety and I fear our New Year day will be about like all the rest. But will fare much better than our Boys who are now engaged with the enemy and I Shudder when I think of the wounded and dieing. I dont know where my regiment is.[20]

CHAPTER 4

One by One the Boys Pass Away

The Hoosiers enjoyed a six month stay in Murfreesboro, their longest period in any one location. Their camp on the east side of town "was made very nice and cleanly [*sic*] and healthy," wrote Sergeant Floyd. "It was laid out city fashion . . . by the formation of the tents into straight and regular rows."[1] They were now a part of Maj. Gen. Joseph J. Reynolds's Fourth Division of the Fourteenth Army Corps, commanded by Maj. Gen. George H. Thomas. The occasional reconnaissance or scout along with minor skirmishes helped the Hoosiers pass the time, as they participated in five different expeditions through Middle Tennessee from January to April 1863, securing forage, taking prisoners, and destroying Confederate supplies and railroads. But such excitement came at a price. In the words of E. W. Freeman, "It does seem that whenever there is anything to be done in the way of scouting, guarding or marching, the 75th is the regiment that has to do it."[2] To make matters worse, "in these excursions the men suffered severely from exposure in the inclement weather," stated one account, "being without blankets or tents."[3]

Despite their relative inactivity in Murfreesboro, the enlisted soldiers of the Army of the Cumberland sensed that they were about to embark on a great campaign. Wesley King, a sergeant in the Seventy-fifth's Company B, wrote a letter home on March 30, 1863, in which he eloquently compared his feelings to those of Shakespeare's Richard III the night before Bosworth Field: "Our grand army here is quiet, but it strikes every one as the quiet that immediately precedes a mighty storm. . . . A great work is going quietly on, strong forts are being erected, regiments are being organized, everything belonging to the army is being remodeled, camp equipage is being reduced and the useless lumber of shoulder straps sent home; inspections are rigidly enforced, reviews are had not for show, but for our idolized commander really to see the backing he has. Everything, Sir, indicates either an onward movement, or a desperate stand."[4]

As 1863 opened, William Bluffton Miller continued to serve as a hospital steward, separated from his regiment in Gallatin, Tennessee.

Thursday Jany 1st 1863
[Gallatin, Tennessee]

Could I be at home to day I think it would be a "happy New Year" in every sense of the word. But when I hear the boom of the cannon again to day I feel Sad and anxious. hope we will be able to enjoy the next New Year day at home. Should our Arms meet with a reverse it may be Severel more yet before we will be permitted to do so. It still rains and is cold and disagreeable. Rumors are favorable in refference to yesterdays Battle and our Army is gradually driveing the enemy but the Stronghold is Murfreesboro and it is not decided yet. Our forces destroyed Laverne and a terific Battle was fought there yesterday. We cant learn any thing certain[.][5] I think from rumor that Bragg is getting a terable drubbing and will get back from his position. We hope for the best any way. I wrote to Newt Burwell Uncle Jimmy (his father) who is in convalescent camp. He was not able to go with the Regiment. I found him out in the camp in the rain and I got an order from the Medical Perveyor to admit him into our Hospital. He has Dropsey and to[o] old for a Soldier.

Friday Jany 2nd

Bragg has left Murfreesboro and our men have taken possession. We have gained a glorious Victory and our anxious moments for the last few days. My Regiment have gone there. . . . I am anxious to get away from here and back where I belong.

Saturday Jany 3rd

The Trains bound North are loaded with our wounded Soldiers. I have not ascertained our loss in killed and wounded but it of course is heavy.

But the Rebels lost as many as we if not more and the[y] retreated on the night of the first toward Tullahoma. The[y] are badly used up and lost their Strong hold.

SUNDAY JAN 4TH

We made a general clean out to day and I went to the Depot to get a Nashville paper. The mail has not been able to get through yet on account of [a] Break in the Rail Road by Morgan. . . . The probabilities are that it will be severel days before we get any mail from the north. The weather is cold and Some Snow. The citizens say it is as cold as it ever gets here. The darkies always go without Shoes and they cant do so now. It is frozen hard now.

MONDAY JAN 5TH

I was to severel Sutlers for paper and Envellops so I could write Letters but it is very Scarce and I did not find any. I was at the camp of the 13th Indiana Battery to see some of the Boys. The[y] formly belonged to our Brigade but are doeing Garison duty here. Our wounded are Still passing through going north untill they get well.

TUESDAY JAN 6TH

. . . The Army is laying Still now at Murfreesboro to rest and recruit its depleted Ranks and prepare for another move. Bragg occupies McMinnville Tullahoma & Hoovers Gap and will remain there untill we move to him again.

WEDNESDAY JAN 7TH

My Old Friend Jimmy Burwell was taken down Sick to day and I fear he will not last many days. . . . I visited Some of our Boys in other Hospitals and found some of them very Sick. . . . There is quite a number from my Regiment in town who gave out on the march after Morgan.

THURSDAY JAN 8TH

I visited the Depot for news and met two of our Boys who came up to Hospital with me. I went with them to see our sick men. . . . Old mr Burwell is very Sick and cannot Survive long unless there is a change.

I think the Symptoms are bad and that he cannot get well. If his discarge papers would come I would try to send him home.

Friday Jan 9th

I did not sleep any last night but Stayed up with Burwell and I put in the day with him. He tried to talk to me but I could not understand him. He died about Six Oclock this p.m. It seams almost like looseing a Father to loose him but I done all I could to make him as comfortable in his last moments. I took charge of his Watch and Knapsack and tellegraphed to Newt Burwell if they wanted to take his body home for burial. I had him laid out in one corner of the Room and will try to keep him untill I hear from his friends.

Saturday Jany 10th

I met Jim Godfrey of my company and I had to let them take Burwell and bury him as the Doctor was afraid of cantageon. I went to the cemetry and marked his grave so I will know where to find him Should his friends want his body. While at the grave my thoughts revert back to the date of examination at Camp Wabash when he was so anxious to go with us and was so full of fun that the Doctors passed him by without hardly looking at him. He was then nearly fifty years old and enlisted through patriotism. He was to[o] old to endure the hardships and gave out on the march from Frankford to Bowling Green. His discharge papers are made out and forwarded to Head Quarters for approval. But here [he] is laid in his last long home away from friends and no one but myself to drop a tear at his burial.[6] And no one but myself could find his grave or tell where his body could be found. It may never be required to know as I dont know whether his friends will ever want to remove him. But I turn away with a Sad heart not knowing how soon I may be brought to this place myself. I wrote to Newt Burwell telling him what was done. . . .

Sunday Jan 11th

I am now entirely alone so far as the 75th Ind is concerned. There are none of our Boys in this Hospital. I took a Bathe in the creek and then went to the Fort where the 13th Ind Battery are and visited our sick in the other Hospitals. . . . I found some of our Boys very Sick and some are improveing.

MONDAY JANY 12TH

I am sick and did not get out untill late. . . . I have Dioreah and feel very Bad. I went to bed early. No mail yet.

TUESDAY JAN 13TH

I am still Sick and was in my Bunk untill after noon. I made out to visit our Sick Boys. It does me good to meet them and talk with them. I[t] Seams to do them good to have me come and see them. It is raining and is a dreary lonesome day and [I] feel homesick but it will not do to let such a thing get hold on me as I See so much of the fatal effects of it. I will guard against it as I could not get home any way. We expected mail but did not get it. I went to bed early.

WEDNESDAY JAN 14TH

It is still cold and rainy it haveing rained all night. There was some Troops marched through town but I did not learn where they are going. I picked up a nice Stick of red Cedar and I am Carveing a Cane to send to "Pa." . . . I feel much better and I hope to be all right in a few days.

THURSDAY JAN 15TH

It is snowing and it is very Sloppy and wet. The train could not get through from Nashville as some Trustle work was washed out. Some of our sick got furloughs and I went to the Depot with them but there being no train they did not get off and come back to the Hospital to stay all night. They were very much disappointed and I felt bad for them. They are so anxious to go home to see their friends. I hope they will get of[f] all right to morrow. The trains do not run through yet.

FRIDAY JAN 16TH

I am Still sick and I went with them who are going home to the Depot but no trains come through and they were disappointed again. I went to the Bakery for Pies for some of our sick men. I had to stay up untill twelve Oclock to night as some of the nurses could not do duty. We get no news from the north as the Rail Road communication is cut off and no Trains can get through. It will soon get so our Rations will be Short unless they can get the trains through. We cant get any Letter paper now and other things are getting Scarce. There was a man killed in an Old Blacksmith Shop near the Hospital. He is a citizen and been buying Hides from the Government. I was down and seen him. He looked horible. He was killed with a club. It is not known who killed him but I dont think it was a Soldier. He is quite an old man and I think is a northren man. He was probably killed for his money. He is rather poorly dressed and dont look as though he had much money about him.

Saturday Jan 17th

No Trains from either way yet. No mail and our furloughed men destined to Stay another night. Some of them fear they will not get to go and it would be very bad as they are so elated I believe some of them would not survive the disappointment. I hope they will get off to morrow. If I cant go myself I like to see others go. I would enjoy a Short visit but I will have to wait a while yet and not lament over it.

Sunday Jan 18th

Jack Lucas and I Started on a scout this morning. We procured a pass out of our Pickets and was about four miles from Town. We hunted for Chickens Butter Eggs or any thing that could be eaten by sick men. But we made our trip for nothing. It is a little dangerous Scouting out Side as we might meet with Rebel Cavalry but we come in about noon. . . . Our furloughed men got off all right. No Trains from the North.

Monday Jan 19th

This is a rainy dreary day. I was in the House all day. Jack & I contemplated another trip to the country but the rain prevented us going. It is better to be in the house [in] such weather than in camp but I am getting So I Can hardly content myself here any more. The time seams so long and I get homesick. I wish they would relieve me and let me go to the front. I asked Doc Brown to let me off but he said he could not spare me.

TUESDAY JAN 20TH

It is still raining and is quite cold. The trains come through and I got Six Letters. . . . I was glad to hear from home once more and from the Regiment. . . . Our Boys are camped on the ground Occupied by the Rebels before the Battle of Stone River. The[y] arrived there the next day after Bragg evacuated and have been there ever since.

WEDNESDAY JAN 21ST

Charles Birch of the 72nd Indiana died last night and we packed his body for shipping north as a relative is here to go with it. I believe he died of pure homesickness and probably if he could of got home a few days would come back all right. He was a nice Boy and was generally liked by the men here. We took him to the Depot but they would not take him untill a Physicians certificate as to the cause of death was procured. So he remains here untill to morrow. . . . I hope we will be able to keep Morgan off the Rail Road now and we can receive our mail regular.

THURSDAY JAN 22ND

I received a Tellegram from New= Burwell asking when his Father died and if he Should bring a metallic case and I answerd it immediately to Louisville So I presume he will be here soon. I will be glad to meet him as any body from "Gods Country" would meet with a welcome from me now. But he is an old acquaintiance and "School fellow" and friend. His politics are [not] just what they ought to be now but that is a small matter and we will not quarrell about that now. I will do every thing I can to assist him in his Sad mission and to get the body of "Uncle Jimmy" away from Southren Soil and back to the land he sacrificed his life to defend and be burried as a christian and Soldier.

FRIDAY JAN 23RD

This was a rainy Gloomy day. . . . I remained in the Hospital the most of the day. I did not go to see our Boys out in Town.

SATURDAY JANY 24TH

Burwell arrived this evening and the Case came on the same train. We took it up town and I had to procure passes to get out to the Cemetary and hunt up the Undertaker and make the necissary arrangements to take up his father and get him to [the] morning Train. Newt Stayed all night with me. We will have to get out early if we Succeed in makeing the Train as it passes here at Nine a.m. It does me good to See some body from home and who can tell me all about my people and Bluffton and how things look in Gods Country. I find he entertains Democratic principles and we had Some pretty Sharp talk on politics. I was once a Douglas Democrat but I am now for the Union "right or wrong" and I dont like to have a man argue with me and defend the Rebels in any way.[7] They undertook to break the union and opend up the war and now let them Suffer the consequences of their foolishness. They must succumb to the arms of the North sooner or later and I am in favor of prolonging the war untill they Surrender and and lay down their Arms unconditionally.[8] Let the Simpathisers of the north howl but I tell Burwell they will See that the old flag will float tryumpantly over every foot of Territory She ever did and that two separate governments will never be tolerated on this continent. He represents the North as ready to raise up (The Democrats) and help the south. I Said to him if that was the feeling the sooner they Showed up the better and we would know then what to depend on and we would Send men there and have a general war. I think a party or Set of men who will encourage the Southern States from the North now are not fit to live under the old flag and the sooner they are put out of the way the Better. This may be Strong language but after seeing severel months of the war I have no simpathies for Rebels of [or] their allies.

SUNDAY JAN 25TH

We were out by daylight and raised Uncle Jimmy but the Train passed before we got him ready to Ship. When we oppend the Coffin he was recognizeable but soon turned black. We put him in the Case and Soldered it down tight so no smell could arise. We found the grave dry and was easier to remove him than we anticipated. The Undertaker took charge of him and will have him at the train in the morning. Newt did not get away and we visited our Sick Boys who were all glad to See him. . . . He finds a great many things here that he did not expect to see. I think he realizes the beauties of the war and I hope it may have a good effect and cause him to view the question in a different light. He dont find much encouragement for his sentiments among the soldiers.

MONDAY JAN 26TH

I went with Burwell to the Train and helped put the Body on the Train. The Train passed at nine a.m. I am some what lonesom since Newt left. But I come back to the Hospital and was there all day. I moved my Bunk into the house adjoining the church. I was at Doc Brown to go to the front to day but he Says I must make up my mind to remain. So I have concluded to be contented and wait untill I am relieved.

TUESDAY JAN 27TH

. . . I was over to the Depot for a Box by Express from home but could not find it. There was three deaths in my Ward and there is one more bad case. Charlie Coolbaugh cannot live long. . . .

WEDNESDAY JAN 28TH

I done my washing. Guss Zerse and I arranged a Bed Room in the House and have a nice room now all to our selves. Charlie Coolbaugh died about three Oclock this p.m. I layed him out and invoiced his Knapsack and put it away. I dont know where he is from but his "Roll" will Show. He was a nice Boy. . . .

THURSDAY JAN 29TH

. . . I was over to the Express Office but our Box has not come yet. I visited Hospital No 4 and did not get to bed untill eleven Oclock. . . . Three deaths to day.

FRIDAY JAN 30TH

There was nothing of importance occured to day. I done about the usual amount of work. . . . My Box has not got here yet.

SATURDAY JAN 31ST

. . . I visited No 4 to day. As I was comeing from the depot this eveining I met Joe Richey who has come after the Body of Harrison Foncannon of the 101st Ind who he says died in No 4. I think it a mistake. I Showed him a place to Stay and then visited the Convalescent Camp where I found Foncannon and he was not dead. I went to the Hotel and told Richey what I had done and talked with him untill nine

Oclock and I went to the Hospital as after the Countersign was out the patroll would not let me pass. A Boy by [the] name of Jacoby died Sudenly in my ward. He was sitting up and fell over dead. He is an Indiana man. It rained all night.

SUNDAY FEBY 1ST

This is a good climate for rain at this season of the year. It is raining yet this morning. I went with Richey to the Convalescent Camp and found Foncannon in the 1st Battalion Co "H." Richey was some what Surprised to find him liveing haveing heard he was very Sick and could no[t] live long. . . . I found Adam Perry very Sick at No 4 and will make arrangements to move him to No 5 to morrow So I can take care of him. He is a member of my company and I try to do all I can for any of our Boys who I find Sick.

MONDAY FEBY 2ND

I went to the Depot to see about my Box after Breakfast but did not get it. I then went to [the] Medical Perveyor for an order to remove Adam Perry to No 5. They did not like to give it but I prevailed on them to issue it. We have a comfortable place now for the Sick in comparison to the other Hospitals.

TUESDAY FEBY 3RD

. . . I got an Ambulance and took Adam Perry to No 5. It is very cold. I fear Perry will not live many days. He is very much discouraged and would like to go home but I fear that is impossible now as no furloughs are granted. I think it wrong to keep men here when they could be sent home untill they get well with less expense and trouble than they can be here and then it would help so many recruit up and be a great gratification to them.

WEDNESDAY FEB 4TH

The long looked for Box arrived this evening and it was in Capt Karns name and I knew I could not get it without an order from him and it would not go on to the Regiment. So I put up a job on the Express Agent. I [im]personated Capt Karns and when I asked for the Box he was very kind supposeing I was a commissioned officer and I did not undeceive him and he enquired where I wanted it and Sent his colored Boy with a Wheel Borrow to take it to the Hospital. Had he known that I was only a "high Private" he would not even let me have it. But so much for being a Captain. I opend the Box and it haveing been on the road since Dec 23rd the things were all spoiled. There was apples in it and they had been frozen and was rotten. I had a new pair [of] Boots in it and the legs were full of rotten apples. The Butter was all spoiled and a large Cheese was rotten. "My dear old mother" thought of me by sending a Basted Turkey but it was spoiled and could not be eaten. The Canned Fruits were nearly all good. I packed all that was sent to the other Boys in a smaller Box and sent it to Murfreesboro. I felt bad to think so many of the good things sent us were spoiled and my heart is full of kindness and thanks to the contributors to know that our comfort is uppermost in their minds. I do think our friends in the north are the best people in the world and I am proud that I can say in years to come that I was a Soldier and fought against wrong and to uphold the "old flag." May the donors live long to enjoy the rich blessings of our glorious land and if I Should not be permitted to see their faces again my thoughts Shall ever be with them in my last moments. I had severel articles in the Box from different friends and also a letter from Nett. I wrote to her this evening telling her that the Box was received and the condition of its contents and I know they will feel as bad as I do to think it did not reach us all right. But they intended it all well and it could not be helped.

Thursday Feb 5th

. . . Add Perry is very Sick and cannot live long. It is very Sad to look at him in the prime of manhood Stricken down with disease and dieing in a foreign land but how many poor Boys have I layed out since I come here. It is an every day occurrence to lay out from three to five and seven. The cemetery is filling up very fast.

Friday Feby 6th

Another Boy has paid the last debt. Adam Perry died this morning. I was by him when he breathed his last and he died without Struggle. I tried to talk with him but could not understand him. One by one the Boys pass away and our ranks are thined out. But others will be called to take their places and they will soon be forgotten. I received a long Letter from Nett Saying that Burwell had reached home with the remains of his father and he had been buried in the old Cemetery without opening the coffin. There was a long funeral of "Soldiers friends" turned out to pay the last sad rights to the dead Soldier. May he rest in peace.

Saturday Feby 7th

This is a beautiful Spring day. . . . We Scrubbed and cleaned up for sunday.

Sunday Feb 8th

Sunday does not differ from any other day with us. If when Sunday comes we have any thing to do it is done as if we were never taught to reverence the "Lords Day." It has the appearance of rain. . . . Col Wolfords 11th Kentucky Cavalry passed through town. They are a fine body of men and made a fine Show. They were going North I presume to keep a lookout for Morgans Gang of Cut throats.[9]

Monday Feby 9th

It is Six months to day since I left home. I[t] Seams as though it was that many years when I think back and think over what has passed and what I have seen and passed through. . . .

Tuesday Feb 10th

. . . I was in [the] Hospital the most of the day. About all the Boys I was acquainted with in other Hospitals have either died or gone to the front and have no place to go only loaf around town and there is nothing to see but Soldiers and I cant content my self long. I write a number of letters for sick men who are not able to write and for those who cant write. I dont know what I would do if I could not write.

Wednesday Feb 11th

My Bunk Mate Zerse awoke me up about midnight by his peculiar actions and I got up and found him Sick with some thing like a Sinking Chill. I called out the Doctors and they soon relieved him. I was up the rest of the night. . . . We had a little game of Eucher this evening and I went to bed leaveing Jack to watch by Zerse who seams some better to night.

Thursday Feb 12th

I got up late this morning. Miss Bates of Indianapolis came as Matron of No 5. She seams to be a lady in every respect and will take charge of the Sanitary department. I was up untill about eleven and Zerse being better I Slept with him in case he should take a relapse. . . .

Friday Feby 13th

. . . I had all the Benches moved out of the Galery preparatory to cleaning it out as "Grey Backs" had got there from old clotheing and we must get rid of them. But it is almost an impossibility as men comeing in from the camps Sick are generally coverd with them. We have a room for batheing them but they get into the Beds in Spite of us. It keeps [us] cleaning all the time. The[y] multiply very fast when they get in and soon Scatter all through the Bunks. I never saw any untill I come here.

Saturday Feby 14th

This is another rainy day and I remained in the house all day. I got a Letter this morning from Nett dated the 7th & 8th inst.[10] I had the Boys mop the Gallery and I answerd Netts Letter to night. The new Sanitary good[s] are here and we will clean out and put them on the Bunks tomorrow and it will help the looks anyway.

Sunday Feb 15th

I Set the Boys to mopping this morning and washing the windows and this after noon coverd all our Bunks with White Spreads. This afternoon Shipley and I took a walk and was out to the Fortifications.[11] They would be more attractive I suppose to a person who never seen any thing of the kind but they are nothing new to me. They would protect the men from an attack but I dont consider them formidable and could be taken by storm. The Fort might hold out a little longer and might kill a good many men before they had to surrender. I have a very bad cold and dont feel very well. It is a lonesom Sunday.

Monday Feb 16th

Our Hospittal looks nice and clean and the white Bed Spreads helps it out. It looks more like home now and I think the sick men enjoy it. I cant help compareing it with the first day I came here. There is hardly one man excep the Nurses that was here when I come. Some have died and others have been sent to their different commands and I see all new faces. We have Severel very Sick men they will probably die.

Tuesday Feb 17th

There is a man from the 129th Illinois a long muscular fellow who we cant keep in his Bunk or even in the house when he takes a notion to go out. There is none of us can handle him and he seams deranged and I dont believe the Doctors know what the difficulty is. I can pursuade him in and can controll him by kindness only and he requires watching. I am the only one [who] can manage him. I keep him in when here but as soon as I am out he has it his own way.

Wednesday Feby 18th

My crazy man keeps me here nearly all the time. But I was at the Depot and met Bill Perry (Adds Brother) who has come to see him. But was teribly Shocked when I told him he was dead and burried. He thinks he cannot remove him home. He is not able financially. He feels very bad about it. . . . Our crazy man got out about ten Oclock p.m and it is dark and rainy and he has no clotheing on but Drawers & Shirt and we cant find him. We are not allowed away now as the counter sign is out and we would be picked up by the patroll if we went out. I expect he will be picked up and be put in the Guard House. We did not know what he was going to do untill he was so far gone that we were unable to prevent him. . . .

Thursday Feb 19th

I carried Adam Perrys Knapsack to the Depot for Bill and he started home. I[t] seamed hard for him to return without his Brother. Our crazy man was returned by the Patroll this morning he haveing been in the Guard House all night and he is very wild to day. We have to guard him all the time. He wont Stay in his Bunk. I answerd Netts Letter of the 18th But got no mail.

Friday Feb 20th

I received a Letter to day containing the Startling intelligence that Father had the Small Pox. I am almost ready to go home on a "French Furlough." I hope none of the rest have been exposed and that he will get along all right. I cant go home and I would not go without a furlough. I come here with an honest motive and because I thought it was my duty and I will remain untill I can go home honorably.[12] I could not prevent any from takeing the disease or do them any good if I was there but I would go if possible. I was out to the Convalescent camp and learned that Harrison Foncannon was dead and burried. I had not heard he was dangerous. . . . We were discussing the Emancipation Proclimation and I find others as well as my self who are afraid of the effect in the north and fear it will cause a war there. A great many Soldiers condemn it on that account.[13]

Saturday Feb 21st

. . . Our crazy man died about eleven Oclock a.m and on examineing his head the Doctors concluded he died from inflamation of the Brain.[14] I think it a case of ignorance on the part of the Doctors and if they had knew what was the trouble he might have been relieved. There is entirely to[o] much experimenting done here by the surgeons.

Sunday Feb 22nd

It is cold and disagreeable and Tom Richey come in to day and I went with him to the Convalescent camp. . . . I answerd Netts Letter of the 15th and sent her some confederate Money. I did not get to bed untill midnight. I got no mail.

Monday Feb 23rd

I am anxious to hear from home but did not get any Letters to day. I did not get up untill Eight Oclock and was on duty from Twelve n untill midnight. I was over to the Depot this evening only a few minutes. One of my Nurses being Sick I relieved him. There is no news from the front this is reliable but all kinds of rumors. I dont think there will be another move made untill our Army is recruited up and reorganized and put in fighting trim.

TUESDAY FEB 24TH

This is a beautifull day and makes me almost homesick. I received a Letter from Nett Saying Pa was convalescing and had only a Slight attack. . . . This is about the only nice day we have had Since I come here. The sun is bright and warm and feels like Spring in Indiana. I asked Doc Brown for a furlough but he did not give me any Satisfaction.

WEDNESDAY FEBY 25TH

This is a change so far as [the] weather is concerned. It is raining. I was at Doc Brown for a furlough again but Said he did not believe I could get one and I will drop the subject. He intimated that if I wanted to risk it I could take a French Leave. But I wont do that. I put in the time reading a Novel called Iron Cross and did not get off duty untill midnight.[15] It rained all night.

THURSDAY FEB 26

I made the usual trip to the Depot but the Train did not get through by reason of damage done to [the] Trustle work by last nights rain. I wrote a Letter to Uncle Jacob Geary and did not go to be[d] untill midnight. I am getting tired of being up half the night right along and if they would only let me off I would go to my regiment immediately. It would be a change and not so monotinus and give a little excitement and variety. It is about the Same thing every day and I look on the same faces with a few exceptions. We get the papers and a few minutes reading will get all the news.

FRIDAY FEB 27TH

. . . There is Some talk of paying us off. We are entitled to Eight months pay and I know there [are] thousands of men here whos famlies need money. But the queary is will the people at home See the famlies of the Soldiers Suffer for the necissaries of life while we are here. I dont believe it. I have more confidence in my friends than that. But we Should be paid off and we could provide for ourselves a little.

SATURDAY FEBY 28TH

. . . We did not mop to day. I went for the news to the Depot but got none of importance. This is another rainy day and I guess we can safely call this a wet month. . . . My friend Zerse leaves here to morrow and I take his place as Stewart.[16] Some of our troops are on the move but we get no news of importance.

Sunday March 1st

March opens up beautifully. This is a nice day. I went with my old Bunkmate Zerse to the Depot. I will be lonely now and I Shall not occupy our old room any longer Jim Nevins Started home on Discharge. I am glad he got out as he is only a "half witted" fellow and never ought have been taken. I enterd on my new duty and dont know how I will get along but I will do the best I can untill relieved.

Monday March 2nd

I received my appointment and Cheverons and made out my first morning Report and put out the prescriptions which is new buisiness to me. I now have entire controll of the Hospital except the Doctors duty. . . . I feel as though I am left alone again and miss "Guss." He was good company and we had a nice time to gether and I feel I have lost a friend.

Tuesday Mar 3rd

I made my morning Report and took it to Head Quarters the first thing and Superintended the cleaning up and arrangeing the Hospital. I was not out in town or to the Depot. I did not get to bed untill ten Oclock. We got no news of importance. I find I have more buisiness than I bargained for and Shall try to get away from here as soon as possible and go to the front.

Wednesday Mar 4th

After the usual Duties of the morning I went to the Post Office for our mail and distributed it to the Sick. . . . I told Doc Brown I Should apply to Regimental Head Quarters to be relieved and he discouraged me. He Says I am foolish to want to go to the front when I can remain here during the war. But if I thought I had to Stay here two years longer I would almost go to Cannada or some other place to get away from here. I am Sorely tired of it and would much sooner cary a musket as be imprisoned in this place.

Thursday Mar 5th

. . . I got a Letter from Nett and one from "Pa." I also got one from Mrs Ashley thanking me for the part I had taken in behalf of her Husband who I wrote the letter for and had such a Strange presentiment of approaching death. She requested me to come and See her should I ever get near her. She enclosed money for me to forward his things to her.

Friday Mar 6th

I answerd Netts Letter after attending to my duty and delivering morning Report. . . . I also answerd Pas Letter and the rest of the day untill Nine Oclock I put in Superintending other matters and then went to bed.

Saturday Mar 7th

This is another rainy day. I made morning Report and Deliverd it. Put up the medicins for the sick and then put in the rest of the day reading a Temperance Story titled "Danger of dining out." I visited No 4 after noon only a few minutes.

Sunday Mar 8th

It rains again to day and after doeing my morning work I wrote a letter to my wife. . . . The Beds were all changed and men furnished clean clotheing and that takes up some time and it changes the gloomy appearances to cheerfulness and Sun Shine.

Monday Mar 9th

Well Monday comes in with rain and I did not go out only to deliver morning Report. . . . No news of importance in the papers and all is quiet in the front.

Tuesday Mar 10th

Mr Joe Richey of Bluffton come into [the] Hospital this morning. He brought Some things from home for me among the rest "Rollies" picture.[17] He came after the body of his Son-in-law Harrison Foncannon. I was out to the Cemetery with him to assist in raiseing him. We did not get back in time to make the morning Train. I was out to see some boys at a Boarding House this eiveining. . . .

Wednesday Mar 11th

Richey took the morning Train for home with the body of Foncannon in charge. I gave him my Letters. An orderly came in and enquired for me when I was out some place. He did not say what he wanted or who he was. . . .

Thursday Mar 12th

I done my work as usual and about noon I got orders to report to my regiment for duty. That accounts for the orderly enquireing for me yesterday. He wanted to know if I was there so he could deliver my order. I was so happy that I can hardly wait untill Train time and I packed my K[n]apsack as soon as possible. I bid all the attachees and sick men good bye and they hated to see me go appearently and I am parting from many friends. But at four Oclock pm I left Gallatin I hope never to return. I am so tired of it. I feel like I had got out of prison. I got to Nashville about dark and was taken to the "Zollacoffer Barracks" which is in a very large unfinished Building that was intended for a Hotel and built by the Rebel General of that name who was killed by Col Frye at Mill Springs Kentucky.[18] We had to Sleep on the floor and make our own Beds. I hope I wont have to stay here very long. I was in the Hospital just three months.

Friday March 13th
[Murfreesboro, Tennessee]

I was called out at three a.m. and supposed I would go on to Murfreesboro. But I learned something. They only take so many men and when they are counted off the ballance have to remain untill the next Train load is called for. This is nothing more nor less than a Prison and I did not propose to remain here any longer than possible. I was not one of the lucky ones and would have to remain another day but by a Strategic military move I managed to get into the ranks of those counted off and marched out with them to the depot. I got to Murphreesboro about noon and went immediately to the camp of the 75th which is south of town on the Woodbury Pike. I found all the Boys that are with the company all O.K. but I miss a number who are absent Sick. . . . I was informed by Levi Keagle that I am brought here on account of a Letter I wrote to Dick Buckmaster and claimed to contain "disloyal Sentiments" or in other words Shows a disposition of insubordination.[19] It was caused by a man professing to be my especial friend who wanted the appointment of "Seargent" over me and reported it to the Captain who applied for an order to have me relieved through Col Robinson. Some of the Boys say I will be "court marshalled." But It does not frighten me any for I cant think I wrote any letter containing any thing of the kind but I will see. My friend Secured the Seargentcy all the Same and he is happy. But we will probably have some things to settle up at some future time. Lieut Starbuck told me that Col Robinson wanted me to report to his tent and I did so. He Showed me the great Letter that Capt Karns had carried to him after demanding it from Buckmaster and after reading it to me asked me if I wrote it. I told him I did and it was my opinions when I wrote it and I had no excuses or retractions to make. He remarked to [me] *That Shows Grit* and also said if others would let such matters alone he ["]would not bother with them." He says I will burn the letter and you can report to your company for duty. I then thanked him and he put my letter in the fire and I went back to the company. The letter refered to the emancipation pro-climation which I do not endorse and never will untill I see farther. If it will help put down the Rebellion any sooner I will think it all right and not before by reason of a dozen Court Marshalls. But I do condemn the parties who were instrumental in trying to get me into trouble and I may have an opportunity to Show as good a record as a soldier as they. But I wont run to beccon[?] of any man for position here much less do as dirty a trick as that for the position of Seargent. . . . I now enter into the dutys of camp life again and feel as though I would enjoy it.

Saturday Mar 14th

This is a nice warm day and we moved our camp farther South and west and we put in the after noon fixing up our quarters. Jim Spake and Levi Keagle are my Bunk Mates. We are camped in a grove of Timber and our Army Streches entirely around the town. I have not had a chance to See the Battle field or Rebel fortifications yet as we are South of Stone River. . . .

Sunday Mar 15th

The rest of the Regiment haveing been paid four months pay I have been expecting my money but have received nothing and it is now over

Eight months since I enlisted. Add Haines and I visited the camp of the 101st Indiana and I seen uncles Will and Charlie Miller. Uncle charlie is Sick and suffering with his foot which was crushed by a Wagon Wheel. He has been examined and reported for discharge as he is not able to do any duty. The rest of my acquaintances are all well. They now belong to our Division and we will be together. . . . We have a good camp and nice Spring Water.

Monday Mar 16th

I was cleaning my gun and done my washing. . . . The army is inactive and no Signs of a move Soon. We do nothing but a little Fatigue Pick[et] or Guard duty and eat and Sleep. We have plenty of rations and are fat and Saucy.

Tuesday Mar 17th

Jim Spake went on Picket and there is no drill. Medsker came and asked me to do some writing for him. I done so but I hope they will let me out of that. I coppied some General Orders for him. . . .

Wednesday Mar 18th

The Boys come in off Picket but we had no drill. I wrote to Charlie Geary and Sister "Sue" and not haveing any thing els to do crawled into the Tent and took a knap. Soldering is very lazy work. We get just enough to do to make is feel as though we were "Borne Tired" and the men will make more fuss over a few hours duty than they would to do a days work at home. Some of them seam to think they come here only to lay around. They dont realize that they are paid by the government to work.

Thursday Mar 19th

I was detailed for Picket duty this morning and our Post is about two miles South on the Woodbury Pike. I am Corporal of Second Relief. Picket duty is done by dividing the men into three parties called "Reliefs" and a corporal has to take charge of each. Then the 1st Relief is scatterd along the line of Stations so many paces apart. Generally about thirty and they are required to walk back and fourth during the two hours they are on duty. They are relieved every two hours which makes two hours out of Six or "two on and four off" as is known in the

Army. The two reliefs not on duty are Stationed in the rear where the guns are Stacked and ready for action if an attack is made on the Posts. They are called the Reserve. In case of an attack the pickets "rally on the Reserve" and all fall back toward camp untill a Line of Battle is formed to meet the attacking party. Genl Rosencrans passed out to review some Troops near our post.

Friday Mar 20th

We were relieved and returned to camp this morning and I went to Murfreesboro for my pay but did not get it. The word come into camp that the second Brigade were surrounded and we were orderd out on a "Double Quick" to Milton where we found the 101st Indiana and other regiments had been attacted by Morgans raiders and had quite a fight.[20] We got into camp about nine Oclock and we layed on our Arms all night. I am very tired and worn out. I dont know what condition or position we occupy. We may have and I expect we will have a fight to drive Morgan away.

Saturday Mar 21st

A reconoitering party is sent out to see where the Rebels are and found they were gone. We gatherd up the Guns left on the Battle field Buried the dead and took the wounded into a house and some Rebel Surgeons come in to take care of their wounded. Morgan got all he wanted yesterday and did not make his appearence to day. Severel men out of the 101st were wounded among them Jim Miller John Clark (Boath legs broken) and Adam Bartlemy Shot in the nose. We left Milton about one Oclock p.m. for our old camp. Morgan undertook to play the same game he did at Heartsville but he found the Yanks wide awake this time and he did not want them as bad as he thought he did. We got to camp about Eight Oclock very tired. . . .

Sunday Mar 22nd

I feel Sore from our march and we will get to rest as there will be no drilling. . . . I was not away from camp and took a good Sleep. There is no preaching in camp. We did not have and Dress Parade. It is a very nice warm day.

Monday Mar 23rd

It rained some to day and we had no drill but Dress Parade. . . .

Tuesday Mar 24th

I went on Picket and we had a very disagreeable day and night. It rained and was quite cold. When we were off duty we could not lay down but put in the entire night without Sleep. This is just the kind of a night that requires Sentinals to keep vigilant watch. I found Jim Mounts of "Co G" asleep on his post. I took his gun. I had to approach him carefully and get the advantage of him before wakeing him up for fear in his fright he would use his gun on me thinkin[g] I was a "Johny Rebb." But I wrenched his gun from him. I did not report him. He would be liable to Court Marshall.[21]

Wednesday Mar 25th

I came into camp about ten am from Picket Duty in the rain. We had the worse kind of a night. I received a Letter from Nett and answerd it. I took a good Sleep and was out on Dress Parade. We received order[s] to prepare for General Review to morrow.

Thursday Mar 26

I cleaned my Gun and packed my Knapsack for Review. The Battallion formed at one Oclock pm and we moved out to a large field South of camp. Genls Rosencrans Genl Thomas [and] Genl Reynolds were present. I never seen Genl Reynolds before. He is an Indiana man medium Size and is a very nice looking old man. I like his appearance.[22] We got back to camp about five Oclock.

Friday Mar 27th

. . . It rained all night and our Sibley Tent leaks and we all got wet. I dont like to sleep in a house that wont turn rain but we will have to put up with it for the present.

Saturday Mar 28th

It is still raining Some yet. This being wash day we had no drill. We were out for Dress Parade. I had a nice Sleep to make up for last night. . . . We prepared for Sunday morning Inspection. No News.

SUNDAY MAR 29TH

We had company inspection as usual on Sunday morning but no drill. I wrote to Nett. It was so cold we kept a fire under the "Tripod" in the Tent. When we have to keep in the Tent all day it makes it lonesome.[23]

MONDAY MAR 30TH

Orders came in to prepare for General Review to morrow by Genl Rosencrans. The troops all around us are orderd out. I suppose the entire "Corps" will be on parade. . . . I cleaned up my Gun and accouterments.

TUESDAY MAR 31ST

We formed about Nine a.m. Generals Rosencrans Thomas Reynolds & Wilder were the Reviewing party. We did not get out of camp untill noon as other Troops were moveing and occupied the road. Our entire Division was out. We were formed by Regiments in open order. Genl Rosencrans and escort rode to the left in front and back in the rear of us and then we "closed up" and formed in colum by company and marched by the Generals. It was a nice Show but I got very tired marching. We returned to camp and Stacked Arms on [the] color line and policed our quarters So if Genl Rosencrans rode through the camp it would look clean. But they did not visit our camp. If they were as tired as we are they were glad to get into quarters and dont care whether our camp is clean or not. To see so many men on parade a person thinks they would be invinceble. This was my first Genl Grand Review.

WEDNESDAY APR 1ST

I was detailed for Picket and we was relieved and come back to camp about noon when orders was for us to be ready for light marching at two p.m. We Started about that time East and crossed Stone river Eight miles from camp by driveing the wagons into the river Side by Side and putting Stringers from one to another and then laying plank on making a Bridge so that we could cross. We camped on the east Bank for the night. We have no Tents or Knapsacks. We cary nothing but our

Blankets and Ponchoes. I dont know where we are to go to but is for scouting purposes.

Thursday April 2nd

We marched Twenty one miles and arrived at Lebanon on the Cumberland River and made our quarters in the Colledge Building. It is a large house and our entire Regiment occupies it.[24] Lebanon is a small town and a county seat. It is a nice location. The buildings are mostly of Brick and are neat. We had good quarters and were not disturbed during the night. The country we came over is some hilly but is about an average in the way of improvements. Planters are about as doeless as they generally are in the South. They depend on the Slaves and they are lazy and ignorant.

Friday Apr 3rd

"Co K" was detailed for Picket and went out to the Post but about noon we were hurried back to town where our men were all out in line of Battle. Some Cavalry had made their appearance South of town which was Supposed to be Rebels but proved to be Wolfords Regiment comeing in. So we were scared before we was hurt.[25] We left Lebanon at Two pm and marched about Six miles toward Murfreesboro but by another rout from the one we come. We camped near a creek I did not learn the name of.

Saturday Apr 4th

We Started about Eight Oclock and reached a Small town called Rome of only a few houses about noon. We camped here all night and got a Splendid rest. The Johnies have been following us all the time but have not made any move to give us a fight. I think we are here to give them [a] chance to try to capture us. We would as soon have a little fun as not if they will give us a chance.

Sunday Apr 5th

We left camp early and made good time and arrived at the River opposite Carthage at noon. We Captured Severel horses and Mules and a lot of Tobacco for our own use. We find Tobacco in twists of a hand and it is nice to Smoke but not good to chew. We marched two miles South and camped for the night. We did not see any Johnies to day. We are a good ways from home (or camp) and if the Rebs jumped onto us we might want help to get out of the Scrape.

MONDAY APR 6TH

We passed through a Small place called Middleton to day where we halted for dinner. After noon we marched Seven miles and camped near Alexandria. We captured Severel prisoners who happend to get in our way also Some more horses and Mules.[26]

TUESDAY APR 7TH

The 75th had the advance to day and we run into Some Johnies and a few Shots were exchanged but no body hurt. We routed about fifteen hundred and thought we would get a fight but they Skipped out. We passed their camp but they were Cavalry and traveled faster the[n] we can. They Showed themselves in the road and on the hills but not close enough to harm us. We kept Skirmishers out in advance all day. We camped about four miles from Liberty.

WEDNESDAY APRIL 8TH

We were on the march early and passed through Milton and Stopped on the Battle field of March 7th for dinner and remaind there some time and I went over the Ground to see the marks of the Battle. The timber bears the marks and the old line of logs occupied by us are just as we left them. There are severel Trenches where the dead are burried. We marched twenty miles and camped on Stone River Eight miles from Murfresboro.

THURSDAY APR 9TH

We waded Stone River and our Quartermaster had rolled out a Barrell of "Rot Gut" Whisky on the west Bank and all were cordially invited to partake as they passed for fear of sickness by being in the water. But I concluded the cure was worse than the disease. But Some of our Boys to[ok] a double portion and was very patriotic the rest of the way to camp. I dont think they were drunk but wadeing the river made them "seasick." We got into our old camp at Murfreesboro about noon where I found Severel Letters and Ma Mollies & Netts Liknesses and some other things from home. They look very natural and I only wish I could See the originals and wonder if I will ever have that priviledge or have I gazed on their faces for the last time. I hope not and that before many months I will get back to them. This is the nineth day on the scout and it seams like getting back home to get to our old camp.

Friday Apr 10th

There was no drill but we done our washing and I was over to get my picture taken but they were so crouded I could not get in the Tent. . . . This is a beautiful Spring day.

Saturday Apr 11th

We had no drill to day. . . . We were musterd to See how many Conscripts to fill our Company it will require. That means buisiness and if there are no more men in the north to volunteer I am in favor of conscripting and make some of the Disloyal Democracy who do so much howling in our rear come out or go South where they belong. If they dont think enough of the Goverment to fight for it let them leave the country and go to Canada or come out like men and fight for the right. There are plenty of feeble men who can Soldier to do the work at home. They can raise produce to supply our Army and with what could be procured from the enemy here we could easily subsist a few months and a united North would crush the monster in a Short time. But the encouragement they receive from Northern Democrats helps to prolong the war. . . .[27]

Sunday Apr 12th

I put [in] the day writing Letters. I w[r]ote to Nett and Pa. We had no drill. I was wondering to night what my friends have been doeing this nice Spring day and [if] they "miss me" at home. They are where they hear the church Bells on the Sabbath and where it is peace and plenty while we hear the Drum or Bugle call to some duty and we dont know how soon we may hear the Sharp crack of the Rifle or the heavy Boom of the Cannon and be called where men do their best to destroy their fellow men. They little dream of what we See and hear. They probably try to Surmise what we endure but they are better off not to know.

MONDAY APR 13TH

I was Corporal of the first relief of Camp Guard and and came off at midnight. . . . Camp Guard is a little easier than picket duty. We go to our Tents when relieved and the Corporal of relief comes and calls us out when our times come to go on duty. We have to guard all the Horses and Quartermasters & Commissary Stores but dont try to keep any body from going out or comeing in. It is more for form than any thing els.

TUESDAY APR 14TH

I was out to Camp Guard Mounting and was relieved from duty and we took our tent down to dry of[f] the ground and air it. But it commenced raining and we had to put it up again. We got orders to prepare two days Rations and be ready to march at a moments warning. It rained all night and we did not move. I suppose there is another scout on hands but where or what direction I cant guess. I would Sooner be scouting as lying in camp. There is more excitement and the time goes faster.

WEDNESDAY APR 15TH

It is still raining but we had company drill and we were marched down to the edge of town and I drew Six months pay $81.00 the first money I have drawn Since I enlisted. The other Boys haveing drew four months before they only got two now. . . .

THURSDAY APR 16TH

I procured a pass to [the] Express office to send my money home but did not send it. I was afterwards detailed for fatigue duty and went to town for Rations. To See the pile of Hard Tack at the Depot I thought there was grub to last a long time but when you look around and see the Soldiers I come to the conclusion that it would soon disappear. But here will be our Base of Supplies for the next move and arrangements are being made now for a move and a number of Houses are used to put Rations in. We also have Bakeries to supply Soft Bread occasionally. It makes the town lively and look like there was lots of buisiness done here. Murfreesboro is or had fifteen hundred inhabitants before the war and is a county Seat. It is situated on the South Side of Stone River and on the Nashville & Chattanooga Rail Road thirty miles South of the former. The country is rocky and the elevation of the town and high Banks of the river gives the Rebel fortifications command of the surrounding country. The natural fortifications are good and then they fortified it Strongly to make a decisive Stand against the advance of Rosencrans. The great Battle commenced on Dec 31st and the Rebel Army retreated on the night of Jany 1st 63.[28] There was more or less fighting from Nashville out but the Battle proper was along Stone river. It was a terable Battle and many a poor Boy layed down his life for his country. I have not been over the Battle field yet but will go over it before we move if possible. . . .

FRIDAY APR 17TH

. . . Nearly all the company are out on duty of some kind. I wrote to Pa and was in camp all day. We are still under orders to march but did not move. There is not men enough in camp for drill and as I was on duty yesterday I did not have to go to day. It is lonesome with the Boys all gone.

SATURDAY APR 18TH

This being wash day there was no drill. After doeing my washing and cleaning my gun for inspection Jim Spake and I went and had our pictures taken. It is not taken very well but is like every thing els here. We have to put up with it. I remained in camp the rest of the day.

SUNDAY APR 19TH

Our Boys are on Picket to day that is my Bunk Mates. We had inspection as usual. . . . The men cary their Knapsacks on picket now for fear of marching orders while away from camp.

MONDAY APR 20TH

I was detailed for Picket duty. I [was] corporal of third relief and did not Sleep very much. The night passed without any unusual accurrence. We picketed on the Woodbury Pike as usual. We were not allowed to have any fire on reserve post which indicates that the Johnies are not far away. But our picket Scouts did not discover any. I [A] detail is sent out each morning to go from the Pickets out side of our lines to see if the Enemy has made any advances during the night. The[y] generally go out about a mile from [the] Picket Line.

TUESDAY APR 21ST

We was relieved and got back to Camp about nine Oclock this a.m. I did not leave camp to day but took a good Sleep to make up for last night. I did not get any letters. No orders to move yet.

WEDNESDAY APR 22ND

I went on Picket again this morning. After our detail went out our Division Started on a Scout and we remained on Picket. Sam Buckmaster and I had a little racket with the Lieutenant Carr commanding pickets. He has been an Orderly Sergeant untill recently he was Commisioned as a 1st Lieut. He did not know how to relieve the post and on Dressing up Gave the Command wrong and a Boy by [the] name of Nevins was about the third man from him and was dressing to the left as commanded.[29] Carr is [a] passionate old fellow and he repeated the wrong command and then struck Nevins across the stomach with his Sword flat wise. When we stacked Arms "Sam" asked me what I would do if "Old Carr" would Strike me with his Sword. I replied I would Stick a Bayonet into him and Carr heard what I said and drew his Sword partially out of the Scabberd and Says "you would" would you (with an oath). I had just set my gun against the stack and I took it up and Carr had got close to me by that time. I brought the gun to a "charge" bringing the Bayonet close to his breast orderd him to hault and he did so seeing I had the advantage of him. I then used some rather strong adjectives to him and told him what I thought of him and he took it like a little man. He said he would report me on our return to camp but he has layed himself liable to dismissall for Strikeing a private Soldier and then he made the first move to strike me and I was on the defenseive and I was not to blame for defending myself. I dont know whether I would used my gun or not but I was not going to let him hurt me. I might under the excitement pushed my Bayonet to[o] far. The Boys all Stuck to me and Said I done right. Carr came to me this pm and Said if [I] did not say anything about it he would not. So we dropped it for the preasent. Now I believe in dicipline and an Officer have controll of his men but because I am a private in the Army does not give an Officer the right to strike or kick me and he will simply do it at his peril when he undertakes it.[30] We have officers that are not competent to command a Corporals Guard (two men) and they are the ones who put on the Style. I find that Soldiering will bring out the principles of an[?] [Officer] and Show him up better and quicker than any thing els I know of. I was on relief No 2 post 2 and we were required to keep awake all night. It is hard to be on duty every alternate night and then not allowed to sleep but I am gratified that our Officers do not intend to be caught *"Napping."* We were four hours on and two off and the hours are long and tedius. The night passed without an alarm.

Thursday Apr 23rd

We came in this am and I wrote to Nett. The Divission returned also from the scout. They had no fighting while out. I did not know but Carr would report me for yesterdays occurrence but I could not think he would after promiseing to drop it as there is some thing in the promise of one Soldier to another. When their word is out it is inviolable and they will keep it Sure. He did not mention it and I guess he wont. . . .

Friday Apr 24th

I escaped detail for Picket this morning and I wrote another letter to Nett. I also received a letter from her. The Scouting party that is out we have no word from yet. But if they had been in trouble we would know it. The "Rebs" have not come after us yet and I presume they dont want us for any thing. I am ready to move when Genl Rosencrans Says the word and we are in good condition to give Bragg another drubbing if necissary.

Saturday Apr 25th

I went on Picket again to day and met an old Boy from Bluffton. Stanly Hall came to our post. I was very glad to meet him. Our orders were strict and I did not get any Sleep. It rained Some to night. The country where we are on duty is very rocky and rough and there is plenty of good places to hide. We have a nice place for the reserve as it is in a crevis of rock and a strong position.

SUNDAY APR 26TH

I come off duty this am. . . . I was not out for Inspection for I just come in from Picket. Some of our scouts returned with a hundred and twenty five Rebel prisoners. They captured them in a Stockade on the Rail Road and they Surrenderd without a fight. They report Bragg as occupying Tullahoma Wartrace and Manchester with troops at Hoovers Gap and say he is strongly posted and will make a Stand on that line. The country is reported mountainous and rocky and will be hard to get over.

MONDAY APR 27TH

I am on picket again. It rained some this evening. I read a Novel while on picket. There was some fireing on our right caused by a few Rebels makeing a dash into a cavalry regiment. We were under arms immediately but they did not make their appearance in our front. The night passed away without any thing else of importance. Some of our Boys captured an old cavalry horse near the Reserve post and thought they would have a ride. Two of them mounted and galloped up and down the line and were haveing plenty of fun but some one scared the old horse and he Shied and threw them off braking Abb Mosures Arm and their fun ended abruptly.

TUESDAY APR 28TH

On returning to Camp I received an Old letter of Jany 29th from Lou Townsend and I wrote to her. It does me good to receive a letter from a friend and it dont make any difference how old it is. It helps me pass the monotony of the Camp to write letters. We like to know that our friends have not forgotten us and a good word from them cheers our hearts and we can endure the hardships much easier appearantly.

WEDNESDAY APR 29TH

The camp was thrown into a little flurry to day by the report that Bragg was advanceing on the Manchester Pike and we formed on the Collor Line and Stacked Arms and then prepared rations to be ready to move at any moment. It proved to be only Cavalry thrown out as a feeler and our Cavalry drove them back and are following them and we are held in readiness to go to their assistance.

THURSDAY APRIL 30TH

I was over to see uncle Charlie Miller this morning and found him very poorly and Uncle Will and I Tellegraphed to Pa to come after him as his discharge papers are expected every day and he would not be able to travel alone. He seams very much discouraged and I am fearfull he will never reach home alive. . . . I also visited Uncle Charlie this evening and found him no better. It seams terible that he cant get home to his family to die. He is failing fast and cant live long and I have to return to my Regiment as military law will not permit me to Stay away over night.

FRIDAY MAY 1ST

The very Sad news come to me that Uncle Charlie died about nine Oclock last night. I went over to the 101st Ind. Uncle Will and I spliced money and by borrowing some we bought a Mettallic Burial Case and Started his remains home. I tellegraphed Pa what we had done. It is a Sad Stroke for Uncle Will to part with his brother here and cant get a permit to go with him. It is hard to realize that he is gone. At home he [was] Stout and rugged but has been going down since he got hurt. He died of Chronic Dioreh. It will be a Sad meeting of friends when his remains get home and how terible for his poor wife when [she] views all that is mortal of him who left her a few months ago in full vigor of manhood and full of patriotism and vigor to battle for his country leaving every thing tha[t] was dear to him behind. What words can express the praise of such noble men. He has sacrificed his life on the alter and it is hoped passed to relms of eternal bliss where there are no wars. May he rest in peace.

SATURDAY MAY 2ND

Rumors in camp that the "Rebs" are advanceing on the Manchester Pike and we have doubled our vigilance and will meet them. If they will come here we can handle them easy but I dont think they will be foolish enough to attack us in our fortifications. I received a Letter from Nett and one from Mollie. Uncle Charlies remains did not leave Murfreesboro untill this morning. It will take them about three or four days to get through. We had no drill but our arms are Stacked on the Color line and ready for immediate action and we may have a warm time some of these days.

SUNDAY MAY 3RD

We had Inspection this morning and formed and Stacked Arms on [the] Color Line. It is getting monotonus to prepare for Battle every day and no Rebs to fight. Stanly Hall come into Camp and I went with him to the 101st Ind. I did not Stay long as we are not allowed to remain away for they might want us. . . .

MONDAY MAY 4TH

We had company Drill this morning and Myself Lee Keagle Patrick Boyle & A T Wilson put our Over Coats in a Box to Send home as it is now warm enough without them. We went to the Express office but there was such a rush that we could not Ship them. . . .

TUESDAY MAY 5TH

It has the appearance of rain. We had company Drill. We got our Over Coats Started and that will lighten our Knapsacks some. We had Battallion drill this pm and I answerd Netts Letter. The marching order[s] are Still delayed. All quiet along our lines.

WEDNESDAY MAY 6TH

It is cold and rainy and we drilled in the rain. We were also out on Battallion drill this p.m. I got a letter from J S Wilson. Capt Studabaker received a dispatch from Pa in refference to his comeing and answerd it that the remains of Uncle Charlie had gone. So he will not come. I wish he could get here and see how we are Situated. It would be a treat to those who dont know any thing about the War. I had anticipated getting to See him but now I will have to wait untill I go home.

THURSDAY MAY 7TH

It is Still cold and rainy but we drilled as usual and dont Stop for rain. It is exercise for us and I like it better than loafeing around camp. Some of our men complain about the drill. . . . I did not go away from camp But got lazy and took a Sleep. I get so tired bumming around camp that I dont hardly know what to do with myself some times. I wish we could move and Stir up the "Johnies" but I might regret it and want some body to help me let them go again. I enjoy better health and [dont] get So lazy when on the march as I do in camp.

FRIDAY MAY 8TH

It was still raining this morning but cleard away about noon. Drilling was all we done to day. I got Netts letter from Louisville Ky mailed there by Pa. He could not get through as Genl Rosencrans orders are to let no person come South now. I am sorry he could not come. I would loved to See him and then he would appretiate the trip so much. I answerd Netts Letter. J V Kennagy come up to day and will now relieve me from the Adjutants office. He looks better than when I saw him last.

SATURDAY MAY 9TH

No Drill to day but washing and cleaning guns for Sunday morning inspection is the order of the day. . . . I visited the 101st Ind this evening and missed Roll Call for the first time. I can say here that I never was absent from camp when detailed for any duty only when detached nor missed answering to my name in the Ranks since I enlisted. No Rebs yet.

SUNDAY MAY 10TH

After Breakfast I was put on extra police duty for being absent at Roll Call last night. That is military and a man never gets any credit for doeing duty and if he happens to commit a little misdemeanor he is put on extra duty or punished for it. I find the American Soldier can be pursuaded better than driven and Some of our Officers who couldent hire a darky at five cents a day at home like to Show their Authority here. They are the most tyranicle and over-bearing and have few if any friends among their men. But others who indulge their men a little have good discipline and plenty of the best of friends. Our Officers have to drive their men and are fussing and fumeing about Something all the time. I would not give a cent for a Soldier that will not stand up for his rights. He never ought to enlist.

MONDAY MAY 11TH

We had company and Battallion drill as usual to day. There is talk that our Divission will move camp about two miles South to the Boiling Springs So as to have more parade ground. There is good news from the Army of the Potomac or Genl Hooker but only a rumor. I did not get any mail today.

TUESDAY MAY 12TH

We struck tents and moved to the Boiling Spring two miles south on the Woodbury Pike. We have a nice Camp near a grove of Timber and Splendid Spring Water. We had no drill but we was out on Dress parade and Capt Sweet of the 105th Ohio was brought out in front of the Brigade and the Shoulder Straps and Buttons cut off him. The Story as told is that on a Scout of Col Halls Brigade Some time ago some of his Boys put up a job on him. He left camp and went to a house to stay and the Boys put on Some citizens clotheing and went and captured him and Scared him by saying they were going to kill him but if he would tell how many men was in Halls command and all other information they wanted then break his Sword they would release him. All of which he did and then come to camp telling what a terible fight he had with the "Rebbs." The Boys returned to camp and heard his Story and then told theirs and he was arrested. He was not liked by his men and they thought he was a coward and wanted to get rid of him.[31] The[y] succeeded nicely as his sentence was that the Straps and buttons should be cut off of him. He [was] dismissed from the Service and set across the Ohio River. He was a nice looking young man and I felt sorry for him to think how he had disgraced himself. But this is no place for a coward and they better get away soon for I think the time is not far away when a man will have to Show his collors. If he cant face the enemy he better go home.

WEDNESDAY MAY 13TH

I was detailed for Picket and left our Boys to fix up camp. We was posted in the woods and in a rough & rocky place. We had a nice day but it rained very hard all night. I had ten men on my relief and kept me on duty about all night. I did not Sleep much. We were not molested by the "Johnies." . . . This is the worst night I ever Picketed. It is dark as Ink and a flash of ligtening lights it up for an instant and then it is like a pall and we cant see any thing. I dont mind Picket in nice weather but I prefer being at home in the house such nights as this. It makes a fellow think over all the mean things he ever done in his life. Standing alone on a Post is lonesome work any time but when it is raining it is awful.

THURSDAY MAY 14TH

We was relieved by [a] detail from the 72nd Ind. . . . We had inspection of Arms. While on Dress Parade Sergt Sweany of "Co A" was brought out and the Stripes cut off his arm and reduced to ranks for curseing Lieut Wheeler of [the] Same company. I guess Sweany was not much to blame but it would not be "Military" to let him escape. The private Soldier has to account for his own Sins and the officers too. That is according to "Red Tape."

FRIDAY MAY 15TH

We policed our quarters this morning and we look quite clean. I wrote to Nett. We had drill at the usual hours and Brigade Drill at one Oclock. We have a nice drill ground. Some of us have been going on Drill without our Cartridge Boxes as they are heavy and cumbersom and of no use in drilling but our Captain got us some distance from camp and then asked how many of us were there without our Boxes and invited such to step to the front and he then inquired for a Non Commissioned Officer and I was the only one. He orderd me to form the men and double quick them to camp for our Boxes and I done as orderd. We went to camp took out all the Cartridges and went back at very "Slow time." He tried to make us run back but we "couldent See it." This Shows up the character of the man. If he had told us before we were doeing wrong we would not repeated it. But he was showing his authority and teaching us poor ignorant privates what it was to have such an intelligent and honorable gentleman for a captain. And then it demonstrated to us that he was such a "brave man" and one who it would not do to set his authority at defiance. Then it taught all of us [to] love him for the lesson. After that we carried forty rounds of Amunition just as long as we expected to have to use it and no longer.[32]

SATURDAY MAY 16TH

Wash day again and prepareing for inspection and no drill. I visited the 101st Ind and uncle will had a letter from Pa which he let me read. I wish we belonged to the Same company as he seams more like a Brother than my Uncle. We could pass many hours pleasently together. I go to see him often and he comes to see me but sometimes it is severel days that we dont see each other. His regiment occupies the left and us the right of the Brigade and it is quite a walk from one to the other.

Sunday May 17th

This is sunday but I dont hear and church Bells nor See any sabbath School children going to sabbath School but instead I see a long line of Breast works lined with Blue coats and the Drum and Bugle call are the substitute for the Bells. The company inspection was all the parade we had. That is done to let the officers see if we know how to keep our guns in order and our clothes clean. If we did not have them to tell us we would not know when Sunday come. A private is not supposed to know anything.

Monday May 18th

Company Battallion & Brigade Drill with dress parade took up the day. I was in camp all day. . . . All quiet in front.

Tuesday May 19th

Nothing transpired to day but the usual drill and dress Parade this evening. I received no Letters.

Wednesday May 20th

We had company drill this morning. Battallion drill and Brigade Drill this pm. Genl Rosencrans was with us during Brigade drill and the drill was a charge on a supposed fortifications and he lead the charge in person. It suppose it was all acted out but the part the Rebels would play in defending their works. There was no body killed and it all looked nice and it is nice enough to play Soldier but the reality is the mischief and what I dont like.

Thursday May 21st

I am on Picket again. We are under marching orders but did not move. I wrote a letter to pay[?] while at the Reserve Post. I only slept about two hours to night. . . . The Sick were sent away.

FRIDAY MAY 22ND

We was not relieved untill about noon. . . . The Regiment was out for drill but I was excused as I was on picket all night. There was no dress parade. We are still under marching orders.

SATURDAY MAY 23RD

This was the day for Brigade inspection. We formed about ten Oclock a.m. We were inspected by Col Hall commanding Brigade. Dress parade but no other drill. . . .

SUNDAY MAY 24TH

Company inspection this morning. I wrote to Nett. We are still under marching orders. I suppose our orders are simply to be in readiness in case the Rebs should make a move of some kind. Or they may be threatening us. We have to guess at it only. But I certainly think there will be a move soon. We have been here so long that if we are going to move I think we better go.[33] But I am not in command and I dont even council Rosencrans So I perhaps dont know what is best. I have concluded to let him run it to suit himself and when he wants me to go all he has to do is say so.

MONDAY MAY 25TH

I was detailed for camp Guard Corporal first relief. Genl Reynolds visited camp and rode around after Corporal Wilsons relief to see that he understood posting a relief. We had considerable fun at Wilsons expense for haveing a Major General helping him to put on his relief. . . . I read a novel "Falkland."[34] The Regiment was out for Battallion drill and Dress parade. Genl Reynolds dismounted at Guard House and played with Little All drummer Boy of company "C."[35] He is a nice friendly old gentleman. He does not think it a disgrace to talk to a private Soldier like a great many men of less rank. Some officers think a private is a mere dog and are here only for them to domineer over and that accounts in a great measure for the feeling existing between the Rank and File. The private soldier does his duty many times because he is compelled to. Not with the free good will that he would if treated as a white man should be. Our sick men were all Sent away which looks like a move again.

Tuesday May 26th

I was relieved from Camp Guard. Our Regiment Sent out the Pickets and there is not enough men in camp to drill. The rest of the Brigade were on drill. . . . I am haveing rather an easy time to day with nothing to do. But it is lonesome with the Boys all out of camp. No news of importance.

Wednesday May 27th

The Pickets came in this morning. I had charge of the detail for policeing quarters and Seely Duffy got saucy on my hands and Capt Karns orderd me to take him to the Guard House which I done accordingly. After drill Duffy was marched out and had to cary a "Rail" through our quarters. This was all done because he Sauced a Corporal. That is "Red Tape" Sure. I could [have] pursuaded him to do as I requested him without arresteng him or punnishing him but that would not be military and then the captain would [have] been deprived of the pleasure it afforded him to see a private cary a fence Rail. Then how much more cheerfull Duffy will do his duty hereafter. Duffy blames me for it and he is my enemy and also the Captains and it was all uncalled for and unnecissary.

Thursday May 28th

We drew Rations with orders to be ready to march at any moment. I was out on Non-Commissioned Officers drill and all the other drilling during the day. . . . The question now agitateing the camp is will we march or is our orders like all the rest. I am ready to go. We will never wipe out the Rebellion by laying here and I for one want to get home. We are in splendid trim to whip Bragg now and drive him further into Dixie. We have a long line of Rail Road to guard and supplies here for a long campaign.

Friday May 29th

No positive orders yet in regard to moveing. The usual amount of drilling was done. . . . I hope we will move as I dont like to be under suspense all the time. We had Dress parade this evening. The atmosphere indicates rain and if we move it will rain Sure.

Saturday May 30th

This is a very wet day. So much So that we cannot drill or do our washing. . . . I made Nett & Rollie each a finger ring from Mussel Shell from Stone River where the Battle was fought. The Shells are very nice and resemble Ivory and are hard. Our Boys manufacture lots of little tokens from them.

Sunday May 31st

Still it rains but we had inspection preparetory to general inspection tomorrow. . . . I put in the day writing and passed the day very pleasently. . . .

Monday June 1st

I done my washing and was not out on officers drill But got ready for inspection. . . . We formed for Inspection at one Oclock p.m. . . . We are Still under marching orders. This was a Nice day but it commenced raining this evening. No important news.

Tuesday June 2nd

The teams was harnessed before day light but we remained on the old camp. We had drill as usual. I wrote to Nett and Sent a Photograph of Genl Rosencrans. I done some writing for Captain Karns. I made out Commissions for all of the Non-commissioned officers.

Wednesday June 3rd

This day finds us still in our old camp. We drilled as usual. Orders came to pack Knapsacks and be ready to move at a moments warning. While on Brigade Drill we perpetrated a Joke on Col Robinson. We had passed out side of the Picket Line and put out Skirmishers and advanceing in line of Battle and supposed we were going to meet the "Rebs." The Colonel gave the command "Load at Will" and we done as he orderd and he discoverd a man capping his gun and made inquiry as to how many had loaded when he discoverd that the entire Regiment had loaded their guns. He was mad and swore some and laughed some. He thought we ought to know the difference between drill and fighting. But we had no way of telling as our orders to march and every thing before look[ed] like moveing. We supposed the Rebs had made and advance and we were going to drive them back. He will learn to use a little more caution hereafter.

THURSDAY JUNE 4TH

I am twenty four years old to day. No orders to move yet. I am on Camp Guard. We drew five days Rations with orders to pack five days in our Knapsacks and three in our Haversacks. It looks as though they proposed to make Pack Mules of us in addition to what we may have to do besides but a private has no soul in the eyes of Some Officers. There has been heavy fireing all day towards Franklin and it may be the prelimenarys of a general Engagement.[36] Let it come but I wonder who or how many of us will be left to tell about it in years to come and think with pride when they Soldiered for the Union. Their names will pass to generations unborne and be blessed by them for protecting the Union. . . .

FRIDAY JUNE 5TH

We are Still in the old camp with Eight days Rations ready to Shoulder up. It rained last night and looks rainy to day. I wrote to Nett and Jake Miller. I was not out for company drill. I went a Short distance to See a man hung. He is a native of this state and report Says he killed a union man and then cut his Tongue out. He was about twenty five years old and not very Smart looking. He claimed he was not guilty. I never saw a man hung before and I dont care whether I ever do again. . . .

SATURDAY JUNE 6TH

It rained all night last night and is cloudy to day. This being wash day there was no drill. We are Still under marching orders. . . . We got news from yesterdays Battle. The Rebs undertook to capture Franklin but were repulsed with heavy loss And our men still hold their position. I would sooner they would attack us here if we could pursuade them to do so. But they prefer fighting on the defensive and we will have to go for them.

SUNDAY JUNE 7TH

Inspection this morning. . . . I took a Sleep and remained in camp all day. I did not get any mail. I read a novel called Biddy Woodhull. This is a terible lonesom day.

MONDAY JUNE 8TH

Officers Drill and Regimental Inspection was the order of the day. There is a rumor in Camp that we are going to Vicksburgh Missippi. I dont believe it for here is where the work is to be done now. We will "whoop up" Bragg and See what he is made of first. If we defeat him then we may go to Vicksburgh but not before.[37] Another Brigade joined our Division. We are now Second Brigade Fourth Division and Fourteenth Army Corps under Genl Geo H Thomas or "Pap Thomas" as he is called. Genl Thomas is a very large man will weigh about two hundred & twenty five pounds. About fifty years old and makes a fine appearance and our Boys think there is no body like him. I always hear men speak of him with praise and we are proud to be led by him. He is one of the main Stays of our department and will lead his men to glory and make his mark before the summer is gone.

TUESDAY JUNE 9TH

Ten months ago to day I left home and I think of that Sad day it causes me to drop a tear. It seams to be a long time ago. I see the Sad faces yet as I Saw them last. Will I ever see them again. I would like to Surprise them not let them know I was about. But I must wait the time. I suppose if I brooded over home all the time I could get homesick. No orders to move yet.

WEDNESDAY JUNE 10TH

It is raining this morning. We are still ready to move but done the usual amount of drilling. The Regiment was formed in "Column by Company" and went to hear a Mr Williams a citizen of Indiana make a Speach this evening. The whole Brigade was out. It was a political Speach. . . .[38]

THURSDAY JUNE 11TH

I am a Camp Guard. It rained Some to day but cleard away this evening. Cap Karns was Officer of the Guard and we had a nice night. I was not out for drill. . . . All quiet in front.

FRIDAY JUNE 12TH

We were relieved this am and C W Beardsly and myself tried to get a pass to the soldiers home in town but did not get it. There was another man to be hung so reported and I went to see it but it was a mistake. . . . No drilling to day.

SATURDAY JUNE 13TH

Nothing but Dress Parade and washing and cleaning up. . . .

SUNDAY JUNE 14TH

This is a beautiful day and the third anniversary of our marriage. Little did I think three years ago that I would be Situated as I am now. If man knew what he was intended for and what trials and tribulations was layed out for him he would Shudder. We had general inspection. I wrote to nett to remind her that I rememberd our anniversary. It rained to night and our old Tent leaked and wet our Beds but we are almost accustomed to that.

MONDAY JUNE 15TH

Nothing transpired but the usual routine of camp. I got a letter from Nett dated the 9th. Well no marching orders yet and I almost think sometimes it is all Bosh[?] and get real discouraged. I have been very healthy since I come to camp and feel "fat & Saucy." I never had better health and I try to enjoy myself. Sometimes I get a little Blue but it soon passes off.

TUESDAY JUNE 16TH

This is a hot day and we retire to the grove of timber for protection from the sun. . . . It makes a fellow sweat to drill as hot a day as this but it [is] nice exercise for us. I like it.

WEDNESDAY JUNE 17TH

Genls Thomas & Reynolds were out at Brigade Drill and looked on. . . . I am not feeling well. The first time since I come back to the Regiment. I done duty all day. I was in camp all day and went to bed early. I hope I will feel better to morrow for if they should move I might be left behind and I dont want that if I can help it. If there is any fun I want to be on hands for my Share of it.

Thursday June 18th

There was severel Shots fired along our picket line and we are in readiness to meet any attack. It rained some this evening. We drilled as usual at the Calls. . . . No positive orders to move. Things begin to look some more favorable towards a move. We drew "Dog Tents" So as to require less teams in our Train. The Shelter Tent is composed of a pice of Canvass about five feet square and two or three men Bunk together and Button them together forming a Letter "A" makeing only Shelter for three. It looks like a small House but I like it better and I believe it will be healthier than to have so many men in a Tent. Each man carrys one piece[?] of the Canvass. We can put up a Tent very quick and can have Shelter from storm any time.

Friday June 19th

Drill at the usual hours. . . . All quiet along our line.

Saturday June 20th

This being wash day we had no drill. I made a table to write on. I done some writing for the Captain. I made Discriptive Rolls for Peter Urton and Mark C Turner Sick men and who are reported as deserters. There was a Sad accident in the 11th Ohio Reget. A man comeing off guard Struck a Shell laying in the quarters with his gun and it exploded killing him and wounding three others.[39] He thought it was a Solid Shot. Men should be more carefull as we have no men to spare and it may not be many days before there will be many killed. I did not get any mail.

Sunday June 21st

I am sick but did not report at Sick call. Beardsley and I built a Shade of Bushes over our Tent. . . . I was in camp all day.

Monday June 22nd

Major John Widmore of the 104 Illinois who was captured with his Regiment at Heartsvill come to our camp. He has just returned from "Rebeldom" where he was a prisoner for five months. I was excused from duty by the Surgeon and got medicin for Dioreah. I formed the company as our Sergeants are all on duty or absent from camp. I remained in camp all day and I was hardly able to move. I dread the Dioreah in the form it assumes here. It reduces a man very fast and if the Army moves I might be sent to the Hospital and I dont want that. I will go if possible. I would think I was going to die sure if I was sent away. But I hope I will Soon be all right or that there will not be any move for a few days yet. I get discouraged easily when I get sick as I have hardly knew what it was untill I enlisted.

Tuesday June 23rd

I am still sick and got some more medicin and was excused. My Eyes are sore and I hope they will soon be well as the Army Sore Eyes are terible. This is the day for General Monthly Inspection. Well our orders to move came at last. We move at five Oclock a.m tomorrow. The camp is all bustle and the Boys are writing home to their friends. Many of us perhaps for the last time. It is a terible thing to contemplate when writing that this perhaps is the last time. I wrote to Nett telling her of our move. We will not march many miles before we encounter the enemy and then if they stand their ground we can expect a terific encounter and some body must be sacrificed. The question is who it may be. But I feel confident that I Shall get through. I cant think any other way. But the great dread is seeing others hurt that I have soldiered with so long. I dont feel as though I could Stand a hard days march but I Shall make the effort or be Sent away. I will not attend sick call in the morning if I can possibly Stand on my feet if I dont go a mile from camp.

CHAPTER 5

Glory Enough for One Day

Pressed by his superiors in Washington to move against Bragg's army, now located along Middle Tennessee's Duck River, south of Murfreesboro, Rosecrans began a general advance southward in late June. The Union commander formulated a bold plan whereby his cavalry and one corps would feint against the Confederate left flank while the other three corps would move on the enemy right. On June 24, Reynolds's division of the Fourteenth Corps, including the Seventy-fifth Indiana, moved out of Murfreesboro on the Manchester Pike. The Fourth Division occupied strategic Hoover's Gap, one of three passes through the mountains on the major roads south of Murfreesboro, and turned back a Confederate counterattack attempting to retake the important access point. By the end of the fight, the regiment had lost only two men wounded, and in fact the entire division had suffered a mere sixty-two casualties.[1]

Reynolds then quickly pushed south to capture the town of Manchester, far behind the Confederate right flank. Bad weather slowed the Federal advance, allowing Bragg to withdraw his forces south to Tullahoma, his headquarters and supply depot. But even there he was not safe. Fearing that the Federals would move south of Tullahoma and cut his railroad supply line to Chattanooga, the Confederate commander was forced to retreat across the Tennessee River to Chattanooga. In a brilliant series of movements, Rosecrans had secured all of Middle Tennessee with a loss of fewer than six hundred men.

On July 1, the Seventy-fifth joined in a reconnaissance toward Tullahoma and its Confederate defenses, only to find both abandoned by the Rebels. The Hoosiers could proudly claim that they were the first ones to reach Bragg's depot, the objective of the campaign, and had played a significant role in forcing the Confederates to retreat to Chattanooga.

The army then settled into camp for several weeks, with little activity except picket duty, drill, and inspections, as the men "were placed in training for the battles before us, like a prize-fighter is trained for a 'set-to' in the prize ring," remembered David Floyd.[2] Finally, in mid-August, the Seventy-fifth began a movement over the Cumberland Mountains to capture the vital rail center of Chattanooga. Despite a hot and dry march, the Fourth Division reached a point near the town of Jasper, west of Chattanooga and close to the Tennessee River. There they were ordered to reconnoiter the river opposite the village of Shell-mound, emplace an artillery battery to control the Memphis and Charleston Railroad that ran through the village and carried supplies into Chattanooga, and establish a possible river crossing site. By the morning of August 22, the Seventy-fifth and a section of artillery had done all that was ordered. While on the river, the regiment exchanged shots with Confederates on the opposite side but also accepted deserters from the Southern ranks who crossed on rafts to surrender. Some Hoosiers even helped compose a force that temporarily crossed the Tennessee River, routed some Southern cavalrymen, and moved toward Chattanooga to test the enemy's strength.

On the evening of August 30, the entire Fourth Division began crossing the river at Shellmound on eight flat boats. The Seventy-fifth then marched southeast to Trenton, Georgia, and prepared to climb Lookout Mountain, part of the Union scheme to encircle Bragg's army in Chattanooga. On the afternoon of September 11, the Hoosiers began the difficult climb and reached the summit that night. David Floyd recalled that a "band was playing a familiar tune, the melodious strains of which caught our ears, while we were on the toilsome march far down the mountain slope, pulling and pushing Artillery and ammunition wagons. . . . To the writer the music of a brass band never before nor since sounded so charmingly sweet—never so inspiring and animating. Marching to the music of this band, we were scarcely sensible of fatigue."[3]

The efforts of the Union forces were not in vain, as Bragg evacuated the city and fell back into northern Georgia and Federal troops entered Chattanooga on September 9. Hoosier morale was high. One soldier wrote that under Rosecrans, "we expect only victory," and he believed that Bragg had taken most of his army all the way to Atlanta.[4]

WEDNESDAY JUNE 24TH
[BATTLEFIELD OF HOOVER'S GAP, TENNESSEE]

The Bugle Sounded Revelie about two Oclock and we got out and cooked Breakfast and Struck Tents and Started about Six Oclock toward Manchester. I was not able to cary my Knapsack and it was put on the wagon. It was a beautiful morning but commencd Raining soon after we Started and did not Stop during the day and night. We had marched about Seventeen miles and had filed off the road to camp when the fireing in front commenced. We were orderd on to the scene of action and formed Line of Battle and drove the Enemy back and occupied the position in Hoovers Gap. The Battle was Spirited while it lasted. It appears the Rebels were being reviewed at War Trace or Manchester by Bragg and left only a few men to Guard this place and Col Wilder drove them out and pursued them Some distance and then re-inforcements comeing up Wilder fell back here and we come in time to assist him and we hold the position with the enemy in our front. I expect the Ball will open up to morrow. We were called out at two Oclock am for Picket and I think it is the darkest night I ever seen. It rained very hard. We kept together by holding to our File Leaders coat tail. We could hear the wounded lying on the Battle field calling for help but we could not get to them. It is terible to Stand on Picket and hear the groans of the dieing at it raining but such is war. Tomorrow will doubtless leave more in that same Sad condition. There is no fireing to night. We are stationed three men on a post and I am near a line of fence with Levi Keagle and J C Milliken. It is mountainous and rocky.[5]

THURSDAY JUNE 25TH

The skirmishing commenced at day light and I Shot at a *man* for the first time in my life and had the same compliment returned. There is a Rebel picket post near ours and they make us keep close to our Trees as they seam to shoot well. Our range is about two hundred yards. The Rebel position is about five hundred yards and on a hill and our position is on the side of the mountain and a high Ledge of Rock behind us. We hold the gap and they cant drive us out without a great Slaughter. We picked up Severel wounded Johnies and among the rest the one that made so much nois near us last night. He has boath Thighs broken. We also got a young Rebel Major shot through the body and he repents of his error and said if he got well he will not fight us any more but I think his days are numberd.[6] We were relieved this a.m. and lay in line of Battle all day. A number of our men were wounded during the day. It rained all day and night. We arranged to sleep in line of Battle and Beardsley and myself arranged our Bunk and carried some Rails and laid at our heads and the water washed the leaves down and formed a dam and awoke us by pouring over our rails into our faces and we got up and found we had a water power strong enough to run a Grist Mill. To Say we are wet wont begin to tell it and I am Sick too. If any body had told me that I could live through this before I enlisted I would thought they were foolish. A number of the dead and wounded were brought in this evening. The Battle was kept up all day between the pickets and our Artillery opend up this evening and there was quite a duel carried on for an hour or two.[7] Our Brigade was relieved by a Brigade of Regulars about ten Oclock and marched to the rear. We are very much fatigued.

FRIDAY JUNE 26TH

The fourteenth Army Corps formed about eight Oclock with our Brigade on the left wing east of the Pike. We could See the Johnies on a hill in our front in line of Battle and could see their heads over the hill from where we formed. The Skirmishers encounterd the Rebels almost as soon as we moved. We drove them before us. We turned over a line of fence and waded a creek almost waiste deep. The Johnies climed the hill and we followed expecting every moment they would open up on us but we made the hill and their line had disappeard and we[re] gone from sight. The[y] were Cavalry and left nothing but their tracks in the mud. Our loss in the two days was about fifty men from the Division. We haulted on the hill and had a fine view of our Army driveing the enemy to our right. It was grand. We left our position about two Oclock pm and took the road to Manchester and marched ten miles and camped for the night. The country is mountainous and the rain makes the small Streams perfect torents. We have got Bragg Started but cant tell where he will Stop. He was completely surprised and beaten out of a Strong position where he would undoubtedly made a Stand if he had not been out Generaled by Rosencrans. It is rather unexpected to us and makes us have the more confidence in the abilities of our Generals. We are only a Short distance from Manchester and our forces occupied War Trace to day and the "Rebs" are giveing away all along the line. Tullahoma the prisoners [say] is Strongly fortified and we may have trouble there. All right let it come and we will meet it manfully.

SATURDAY JUNE 27TH

We started again this morning and a march of Six miles brought us to the north Side of Duck River and the Enemys fortifications are but a Short distance away. We haulted about two hours and then crossed the River on a temporary Bridge as the Rebs haveing burned the old one we constructed one out of poles to cross the Troops on. We took possession of the Town and fortifications as they were evacuated. There was heavy cannonadeing all day to our right and we thought some of our Corps had been engaged in Shelling the Johnies. Our teams and Artillery did not cross the river but Correlled in the Bottom untill a Bridge can be thrown across. We camped in an Old Rebel camp inside of the Breast works. Manchester is a small town and is situated on a high Bank and has a commanding view of the surrounding country and the Rebs might have made quite at fight here. But they seem to be better on the run than fighting. It still rains and makes the roads bad and the Wagons & Artillery cut them teribly. I feel better and Stood the march very well for a Sick man.

SUNDAY JUNE 28TH

We did not move to day but drew the loads out of our guns and cleaned them up. I received a Letter from Nett. We had Inspection after noon. We dont look nor feel as nice as we did when we started as it has rained on us nearly all the time. Our Corps all came up today and the Teams and Artillary crossed the river and we got our Knapsacks. We will not remain here long for I think Genl Rosencrans is going to push Bragg untill we get a general engagement and from the indications "Bragg" will not fight untill he gets the advantage of us in position and when it does come there will be mourning all over the land. Still the prisoners Say we will get a Battle near Tullahoma.

MONDAY JUNE 29TH

Troops were moveing early but we did not get on the road untill nearly noon being in the rear guarding [the] train. It commenced raining while we were in the Stree[t] and it beat any rain I ever seen. The Street was a perfect river and it nearly drounded us but we had to take it.[8] It rained all the afternoon. We marched within about four miles of Tullahoma and camped on a tributery of Elk River. The Stockade was deserted. We camped in a thicket of Small Oak timber. We marched on the Rail Road. There was heavy fireing and the cannonadeing was terific. The Rebbels keep falling back as we advance. We sent our Knapsacks back to Murfreesboro So we can move faster. Heavy Skirmishing in front this evening and I dont know what to morrow will bring fourth.

TUESDAY JUNE 30TH

We were ready to move early this morning. There was heavy Skirmishing soon after leaveing camp and we expected a hard Battle to day but only moved a Short distance. Reports of all kinds in refference to the proceeding and their forces are in camp. . . . The report that Col Wilders Brigade had been captured but was contradicted and I dont believe it. We Still expect warm times to morrow from the movements to day. We have plenty of mud and our trains can hardly move at all. No mail come to us. I presume the cause of the delay is the repairing the Rail Road so as to supply us. The Rebels destroy all the Bridges as they retreat and our enjineers have to repair as we advance.

WEDNESDAY JULY 1ST
[TULLAHOMA, TENNESSEE]

We Started for Tullahoma and we were all expecting a fight sure as it was promised to us ever since we left Murfreesboro and they are reported to be concentrated. We left our camp determined to do our duty and stand up to work as long as there is enough left to make a fight. We came in to the fortifications south of town. When we got within range of the works the timber is all cut down the tops fell from the works and the limbs are Sharpend forming a forest of pickets for us to climb and would prevent moveing with any rapidity and they could rake us. Cos K & E were orderd out as Skirmishers and we advanced as rapidly as possible. We encounterd some "Rebel" Skirmishers and drove them before us and advanced to the works. Who can discribe their feelings advanceing on a line where he expects every Step will bring death and distruction all around. But we crawled on and under and over the timber and the large guns frowning on us from the works. But we reach the works and find that the enemy is gone and with a Shout we mount and turn and look back and see our Regiment in the first line and One Battallion after another to the right and left as far as the eye can see and behing them the 1st and 2nd lines in battle aray comeing on. When we mount the works the Adjutant comes down the road with our flag and we rush into town and plant it on the fort an[d] on the highest hill. Then we lay down on the hill and watch the advance of the Army and fineally they file off in to the different roads and march into town. The 75th Indiana is the first Regiment in Side of the Rebel works. That is glory enough for one day but I am very tired. I am very agreeably disapointed and yet I had made up my mind to See a fight and feel like I would sooner they had Stayed. But they are gone and all their boasting goes for naught. Tullahoma is a strong point and the natural defences are splendid. There is not much Town but is about an average of Southern towns. The citizens have all "Skipped" out for fear of the Battle and the houses are deserted. We got a number of prisoners and a lot of Corn meal with Some tents and camp and garrison equipage that they left in their haste to get away. There is a number of "Seige Guns" in the forts.

THURSDAY JULY 2ND

It seems that we are going to keep the Johnies on the jump as we started in pursuit and marched about Eleven miles. As we had the advance yesterday we are guarding [the] train to day. There was Skirmishing all day with the rear guard but they did not hault only when we pushed them to[o] hard and then they form and threaten us. We capture a great many Straglers and it is reported that we made a haul on them to day of Twenty five Hundred to day and five hundred wagons but it is only a rumor. We camped on Elk River about Seven Oclock pm. We are camped in a grove of timber and have a nice camp and good water. We are about five miles east of the Rail Road. The Roads are so bad we travel very Slow but perhaps as fast as the Johnies would let us.[9] But we kept them moveing to day. They must be discouraged as they are retreating all the time.

FRIDAY JULY 3RD

Geneal Rusaus Division waded the river by holding on to a Rope Streched across.[10] They had lots of fun. We moved about ten Oclock and went west to the Pike so the Teams could cross on the Bridge. It commenced raining Soon after we Started and continued all day. We were in the rear of Wagon Train. We marched about five miles and camped near the Stockade where the fight was yesterday. The Bridge is burned and we will have to build one before we can cross. The flooring is all burned off. There was some Cannonadeing to day. We have good Spring Water. Four of us crossed the river and found some "*Rebel Hogs*" and I Shot one and when we come to Skin him found him to be an old B-male and smelled very loud but we was out of meat and Skinned out the hams and went to camp. Genl Rosencrans was where we crossed the river and asked us if it was a black hog and we told him it was and he replied by saying "black hogs were dangerous and not to let them bite us.["] But when we come to cook him we could hardly stay in camp and hungry as we was could not eat it. Rations are very Short.[11] This part of the country has some hills but not what is called rough. But in our front a few miles are the Cumberland Mountains and it will be a rough country and looks like it would be impossible to get over them. Elk River is a small Stream at this point. The soil is Sandy mixed with Red Clay.

SATURDAY JULY 4TH

The Aniversary of our National Indipendence finds us on Elk River ten miles south of Tullahoma. This was a nice morning. We waited for our Division Train to come up and did not move untill about Eleven Oclock and marched about two miles when my company was orderd back to help the Supply train up. We only moved about three miles but it was dark when we got to camp and we had a hard time pushing the wagons through the mud. The mail come to us but I did not get any Letters. Our Boys feel good over the news of "Lees" defeat at Gettysburgh Pa.[12] There was cannonadeing in front but Bragg is still on the go. I found some Huckle Berries along the road. We drew two days rations and it consisted of four Crackers one fourth lb meat and a Spoonfull of Coffee.

That is small for a man who feels like he could devour a government Mule. But we go on the pri[n]ciple to live while we can and eat it all up and then Starve untill we draw more. A man can eat all we drew to the man at one meal doing such duty as we do.

SUNDAY JULY 5TH

It is still raining this morning and continued throughout the day. Lightning Struck a Tree near the foot of our Regiment and made things jingle but did not hurt any body. We drew two days rations of Beefe. Our Bed came very near floating away to night. Keagle and I was out hunting Huckleberries and got lost but Some Cavalry men helped us out. Our camp is in a grove of Saplings and very wet place. I dont want to Stay here long for fear of floating off. We will not have to go very far untill we will be high enough. For a few miles will take us to the mountains. There is no trouble about water as we have plenty.[13]

MONDAY JULY 6TH

Still it rains and terible muddy. We moved our camp about noon to higher ground. As we climbed the hill I looked back over the country we came over and was surprised at the view. We are at quite an Elevation and can see all over the surrounding country. It was a grand sight. We camp in regular order and as our Rations were Short and our Train back Some of us went out to forage. We got a Calf and a good hog (Strays) and Supplied us with meat.[14] The sun Shone very hot. We are camped on a level piece of Ground on a Spurr of the Mountains and a nice camp and plenty of Spring Water. It quit raining and I do hope it will not rain for a month. We have been Soaked for two weeks.

TUESDAY JULY 7TH

As we were not going to move some of us went for Dewberries. We found plenty of them and gathered about a Bushell. There was hundreds of men in the field and all was supplied. Our Train is still behind. Report in camp that Vicksburgh had Surrenderd and the confirmation of Lees defeat and Severel guns was fired in honor of the victories by our Batteries.[15] It rained all night and some of our Boys went back to the river to help the Supply train up the mountain and I hope they will get up for we are getting hungry. I believe when a person knows he has nothing to eat he will get hungry quicker than if he had plenty. I believe I always had enough to eat all my life untill the last few days. We have no bread of any kind to night but one of our Boys got some middlings or Shorts and we made cakes out of it and a man had to have a Stomache like a Corn Sheller to dijest it.

WEDNESDAY JULY 8TH

Some of our Teams come up this morning and we drew two days rations of Hard Tack. News good and Cannonadeing all around us. We did not move and I done my washing and wrote a letter to Pa and one to Nett. I sent them the Atlanta Intelligencer. The rest of our Train came up. It rained this evening. . . .

THURSDAY JULY 9TH

The sun come up clear and it is very hot. We had no meat of any kind for Breakfast. This is about the only day that it failed to rain a little since we left Murfreesboro. . . . We have been smelling something in camp for severel days that smelled like putrid human flesh and went in Search of and found five dead Johnies who were carried among some rocks by their men and left unburried and we burried them as best we Could. We could not handle them and we dug holes and rolled them in with the Shovels and coverd them up. Some of them was partially eaten by hogs. They were Cavalry and was killed in a fight severel days ago on the ground where we are now camped.

FRIDAY JULY 10TH

I went with Some other Boys for Apples and Berries and we did not get back to camp untill about noon. We were out Side of our Pickets [and] did not see any "Johnies." We got a half bushel of Apples and only about a half gallon of Berries. The news from the Potomac is good and the surrender of Vicksburgh was confirmed. There was about a hundred & fifty Johnies came in and surrenderd.[16] There was talk of a move but no orders came. . . .

SATURDAY JULY 11TH

There was a very heavy dew and it has the appeerence of rain. No marching orders. All quiet along our front. . . .

SUNDAY JULY 12TH

On Picket to day for the first time since we left Hoovers gap. It rained very hard afternoon but was not a very bad night for Picket duty. No move.

MONDAY JULY 13TH

We was relieved about nine Oclock and went out for Berries. It still threatens rain. Our Boys are all out of Tobacco and I asked Col Obrien to go to Elk River to the Sutlers. He sent a detail with me with orders for the Sutler to come up immediately or not at all. But we could not find him and after gathering some Huckle berries we went back to camp where we arrived about dark. We were tired over our tramp but had plenty of fun.

TUESDAY JULY 14TH

I was in camp all day. No orders to move yet the report is that the Tunnel in the mountains is obstructed and it will have to be cleaned out before we can advance and the wagon roads are full of timber. . . . Bob Davis came into my tent and we made us a house out of polls and have nice comfortable quarters. We build a Pen of polls about four feet high and use our Shelter Tents for a roof.

WEDNESDAY JULY 15TH

Lieut Starbuck Sergt Ryan and myself went for Berries and gatherd a nice lot.[17] . . . Our mess concluded we would make a Blackberry Pie and Davis got some flour of the commissary and I made the pie and we baked it in an iron oven and it eat Splendid. It was a change and probably not as palletable as if our wives or mothers had made it. But we thought it was all right. It was a change from "Hard Tack" & Sow Belly. We had Battallion Drill for a change this pm.

THURSDAY JULY 16TH

It is cloudy and quite cool. We had company drill So we would not forget how. Also Battallion Drill this pm. . . . There is talk of a move up the mountains. It looks like it was going to be considerable of a task to pull our wagon train and Artillery up. But I have confidence enough in our Army to think we are invinceable and the Rebels cannot Stop our victorius march and if they cant meet us in Battle in a country with so many natural defences and almost impassible beariers what can they do when we reach a level country without these advantages. It looks as though it is foolishness for them to prolong the war with so many discourageing circumstances. I was opposed to the Emancipation Proclimation of President Lincoln when it was issued but now I endorse it heartily and it gives us advantage of them in this. That they must run their Slaves south to help eat up their Supplies which are Scarce at best or we will make Soldiers of them and I am not very particular if they put them in the front rank as they can stop a Rebbel Bullet as well as a white Soldier.[18]

FRIDAY JULY 17TH

We had the usual drill and Bob Davis being Sick I done our washing. I answer[ed] Netts Letter of the 5th and as our mess likes pies I baked two. We Signed the pay Rools after dark so as to get our pay tomorrow. I had a severe attack of Cholic and was sick all night (too much pie). I did [not] go to the Surgeon for medicin but worried it through.

SATURDAY JULY 18TH

I feel very bad this morning from the way I passed the night. I was out on drill all the same. I dont like to go to sick call if I can help it. . . . We received four Months pay and I sent Net[t] Fifty dollers by allotment Roll. The way that is done we pay what we want to Send to the Captain and they place our names on the Roll and then the Roll and money is given to the pay master and a duplicate roll is sent to the home Bank and our friends get the money there. The money we pay back goes to pay off other Regiments. No money passes over the road home and the paymaster does not have to cary So much with them for if the Johnies dont like us they like our money as it is better than their own in the heart of the Confederacy and they would rather have it.

SUNDAY JULY 19TH

Company Inspection was our Sunday duty. . . . Jim Morgan of the 101st And Levi Keagle and myself Scouted for Some Pork and found a nice Hog with Southren principles and took him in and feasted off him.

MONDAY JULY 20TH

. . . This is a hot day. We had only company drill as it is to[o] warm for the Field Officers to leave their Tents. It Seams the more pay a man gets in the Army the less duty he is required to do. I paid one dollar and twenty five cents for a pair of Suspenders worth about Twenty five cents. My Bunk mate Beardsley is on Picket and I carried his dinner to him. I received Netts letter of the 12th July Saying the Home Guards would have to come into the Army. "Bully." They will get to see the "Ellephant["] walk off on his ears. I wish they would force every able bodied man in the north to go into the Army regardless of politics. We could soon wipe out the Southren confederacy if we had a united north.

TUESDAY JULY 21ST

It rained hard last night and is still rainy. We drilled as usual. I was in camp all day. . . . News good. It seams it was a general move of our Armies when we left Murfreesboro. It is a grand thing and we have Surely been successful and it prevents the Rebels from reinforceing any one point as the[y] must defend their entire line. When if only one of our Armies moved the Rail Roads could run Troops from one place to another and defeat us in detail. But the plan adopted now will certainly compell them to ask for terms or their entire country will be laid waste. Our Generals are not so particular about protecting Rebel property and I think that is a senseable move. If we continue to place a Guard at every house they can hold out much longer than if we make them feel the effects of war.[19]

WEDNESDAY JULY 22ND

We had drill as usual. Our teams went for Rations. I understand they go to Deckhart Station only Six miles and if the Rail Road is repaired that far we will soon move again. George Whitestine of "Co E" was buried to day in "honors of war." He died in camp and was burried at the foot of the mountains with nothing to mark the place. He was a faithfull soldier and a good Boy. Another Sacrifice on the alter of his country. He Still lives in the hearts of his comrades and as they march on to duty they will think of "George" in his narrow Grave. I was detailed for picket this evening.

Thursday July 23rd

We returned to camp from Picket about day light and left camp about five Oclock am. and Started up the mountains to cut the timber out of the road that the Rebels had fell into it to impede our advance. The passes through the rocks was pretty well filled up. We had about two miles to clear out and haulted for dinner and then sent Scouts to ascertain if there was any more and they reported the road clear and we started back to camp where we arrived about five Oclock p.m. with no other adventure than killing a number of Yellow Rattlesnakes. One of our boys Shot one about five feet long. They are very plenty but are cowardly and will run unless crippled. . . .

Friday July 24th

This camp is called "Camp Winfield" and we did not get marching orders. This is another hot day. We had no drill but rested over our work yesterday. . . . The water is getting Scarce and there is a rumor in camp that we will move to morrow to better water. I am ready to go as I am tired of this place and it looks more like doeing Something when we are moveing and I feel better.

Saturday July 25th
[Decherd, Tennessee]

We got orders to be ready to move at two Oclock pm and Started precisely at that time. We passed through Deckhards Station where there is only a few houses and camped about a mile and a half South of town. We have a beautifull place to camp and splendid water. One year ago to day I enlisted. I did not think then I would have to s[t]ay this long but I dont know whether the war is any nearer over only in time. It looks as though it might close up but when I think what we have before is The country we have to pass over and the Rebels in our front I get discouraged and think they may continue the struggle some time yet. They have shown that they are brave and will resist to the last.[20]

Sunday July 26th

Supposeing we would remain here a few days we carried lumber about a mile and made us a house. . . . It has the appearance of Rain. We did not have inspection. Our camp looks nice and comfortable as we have learned to make our selves so if we dont stay long in a place. A Soldier always lives fast while he can and only starves when he cant avoid it. There was preaching in camp but it is very hard to get the majority of the men to meeting. They have to[o] much to attend to (They Think So) and if the Captains form their companies and compell us to go it is all right and they have a good congregation and not otherwise. I think there is a time for everything and dont o[b]ject to the meeting part but praying would never lick old Bragg without the assistance of a little Gun Powder.

MONDAY JULY 27TH

It is cloudy and rainy this morning but cleard away about ten Oclock. I made a ring out of Laurel Root for Rollie. We had no drilling. We got orders this pm to move tomorrow morning. I went to the creek and took a Bath. Well we will have to leave our nice quarters again. It seams provokeing to think we worked so hard to fix up yesterday and now have to leave. . . .

TUESDAY JULY 28TH

The sun come [up] very hot and we did not move. I made a ring for Christ Lew. . . . I visited the 101st Indiana. We have orders to move at Eight Oclock am to morrow. So we will stay another night in our nice camp and then we will have to leave it.

WEDNESDAY JULY 29TH
[UNIVERSITY HEIGHTS, TENNESSEE]

We "pulled out" at Eight Oclock and our camp was left in a terible plight. Our Boys Set fire to the camp and we bid it a good bye in that condition. We returned to Dechards Station and then started east and Struck the pass we cut out a few days ago over Red Hill. We marched about ten miles and camped at University Heights where Genl Sheridans division of McCooks Army Corps is camped who we are to relieve.[21] The Scenery was grand as we looked back over the valey we have left and now we are about two thousand feet above the valey. But with a few exceptions the top of the mountains are level and we find nice camping ground. We filed to the left of the road and camped in the woods. A Short distance from us is a ravine where the springs are located and gush out of the rock where wooden Spiles are inserted and runs the water out in numerous small Jets and we can fill our Buckets by placeing them under a Spile. It is splendid water and we are glad of the move. I bought some new potatoes from one of the soldier Boys. Our meat Rations run out and we done without for supper. It was hard work for me to climb the mountains and made my feet very sore. . . . We did not pitch our tents as we will move camp to morrow when Sheridans men move out. They are going on south. Bragg will make his stand at or near Chattanooga so prisoners report and we will have to march some distance yet before we meet him. Some say he is getting us to cross the mountains where we cant retreat and will then defeat us and capture the entire Army. But I think when he captures us he will want some body to help him let us go. I dont fear that and if we only can catch him we will give him all he wants to get away with.

THURSDAY JULY 30TH

We moved our camp this morning to the edge of the Ravine and on the north Side and the 101st is camp[ed] across and but a Short distance from us. We are in a grove of timber and one of the nicest of camps. Sheridans men moved about five am. We worked about all day cleaning off our camp and fixing our Bunks. There are so many poisonous varmints here that we have to raise our Bunks off the ground and burn all the Brush and leaves to kill them. We carried our lumber about a half mile. Rails are scarce (none) and we burn green wood and have plenty of it. . . . This place takes its name "University Heights" from there being the foundation of a large Female College here and the war has stoped the work. It was called Red Hill before. The nice water and mountain climate makes it a beautiful location for a School and very healthy. The corner stone of [the] University is of Grey Granite and the Boys are makeing orniments of it.

FRIDAY JULY 31ST

We put in the day grubbing Grading and policeing our camp and it is the nicest place we have had for a long time. All the water will run down the hill and away. We will remain here some time so report says. But about the time we get fixed comfortable we will move I expect. I bought Some apples of a citizen. They come into camp to trade with us. . . .

CHAPTER 6

Chickamauga and Furlough

Despite the success of the Army of the Cumberland in taking Chattanooga, the Confederates were far from beaten. Unfortunately for Rosecrans, three of the Army of the Cumberland's corps became widely separated as they advanced into northwest Georgia, allowing the outmaneuvered Bragg an opportunity to move quickly and destroy each in detail. Fortune smiled on the Federals, however, for Bragg's subordinates botched two attempts to crush portions of the dispersed enemy army. Finally realizing his perilous situation, Rosecrans quickly ordered a concentration of his forces before Bragg seized another opportunity to strike. Soon the Union corps had closed within supporting distance of one another on the west side of Chickamauga Creek.

The Seventy-fifth moved down the eastern slope of Lookout Mountain and into McLemore's Cove, then to Pond Spring on Chickamauga Creek, where the Hoosiers enjoyed three days of rest. The respite ended at 4:00 p.m. on September 18, when the men shouldered their muskets and left Pond Spring on a critical forced march. Having failed to prevent the Federal concentration, Bragg's objective now was to cross the Chickamauga, turn the Federal left flank, and get between Rosecrans and Chattanooga. In the late afternoon of September 18, his men skirmished with Union cavalrymen but were able to push across the creek in force. Bragg's troops continued to cross through the night and were ready to begin the battle in earnest the following morning.

As the Confederates crossed the Chickamauga, the Seventy-fifth and the rest of the Fourteenth Corps marched north to Crawfish Springs. There they were ordered to continue moving through the night in order to secure the Lafayette Road to Chattanooga and establish the Union left flank. "It is almost

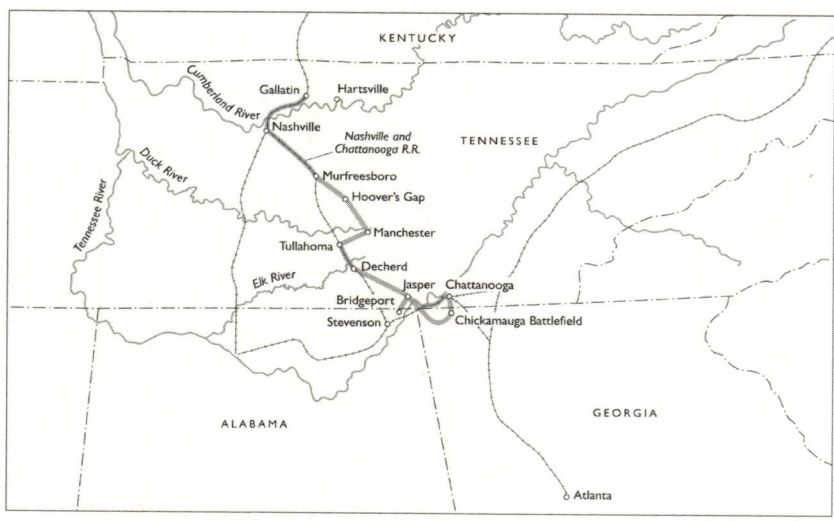

MAP 2. Travels of William Bluffton Miller in Tennessee and northwest Georgia, 1863.

miraculous that during that fearful night we did not meet with some dreadful accidents," wrote a member of the regiment. "Here and there fences were set on fire, and the columns of marching troops, at one point, would penetrate the lurid light which illuminated their pathway, and at another would plunge into the impenetrable darkness." Making matters worse, "hundreds of wagons . . . and immense trains of artillery . . . intermingling with the marching infantry, would choke up the narrow way." The air was full of the "deep dull rumbling of the artillery wagons, the clanking of arms, [and] the thousands of subdued voices of men marching at midnight near the enemy."[1] One Indiana soldier had more vivid memories. He recalled that they set fire to "every thing that would burn and for miles on either side we could see fire. At times the heat was so great we could hardly keep in line."[2] Two divisions of the Fourteenth Corps made it to their assigned places by the morning of the nineteenth, but the division of Joseph Reynolds was still marching north, trying to arrive in position, when the Battle of Chickamauga officially began.

After the night march, the Seventy-fifth halted for breakfast, but soon the command to form ranks was given again, as the rattle of musketry was heard on the Union left flank. In the early afternoon of the nineteenth, General Reynolds and his men arrived on the battlefield. The Fourth Division was quickly split apart. Corps commander Thomas ordered one brigade to move into the Federal line of battle. Gen. John Palmer of the Twenty-first Corps appealed to Reynolds for help and was given three regiments from the other brigade. Reynolds was left with only the Seventy-fifth and an artillery battery, so he decided to place these units in reserve near the center of the Federal line. The logical position for this remnant of his command was Brotherton Ridge, a height running parallel to the Lafayette Road, the main artery to Chattanooga.

These troops would not remain idle, however. When part of the Union line gave way, the reserves were called into action. At nearly 3:30 p.m., General Palmer ordered the seven hundred Hoosiers to charge and meet the advancing Confederates. The woods rang with cheers as the Seventy-fifth men rushed to meet the enemy.[3] They surged forward "in fine style" and drove Brig. Gen. John C. Brown's Confederate brigade back a "considerable distance," in the words of General Palmer. "The officers and men of that regiment deserve great credit for their gallantry in this affair," he reported.[4]

Now in position on the east side of the Lafayette Road, Colonel Robinson received a warning from General Palmer: the enemy had been merely startled by the charge of his large regiment, and they would return. He told the Hoosier colonel that his raw troops would be unable to hold them but should "keep up appearances" as long as possible. Palmer was correct— their initial success was only temporary.[5] At about 4:00 p.m., Brig. Gen. William B. Bate's brigade assaulted the Hoosiers. Robinson's men and the other Federals east of the Lafayette Road made a brief but determined stand, but eventually they were flanked and forced to retire in confusion back across the Lafayette Road to Brotherton Ridge, as the Confederates pushed away all opposition. Colonel Robinson met General Palmer again and reported that his regiment had been destroyed and had only fifty survivors. The rest, explained Robinson, were dead or prisoners.

Palmer reassured the colonel that his men had merely "taken care of themselves" and would soon return, and he backed up his prediction with a bet of ten dollars. Palmer won the bet.[6]

Now General Reynolds and the rallied troops on Brotherton Ridge attempted to hold the line and keep the Confederates from breaking the Union center. Their efforts were in vain, however, as by 4:30 the Federals had been driven off the ridge by three enemy brigades. The Hoosiers moved north up the Lafayette Road to nearby Poe Farm and there helped establish a new defensive line to halt the Rebels. After the men reformed, the Indiana officers, "with tears in their eyes and determination on their faces," begged in vain for the chance to reclaim the lost ground. Thanks to help from twenty artillery pieces, the Union soldiers stopped Bate by 5:30. When Federal reinforcements arrived, the Union center was restored. Speaking of the Confederate attacks, Sergeant Floyd wrote, "Onward they madly rushed, yelling like bloodhounds upon the trail. Every moment had its peculiar sound of terror—every spot is ghastly sight of destruction and horror."[7]

Darkness finally ended the slaughter. The moonlight cast shadows over the dead and dying, and only the groans and prayers of the wounded broke the stillness. "The wretched spectacle of these men, as they lay cold and stark in the moonlight . . . and the wearied, haggard, jaded and hungry heroes, with smoke-begrimed faces . . . as they lay asleep in the midst of the dead and dying . . . impressed the sombre coloring of a picture upon the writer's memory, that will never be erased," wrote the regimental historian.[8]

The Confederate plan on the morning of September 20 was to begin the assault on their far right and have each division in turn attack on down the line. Early on Sunday morning, the veterans of the Seventy-fifth, in line near the Poe House, began constructing simple breastworks, consisting of a few old rails and decaying logs and stumps piled up in front of their position. "Not having picks, spades or axes . . . we built a rude line of works about hip high, little thinking we would remain in this position all day," a member of the regiment noted. The same soldier recalled that the men soon sat down to discuss the previous day's fight. "Some felt proud," he wrote, "some as though we might have done better, but we did all we could."[9] With their defenses in place, the Hoosiers hurled back the first Rebel attack against them then enjoyed a brief lull.

Disaster soon struck the Federal army. Thomas Wood's division of the Twenty-first Corps pulled out of the Union battle line to plug an imaginary gap, only to create a real hole. A massive attack by Gen. James Longstreet's eight Confederate brigades (eleven thousand men) into that void wrecked the entire Union right flank. By about 1:00 p.m., the Seventy-fifth found no Union troops in position on their right; in fact, *they* had become the right flank of the Union line. By 2:00 p.m., the Army of the Cumberland was fighting in two large groups—one emplaced on "Horseshoe Ridge," a defensive position west of the Lafayette Road, and the other, including the Seventy-fifth, in a "bull-pen," as the men termed it, with the enemy on three sides of their horseshoe-shaped line east of the road. Both segments came under heavy Confederate attack, and soon all the Federal ammunition was gone, except the rounds collected from the cartridge boxes of the dead. "But for this circumstance," believed General Reynolds, "we could have maintained our position indefinitely."[10] A lull in the fighting ensued, although the deadly fire of sharpshooters continued, one of which killed the Hoosiers' brigade commander, Col. Edward King.

Now all that was left was for the Federals to attempt to withdraw up the Lafayette Road toward Chattanooga, to save themselves from being "gobbled up."[11] Just as sundown was approaching, Reynolds's division "moved to the assault with the accuracy and precision of an evening's dress parade" to open the road. "Our ranks were well closed, our steps elastic, and our faces were lit up with the hope of success, whilst shot and shell ploughed the ground around us," wrote a participant.[12] The division successfully drove off the surrounding Confederates and cleared the road to the north. The Seventy-fifth's brigade then held a road branching off to the west, leading to McFarland's Gap and Rossville, so that their portion of the army could safely withdraw from the field. "We ran all the way [to Rossville]," wrote

James Essington, "tired, footsore, hungry and thirsty, but thank God we were not captured."[13]

By the end of the Battle of Chickamauga, the veterans of the Seventy-fifth Indiana could proudly state that although the Union army had retreated, the regiment had fought its first major battle and lost a total of 138 men killed, wounded, captured, or missing, the highest loss of any unit in Reynolds's division.[14]

The Hoosiers arrived in Chattanooga on the morning of September 23 and began to construct new fortifications while improving those left behind by Bragg's troops. "[We] now defy the whole confederacy," Capt. Samuel Steele confidently wrote, but as the Confederates closed in around the city, their siege lines gradually began to choke off the flow of vital supplies to the Army of the Cumberland.[15] Union troops in Chattanooga were soon so desperate for food that they stole rations of shelled corn from army mules and actually shed tears over moldy and condemned hardtack crackers. Wood for fires began to give out as well, necessitating the hauling of fuel from the enemy lines or from far up the river. To make matters worse, Confederate artillerymen threw rounds at the Union defenses, though they did little damage.

Despite the defeat at Chickamauga and the gloomy outlook for the future, at least some Hoosiers were proud of all they had accomplished. S. W. Payne wrote an optimistic letter home in late October in which he summarized the Tullahoma and Chickamauga campaigns:

> We have reached this place through rain and mud, stifled by dust and scorched by a burning summer sun—by wading streams and climbing rugged mountain heights—by weary marching by day and often by night—and at last meeting the foe on unequal terms, striking him blow for blow and then *cutting our way through his forces*. It took just three months of labor to accomplish this. Thank God we are here and glad of it. We have achieved a great success in getting here. After the lapse of a month we are doubly assured that our position is a good one and that it is beyond the power of the *Confeds* to drive us hence.[16]

While under siege in Chattanooga, the Union army was reorganized and several segments assigned new commanding officers. The Hoosiers of the Seventy-fifth became part of the Third Division, Fourteenth Corps and lost their division commander, General Reynolds, who was promoted to chief of staff. His replacement was Brig. Gen. Absalom Baird, who was destined to lead the division for the remainder of the war. The Army of the Cumberland was given to Major General Thomas, the old Fourteenth Corps commander, while his corps was placed under Gen. John M. Palmer. Most important, overall command of the Federal effort in Chattanooga was assigned to Maj. Gen. Ulysses S. Grant. By late November, Ed Freeman of the Seventy-fifth was able to confidently report that "all are in good fighting spirits" and told his readers to "look for important events to transpire in this locality before long."[17]

The newly arrived commander moved decisively to break the Confederate siege. In late October, he sent troops to capture strategic Brown's Ferry and open a shorter supply route from the Tennessee River. Finally, with the arrival of Gen. William T. Sherman's Army of the Tennessee, Grant began large-scale operations. First, on November 23, he ordered part of his army, supported by the Seventy-fifth, to move forward and test the strength of the Confederates on Missionary Ridge, and they succeeded in capturing Orchard Knob, a wooded rise about halfway between the city and the height. Grant then planned to move against Bragg's flanks by threatening the Confederate left on Lookout Mountain and storming Tunnel Hill at the northern end of Missionary Ridge to break Bragg's right. In the meantime, the Army of the Cumberland would hold the attention of Bragg's center along Missionary Ridge.

The following day, Union forces dramatically seized Lookout Mountain, and cheers rang out as the Stars and Stripes were raised on that point. The Confederates withdrew to Missionary Ridge, and on the twenty-fifth, Grant planned to assault that position. He ordered the troops who took Lookout to move against the left flank of the Missionary Ridge line at Rossville Gap while simultaneously attacking Bragg's right at Tunnel Hill.

Unfortunately for Grant, the Federal drives against both flanks bogged down. The Federals on Bragg's left were delayed in crossing Chattanooga Creek, while Union troops attacking at Tunnel Hill faced stiff Confederate opposition. To help with the Tunnel Hill effort, Grant sent Baird's division to reinforce that end of the line. No sooner had they arrived, however, than they were ordered to move back to the Union center. Grant was sure that the Confederates were now rushing reinforcements to Tunnel Hill and had consequently weakened their center. Now if the Army of the Cumberland could demonstrate against Bragg's center, the Southern commander would recall his troops to meet the threat and hopefully give the Federals a chance at Tunnel Hill.

Baird's soldiers returned to their former position about 2:30 p.m., and there the Hoosiers waited for the signal to attack. About an hour later, when six cannon shots were fired, the Federal line surged forward across the undulating ground "like a prairie fire" toward the ridge.[18] "Never before did I see the 75th so anxious to go into battle as they were at that moment," wrote Hoosier James Essington.[19] The Federals overran the first line of Confederate rifle pits, as Rebel cannon on the ridge fired rapidly and were greeted in reply by Union guns in the Chattanooga defenses. "There never was witnessed a sublimer spectacle," wrote Sgt. David Floyd.[20]

Now at the foot of Missionary Ridge, the Federals realized that to remain there would be suicide. After a few minutes of catching their breath and reforming lines, the Union troops surged up the ridge. "My brigade moved at once with cheers and a hearty good will," reported Col. Ferdinand Van Derveer. "The precipitous ascent, the enemy's sharpshooters in front, and the terrific enfilading artillery fire upon each flank were forgotten in their eager haste to storm the heights," he added.[21] The Seventy-fifth advanced up the steep slope and through deep gullies, with brush, rocks, fallen trees and enemy fire adding to the difficulty. "Every man was left to his own resources, bravery, patriotism and generalship," wrote a member of the 101st Indiana.[22] Despite the obstacles, the division reached the crest and began moving along the ridge. While enjoying a brief rest, Colonel Robinson noticed Federals and Confederates battling over an artillery piece belonging to a Florida battery. Robinson ordered his men to rise, fix bayonets, and charge. They captured the cannon and drove the enemy away. Colonel Robinson then grabbed the regimental colors and waved them to cheer his men "to the verge of insanity."[23]

Darkness ended the action with the Confederates in full retreat and the Union troops encamped on the crest of Missionary Ridge. Casualties in the Seventy-fifth had been light—only nineteen out of more than three hundred men engaged. The victory had been complete, and the Hoosiers had done well, helping to erase the defeat at Chickamauga. In the words of Colonel Robinson, "Their justly earned laurels upon more sanguinary fields did not depreciate in the action before Chattanooga. They met the enemy, as upon former occasions, determined to defeat him at all hazards."[24] Colonel Van Derveer complimented his men as well: "In this action my brigade fully sustained the reputation it had won at Chickamauga. None flinched from their duty."[25]

William Bluffton Miller, badly wounded at Chickamauga, spent the last months of 1863 recuperating in the hospital and at home and missed his regiment's heroic charge up Missionary Ridge. He rejoined his comrades shortly before the end of the year. The spring of 1864 would find them all back in northwest Georgia.

SATURDAY AUG 1ST

General Inspection at Nine Oclock a.m. and company inspection this evening. . . . We had no drill. I was out of camp for Laurel Root. I bought some Apples and new potatoes. It rained very hard this evening. . . .

SUNDAY AUG 2ND

I bought some honey from a Citizen. I wrote to Nett and Sent a little Book made out of Granite to Rollie. . . . It rained some. I was out to our Picket line but could not get out. We had two Inspections to day. We pass the most of our time down at the creek working Granite. There is all kinds of little trinkets made by rubbing it on the Sand Stone where the water runs over them. It wears the Granite away and leaves a smooth Serface. It shows the Yanke[e] inginuity to go down and See them working. There are hundreds of Soldiers there all the time and they will be makeing different things. Some of them are very handsome. Then it whiles away the tedius camp live and is a sort of recreation for body and mind. This is a nice warm day but we have a nice mountain breeze nearly all the time.

MONDAY AUG 3RD

I put in the most of the day working Granite as we have no orders to drill yet. We had Dress Parade this evening. . . . We received [orders] to commence the company drill twice a day. No news of importance.

TUESDAY AUG 4TH

Companys E & K drilled to gether as neither had men enough as the Boys are on Picket. I did not write nor get any letters.

WEDNESDAY AUG 5TH

Company Inspection and Dress Parade constituted our duty to day. No mail for me to day and I did not write a letter.

THURSDAY AUG 6TH

I received Netts Letter of the 30th July and did not answer it as I was detailed for Picket. I got a Letter from Jim Spake.

FRIDAY AUG 7TH

I received Netts letter of Aug 2nd informing that Rollie was very sick of Flux. We was relieved from picket by a detail from the 105th Ohio. Our Knapsacks came up to day and my things were all right but two pairs [of] Socks which had been taken out. We received orders to prepare for general Inspection. I got a letter from Lou Townsend of the 2nd speaking of Rollies sickness and I feel to night as though I would give any thing to be at home. I am very Sad and lonesome. I can stand it very well if my folks keep well. It has been so long since I seen my little family that I almost forget how they look. I hope the next letter will Say Rollie is out of danger [if] not entirely well.[26]

SATURDAY AUG 8TH

We had warm Biscuit for Breakfast. I cleaned my gun for General Inspection at Eight Oclock a.m. After inspection I was Sent on Picket to relieve the Boys of the 105th Ohio so they could draw their pay. The[y] returned and relieved us this evening and we returned to Camp. I got a half bushell of potatoes while on Picket. We live splendidly here. Plenty to eat.

SUNDAY AUG 9TH

We had Inspection twice to day and dress parade. I received Lou Townsends letter conveying the Sad news that little Rollie died on the evening of the 4th inst at quarter to Six. Who can till the feelings of a Soldier far from home and friends whe[n] he receives and when it comes one year since he left them that one of them has passed away. Oh the anguish and Sorrow I feel to night. One year ago to day I left my dear wife and Baby seven months Old to battle for freedom with the fond antici-pations of pleasure when I should return to them when peace reigned supreme. But now my Babe has passed away and I shall never see him more and then to know thay my wife is left alone. I know She is among friends and will be taken care off but there will be a wound that nothing but time can cure. She will miss him more than I will as my absence [has] been so long that I can hardly rea[l]ize that I ever had a child. But Sad as I feel I shall try to do my duty to my country and console myself as best I can. Trusting in him who doeth all things for our good. I hope the war may Soon close and we can return to our homes and dear ones and enjoy their company as in days gone by. I will write to Nett to morrow and advise her what to do. I know it will be So lonesome to keep house alone now that She has no little boy to keep her company.

MONDAY AUG 10TH

We drilled as usual and I wrote to Nett. I was over to the 101st Ind this p.m. and then cleaned up for inspection to morrow. The officers dont intend we Shall get dirty as we have from one to two inspections dai-ley. Some of them know about as much about a gun as a hog does about war but they can put on the Style all the same.

TUESDAY AUG 11TH

Drill as usual. Orders came for our Regiment to go to the Picket line and after we got there found out it was for a Brigade Drill. After "Brushwhacking" around in the Brush for an hour we marched back to camp. It was wet and we all came back "sprinkled" and there was plenty of Shoemake and if we are not all poisoned more or less I Shall be happy. It was the bigest piece of foolishness [by] a set of officers who cla[i]m to have comman sence I ever knew to be perpetrated. Time will Show whether I am right or not. . . .

WEDNESDAY AUG 12TH

Drilled as usual and I wrote a letter partly to Nett. I made a Diamond out of Granite for Christ Lew. Our mail did not get in as the mail Train was ditched and did not get to Dechard Station in time for our pm to get through before the countersign out. So I got no Letters.

THURSDAY AUG 13TH

Our mail came in this morning and with it a letter from Nett requesting me to send her Rollies picture that I have. I finished my letter commenced yesterday and enclosed the picture for her. Her letter was Sorrowfull and it made me feel badly for her to think how lonely She must be. It rained some. I made a heart out of Granite for Christ Lew. There is talk of a move in camp but no positive orders yet. But I think we better be going and catch Bragg as soon as possible. No news of importance.

FRIDAY AUG 14TH

I am sick and had to report at Sick call and was excused from duty. . . . Beardsley done my washing for me as I was not able to do it myself. No orders to move yet. I notice severel of the Boys besides me who are poisoned from Shoemake from the Brigade drill a few days ago. I only wish some of the Officers that caused it had a little of it and they would know how pleasant it is. I hope it will soon get well and they wont get me in another Such a Scrape. I will prefer extra duty hereafter.

SATURDAY AUG 15TH

I reported at sick call and was excused from duty again to day. My face is very sore and I have a bad head ache. . . . There was Inspection but I did not go out. We get no news as our Armies are laying Still. I think the cause is the Battle of Gettysburgh crippled the Army of the Potomac so the[y] will have to recruit up before they can move and we are only holding our position untill our Rail Road is in running order and when everything is ready we will all move to gether again. It all depends on concert of Action and they cannot concentrate their forces at any one point. The country we are traveling over now could not be campaigned over in any other way. If Lee could reinforce Bragg they would get men enough here to drive us back and vice verse. But it keeps Bragg buisy and all he can do to hold us in check and Lee has his hands full while Genl Grant on the Mississippi is keeping them employed there. It rained some with heavy thunder. I was in camp all day. . . . I had some ripe Peaches.

SUNDAY AUG 16TH

I visited the surgeon again this morning. I dont feel much better. I wrote to Nett. Wilders mounted Brigade came up to day and there is strong talk of a move. . . . I hope they will not move untill I get able to go. I dont want to be left behind as I want to see Bragg get the drubbing we had laid out for him. I would feel bad if the Regiment should pass through a Series of Battles and I could not say I was along. I may be hurt or killed but I am willing to risk it. I think I will be all right in a day or two. I Shall try to go if possible.

MONDAY AUG 17TH

I am Better this morning. The Bugle Sounded "Roll Call" before day light and we got orders to be ready to move at Seven Oclock a.m. That is the best medicin I can take and it will cure me almost immediately. We Struck Tents and Started towards Jasper. We did not get off the mountains untill nearly dark. The valey in our front was grand. We passed the 1st Battallion of Pioneers about half way dow[n] the mountain where they were in camp. Two miles from the top down into the valey and some places very Steep descent. We camped on Battle Creek about dusk about a mile from the mountains. We camped near a line of fence and after we Stacked Arms the Rails began to walk off and Col King commanding Brigade Sent an Aid Decamp to Col Robinson to order us to go to the mountains for wood. Col Robinson rode to Col King after telling us to take the rails and Said Col King you are doubtless aware that my men marched twenty miles to day and they are going to burn those rails and if you want my Sword you can have it. Col King replied tell your men to burn the "top rails." We did so but the fence was all gone in the morning. This little accurrance demonstrates the character of the two Colonels. One would make us cary our wood a mile after marching hard all day and protect Rebel property and Sacrifice his men while Col Robinson had some feeling for us and Stood up for his men and made friends while Col King call[ed] a curse from every man in the Regiment. Some officers think the private Soldier is nothing but a dog and treat them accordingly and if there was no privates we would have no use for Officers. About all some officers are real good for is to draw their pay. We get water from the Celebrated "Blue Springs." This valey is called "Sweedens Cove." It is very rich and fertile and peaches by the Ton. We had a hard days march it was so rocky and I am very tired and foot sore. The mail did not come up.

Tuesday Aug 18th

The sun up hot and no orders to move yet. I went and got a mess of Roasting Ears about day light. There is plenty of corn and almost all kinds of produce and we will not Starve while we remain in Sweedens Cove. There is a peach orchard near here in which is said to be three thousand bearing trees and our Boys improved the opportunity to day. There was four men detailed of the company to go for peaches. We got marching orders about noon and Started nearly east following Battle Creek and we camped near the creek to night. We are surrounded by mountains now and the scenery is grand to me who was borne and raised in a very level country such as Wells county Indiana. I carried my Knapsack to day So I think I am improveing fast. The Rebels were reported only Six miles from us when we Started but if there was any they left before we Seen them.

Wednesday Aug 19th

This morning Still finds us on Battle Creek and prospects for a very hot day. . . . We had plenty of Green Corn & Peaches. . . . There is rumors that we will remain here a few days but nothing reliable. We have plenty of supplies and we make some of the old planters feel the effects of the war as we forage and take any thing we can eat.

THURSDAY AUG 20TH

There was two men detailed for Corn & Peaches and we did not move. Our Brigade Teams went to Tracy city for supplies. We had company Drill and Dress parade. It will not take us long to clean out all the forage and eatables in this valey and I don't think we will remain here very long.

FRIDAY AUG 21ST
[JASPER, TENNESSEE]

. . . Orders to move came about Eleven Oclock and as our Teams are not hear we left our Camp and Garrison Equipage in camp under Guard and "skipped" out for Jasper Six miles where we camped about dusk. I was detailed for fatigue duty after we camped but it did not last long. This was a terible hot day and rained Some this evening. Jasper is a county seat but not much of a town. We have been marching nearly due east Since we came down off the mountains and must be severel miles from the Rail Road. We are not many miles from the Tennissee river.

SATURDAY AUG 22ND

Report came to camp that about three hundred Rebel Cavalry lay between us and the River and my Regiment with one Section of Capt Harrises 19th Indiana Battery was orderd out to "gobble" them in.[27] We went cautiously and quickly but they crossed the River and had Skipped out. We filed off the road into a corn field on the bank of the river and kept hid from view from the opposite side. We are now at Loves Ford opposite Shell Mound Station on the Nashville and Chattanooga Rail Road. We kept quiet to see if the Johnies would not run a Train over the road as they are going to Chattanooga and running all their supplies there. But about Eleven aclock pm one gun from the Battery commenced Shelling the coverd Bridge at the mouth of Chickamauga creek and the other Shelled the Station house but there was no reply from the Rebels. And Three of our Boys with Leut [?] Conkling of "Co D" crossed over in a Canoe and Set fire to the Bridge which was entirely destroyed. "Co K" (My co) with D & E supported the Battery. The night was very dark and it was a magnificent Sight when the Bridge was burning to look a cross the river and observe the reflection on the mountains on the oposite and then the little boat returning with those brave Boys who had ventured across the river. They did not know what was awaiting them and we could not assist them if they had been attacked. We could see lights spring fourth at the houses after our Battery fired the first round. The citizens did not know the Yankees were so close to them and were no doubt surprised. We will cross the Tennissee at this point but how or when I dont know. The country opposite looks like that we have come over and Deserters say it is worse and that Chattanooga is situated in a very rough Section. We are only about thirty miles from there now.

SUNDAY AUG 23RD

About day light we noticed two men come down to the river opposite and Showed a "White Flag" and soon stripped and lashed their clothing on a Board and started over. A detachment under Cap Karns went down to where they landed and they proved to be deserters from the 41st Missippi and detached to a Regiment of Rebel Sharp Shooters. They claim their cause is lost and they were tired of the war. Their name is Wilder and are brothers and live near Corrinth.[28] They say we will have a battle at or near Chattanooga. That it is a strong position. But we have come so far and drove them from so many strong positions that I am not scared yet. We were relieved and returned to the Regiment back in the woods. We live on Corn Beans & fresh pork. We have a large iron Kettle and large enough to cook for the entire Company. Genl Rosencrans rode by us this evening and enquired if we had plenty and our Boys invited him to dismount as our mess was about cooked but he declined and passed on. We can look across into Alabama & Georgia. . . . I am getting fat again.

MONDAY AUG 24TH

Company "K" was sent on picket and I was not on duty but was at the Reserve. We relieved company "B." . . . I went with S A Karns and "Zack" (our darky) to get a "Bee Scap" but they were all gone. Our Battery kept Shelling the valley across the River. The "Johnies" fire on us as they are picketing and we see them. We keep hid in the Cane & Brush. It is about five hundred yards across. We exchange papers with the Johnies by swimming out half way carying the papers in our mouth. They are honorable and wont fire on us if the[y] agree not too. One Sharpshooter climbed a tree and kept fireing at the Battery Boys and fineally the gunner turned an "old twelve Pounder" on his tree and cut it off and let him into the river. The last we seen of "Johnie." He did not swim out and was undoubtedly killed. Capt Harris threw severell Shell into Shell Mound Station house. Our gunners keep the Rebels awake. We exchange a good many Shots.

TUESDAY AUG 25TH

It is thirteen months to day since I enlisted and it finds me still on the north side of the Tennessee. We was relieved by Co G and returned to camp. I got some nice Honey and we still have plenty of Corn & Peaches. We moved camp back over the Fill into a thicket of Small Oaks. . . . Our Teams come up with five days rations. I did not get any letters. The Rebels are Still Seen and our Boys keep fireing on them. The news is very Scarce and we may remain here a few days. Our orders are to clear up our camp which looks like remaining. But we cant tell anything about that. We may move to morrow but I hardly think we will.

WEDNESDAY AUG 26TH

Levi Keagle & I went to the river to see the Pioneers raise Some old flat boats that was Scuttled by the Rebels. One company crossed the river on a Flat and we supposed the Rebs would fire on them but they did not fire a Shot. The[y] landed and "deployed" and drove the Johnies back. That gives us a hold on the south Bank without any resistance. It seams remarkable that they will allow us to advance as they do. Our teams returned for our Camp & Garrison Equipage left on Battle Creek and came back about noon. We cleared off our camp and pitched Tents. It was a big job but we will have a nice camp when we get the grubs out and policed. . . . We discovered a bright fire on to[p] of the mountains across the river to night and we cant account for it unless it is a Signal light. Our Battery tried to throw a Shell to it but it is to[o] high to elevate the guns to.

THURSDAY AUG 27TH

We finished policeing our quarters. The camp is on very low ground. Severel Deserters came [to] it and surrenderd. The light on the mountain last night was their camp fire. They report that Braggs Army is teribly demoralized and discouraged. But say we will have to fight before we get Chattanooga. I went and took a nice Swim in the Tennessee. . . .

FRIDAY AUG 28TH

I was on pick[et] at the river to day. We had I[?] nice place and as the Johnies have left the other side we put in the [day] fishing. Severel deserters and one conscript came over. The Conscript was from Atlanta Georgia. There is no fireing. Word came to camp that about fifty "Rebs" were hid in the mountains and four companies from the 75th Ind and Six of the 101st with Artillery me[n] for Scouting crossed the river about Eight Oclock this p.m.[?] to capture them. The Guides relieved the Rebel pickets and our men pushed forward to their camp and captured only Six of them with thirteen horses and some Arms. It was very dark and they slipped away into the hills. Our Boys did not get back to camp untill about daylight. They came to camp with plenty of forage and lots of chickens.[29] I had a long talk with a Rebel by name of "Guage" who claims to have been a Major.[30] He is a bitter "Secesh." He says they are not whipped yet and the war will last some time longer. We had some Saucy talk and I have concluded that he is more of a "Spy" than a soldier and Should not be allowed in or around our camp. He claims to live near here and that our men are killing his hogs and distroying his corn. I told him I thought that was all right as he could contribute to the good cause. Deserters report Bragg evacuateing Chattanooga as fast as possible.

SATURDAY AUG 29TH

I seen the largest Snake here this morning I ever "saw loose." He was a monster and as he Showed a disposition to run from me I concluded to let him go peaceably. He is like "Jeff Davis" "wanted to be let alone" and did not attack him. We were relieved at Nine Oclock am and returned to camp. It is all quiet along the lines. We had company inspection this evening. . . . Quite a number of deserters came over to day. They Say the war is over and I have no doubt they think so. But I cant agree with them for I think there will be a terible Battle in this department within the next thirty days. There is a large Smoke South of east from us toward Chattanooga and we surmised that the Rebs are burning the Town or Supplies they cant move.

SUNDAY AUG 30TH

A number of deserters came in to day and Sixteen was Sent to Jasper and among them Major Guage[?] as he stiles himself. Our Officers concluded to take charge of him for a while. I answerd Netts and Mollies letters. We had Regimental inspection. We received orders to be ready to cross the river during the night with one days rations. We started from camp about ten Oclock and was ferried across on Flats with the rest of our Brigade and started up the river near the Rail Road towards Chattanooga. It was very dark and the road rough and rocky and hard marching. We were on the road all night and arrived at "White Side" or Running Water about day light where we found the Rebels had burned the Bridge. The Bridge spanned the valey from one mountain to the other and was coverd and Iron roofed. It is about one hundred and fifty feet high at highest place. Our Cavalry captured Severel prisoners. The Bridge here cost a mint of money and Severs the Rail Road and will take months to rebuild it so the cars can pass over and should we take Chattanooga our supplies would have to be carried over the mountains by wagons.

MONDAY AUG 31ST

Some of our men climbed the Sugar Loaf mountain on the east side of the valley and started some coal cars down the track and the[y] came like ligtening and would jump the track and come down the mountain with a terible racket and made fun for the Boys. After breakfast we started back to Shell Mound but did not recross the river but camped in an old Rebel Camp near "Nick a Jack" cave. I was over and explored the Cave and I find that there is plenty of Salt Peter here and the Rebels had about four hundred Slaves to work here leeching the clay and working it out and Shipping it to Chattanooga where it is used in manufactureing Gun Powder to Shoot Yankees with. They have tracks layed all through the cave to wheel the clay out and their Leeches are in the mouth and the refineries out Side. I was back in the cave some distance and it is a rough dismal place and I observed Torches all through it. Some above and some below me. If a man Should Step off of the plank it is no telling where he would land. Report says the cave has been explored for a distance of Nine miles into the mountain but I dont know how true that is. This was a hot day and the roads were very dusty. . . . Our Camp and Garrison equipage was not brought over the river to day. I dont think we will return to our old camp north of the river but go on South.

Tuesday Sept 1st

We moved our camp close to Depot House and the rest of our things were brought across the river. I went over for my Knapsack myself. "General Turchins" Brigade crossed over.[31] I see they are getting about all of the 4th Division across now. . . . We moved camp on account of Small Pox being in a famly near camp. I remained in camp to guard our things and did not get to the new camp untill nearly night. We did not put up our Tent but slept in the Commissary Tent. There was a man by name of Robert Cummings of Company "I" drowned in the river while batheing this evening. There was five hundred men in the river but assistance did not reach him in time to save him. He drounded near the middle of the river.[32]

Wednesday Sept 2nd

. . . Robert Cummings body who was drownd yesterday was recoverd and burried in "honors of War." . . . All of our things were brought over which looks like a move soon. There are lots of soldiers camped in the valey here now. I was out for corn but it is getting scarce and hard to get. I got no mail. The positions of the Corps now is Critendens is approaching Chattanooga from the north. The 14th Corps crosses here and McCook crosses at Stepenson and Bridgeport below us. I think we are going to the rear of Chattanooga to cut the Rail Roads and cause Bragg to evacuate or surround him and lay Seige to him and cause his surrender. I merely guess at it.

Thursday Sept 3rd

. . . We got marching orders about noon and started South toward Sand Mountain and Trenton. We got stuck in the mountain pass as our Teams can hardly move. It got dark on us about six miles from camp and we layed down in the road and slept. This is the roughest place we have found yet. The pass is narrow and coal mines all around us. On one side it is purpendicular hundreds of feet hight and on the other is the valley hundreds of feet below with only a narrow road up the mountain. If the Rebels cant hold such passes as this what can they defend. Genl Turchins Brigade is in advance and keep us back. . . . I did not get any mail nor much Sleep to night.

FRIDAY SEPT 4TH

I cant say we left camp this morning as we were in the harness all night. But we moved on and crossed the Sand Mountain Range and about five miles up the valley and camped about three Oclock p.m for the night. This is rough Sure to have no place to sleep last night and march untill afternoon before camping or stopping for any thing to eat. But a detail was sent out for forageing and brought Potatoes Yams & chickens that the Secesh planters generously contributed at the Sugestion of the Yankees with "Guns" on their Shoulders. They are very clever that way when they cant avoid it. This valley seams to be in a good prosperous condition and we can live here as long as it holds out. Our teams did not get up. . . . There is something in the "Air." Bragg must fight or run soon. Reported that he has been reinforced by a Corps of Longstreets from the East.[33]

SATURDAY SEPT 5TH
[TRENTON, GEORGIA]

We did not move untill after noon and then moved to Trenton. We are now in the State of Georgia but only a short distance from the Allabama line. Our orders are very Strict and no Stragling allowed. We can see the Johnies on the mountains watching our movements but dont come close enough to interfere with our march. Report Says that Chattanooga is not evacuated yet and deserters Still claim that we will get a Battle near there and it is confirmed that the Army has been reinforced by Longstreet. I am satisfied that if we succeed in defeating the Rebel Army here it will almost be decisive and almost crush out their last hope. But if we should meet with a reverse and have to retreat it Seams to me we could hardly get away. Everything depends on our success in the next few days and not very many for we are drawing the lines so close that they must defeat us or their cause is lost in this department. Their men are deserting by hundreds to us and are very much disheartend and we all well know the consequence of a defeat and every man will do his whole duty and stand to the work manfully. There was some Cannonadeing in the direction of Chattanooga to day. I would not be surprised now if the "ball" should open up any moment for our maneuvers all indicate it. Signs of Battle are plenty and orders are strict and we are kept together.

Sunday Sept 6th

We did not move but not a man was allowed to go away from his command and we were ready to "fall in" at any time. There was some Cannonadeing towards Chattanooga. Report Says a Brigade of Rebels hold the pass in our front and also that Bragg still holds his position. General Rosencrans Head Quarters came up to night. Colonel Robinson also joined us to day. We did not get any mail nor papers. Trenton is a Small town and is almost deserted. It is in Lookout Valley. The country Surrounding the town is level but mountains any way I look. I dont think I would want to live in this country as I cannot get out without climbing. If we should have to retreat I think we could hold some of the places in our rear. There is iron ore all along these mountains.

Monday Sept 7th

I was detailed as a Head Quarter guard and orders came to move about noon. We moved a few miles and camped near a new Iron Furnace being built by the Rebels to work the Iron ore into Shot & Shell. I was in the rear and did not get to camp with the Regiment but remained at Head Quarters all night. We could see Rebel pickets on the mountains but at a safe distance. There was more cannonadeing towards Chattanooga. I got a "Nashville Union" but the news was very meager and I presume it is kept back by our General officers as that might do us an injury if our movements were published and is therefore suppressed. But I think there will be plenty of News and very Sad news to be published ere long. No mail.

Tuesday Sept 8th

We were relieved from guard about nine Oclock a.m. and returned to camp. The 75th did not move but relieved a Pennsylvania Regiment who were guarding a mill on Lookout Creek and they followed their command to the front. Some of our Boys were out forageing and returned with fresh meat. We saw some Rebs on the mountains. The news of Genl Negleys Divission fighting at Lookout Gap came back and we expected to move forward but as we did not move he must have held his position and drove the Johnies away.[34] We put up our tent this evening to shelter us from the heavy dew. We got no mail. It was a very hot day.

WEDNESDAY SEPT 9TH

. . . The Post Master reported we had fifteen minutes to write and I wrote to Nett as I may not have another opportunity. It seams Sad when I take pen and paper to write that such thoughts are upermost in my mind but when I reflect on the circumstances Surrounding me and know what I will have to pass through it is hard to avoid such feelings. There was great cheering in our camps this evening over the news that the 93rd Ills enterd Chattanooga to day. Another Stronghold has fallen and comparitively without a Struggle. That alters our position now. If we should meet with a reverse we can use that for a base to fall back to. Our forces would have to be teribly demoralized if we cannot hold that position. The Rebels claim it is the key to Georgia and now they have evacuated. But I still think there is a Battle to be fought yet not far ahead but I cant locate it. We have orders to be ready to move at three oclock a.m. tomorrow with two days rations. But who knows where we are going. Some think we will go to Chattanooga but I dont believe it.

THURSDAY SEPT 10TH

We Struck tents and Started early and went about a mile on the wrong road and had to counter march and Struck Lost Cove. We was on the road to LaFayette but now we climb Lookout mountain. We marched about ten miles and stoped about three oclock p.m. at the foot of the mountain for the night. I was out for Sweet Potatoes but did not find any. We are only a few miles from where Genl Negly had the Skirmish a day or two since. We have a good camp and good water. Some of our men came in with fresh meat. . . . We heard no fireing to day. . . .

FRIDAY SEPT 11TH

We did not leave camp untill after noon and we passed Brannans Division at the foot of Lookout.[35] We started up and each company was detailed to help the wagons up. It was a long Steep climb and we pushed the wagons before us and did not reach the top untill midnight and we were a tired set of men. There was heavy musketry in front while we were climbing Lookout and I think the Johnies are there in force and will resist our march to morrow. We went into camp at the summit and layed down with orders to move at four Oclock a.m. only four hours rest for us to night dont look like a very long time to us. But to morrow will bring fourth something. We are orderd to have two days rations and a hundred and twenty rounds of amunition and that all indicates buisiness. Well if the time has come for us to meet the enemy in a pitched Battle I am glad of it for we will then get the neaded rest over our campaign and we will teach them another Stone River lesson.

SATURDAY SEPT 12TH

Revillee at four Oclock and we started without our Teams. We crossed the mountain and decended into the valey and in about five miles came up with our advance which was driven back yesterday about three miles. This is a rough and rocky place and our position is along a line of fence. We chinked [?] it up for protection. We lay in line of Battle the rest of the day awaiting an attack but it did not come. It is reported that one Corps of Rebel Infantry with Wheelers Cavalry occupy a gap in the mountains ahead of us and I suppose that being the case we will drive them out if we can.[36] Our loss yesterday was only about fifty killed. Some say the Rebels cant get out only by running over us and if that is so they will never get out for we have plenty of help close at hand and the mountain in our rear. I dont believe that for they have always managed to get away. We will give them a warm reception if they will only come and see us. . . . We lay in line of Battle all night with our guns all loaded so as not to be surprised. There was no fireing in front or in our hearing only an ocasionall picket Gun.

SUNDAY SEPT 13TH

We were called up before day light and was in line of Battle with Knapsacks packed ready to sling if necissary. But the Rebels did not put in an appearance. We moved to the front about three miles to the foot of [the] next range of mountains where we joined Wilders and Turchins Brigades of our Divisson. We fortified another line of fence and lay in line of Battle. A couple of our boys concluded that if we couldent get a fight out of Bragg that they would get up a little fight of their own and had a little fight accordingly but neither was hurt very bad and the only harm done was the kicking over of one Stack of Guns. The[y] were charged but fortunately did not fire. The Captain restored order and all is now peace. The fight was the result of throwing Corn Cobs and

Tennissee Corn Bread at each other. The parties was Silas H Wentz and
Andrew J Brickley. No mail.

MONDAY SEPT 14TH

We moved North east about five miles to pond Spring where we captured
a Post Office and some of our Boys got some rich Letters. We surprised
about three hundred Rebel Cavalry in a Sweet Potatoe patch and they
were teribly frightend and left their potatoes in the field. They did not
know we were about. We could see the Johnies occasionally but they did
not disturb us. They have disappeard from our front. I was sent on Picket
after dark and we had considerable trouble establishing lines. Our orders
was very Strict and we was told the Rebels were near us. I had Sixteen
men on my relief and we picketed along a fence. Our reserve was at the
forks of the road and my relief is about a mile long when Stretched out.
One of my pickets got alarmed by hearing something walking in the
Brush. He haulted it and when he commanded it Stopped. Then it would
start up again. It done so untill I heard him cock this gun and I said to
him dont Shoot untill you see something to shoot at and Shortly a calf
came walking out of the woods. We had a laugh at his expense. The night
passed quietly. I was out forageing for a hog and got a good one. Well it
dont look so much like a fight now as it did. But cant think it is over yet.
I did not get any sleep to night. No mail came up.

TUESDAY SEPT 15TH

After it come day light we were orderd forward to extend our lines and
see what is in front. We advanced about a quarter [mile] to an elevated
position and can see a line of Pickets but not close enough [to] tell what
Army they belong to. Some troops made their appearance comeing
down the mountain from the north and Col King orderd out the 68th
Ind and 105th Ohio to ascertain who they are. They moved out a bout
a mile and run in to Genl Palmers Division of Crittendens Corps and
returned to camp.[37] They camped and threw out pickets and now there
is a double line here. There is fireing along our line south of us and the
Johnies are reported and "Pigeon Gap" and strongly posted. We had
plenty of Sweat Potatoes but I had no Coffee and very poor water and
returned to camp this evening with a severe head Ache[. . . .] Genl
Rosencrans was reconoitering around camp and report says he has

demanded Bragg to surrender and given him two days to do so. That is only a "Grape vine." But I think five more days will not pass before he will Surrender or retreat or we will do one or the other. This evening finds our Troops concentrated and there is "Music in the Air" some place. There is a large force of Rebels in our neighborhood and if they have been reinforced as reliably reported they will fight. I think the preliminary Skirmishing has commenced now.

WEDNESDAY SEPT 16TH

. . . It rained Some to day. "Pond Spring" is a curiosity. It appears to rise out of the hills and is grown up with a moss or weed that lays on top of the water which gives it the appearance of a "Frog Pond" in Indiana. There is a bench walk constructed from the north bank to the center about a hundred feet long and at the end of that seams to be a hole where the water comes up. It is severel feet in diameter and has been Sounded hundreds of feet deep without Striking bottom. The water is pure and Soft. The outlet is a creek on the East. There was fireing to the south of us all day. No mail came.

THURSDAY SEPT 17TH

Orders came for a detail of Twenty men from the company to go to the right and relieve Genl Turchins men who had a fight at Baileys Cross Roads.[38] We started about noon and met our Ambulances comeing in with the dead and wounded. We relieved Turchins men about sunset. I was sent with Wm Starr and J C Milliken on picket and it was dark where we was posted and we could not see what we have in front. Our orders were for one to Stand while the others slept as they could not relieve us. We could hear the Rebs in their camp and they are so close we can hear them talking and swearing. They are moveing camp from the noise. I Stood my severel tricks and tried to sleep while the others were on duty but I have to[o] many things to think about. It is trying on a mans nerves to be placed in this position. Out in the woods with but two companions and them sleeping and in hearing of the Enemy and not knowing what a moment may demonstrate. It causes a man to think of all the mean things he ever done in his life and he will keep his eyes and ears open. A little circumstance occurred to night that frigtend me teribly. I was leaning against a Red Oak tree and every thing quiet when I thought I heard the brush rustle in my front. I was all attention as I could not See very far. Soon I heard it again. This time I am certain and fineally a third time accompanied with a "*Whee-e-e-Who Who Who oh*" and I felt my hair assume a perpendicular as I thought a "Reb" had me sure. I stepped back and about ten feet up in the tree a clear Sky deleniated the out lines of a "*Screctch Owl*" perched on a limb who was the innocent cause of my alarm. I "Smiled a Smole[?]" and held my position manfully untill relieved. I tell this to illustrate the nervous condition I was in and I dont know but if any body else would done as I did. I knew what it was in an instant but his scream went through me like a Shot.

FRIDAY SEPT 18TH

Day light brought the Rebel Skirmishers into view and we put in an hour or two Skirmishing with them before we was relieved. The Rebel camp is about a quarter mile from us but hid by a cornfield. I was surprised to see a Johnie come to the Cornfield fence and lay his gun on the top and Stand there in plain view with his head and shoulders exposed. He either did not know we were so close or was very brave. It is about two hindred yards to the fence from us. One of our Boys took a rest off a log and took deliberate aim and fired and missed him but he did not wait for another Shot but retreated in good order. We was relieved by a detail from Genl Crittendens Corps and went to camp. We got dinner and drew three days rations with orders to be ready to move. It was about dusk when we Started and I find all of our Troops on the move. The night is rather dark but the woods are afire all along the road. We are going north east or nearly towards Chattanooga. Our teams left us during the night and we marched all night but could not move very fast. There is Something up. If Chattanooga is evacuated and Bragg had left this Section there would be no necessity for our marching all night just to go there and I think we will see the Elephant before many hours. Brannans Division is in advance of us. There has been no fireing during the night but things look suspicious.

SATURDAY SEPT 19TH
[BATTLEFIELD OF CHICKAMAUGA, GEORGIA]

We haulted near Crawfish Springs for Breakfast and I wrote up my Diary for yesterday. The mail camp up and I got some letters from Nett and others. While laying in the road the fireing commenced in front and we fell into line and pushed forward. We moved perhaps two miles and filed off to the left of the road and layed down while the Battle raged in our front. We are now in reserve and are to support or reinforce any part of the line that may Give away. We were in this position for some time and then went off by the right flank and took a circle and haulted at the road and faceing east. About Eleven Oclock a.m. the 1st Kentucky Infantry was pressed so hard they gave way and left a part of Battery "F" 4th Ohio Artillery expose[d] to capture. The Rebels charged and came for the Artillery. Our command was "Fix Bayonet" and the race was for the Guns one of which was fast on a Sapling and nearly all the horses were dead and only a few of the men left with their Lieutenant. We got to the Battery first and broke files around them and met the enemy "face to face." They haulted and we opend fire and they began to waver and fineally broke. But our regiment had received a volley from them that left its impression on our ranks. But we followed them up for some distance before they reformed. Then we fought them back and fourth over the field or through the woods rather during the day. The rattle of Musketry was dreadful and to see the men lying dead and dying on the field and being run over by Artillery and lines of men it was perfectly appalling. The first man killed from my company was Andrew J Harter and he was killed about the time we reached the Guns or soon after we crossed the road. There are many incidents of interest on the field that came under my immediate notice Some of which should occupy a space here and I will insert some of them. When we passed the Battery we rescued the[y] had double Shotted the Guns and the gunner fired them into the ranks of the Rebels at Short range and they were three or four lines of Battle deep and the Shot mowed a road through their ranks that a Six mule team might be turned around in them. It was terible to behold. It seamed like they had almost annihilated them. Some were only knocked down from the force of the Shot but many of them never left there. I noticed a Rebel Sitting against a tree near us at one time with a handkerc[h]ief trying to tie up a wound in his thigh. I merely remember of glanceing at him and only a moment after I noticed he was dead. Some random Shot had found the vital spot in his body. One place I noticed the colors of some Regiment lying and I dont think fifty dead men is an over estimate laying around them. The Battle raged all day without ceaseing untill about five Oclock when I was Struck by a minnie Ball passing through my right thigh and lodgeing in my left one.[39] It did not fracture the bone or knock me down but disabled me so I could not walk. When it first Struck me I did not think I was seriously hurt. I was in the act of Stepping when I was Struck. I fired the charge from my gun and loaded it again and our line fell back and I undertook to follow but my legs refused to carry me and I inserted the Tompion into my gun and used it as a crutch.[40] I managed to get back and Surgeon Dixon of the first Kentucky dressed it and orderd me off the field.[41] I hobbled back and kept from being captured. Hamp Case the drummer Boy of my company came along with a Lieutenant who was wounded and he left him and took charge of me. Our men kept falling back as the Rebels pressed them and fineally came out into the open field and from where I was I could see the Battle. The Rebels Seam[ed] to be desperate. Some say they are drunk and they made one charge after another and our men made terible havoc in their ranks. They kept up the fight untill darkness put a Stop to it. There was heavy fireing to our left untill nine Oclock to night. I was taken up about that time by the Ambulance train and taken to Crawfish Springs near where we breakfasted this a.m.[42] Isaac Fields a Boy from my company got with me and our wounds was dressed after we got to the springs about eleven Oclock p.m.[43] This has been a terible day to the American Nation and many bitter tears will be Shed north and south for the dead of Chickamauga. There are thousands of men in the prime of life who this morning felt they were destined to live to a ripe old age who to night are lying on the Battle field Stark and Stiff and who will be coverd where they fell with a few shovels full of dirt and left to rot with nothing to mark the place where a hero perished for his country and that the government might live. They will not answer to Roll Call in their respective companies any more and the report will be "Killed at Chickamauga Sept 19th 1863." And how anxious will our friends Scan the columns of the Newspapers to see who is among the missing. I found Andrew J Brickley here and neither of the Boys have any Blankets but I happend to have mine. The Boys all lost their Knapsacks in the Battle. The night is cold and lots of our wounded men will chill to death. There is wounded men all around me and the moans and cries are heart rending. I Slept cold and had to divide my Blankets with my comrades. Our loss is heavy but the Rebels must have lost hevier as we fought on the defensive most of the day. We fought Longstreets men. We can tell them by their dress being uniformed in White Jacket and Blue Coller and cuffs and Blue pants. They are much better clothed than Braggs Army. I dont believe Genl Rosencrans intended to meet the Johnies here but was trying to get to Chattanooga but it was forced on him by Longstreet and the only thing worries me is Are we defeated and will we have to relinquish our hold. I sincerely hope not. Our men held their ground and we occupy about the same position we did when the Battle began. Genl McCooks Corps is now in position and I think to morrow will place things in a different light. But it looks very discourageing to me here on my back and cant assist our Boys and if our forces have to retreat what will become of us. If they get me they will have to run for it for I dont intend to be captured if I can possibly avoid it. Beardsley come to see me before I was taken off the field and Says my company lost in killed and wounded twelve all told. There are a number missing but they cant account for them. Some of them are probably killed and wounded.[44] I have no chance to write home.

SUNDAY SEPT 20TH

The Battle opend up along our lines about Eight Oclock a.m. and the Rebels made the attack. I lay here listening to the musketry and Cannonadeing and it is terific. I set up and wrote some in my Diary. About noon our Cavalry formed near us and word came to us that our forces could not hold their position and those who could get away had better start. I do not want to be captured and I did not think I could move at all but the excitement made me make the effort. I got a crutch or Chestnut fork and hobbled out and after geting warmed I managed to keep out of the way. Ike Fields kept with me and about Sunset some Boys out of the 26th Indiana Shot a hog and we camped with and Shared our Bread with them that we got out of a wagon along the road that was broke down and left.[45] It was lucky for us for we were out of rations as we lost it in the Battle. Some of the musicians from the 101st Ind camped with us. We got along very well but I am very Sore and loss of Blood has weakend me. The road was full of wagons and ambulances going to Chattanooga and there are all kinds of reports as to our defeat. Some thinks our Army will be annihilated but I dont fear any such result. Rosencrans keeps up the fight and disputes the ground inch by

inch and if we was so teribly defeated our Army would retreat faster. I
think our forces will hold Chattanooga any way and that will be our
base for another campaign. The Johnies captured the field Hospital
where we left this morning and all the wounded that could not get away
so I was told.[46] I am now only three miles from Chattanooga and I hope
will be picked up by the ambulance train. The road is full of teams and
our divission Ordinance Train is correlled near us. I fared very well to
night considering the circumstances. Of course I dont fare so well as if
I was at home with Some one to take care of me but a man dont know
what he can endure untill he is tried. Walking has greatly inflamed my
wound. I dont think our Army has been driven back very far from the
fireing. The[y] must occupy nearly the same position they did yesterday.
I am sure Rosencrans will beat Bragg some way as he has always done
it. I have implcit confidence in his ability to cope with him and
Longstreet combined and come out all right yet. The man who has led
us over the rough and rugged country and out Generaled the "Johnies"
is [the] man the united States government can tie to.

MONDAY SEPT 21ST
[CHATTANOOGA, TENNESSEE]

I could not go this morning as my legs are very Sore and I cannot even
Stand up. Ike Fields went to our Ordinance Train and told Sergeant
Briggs that I was played out and he Sent the Captain in charge of
Ambulances after me. They took me to Chattanooga. When we arrived
in town we found it full of wounded men. The Buildings are full and
they are even lying in the Door yards and we were orderd to get across
the river.[47] Our Regimental teams came along and Jacob V Kenagy and
some of company "E" Boys put me on Mogg Thomases wagon. Doc
Tumbleson got on the wagon and dressed my wound while we were
Standing in the Street. The sun was hot and together with the jolt of
the wagon I got sick. We did not get across the Pontoon Bridge untill
nearly dark. When we got to a camp the Boys helped me out and I
fainted for the first time in my life. The excitement of the past few days
with the exertion and over taxing of Body and mind has about pros-
trated me. I remained with [the] teams and the Boys took good care of
me. The cannonadeing is Still going on but report says our Army is Still
gradually falling back to the city of Chattanooga and punishing the

Rebels teribly. I was orderd to be ready to go to Bridgeport to morrow morning. I am reported in Cincinnati papers as wounded and a prisoner. What will my friends and especially my wife think when [she] Sees that. Only a Short time ago She burried our Babe and now when She thinks I am gone I know She will feel terible. I have no chance to write to her but will do so as soon as possible.

TUESDAY SEPT 22ND

The Boys helped me out to the road thinking to put me on the wagon Train to go to Stephenson but they were all loaded with the wounded and after laying there untill evening we returned to the wagon Correll for the night. Report says Rosencrans occupies a position at Chattanooga that he will hold. The fighting Still continues but not so heavy. They are getting tired of it I guess and will give it up soon. . . . My wound is very Sore and I cannot dress it myself and it has not been dressed since yesterday. They Say it is Sixty five miles to Bridgeport and we will be comp[e]lled to ride over the mountains in a wagon. I dread it and cant tell how I can Stand it. But we cant be cared for here and if we could I dont see how the Army can be supplied. All the Supplies will have to be wagoned over the mountains. But I think I have stood considerable thumping around and still live and I have no doubt I can live through it. I have not heard from the company since I left it and dont know how many of them are left to tell the Story But I hope for the best.

WEDNESDAY SEP 23RD

I was carried out to the road again this a.m and in a Short time was picked up by the Ambulance Train [and] was taken to General Field Hospital over Waldrens Ridge.[48] Here is said to be over fifteen thousand wounded Soldiers. It looks like a large estimate and I dont know how true it is. But Suffice to Say there is a great many. I was put into one of Genl Wilders Brigade wagons when I arrived and was taken out again and in a few minutes was again put in a wagon and Shortly after we Started for Bridgeport. The teams are orderd to drive twenty four miles a day and it is terible on men like myself who cant walk to ride over such a rocky road. We made the summit of the mountains before dark and could look back and see our Army around Chattanooga. The train Stopped to burry a Soldier who died and we had a good opportunity to view the position. There is Still Some cannonadeing and Skirmishing as the Rebels occupy Missionary Ridge on the East and Lookout Mountain on the west Side of the city while our forces occupy the town. The Battle is comparatively ended for the present. We crossed one range of mountains and camped in the "Sequatchee" valey after fording the river. It was dark when we camped. There is severel Boys from the 101st Ind in my wagon. Among them Lieut Wilson of "Co G" and John Markley of Co "B." There is thirty teams and ten men in a wagon which makes three Hundred wounded with the wagon train.

THURSDAY SEPT 24TH

We left camp early and had a much better road to day. The collored people along the road was very good to us and one old Darky woman gave our wagon load a plate of potatoes and they were cooked nice and I could not help but think that although her Skin was black her heart was all right. We Struck a mountain pass after noon and crossed the range and camped at Jasper. We got into a house and had good quarters. The country we traveled through the valley is beautiful and the plantations are large and the Soil fertile and had not been damaged much by the war. The citizens are all Rebbels and claim we will have to leave here. They Say Bragg has been drawing us on and I think he has made a bad draw for their cause for Rosencrans will hold Chattanooga as sure as fate or loose his entire Army.

FRIDAY SEPT 25TH

We pulled out early and some of us did not get any breakfast. We reached Bridgeport about noon and was taken to the Hospittal on the hill west of the Station house (for that is all of the town) and furnished Some boiled Beef & coffee and as we was hungry it went first rate. After dinner we was taken to the rail road and put in freight cars. We were layed in the cars as close as possible. There is about a thousand wounded on the train. We run down to Stephenson and remaind there untill Some time in the night. I was so worn out that I went to sleep and did not waken untill we had passed Cumberland Tunnel and I dont know the time of night. This is more comfortable the[n] being pounded around in a wagon.

SATURDAY SEPT 26TH
[MURFREESBORO, TENNESSEE]

Our train reached Murfreesboro about Nine Oclock a.m. and orders were to take Eighty of us off to be cared for here. I did not feel inclined to get off as I wanted to get as far north as possible but through solicitations of the Chaplin of Hospital No one I consented and Fields and I was put into an Ambulance and taken to Hospital No one. We are in the Female College and have a very good place. My wound was dressed after we got our dinner the first time since it was dressed Monday last on the wagon at Chattanooga. It is in a bad condition the cords haveing contracted and leaveing it crooked. It is badly inflamed and sore. The Surgeon is a "Jew" and he examined it and put a brace on it to draw it Strait again.[49] I am weak from loss of blood and tired to death but otherwise I feel well enough. I think a few days rest will help me. If I can only save my leg from amputation I shall be happy. I am laying by a Rebel Captain by the name of Pedigrew who was wounded at Hoovers Gap in June and he lives at Franklin when at home. He is a bitter Secesh and I am fearfull that we will quarrell unless he keeps his mouth Still.[50]

SUNDAY SEPT 27TH

I managed to write a few lines to Nett to let her know I am Still alive. I know it will be a welcome letter to her as it is the first since the Battle. I have no doubt she thinks I am a prisoner and dont know how bad I am hurt. . . . I have [no] word from the Regiment since I left it. I feel much better from last nights rest and am in hopes I will soon be able for duty again. I dont suppose we will get a furlough. Some of our men think we will get to go home. I am sure it would be a great gratification to me to be at home while I am disabled but I shall not count on it and will not be so badly disappointed if I Should not get one.

MONDAY SEPT 28TH

. . . It is terible on me to be confined here. If I was Sick it would be different but I am healthy and that will help me out. I will try and not get discouraged. Quarreling with this old "Reb" captain helps me while away the time. He is an illnatured old dog and I like to tease him. He says if he gets well he will fight us again and I tell him there is no danger. That he is going to die Sure. I feel as though I dont care if he does and I do think the chances are against him. No news of importance.

TUESDAY SEPT 29TH

I feel very well this morning. . . . The visits of the Surgeon is an every day occurrence and not worthy of Note. Deaths are the same and not being acquainted with those dieing it [is] not so much thought of as if a friends dies. We get no news only Rosencrans holds Chattanooga with the Rebels occupieng Missionary Ridge and Lookout Mountain.

WEDNESDAY SEPT 30TH

I fell out with our "Jew Sergeon" this morning and had a notion to cane him. He pulled the Bandage off my leg and hurt me without a cause and I got mad. He says he wont have any thing more to do with me. I dont care. He is as ignorant as a mule and puts on to[o] much "Stile." I told him I thought he graduated rolling whiskey barrells in a Drug Store cellar. He comes into our ward and sits down an[d] enquires of the nurse how this or that patient is without visiting and examineing for himself and I think that he dont care whether the Boys get well or not. My wound commenced bleeding and kept it up all day. I wrote to Nett to send me a pair of Boots and sent her some flower seed and a lock of my whiskers as my hair and whiskers was very long not haveing Shaved during the march. The right side of my face is bruised I suppose from the concussion of the gun as my shoulder is lame and I cant account for it otherwise. . . .

THURSDAY OCT 1ST

My wound has been bleeding freely for twenty four hours and I sent for Dr Threlkeld Surgeon in charge and explained the difficulty with "Currly" (the Jew) and he said I had not been treated properly and Sent Dr Link an Indiana man.[51] He examined it and says there is danger of looseing my leg but says he will probe it and can then tell more about it. . . .

FRIDAY OCT 2ND

Dr Link put me under the influence of Chloroform and examined my wound and opend it up. He thinks he can cure it now but if "Currly" had run matters a while yet I would either died or been minus a Leg.

The[y] better put such fellows in the ranks and they would be of some service to the government. There is reinforcements going through on the cars. Trains pass about every half hour and are loaded with Soldiers. We can see them from the windows. The 41st Pennsylvania passed and they say the 20th & 21st Army Corps of the Army of the Potomac are all going to Rosencrans.[52] If that is so the "Rebels" will soon be on the run again and our Boys will drive them into the Atlantic Ocean or Gulf of Mexico. I hope they will and drownd all of them.

SATURDAY OCT 3RD

The air feels like fall and is very pleasent and makes me wish I could be out but I have to keep still. It is terible hard for me to keep in the house. My wound looks and feels better. The reinforcements are still going through to the front. Two Chaplains with two citizens from Indianapolis who are sent here to look after the Hoosier Boys visited us. They were sent here by Governor Morton. He will look after us and try to help us all in his power. He is very popular among Indiana Boys and is certainly a model Governor.

SUNDAY OCT 4TH

The wagons have been going all night and the excitement runs high. The citizens are all in the fortifications and it is all caused by the report that Wheeler or Morgans Cavalry is near town. . . . We concealed all our valubles such as watches and money So I[n] case the Rebs come they cant rob us. Well I dont suppose they will hurt us if they do and they cant take us along unless they haul us and they will not undertake that as our men will be after them. The day passed and they did not come.

MONDAY OCT 5TH

The excitement is still at fever heat and Citizens and Negros are moving to the Forts. I can sit on my Bunk and See them going across the flat. The Chaplin orderd all the men who could possibly get out to go to the Fortifications and it about cleaned out my Room. The Wardmaster would not let me undertake it. Report that the Rebs are only three miles from town and that mail is stopped for ten days. That is the worse part of it for me for I like to hear from home. About four Oclock this pm. a lot of

Cavalry came dashing into town and then there was fun to see them going for the fortifications. Our Hospital men with their Gray Gounds on led by Doc Miller made a gallant charge and was followed by citizens and darkies. There was Some very funny little incidents happend and we enjoyed the fun and laughed untill our Sides were sore. We supposed of course it was Rebel Cavalry but it proved to be Col Wilders Mounted Brigade and we were safe. They were dusty and looked more like "Rebs" than "Yanks." But it is surpriseing to see how sick men can run when they are scared. Some who made the best time could not possibly get off their backs if orderd to the front. It was said the Rebs came up to the edge of town and one of them Shot a little girl in a door yard but I cant vouch for that. There was an old Rebel Shot at the Court House by a Provost Guard. He had sent word to the Rebels that the town could be captured and when put under guard swore he would help the Rebs if they come and was very insulting and the guard Shot him dead. The Rebs captured some of the 33rd Indiana and burned a Rail Road Bridge near town. Our mounted men have followed them from Chattanooga and Captured and killed about a hundred. Our convalescents came back this evening bringing their Guns and accouterments along in case they should have to go back. The chaplain commanded the Squad. Some of them was on crutches but they could Shoot. . . .

TUESDAY OCT 6TH

My wound is very Sore to day from wearing my Pantaloons. It is very cool with a heavy frost. The Cavalry had quite a fight north of town a few miles and some of their wounded were brought into Hospital. The Rebels are on the run and are trying to get back South again. They think it is getting a little to[o] warm here. I wrote to Nett but got no letter.

WEDNESDAY OCT 7TH

I got out of my bunk and Hoover made a Stirup[?] for my foot and I hobbled around a little. I am so tired of lying on my back I cant hardly endure it. There is nothing to pass the time. I read untill I cant hardly see and Some times take a hand in a game of Eucher or Old Sledge for amusement. We get no news and I have no letter from home. The papers have nothing in them.

THURSDAY OCT 8TH

I wrote to Nett. We got but two meals to day. I Spent all the money I had
and will now have to depend on the Hospital Grub all together. Ike Fields
received a letter from his Father with five dollars enclosed. The first word
from Bluffton since we come here. The Band played a piece of music that
I heard in Bluffton and it made me feel almost like I was at home. We got
Pie for supper from an old darkie woman. I also got some Apples. I asked
the nurse for my Boots So I could go down to meals and he thought I was
getting well to[o] fast and said I had better wait awhile. I hobbled out into
the hall but I find it does not do me any good to try to walk and it makes
my wound much worse and I will have to keep quiet. I feel first rate otherwise and that is why I cant keep in bed. There is a report that the Rebels
captured Shelbyville but they cant hold it if they have. I expected a Letter
from Nett and I feel disappointed. If I could only get a Letter I would [be]
more contented. There certainly has been time enough since I wrote from
here to get a reply if she answerd it promptly. But I will just have to wait
untill I get one and make the best of it.

FRIDAY OCT 9TH

Fourteen months ago to day I left home in the best of health little thinking that to day would find me in the condition I am in. This is a beautiful day and as I look out I feel like jumping up and running around. I
have a "Jaw" with Hoover (my nurse) about my clotheing but he Says
I cant get them yet. He thinks I would walk to[o] much and perhaps he
is right. I was delighted to receive Netts Letter of the fourth. Eagerly I
perused it. She says Stiffys friends received a letter from "Ez" Saying I
was wounded in boath Legs but he did not know how bad and then they
did not hear any more untill She received my letter from here written
Nine days after I was wounded. She Says the suspense was terible and
I know they must [have] looked anxiously for a letter from me. I would
like so much to surprise them by going in on them without letting them
know I was comeing.

SATURDAY OCT 10TH

Wm Thorp one of my company come back from home where he was
on furlough. He says Pete Urton was arrested at home as a deserter by

the home Guard. I hope they will bring him back and make him serve his time with Ball & Chain for of all men I most dispise a man who will desert his command after takeing the oath of allegiance. There was some more wounded men came into our room and Some of them have gangreen in their wounds. I dont know whether it is contagious or not. No News and no mail for me.

SUNDAY OCT 11TH

. . . We got but two meals to day and Ike got a Pie down town. I have no money as mine has not come. But Ike has some and he divides with me. I dont like this two meal buisiness. I am healthy and I get terible hungry. Reinforcements are Still going to the front and we will hear from them Soon. There was preaching in the dining [?] hall but I could no[t] go as they wont let me have my clothes yet.

MONDAY OCT 12TH

We got a new nurse as our old one was made wardmaster in place of "Jim" who licked my "Jew Doctor." I wish he had given him one for me as it would save me the trouble as I will give him one when I get able to be out if I can find him. He dont come into our room any more. I got Sister Mollies Letter of the 7th. This was a rainy day and it gives me the "Blues." I want away from here. I would rather be chaseing "Old Bragg." There is more variety in it especially if a fellow gets Shot in the Leg. I wish I knew how long I will have to endure this.

TUESDAY OCT 13TH

The Doctor talked very encourageing to me to day. He Said I must be very carefull or I might have to stay here intill Spring. He thinks I dont keep quiet enough. I suppose he knows but it is impossible to lay on my back all the time. It would kill me and I would as soon die on my feet as on my Bunk. I think I could get around some if the[y] would let me. I would like to go down in the yard but I cant go out in Drawers and Shirt. . . .

WEDNESDAY OCT 14TH

. . . . My wound was very painful all night and seams to have quit dischargeing. That is some Sign of Gangreen and I am uneasy about it. I had

Doc examine it and he Said it did not look so well and did not encourage me much. He scolded me again for not keeping quiet. He is a "man after my own heart" and I cant get angry with him and I Shall do better hereafter. I dont want to stay here and I guess it is best to keep quiet.

THURSDAY OCT 15TH

I answerd Lou Townsends letter this morning. Doc Says my wound looks better and it dont pain me so much. I rested very well last night. . . . Report Says that Nashville is full of wounded and dont get any care. I guess we were wise for stopping here as we have a very good place and plenty to eat and good beds.

FRIDAY OCT 16TH

They took our names and the commands we belong to this morning and the talk is all wounded men will be furloughed home. I think myself we have earned one and there we could take better care of ourselves among friends and would soon get well. I thought I would certainly get a Letter from Nett to day but I was doomed to disappointment as usual. It is a week since I received one. It rained Some.

SATURDAY OCT 17TH

. . . I was down Stairs for the first time. Some Secesh women come in to see us to day. The[y] send in provission to the Rebells here but dont give us Yankees any thing. My experience is the women are more spitefull than the men and I dont Care as I dont expect to run for office or marry here and they can treat me with contempt if they choose.[53]

SUNDAY OCT 18TH

. . . The Surgeon gave me Tinct of Iron to put on my wound and it hurt me teribly. He claims it will kill the poison and if the gangreen is there it will stop it. I did not attend the meeting. I like the Chaplain very much. He is a Methodist.

MONDAY OCT 19TH

My wound looks some better but I continue to use Tinct of Iron on it. . . . It is nearly two weeks Since I had a letter from home and I am very uneasy about it. I fear they are sick. We got no news from the front and I think there will be a move made soon.

[TUESDAY OMITTED]

WEDNESDAY OCT 21ST

Corporal Henry Parker of Co A 87th Indiana died in my room of wounds received at Chickamauga. Report is confirmed that Genl Rosencrans was removed and "Grant" takes the command of the department. The reorganization puts my Regiment in the Second Brigade Third Division fourteenth Army Corps. Still no Letter from Nett. I guess She must have forgotten me or is Sick. Time will tell.

THURSDAY OCT 22ND

. . . My wound is very Sore and painfull and Doc put Bornine on it. If that dont hurt then I dont know. It cooks the flesh like a red hot Iron and hurts about as bad. But it will remove any Gangreenous matter. Gangreen is said to be the first Stage of Mortification and must be checked immediately or it will cause death Shortly.[54] No news from Chattanooga.

FRIDAY OCT 23RD

. . . Doc Says my wound looks healthier to day. I am discouraged for one day it is better and the next worse. But I suppose I will have to be patient and it will heal all right. It will take it a long time to get well and regain strength as it seams weak. The Ball passing through the main cords of the leg is what makes it weak now. No news from the front.

SATURDAY OCT 24TH

I did not attend preaching to day as I had to have another application of Bornine and I am very Sore from its effects. . . .

SUNDAY OCT 25TH

There is preaching again and I went down Stairs. . . . There is a report that the Rebels are at War Trace and threatening this place. But it must be only a small command or our Boys would be "whooping" them up. I dont think they will come here. They might capture the town but our Forts would make it very warm for them. They could shell the Town. It might expose us but our men would be carefull where they Shelled and can See the Hospital Flag on the Building.

MONDAY OCT 26TH

I wrote a Letter for a Boy from another Room by name of Patterson to his parents. I write a great many letters for those who have never learned to write and some who are not able and I like to accommadate them in that way. It passes the time for me. . . .

TUESDAY OCT 27TH

There was no Trains to day as there are Stragling parties of Rebels scat-terd through the country and it is not safe to run trains. The ward mas-ter told me to day I would be furloughed home. I dont know whether he knows or not but I hope he is right. I would enjoy a Short visit among my friends if only for a few days. No news of importance that is reliable.

WEDNESDAY OCT 28TH

My wound looks and feels much better. I got a man to make me a pair of Crutches and can get around some. I can get my clotheing now when I want them. An old darkey woman mended my Pants that I was wounded in to day. I received a Letter from Nett and wrote to her. The report that the wounded will all be furloughed is confirmed but I did not tell Nett I would get home for fear of a failure and then I want to surprise them.

THURSDAY OCT 29TH

I managed to get down in town with Dora Williamson for the first time. It does me good to get out but I was terible tired when I got back. We bought Some Apples. . . . It rained very hard all night.

FRIDAY OCT 30TH

The Wardmaster told me my Furlough had gone to the Medical Purveyor for approval.[55] That does look a little like I might get home but I will not build up on it untill I get Started any way. It is still raining. . . . No Rebels around here now.

SATURDAY OCT 31ST

I got no Letter from home but received a letter from J. V. Kenagy and answered it. He gave me the Regiments composeing the Second Brigade viz. Second Minnisota Ninth Thirty fifth and One Hundred & fifth Ohio. The Seventy fith Eighty Seventh and one Hundred and first Indiana. They are the 2nd Brig 3rd Div & 14th Corps.

SUNDAY NOV 1ST

. . . I did not attend Preaching. It is such hard work for me to get up and down Stairs with Crutches. . . .

MONDAY NOV 2ND

I learned by the papers of the death at Nashville of the death of Sergeant John T. Cartwright of my company. . . . I was down to the Express office for a Box that is comeing from home but did not get it. Some of the Boys Furloughs come back approved but mine was not among them but I begin to think I may get one. If I do I think I will feel to rejoice.

TUESDAY NOV 3RD

. . . My wound is healing very fast now and I think if I get home a few days I can Shoulder a gun again. I dont know whether it will make me cowardly or not. But I guess I can face the music again.[56]

WEDNESDAY NOV 4TH

Our Furloughs did not come. I begin to feel anxous now. Who could help it to think of the exquisite pleasure of meeting dear friends after being away nearly fifteen months and passing through the "Mill." . . . I dont get any letters from the company and I would like to hear from the Boys.

THURSDAY NOV 5TH

Our Furloughs came on the Nine Oclock train and as they were to take effect from to day I concluded to start immediately for home. We will get a train at 5 30 p.m. Ike Fields did not get a furlough but Dora Williamson did and we went to the Post Quartermaster for transportation and Start on the Journey with only five dollars in money which I happend to have.

Capt Williams furnished us tickets and we arrived at Nashville about dark and went to the Soldiers home for the night. Nothing of any importance occurred but I find it is going to be a task for me to make the trip but the pleasure of meeting friends again will stimulate me. I can hardly realize it is possible. I could not sleep to night for thinking about it. We went to Capt Stewart post Quartermaster at Nashville this eve for transportation Tickets to Louisville Ky so we could take the 7 am Train.[57]

Friday Nov 6th

We pulled out of Nashville at 7 a.m. and arrived at Louisville at Six p.m. and Stayed at the Soldiers home. There is a train leaves Jeffersonville for Indianapolis at 9 p.m but we could not get our transportation in time and will not get away from here untill tomorrow p.m. It is quite a disappointment and I fear now we will not get home before Monday when if we could [have] left here to night we would [have] got home Saturday. We passed our old camps at Lebanon Junction and Shepherdsville. We have done well so far with the money not haveing paid out any thing for Rail Road or Hotel Bills. Our fare has not been extra but good enough for soldiers. Those Homes have been established for the accommodation of Soldiers as I find some Hotel keepers who would hardly let a Soldier Sleep in their Beds. It is well enough to guard against the Grey Backs but we was particular and drew all new clotheing so as not to cary any home with us.

Saturday Nov 7th

We remained at the Soldiers Home untill after dinner and then crossed the River to Jeffersonville where [?] we got tickets to Ft Wayne for our transportation. It makes me feel almost like I was at home to be in my native state again. We arrived at Indianapolis just in time for [the] train to Peru where we arrived about mid night when [?] we was informed we would have to remain untill Monday. The passenger trains have all gone east and they wont let us ride on a freight. It was a terible disappointment and we went to the Keller House to stay all night.

Sunday Nov 8th

Dora and I held a council of war and after dinner we took our Knapsacks and went to the Depot resolved to try to get to ride to Ft Wayne. There was a wreckers Train pulled in and they had an Old Second Class coach that they had taken out of the ditch. I Stated our case to the section Boss and appealed to his Sympathy to let us ride. He said it was strictly against orders but to get into that Car. He refused to take our Tickets or money and we rode for nothing. Now this man risked looseing his situation to accommodate us and he is about the only man we have met since we started that has Shown us any favor and I Shall always think well of him and should he ever be placed in a condition that I could favor him I would take pleasure in helping him out. He is certainly a gentleman. Well we have stolen a march on the Rail Road and will be ready to take the stage in the morning. We stayed at the Main Street Exchange all night. We had a rough ride as they run like Sixty and we got off the track once. Then there was nothing in the car but us and a lot of old Iron. I thought some times I would rather take it a foot and be much Safer any way.

MONDAY NOV 9TH
[BLUFFTON, INDIANA]

We took the Stage for Bluffton and arrived there about two Oclock p.m and I am about played out but a few days rest will make me all right. The Stage drove up to Pas and Mother come out to see who was comeing to their house and little thinking it was me and I never shall forget her look of surprise when She Saw me nor the hearty welcome she gave me. It was not long in being generally known that I was at home and soon Nettie [?] came and was as much surprised as any of them. The room Soon filled with friends and neighbors to see me and hear from the Boys who are in my company but I cant tell them much about them it haveing been nearly two months since I left them and they were then engaged in a terible Battle. But I lay on the sofa which was prepard for the occasion and talked with my friends and I dont think I ever passed a day more pleasant in my life. Here I find sympathy for us and our cause and a feeling that can be appretiated by the soldier and makes me feel proud of being called a soldier. My wounds demonstrate to my friends that I have tried to honor the calling and done my duty. Friends kept comeing untill late at night and I am very tired. But I will be all right before the time arrives for me to return to the Army. But I miss my little Boy of Seven months old when I left and he would nearly [be] two years old now. I find the rest of my relatives in good health. Bluffton looks natural so far as I have seen and I noticed many old friends on the street who look natural. My wound is very sore from the effects of my journey but looks healthy.

TUESDAY NOV 10TH

I remained at Fathers all day and there was a great many came to see me and I passed the day very pleasantly. Many invitations to visit were extended and from now untill the first of December the time was passed in visiting friends and not a day passed but we was invited out. We generally Stayed at nights at my parents or Father Karns. A great many questions were asked about the Army and as Soldiers like to rehearse their adventures and I was not an exception to the rule I entertained the people as well as I could. Some times the political questions would come up and some would express themselves as Surprised to know I was not a Democrat as I was when I went out. I tell them I am as much a Douglas Democrat as I was in 1860 but my Democracy does not consist in being a "Rebel" against the Laws and Goverment. I had severel warm discussions and talked in a way that some of [them] here dont like but that makes no difference. I tell them there is no political parties. It is a disolution of the Union and tryumph of Secession or their Surrender and the tryumph of Law and order. I dont care who it may hit I class all who oppose the union Army as Rebels and I can give them no other name. I dont know any Southren Confederacy as they call themselves. I find a number of friends who call themselves Democrats who entertain the Same views in regard to the war as the Johnies and they are proud to be called Rebels and I cant call those here anything els. There is this difference. The Rebs come out manfully and Sacrifice their lives for their opinions and Show themselves to be men while those I find here only talk and have not got the courage to take sides openly. One man asked me if I endorsed every action of President Lincoln. I told him I did not and supposeing he would get an item asked me what he had done that I did not indorse. I simply replied to him that [I] condemned him for not hanging Valandingham and all the rest of such men north.[58] He thought I was hard on him. But I find he entertains the same views that the "Rebs" do and I advised him to go south and Show his manhood. I dont pretend to know who are democrats and I speak out frankly my opinions in any kind of a crowd. But I find many good true and loyal men here some who are to[o] old to serve in the Army. But of all the men I most despise are those who run to Canada when they are drafted. In a discussion on the Emancipation Proclimation one man asked how I would like to have a negro Sit on a Jury for me. I told him I Should not object on account of color if the man was intelligent.[59] Another asked me derisively how I would like to wait at the polls untill a big "Buck Nigger" voted before I could deposite my Ballott and I replied that I did not favor negro sufferage but I would much rather wait on the blackest Nigger in America to vote as one of those "Cannada Vetrians." It seams he had been there and he began makeing excuses but I seen it hit him and remarked that what I said was from the heart and I had nothing to retract.[60] I find many here are ready to rejoice over any reverse the Union Army may meet with and they call themselves Democrats and I can say if that is Democracy God forbid that I should ever have any of it. My wife and I was invited to dinner one Sabbath and after attending church we went there and when I went in I noticed the party without one exception was composed of these Democrats. I concluded I was insulted and made up my mind that if the political questions were brought up I would say my say and then leave but there was nothing said that I could take exceptions to and the day passed very pleasently. One Old Democrat expressed himself rather freely one day to me when I had not been addressing my conversation to him and I Said to him that it would not do for him and I to argue politics and that I would not Say any thing to hurt his feelings but he must not put in again when I was not talking to him or we might have some trouble and he kept away from [me] during my Stay at home. I was told soon after I got home that a certain man had said once when he heard one of my letters read that if I had been present he would have "slapped my face." The friend who told me would not tell me who it was as he said it would only make trouble and I said to him if it was a Boy or a woman I did not care any thing about it but if it was a *man* I would like to know who it was. On the day before I was to return he told me who it was and I met him soon after on the street and I repeated the remark to him and told him if he felt like it I would say to him he had better attend to it at once as I would leave to morrow. He denied the whole buisiness and Said I had always treated him Gentlemanly and he had tried to treat me so. I knew he had said it for the man who told me was a man of truth and I told him I believed it but as he backed down it was all right. I dont think [I] am quarrelsome but I consider all "Rebels" my enemies. Many pleasing little episodes occurred during my Stay at home. The good and Loyal women got up a nice supper in the Good Templers Hall one night and as some more soldiers had come home we had a splendid time. I will often think of it when I return to the front and bless them for their kindness. I attended the Good Templers Lodge Severel times and was always welcomed kindly and enjoyed the meetings. But all things have an ending and my time expired and the thirtieth day of November was my last at home and as I reflected over the pleasent time at home and what was in waiting for me when I returned to the Army to Serve Nineteen months yet unless the war should terminate it makes me feel Sad. We took Tea with Aunt Eliza Covert and Uncle and Aunt Townsend and My Father and mother were present and we had a nice time. But my mother seamed very Sad and I know the cause to[o] well. When I went away before I had not the least idea of war but now I know what is before me and the experience is a good teacher. But I am Sworn to Serve three years or during the war and I Shall go back to do my duty and Serve my time honorably and faithfully and if permitted to return I can enjoy my home and friends and not be afraid to look any man in the face and tell him I soldiered during the war of the Rebellion in the Union Army and for the Union one and inseperable and that Freedom might live to the Abolition of Slavery and all men regardless of collor may be free. We returned and Stayed all night at Fathers. A number called during the evening to say good bye to me. We did not retire untill late.

TUESDAY DEC 1ST

Sad very Sad! was the parting from my Wife Mother Father Sisters and friends this morning and hard for me to bear up under. When I started from my old room to go down Stairs I turned around and took a last look at it and wondered if it were possible I was leaveing it for the last time. It is the room I have accupied almost all my life. My mothers last words ring in my ear as I kiss her a farewell. *"Will I hate to see you go back again"* but duty calls and I must away and why dwell on the heart rending cries of dear friends. . . . I am not able for duty and I may get an extension of Furlough at Indianapolis and if not I will proceed to

Murfreesboro and report to the Hospittal. We arrived at Ft Wayne about 2 Oclock pm and Stopped at the Main Street Exchange as we do not get a train untill about 4 40 a.m to-morrow. Dora Williamson is along and we are going to try to ride on our Tickets to Peru that we come home on as the Section Boss would not take them up. Politics got pretty high on the Stage as we had an old Democratic Secesh in and we made it warm for him to the amusement of the other passengers. We advised him to go south and don the "Grey" and help his bretheren out of the dirty Scrape he had helped them into and Show himself to be a man in the front instead of barking cur in the rear. We talked very insulting to him and fineally advised him to "dry up" or we would compell him to foot it to Ft Wayne. He subsided and we run the craft through and I concluded he was glad to part ccmpany with us and we had no regretts at leaveing him.

WEDNESDAY DEC 2ND

The Porter called us up and we took the train at 4 40 am and on presenting our Tickets the conductor refused to take them and pass us through and we had some trouble as he talked of Stopping the train and putting us off. But there was a number of soldiers on and they would not suffer it and the Conductor concluded to let us ride. We got Breakfast at Peru Station House and reached Indianapolis at 11 am where I met Jim & Magg Spake and Call Karns and went with them to Camp Burnside and Stayed all night. The Boys belong to the Vetran Reserve Corps and are on duty Guarding Prisoners in Camp Morton.[61] I went to Colonel Oatis and talked with him about extending my furlough but he said he would like to do it but his orders were not to do so for any men. So I will leave here in the morning for Dixey. . . .

THURSDAY DEC 3RD

I took the train from Union Depot for Jeffersonville at 9 a.m. and got there at dark. I was detained at the ferry on account of a lot of Rebel prisoners crossing. There is about Eight Hundred who was Captured at Lookout Mountain and Missionary Ridge Nov 25th. They are takeing them to Camp Chase Ohio.[62] There was a couple of roughs on the ferry who were going to have a Shooting match but was prevented. They drew Revolvers and talked very loud. It was about 9 Oclock pm when

I got to the soldiers home and it was crouded with Soldiers who have been at home on furlough. We are close to the Nashville Depot. I met Ike Fields here going home.

FRIDAY DEC 4TH

I got my ticket for Nashville but the Train was so crouded that I concluded to wait another day. I run around town and went to the Ferry with Fields. The Home is full and I Shall try hard to get off in the morning. Louisvill is a nice city and the war makes it lively. I took a look at the old Hoosier State across the river. Our Army has again met the Rebels and defeated them badly and the papers are full of the Battle. Hooker drove them from Lookout and the Army of Sherman drove them from Missionary Ridge and they are on the jump as usual.[63]

SATURDAY DEC 5TH

I took the train at 7 am and had an all day run arriveing at Nashville at Sun set. Robt Davis met me at the train. They proposed to take me to the Zollicoffer Hotel but I refused to go and my furlough not being quite expired the[y] did not insist and I went with Bob to his quarters in Convalescent camp and Stayed all night. I expected to remain here over sunday and I dont propose to be confined in a military prison. I want to see some of Nashville.

SUNDAY DEC 6TH

I went with Davis to the State prison to see Jake Miller as he is on duty there guarding Rebel prisoners. We were down to the Boat Landing and at the State House. It looks more like a Fort than a place to make Laws. Nashville is a nice little city in times of peace but it looks very much dilapidated now and the Streets are badly cut up with government Supply wagons. I remained with Davis and tried to pursuade him to go with me and I would go on to Chattanooga but they would not let him go. He is not very rugged yet.

MONDAY DEC 7TH
[MURFREESBORO, TENNESSEE]

The train left for Murfreesboro at 7 a.m. Davis come with me to train. I got through about ten and reported to Hospital No one and got an old

Letter from Capt Karns and two from Nett. . . . I also found my Box all right. I was assigned to my Old Room (McIntyres) in Ward "B." I found a number of the old Boys here yet and especially my "Reb" Captain Pedigrew. He says he cant live long and he does look as though his days was numberd. . . . It made me homesick on entering the Hospittal. I cant stand it here. I Shall try to get to the front. I cant march but could do some light duty and be with the Boys.

TUESDAY DEC 8TH

. . . This is a rainy dreary day and I am terible lonesom. I wrote to Cap Karns. I will Surely die if I have to remain housed up here. Doc Link wanted me to do Some writeing for him but I refused for fear I could not get away. I told him I wanted to go to the front but he Says I cant get through if I started as they are all examined at Stephenson Allabama and if they cant do duty are put in convalescent camp. I would as soon stay here if that is the case.

WEDNESDAY DEC 9TH

This is a beautifull day. I wrote to Nett and did not go out of the Yard. We are required to have a pass and I dont like to ask for one although they never refuse to let us out. I read a novel tilled "Sweeny Todd or the Ruffian Barber."[64] . . .

THURSDAY DEC 10TH

. . . Doc Link was at me again to do some writing in his office and tried to pursuade me that I would not be able for duty for a long time and said I might have to be transferd to the Vetran Reserve Corps and I told him I would go to Cannada if he put me there. I dont ask them for charity and if I cant do duty let them discharge me and I will try to make a liveing at home. This is a nice day and I would like to get away from here. There is a report that mead defeated Lee again but nothing reliable. I was in the hospittall all day. . . .

FRIDAY DEC 11TH

I was at Doc Link to let me go to the front and he Said he would let me know to morrow. I made a finger ring out of a Button. I wrote a letter to Pa. I never was homesick before and I dont know that I am now but

I cant Stand this confinement much longer. I am almost tempted to go
to the Depot and mount the first train [that] comes along and go to the
front. But I Shall torment Doc untill he gives his concent. I am afraid
they will transfer me to some other command.

SATURDAY DEC 12TH

Glory! I pursuaded Doc Link and got his concent to go to Chattanooga
Monday. I received a Letter from Nett. This is a very rainy day and I
thought perhaps I was foolish to want to get away from here to camp
out in mid winter when I could as well stay here but I will risk it rather
than tolerate this prison any longer. Dora Williamson and I went down
town to get some little articles preparatory to moveing. I have some
very good friends here that I hate to leave but friends must part Sooner
or later.

SUNDAY DEC 13TH

General Inspection this morning and we had to be cleaned up and be
on our Bunks. The Surgeon took a look at me and asked me what ailed
me I told him I had been wounded but all I required now was plenty of
"hard tack & Sow Belly" and I would pull through. . . . I Sold some
things I did not want to carry along and made other arrangements to
leave. When I think it all over and see the familiar faces here it Seams
almost like leaveing home again. Then I know I will See hard times
again. Doc thinks I cant get through as I am very lame yet and use a
Crutch and Cane but I will play it on them if possible as I dont want to
stop at Stepenson.

MONDAY DEC 14TH

I got up early and got ready to go. After berakfast we had to report to
the Medical Director to get orders for transportation and then to the
Provost Marshall and it consumed so much time we missed the
Passenger train and the freights refused to haul us return to the hospittal and stayed all night. I did not get any mail nor write any but I read
the Presidents proclimation.[65]

TUESDAY DEC 15TH

We reported to the Provost Marshall and missed the Passenger train again but we climbed a freight and the Conductor tried to put us off but we stuck to it and he fineally pulled out. There is about twenty of us under a Sergeant from the 28th Wisconsin and he is no better than a wooden man. We got to Stepenson about 9 Oclock pm and had no place to go but spread our Blankets down on the porch at the Depot House and slept. It was a little cold and rather a hard bed but better than none.

WEDNESDAY DEC 16TH

We got transportation to Bridgeport this morning and we had to report to a Surgeon and the Sergeant got me near a Stump where I hid my Crutch and cane and when the Surgeon came along all I had to do was Stand up in the Rank and he passed along and went into his tent and wrote an Order for us to go on to Chattanooga. We drew three days rations and crossed the river on the pontoon Bridge and I came very near getting Set into the river. We passed a detail of Soldiers who were hauling over some Artillery and they had five poor old horses to one gun and I was carying a Cracker Box and the leader reached for it and jostled me and came very near knocking me into the river. We found an old engin across the river hitched to some old flat cars about ready to pull out for White Side and we got aboard. The Bridge across the river was burned here and the cars cannot cross yet but in a short time it will be all right again. We soon got to White Side and here we got off and have thirteen miles to "hoof it." We went only five miles and stayed with an old citizen all night. I got with Severel of our Boys among them Lieut Chalmers of Co.G Beam & Cacy of Co A and Bill Tharp of Co F.[66] I could hardly travel and the boys stayed with me. I find it is very hard work for me to even hobble along the Rail Road and it was about all I could do to get up the mountain at Whiteside.

THURSDAY DEC 17TH
[CHATTANOOGA, TENNESSEE]

We started early and it rained on us. We had a Smooth road by following the Rail Road. It was very hard work for me to get along but the Boys Stayed with me. We reached the 75th after noon near Chattanooga. I found the Boys all well but Wm Starr. This was a cold night. I Slept with J V Kenagy in the Captains tent. We are camped in the valey between Lookout Mountain and the freight Depot and have a nice camp but have to go to Lookout for wood and the Boys use a pair of Car Trucks to haul it on the Rail Road. When I look around me and see the mountains and hills recently occupied by the Rebels and the strong positions that our Boys drove them from it hardly seams possible. Lookout on the West Eighteen hundred feet above us and Missionary Ridge circles around on the South and East Six hundred feet high with a heavy line of fortifications at the foot entirely encloseing us in it formidable. But our men under Genl Hooker in the Battle above the clouds drove them off the Mountain.[67] While Sherman & Thomas charged Mission Ridge and defeated them and took possession of their Artillery and turned them upon their flying ranks. Never in the history of Nations was there such a victory achieved. Our Boys live on one fourth Rations but the Rail Road will Soon be re-built and then this will be our base for another advance. But when the Rebels can make another Stand I cant See as there is no such country to pass over as we captured in the last few months. Chattanooga is ours now Sure.

FRIDAY DEC 18TH

My Regiment went over Mission Ridge to guard a Bridge across Chickamauga Creek but I was to[o] lame to go along and remained in camp. I dont know what I will do now as I could not march. But I dont think we will leave here for some time perhaps not untill Spring. The Army will re-organize before another campaign and the Rail Road will have to run supplies here and the Bridge at Whiteside will require considerable work and if the cars run in here in two months it will be as soon as I think they can do so. I hope in that time I will be able to march for I dont want to go to the rear. I wrote to Nett but did not get any mail.

SATURDAY DEC 19TH

Capt Karns and I took a walk to see some of the defences of Chattanooga and I find the Yankees have not been Idle Since they took possession. Besides the natural defences they have built severel Forts and numerous lines of Fortifications and if the Rebels could not hold it when in their possession I dont think they have men enough to re-take it and hold it.

We was over some of the Battlefield of Nov 25th and at Orchard Knob the place where Genl Grant was during the Battle and it gives a splendid view of the Situation. The fight was conducted as follows. Genl Hooker with the 20th and 21st Corps crossed the Tennessee on the Pontoon Bridge the night before and marched down the river and recrossed below Mockisin Point and Lookout and in the morning the Rebels discoverd him encamped on the Western Slope and the adjoining hills. Genl Sherman also crossed the river and marched up and recrossed at the foot of Missior Ridge and Genl Thomas remained in camp in the valley. Genl Hooker began the attack and drove the Rebels around the mountain on the east side forcing them to evacuate Lookout Point in haste. Genl Sherman attacted the end of the Ridge and the Rebels concentrated there to meet him which was a fatal move for it weakend their center. Thomas was orderd to take the line of works at the foot of the Ridge and hold them out our men without orders after storming this line did not hault but commenced climbing the Ridge after the Rebels and they were so teribly frightend that they stampeeded by the time the[y] reached the summit. Thomas Swung around so that his line faced Genl Sherman and attacted Hardee in the rear placeing him between the two fires and the consequence was they Stampeeded and got in a terible hurry to get out. The Slaughter was terible and the Rebel lines melted like snow under a July sun. They threw away their arms and left their Artillery and got away the best they could. It was more than our men expected. Our Generals expected to have a terible Battle but the planning was good and worked like a charm. The Rebels on Picket after they drove Rosencrans in here used to hollow Chickamauga and called our Corps "Thomases Pets" and going up the Ridge our Boys retalliated by hollowing at the flying Johnies "Here is your Thomases Pets and we will give [you] Chickamauga." Our Boys calls it the Battle of Mission run (instead of Ridge). I done some writing for the Capt makeing of Clotheing Report. I slept with him.

SUNDAY DEC 20TH

. . . I cooked Breakfast for Capt and I as our Darkie was in the Guard House. There was a report that five of our Boys was captured by getting to[o] far from the Regiment but nothing reliable. I hope it will not prove true. . . .

MONDAY DEC 21ST

I commenced writing for Capt Karns as Wiley has gone home on furlough and the duties of Orderly Sergeant has been neglected and the
company Accounts have not been adjusted. There is considerable writing to be done and I can make myself useful in that way. I read Jeff
Davises Proclimation and he seams to be full of fight yet and I guess we
will have to whip him some more. But I dont see what or how he expects
to gain anything by prolonging the struggle.[68] They are sacrificeing lives
and property in a hopeless cause for they must Sucumb sooner or later
and Submit to the powers that be. This is a nice warm day. . . .

TUESDAY DEC 22ND

The wind blowed very hard and cold and makes is disagreeable. It froze
some last night which is a very unusual occurrence in this country. I finished one quarter of Clotheing account.[69] . . . I bought a Nashville paper
but the news dont amount to much. Our Boys are still at Chickamauga
Creek and I dont know how long they will remain. The camp seam
deserted as there is only a few of us convalescents in camp.

WEDNESDAY DEC 23RD

It is cloudy and cold this morning and looks as though it might Snow
but I guess it wont do that. . . . We got the report that the Rebel Genl
Longstreet was killed and his command was defeated with heavy loss.[70]
The loss said to be twelve thousand but I fear that is to[o] good to be
true. The Nashville papers dont Say any thing about it. It dont seam
right to rejoice over the death of any body but in these war times it
makes me feel a little elated over the misfortunes of the Rebels and I
believe I will give my old military hat one toss if that report proves to
be true for I[t] removes one of their best Generals from the field. I was
writing all day for the Captain and remaind in his tent all night.

THURSDAY DEC 24TH

This is a beautiful Morning but tolerable cold. I was writing all day. . . .
This being "Christmas Eve" my Stocking should be hung up but I dont
think there would be any thing put in it as "Santa Clause" is afraid to
come here. But some of the Boys are haveing some fun Shooting. I hear

musketry all around in the camps. The report of yesterday is not confirmed.

FRIDAY DEC 25TH

Christmas finds me in Chattanooga. This is a cloudy cold morning and I did not get up very early. Every thing is quiet and the Regiment being gone there is no duty or drilling to do. Our Christmas Breakfast consisted of fat pork Some cold Beans and a few crumbs of Crackers. Seargt Ginger came for me to go with him out to the Regiment with the teams to issue rations to the men and I took the mail out to the Boys.[71] The Boys had hominy made and I appretiated it. It was splendid. It was dark when we got back and I was very tired & lame. We crossed Mission Ridge and I picked up a spade which we brought back with us. We found the Boys all right and the reported capture was not true. It commenced raining this evening and it was a wet night. . . . Missionary Ridge still Shows the marks of the recent Battle. The Ridge on top is very narrow and slopes off to the East abruptly and there is some Cannon with the carriages broken lying around and the timber is marked with Bullets and the Grave Trenches Shows where the Battle was the fiercest. We have a splendid view of Chattanooga and the valey from the summit of the Ridge. There is Some rummors in camp from Knoxville but nothing to rely on. Well this thing of liveing on Short rations is not very pleasent. We get just enough to make us illnatured and feel mean. We draw one day to do four. I am not sick and could stand a little more feed. But it cant be got through untill the Rail Road is completed. The poor mules are Starveing to death by the hundreds and eat up the Wagon Boxes and anything els that they can get hold of. But we will hold on or starve. We dont want to have to do any of our work over. The next move from here will be to Atlanta as the Rebs have a strong hold there.

SATURDAY DEC 26TH

It is still raining. I made out the pay Rolls which took me all day. . . . It is getting terible muddy.

SUNDAY DEC 27TH

Doctor Shaffer our Assistent Surgeon was in our tent telling his adventures in Richmond as a prisoner. He was captured at Chickamauga. He did not form a very good opinion of the Davis Government or the way they treat prisoners of war. . . . The wind blowed hard and came very near capsiseing our Tent. Our Boys have not returned to camp yet and it seams lonesome without them. I wish I was able to be with them but I have to put in the time the best way I can. I have been writing for Capt and while I am at work I do well enough. It is hard work for me to hobble around and the weather is to[o] bad to be out.

Monday Dec 28th

It is cloudy and cold with Strong wind and awful muddy. I bought an Indianapolis Journal but the news was meager. The Adjutant came to me hunting Some one to detail as a clerk at Division Head Quarters and sent me to Major McCole and he wanted me to go. He Said I could not do duty with the Regiment as I could not march and there I would have a horse to ride and light duty. I did not know what to say for fear I cannot fill the position but concluded to try it. . . . The Regiment is still on duty at Chickamauga Creek.

Tuesday Dec 29th

This is a nice morning and I was writing when an order came for me to report at 3rd Division Head Quarters to Major James A Conly Division Inspector which I proceeded to do and succeeded a Boy by name of Lousbury of the 14th Ohio who has Vetraned and going home on Furlough. My duties are numerous but principly writing.[72] We are quarterd near Cameron Hill and nearly a mile from the Regiment. I have an officers Tent to myself and a very nice place. I returned to camp for my Knapsack this eveining. . . .

Wednesday Dec 30th

. . . I forwarded Inspection Reports to Corps Head Quarters. I have to keep up Genl Bairds file of General printed Orders and met him for the first time.[73] He inquired the cause of my being lame and where I belonged &c. I did not get a letter to day and I am getting anxious to hear from home. I did not get a paper and consequently no news from Knoxville. The Rebs haveing that place under Seige the interest all centers there now. But I dont think [they] can capture it. I did not go back to camp to day but remained in the office all day. It is a long walk for me. I did not do much writing to day.

THURSDAY DEC 31ST

This day is the last of this eventful year. One that I Shall always remember. It has been the bloody year of the war so far. The hardest battles have been fought and every inch of ground contested but the Rebels have been beaten at every point. The only great reverse was at Chickamauga and we then held the objective point Chattanooga. But it is Sad to think how many Brave and noble men have been killed and burried in unknown graves. And hearts of many wives mothers and sisters have been grieved and the orphand children are Strewn all over our once happy country. I done my usual morning duties. . . . It commenced raining very hard about 10 Oclock a.m. and kept it up during the day. There was a heavy mail came and I went to camp but none came for me. The wind blowed hard and cold and it was dark when I left the regiment to go to Head Quarters and I met with an accident. I took the Rail Road track to Town and the men had left the Car Trucks on the track [and] I could not see them and fell over them and Struck my face on the gravel and bruised it very bad. I had a cane in one hand and the other in my pocket and could not save my self. I saw numerous Stars but I got up and toddled on and reached my tent before I could see how bad I was hurt. The wind blowed so hard I had to get up and stake my tent down to keep it from blowing over in the night. I Bunk with Division Surgeons clerk by name of Isaiah V Bates from the 19th Illinois. I close this year with the prayer that the new year may bring peace and tranqulity to our country and put a Stop to the terible bloodshed now going on and that soon we may be a united and happy people. "So may it be."

CHAPTER 7

Paper Coller Service

The Hoosiers enjoyed drill sessions and picket and fatigue duty in Chattanooga through December 1863 and January 1864. The only real break in the monotony came in late February, when Baird's division and others moved through Ringgold, Georgia, to test the Confederate defenses at Rocky Face Ridge, west of Dalton, where Bragg had retreated after the Missionary Ridge debacle. This time it was not Bragg opposing them but the new commander of the Confederate Army of Tennessee, Joseph E. Johnston.

Instead of returning to Chattanooga, the Seventy-fifth was posted at Ringgold, about twenty miles southeast of the city, to perform outpost duty in front of the Rebel army. Their location near the enemy required constant vigilance and led to a "religious awakening" in the unit's camp, with prayer meetings and the conversion of a large number of men who were then baptized in East Chickamauga Creek.

In late April, the Seventy-fifth, now again under the command of Lieutenant Colonel O'Brien (Colonel Robinson having resigned the month before), launched another tentative advance to feel out the Confederate positions near Dalton. A mixed force of infantry and cavalry drove the Confederate pickets toward the town of Tunnel Hill, in front of Dalton, but the outnumbered Yankees soon withdrew.

During the first part of May, preparations were made in earnest for the campaign to capture the important city of Atlanta. Maj. Gen. William Tecumseh Sherman, now commanding the Union Armies of the Cumberland, Ohio, and Tennessee, ordered arms and equipment inspected and surplus baggage and sick men sent to the rear. Sherman's three separate armies, plus several cavalry divisions, totaled about 110,000 troops. They would face General Johnston and the 63,000 members of the Army of Tennessee.

The Seventy-fifth began the campaign with just over 400 men, a far cry from their original strength of 1,000. The Union advance began on May 6. Moving in force against Rocky Face Ridge, Thomas's Army of the Cumberland kept the Confederates occupied while the Army of the Tennessee moved through Snake Creek Gap and outflanked the left of Johnston's line. Johnston withdrew south and went into position outside the town of Resaca. Although deployed in line of battle several times, the Seventy-fifth experienced only minor skirmishes during the first few days of the campaign. On May 14, the regiment came under artillery fire as they drove the Confederates in retreat toward Resaca but suffered only light casualties.

At Resaca, the Fourteenth Corps and most of the remainder of the Union army made attacks against the Confederate defenses while a portion of Sherman's force flanked Johnston again. The Confederates fell back, first to Calhoun, then to Adairsville. Johnston then sought to divide his forces and lure the Union armies into a trap. He sent part of his army toward Kingston, the remainder to Cassville, and waited for Sherman to divide his troops as well. If all went according to plan, the Confederate forces would reunite at Cassville and crush the Federals marching to the town, possibly forcing Sherman to retreat or at least halt his advance. Concentrated at Cassville, Johnston's army came under an intense artillery bombardment, and the Confederate commander ordered his men to abandon their positions and withdrew to Allatoona. The Hoosiers moved in pursuit through Resaca, Calhoun, Adairsville, and Kingston.

Johnston's army moved to a new position along a line stretching from Dallas to New Hope Church to Pickett's Mill. Although Union assaults on New Hope Church and Pickett's Mill failed miserably on May 25 and 27, Johnston's Confederates, believing they were about to be outflanked again, retired to yet another defensive position. The Hoosiers finished the month of May in the rear of the line of battle, guarding the army transportation train, and so were spared being involved in the costly assaults. They returned to the front and faced the Confederates on Pumpkin Vine Creek, near Dallas, and skirmished with Johnston's men until the Rebels abandoned their earthworks.

The Confederate Army of Tennessee then established
defenses along the Lost, Pine, and Brush Mountain line. The
Hoosiers faced Johnston's men again at Pine Mountain, only
to have them withdraw as the Federals moved around the
mountain. "At this time the pick and the spade were as essen-
tial to successful warfare as the gun and cartridge-box," wrote
Sergeant David Floyd, and these "inseparable companions"
were put to good use on many occasions during the campaign.[1]
Both sides dug in whenever they halted, and for the rest of June
the men would advance then build earthworks and skirmish
with the enemy.

As the Confederates fell back a short distance toward
Kennesaw Mountain, the Hoosiers faced their first serious test in
the campaign. On June 18 the soldiers of the Seventy-fifth
marched toward a new Confederate line of works on Mud Creek.
Moving in a violent thunderstorm through marshy undergrowth
and woods, the unit slogged across Mud Creek, only to enter an
open field facing the Confederate fortifications about 350 yards
away. While Union skirmishers kept up an incessant fire, the
remainder of the force began to dig their own fortifications.
Working hard and fast, the Federals built their defenses literally
in front of the enemy, who were occasionally able to respond with
a few shots. After an Ohio battery arrived on the scene, an
artillery duel ensued, the roar of the guns mingling with the
sounds of thunder. Despite the effectiveness of the Union fire,
some Rebel artillery rounds tore through the new Union lines.
"Down we go," wrote Hoosier James Essington, "lying as close to
the ground as possible; in a few minutes the Rebs have torn our
works to pieces, but we flatten out a little more." The Seventy-
fifth, he added, "never hugged anything before as they did old
Mother Earth at that time." Sergeant Floyd agreed: "Probably
not during our entire term of service had we as great a desire to
take the horizontal position upon mother earth face downwards,
as on this occasion."[2] Their courage paid off, however, for by the
next morning, the Confederates had retreated to Kennesaw
Mountain.

The Seventy-fifth followed, and once more the men dug
trenches facing Johnston. Skirmishing again ensued and

casualties mounted as the men kept close to their muddy ditches and tried to avoid the deadly fire of sharpshooters. The men contested "every foot of the ground by hard fighting amid dense forests, rain, mud and difficult ravines," a member of the 101st Indiana recalled.[3] Luckily, the Hoosiers were not called upon to participate in the disastrous Federal assaults against Johnston's lines on Kennesaw Mountain on June 27 but were eyewitnesses as the men of the Army of the Tennessee, supported by the other Union armies, hurled themselves at the entrenched Rebels. With the failure of these attacks, the Hoosiers settled back into their earthworks.

Trench life during the Atlanta campaign was a unique experience for the Federal soldiers. The Union lines were often "so close to the enemy, that no one on either side could show his head above the works without getting shot." Men would hold a cap or hat on a bayonet above the entrenchments to be pierced by a bullet as a relief from the boredom.[4] If a man was foolish enough to expose himself during the daylight hours, he heard the "zip zip" of bullets from the Confederate lines, a deadly signal for him to return to his earthwork "home." A log ten or twelve inches in diameter, known as a "head log," was placed on top of the earthworks to protect that part of the body, but the log was elevated some five inches with chunks of wood in order to allow a space to shoot through if needed.[5] Away from the earthworks there was always the chance of death by artillery fire, although the men quickly learned how to tell where a shell was going and when it would burst.[6] Any movement of troops was done at night to avoid unnecessary casualties.

Two uncommon occurrences broke this monotonous routine. On one occasion, after working on their trenches under artillery fire, the men of the 101st Indiana and presumably others in the brigade were given whiskey. More than half of that regiment refused the ration, instead giving it to more interested comrades, but no doubt the others thoroughly enjoyed the unusual "ration."[7] Having helped the living, the Federals then turned to aiding the dead. A truce was called on June 29 to bury the fallen, and in the midst of this brutal existence, the men in blue and gray mingled like friends, a "sad and strange" sight, only to resume killing each other when the truce ended.[8]

As his comrades endured the hell of active campaigning, Miller, still not fully healed from his Chickamauga wound, remained behind the lines performing "Paper Coller Service," wielding a pen and paper rather than musket and bayonet.

FRIDAY JAN 1ST 1864
[CHATTANOOGA, TENNESSEE]

The new years Morning comes in bright and fair but the wind still blows fiercely. It has a terible sweep up the river and Stirs things around lively. . . . I was in the Office all day. I am many miles from home and I wonder what they are doeing this New Years day. I have no doubt they think of the absent and are praying for our return. It is not long since I was with them a few short days and I often think of it with pleasure. It is only one month ago but it seams much longer. Will another New Years day find me Still a Soldier. Who knows but ere that time rolls around I may be with the number who have Sacrificed their lives on the altar of freedom. We dont know what is destined for us or we might Stare with horror on the spectacle. It is best we should not know. But we must take is as it comes without complaint. Our Mess here is composed of the following Boys viz: C. H. Walbridge of Toledo Ohio Geo W Farley Toledo Ohio members of the 14th O.V.I. Samuel Mier St Paul Minnisota O. H. Mevis St Paul Minn. Member[s] of 2nd Minnisota George Brown of Cincinnatti Ohio I dont know his Regiment I. V. Bates Peora Ills of the 19th Ills V.I and myself. We hire a cook and mess together. "Darkie Joe" one of the blackest and dirtiest looking "Niggers" in America "Sloshes" up the "grub." He is big and stout. Wears no fourteens Shoes and never laces them up and his feet look like Saritoga trunks. We draw full rations here and have plenty and to spare. I wish some of the Boys had some of our rations but I dont know how to get it to them.

SATURDAY JANY 2ND

It is very cold this morning and I did not get up until about Eight Oclock. I slept cold all night. . . . I coppied some orders for the Adjutant

Genl to help the Boys out of their drag. I also had a lot of printed orders to distribute. I was in the office all day. . . .

SUNDAY JAN 3RD

I distributed a lot of orders this a.m. . . . It is cold and it sleeted some and makes it disagreeable to be out so I remained in the Office Tent all day. I wrote untill about ten Oclock p.m. . . . I like my position very much but cant say that much for Major Connely and the reason is he is a "nabob" and punnishes to[o] much "rot Gut" Whisky.[9] He is small in Stature but large in his own estimation. I have concluded if he could be bought at my estimation of him and Sold at his there would be a grand speculation in it. But I am under him and am not supposed to know any thing as I am a "private."[10]

MONDAY JAN 4TH

I sent out the picket circulars with letters of advice and then finished my letter to Nett. This a cold Sleety day and very disagreeable to be out. I was in the Office all day. I dont have work enough to keep me at it all the time but I have to be here when wanted. I dont go away at all without permission from Major Connoly. A Soldier is supposed to be always at his post to do the bidding of his superiors. He never gets any thanks for the good things he does and is always cursed for any mistakes he may make. I mailed my letter this evening.

TUESDAY JANY 5TH

General Orders Military Head Quarters Dept Cumberland come in and I distributed them. . . . I also commenced a letter to Pa but had to quit and go to work on the Quarterly Inspection Reports and I was at work the rest of the day. No news of importance.

WEDNESDAY JAN 6TH

It is very cold. There was a heavy mail came and I got two letters from Nett of Dec 23rd & 27th. . . . I am not feeling very well but I was glad to get a letter once more. I have been changeing my place of Stopping so much it is almost a wonder they can find me at all. But I hope my mail will come regular now. It is a great pleasure to get word from home.

THURSDAY JAN 7TH

This is a cold morning and cloudy. I received an old Letter from Nett forwarded from the Hospital. It has been a long time a comeing but an old adage is better late than never. I had a lot of printed orders to distribute. . . .

FRIDAY JAN 8TH

There is quite a snow on the ground and it Seams almost like Indiana. Major Conly Starts home to day on leave of absence for twenty days. I made out monthly reports to day which kept me at work. No mail.

SATURDAY JAN 9TH

I was writing buissy[?] all day. I did not leave the Tent only to eat. The Major has not got off yet. I dont know what the trouble is. I did not write any letters nor receive any.

SUNDAY JAN 10TH

I was at work on Inventory and Inspection Reports for condemned Ordinance Stores of the 105th Ohio. The Major Started for home to day. I was over to the company for my ration fund which was two dollars and fifteen cents. That looks like a very Small amount in comparison to the amount of Starveing. If I understand this is an allowance made in the regulations for rations not drawn. We are allowed so much of different kinds of food and if we dont get it should have the price of it in money and this is my Share since comeing into the Army. I[t] Seams to me there must be a little Steal in this matter. But that is military I suppose. I know we have missed drawing more than that amount to the man since I became a Soldier.

MONDAY JAN 11TH

I finished up my Reports and then wrote a letter to Nett. I distributed some orders. I got no mail. Jake Kenagy come over to see me and spent the evening in my tent. I like to have the Boys come to see me. The Regiment is now in camp at the place they was when I left them haveing returned from picket duty on Chickamauga Creek.

Tuesday Jany 12th

I had plenty of work to day but went over to the Regiment this evening and got Netts letter of the 1st. . . . There is no news. The weather is quite Moderate for winter.

Wednesday Jan 13th

I was writing nearly all day. . . . This is a cloudy day and has the appearance of rain. The Band of the 15th Regulars came to Head Quarters and Serenaded Genl Baird to night. . . . There is a "Grape Vine" circulateing that we are going to move. We may move a Short distance for guard duty as we are to[o] much concentrated here and I think we may move to some post a few miles out for protection. But that will be all. We could not campaign now.

Thursday Jan 14th

General Washingtons Birth day was celebrated by the Cars running in to Chattanooga for the first time since we occupied it.[11] Now we will get full rations. The Boys boarded the cars and helped them selves to "grub." They found Some Sanitary Whisky and some of them got terible drunk and had a jolly time. The Q.M. reported it to Genl Rosencrans and the only reply he got was "The Boys are hungry." I dont approve of the proceeding but they have lived on Half and quarter rations since in September and I dont blame them much. This is a beautiful day. The mail came this p.m and I received a letter from Nett of the 3rd & 4th containing Some Glee music and among it the new songs "Rally around the flag Boys["] and "Brave Boys are they.". . .

Friday Jan 15th

I answerd Netts letter but not haveing any letter from home for some time concluded to not write them untill they answer some of mine. It is a Sad disappointment when we dont get letters from our friends promptly. . . . No orders to move yet.

Saturday Jan 16th

I hadent much to do to day and read a novel the "White Lady" and I spent the evening with the company but got no mail.[12] . . . The first

Passenger train came in about dark. It seams like buisiness to hear the Cars Whistle again. It seams like we are nearer home whe[n] we know communication with the north is opend up and unobstructed. Then it brings us supplies plenty. But we have a long line of Rail Road to protect and a few minutes work on the track of the Rebels might cut us off any time. But they will have to be very Sly if we dont catch them at it.

SUNDAY JAN 17TH

I wrote to Nett and Sent Aunt Affie Bulger a ring made from Laurell Root off "Lookout.". . . . Some of our boys went up on the top of Lookout. No passenger Train come through to day.

MONDAY JAN 18TH

This was a wet morning but turned cold towards evening. There is a report that Genl Davises Division had a fight yesterday but no particulars.[13] . . . This is a cold night.

TUESDAY JAN 19TH

. . . This is a nice day. There is still rumors of a Battle but nothing confirming the report.

WEDNESDAY JAN 20TH

This is a beautiful day and I did not have much to do. . . . The mail train was ditched and did not get through. No news.

THURSDAY JAN 21ST

This is a nice day for January. There is rumor that Longstreet was defeated and had to raise the Seige at Knoxville but nothing reliable.[14] Some of our Troops moved to Fort Wood. . . .

FRIDAY JAN 22ND

This is another nice day and the cars came through again. . . . There are rumors that Genl Johnston (Braggs sucessor) is advanceing towards Chattanooga and I notice fatigue details are heavyer than common. Large details are working on the fortifications and there may be something in it. But I cant think he will attempt to take this point. The time was when

[he] might have taken it but that time has gone by. If they have men enough to flank us they might play the same game we did but that would not be [a] very safe move. A Small garison here would hold the place against a direct assault and the ballance of us would attend to them.

SATURDAY JAN 23RD

There is a detail of Seven hundred men from our Divission to work on the fortifications to day. I was over to the Regiment this evening and received a letter from Pa and one from Nett. I did not leave the company untill twelve Oclock and then had to look out for Patroll as the countersign was out. Some of our Boys got a little to[o] much whiskey and there was music in the air. I got back to Head Quarters all right.

SUNDAY JAN 24TH

Division Post Master Coppage and I went up on Cammeron Hill to take a view of the country.[15] This hill is three or four hundred feet hight and the 16th U.S collored Regiment are building a Fort on the summit. It would be a terible place to Storm and it commands the valey across the river for miles. They have Scalped the hill on the north side for a hundred feet which makes it steep and smooth. The men work with ropes around their bodies to keep them from Sliding over the ledge. It looks as though a person [could] easily throw a stone into the Tennissee river from here but we tried it. The stone would drop down behing the ledge and we could not see where it struck. There are thousands [of] mule carcasses scatterd along the river that starved to death this winter. . . . This was a beautifull day but I was lonesome.

MONDAY JAN 25TH

I distributed some Genl Orders this morning and then wrote to Pa. There is considerable Stir in town by teams hauling out Rations to different Camps. C H Wolbridge and I drew rations for our mess. "Chett" got a little "Juice" and was a little "off." . . .

TUESDAY JAN 26TH

There is a rumor that our Division is going to Knoxville but nothing reliable. . . . The Glee Club from the 79th Pennsylvana came and Serenaded Genl Baird and sung some nice Glees. No news.

WEDNESDAY JAN 27TH

There is still talk of us going to Knoxville. I was at the Depot and learned that my Regiment had gone to Harrisons Landing on a scout. One of our clerks Geo Farley was put in the Guard House for going to Lookout without permission. He is rather large for his clothes any way and perhaps it will do him good. . . .

THURSDAY JAN 28TH

. . . Wash Wandell and Nelson Fulton of the 22nd Ind came to see me. They are going home on vetran furlough. I was over to the Regiment. They came in from scouting to day. . . .

FRIDAY JAN 29TH

I was makeing the monthly Abstract of Ispected property for January to day. . . . This was a pleasent day. Capt Johnston Started to Nashville to day for more Horses.[16] No news.

SATURDAY JAN 30TH

I worked all day on my reports. I visited the regiment this evening. It rained some to day. . . .

SUNDAY JAN 31ST

Wandall & Fulton of the 22nd called to see me again. They are awaiting Transportation and their Regiment is in the Barracks. . . . No news.

MONDAY FEBY 1ST

It rained some this morning but afternoon was clear and warm. I worked all day on Monthly Report. . . . There is no news and our routine is about the same each day and not very interesting.

TUESDAY FEBY 2ND

This is a nice morning but a little cold. . . . I received a letter from Nett of Jan 11th. It has been a long time on the road but nevertheless was welcome.

Wednesday Feby 3rd

I was at work all day on Reports and finished them about Nine Oclock to night. . . . We did not get any mail.

Thursday Feb 4th

I worked on Abstracts all day. . . . No news.

Friday Feby 5th

I finished and forwarded my Abstracts. . . . I was over to the Company this evening.

Saturday Feb 6th

I did not have much to do to day. . . . The Freight Depot burned down to night with its contents. There was a large amount of Clotheing in it and other commissary Stores. That is a good way for Quarter Masters to settle when they get behing with the government. All they are required to do is to burn up what they have on hands and their Books and then make their Reports accordingly. The Private Soldiers are the only sufferers as they have to wait untill the deficiency is made up by Shipments.

Sunday Feb 7th

The third Brigade was out on Review for a change as it is sunday. . . . I send Nett some Valuntines. I went over to the Regiment and find a rumor that our Division is going to Dalton but no orders.

Monday Feb 8th

George Farley the clerk who was put in the Guard House for going to Lookout without permission was sent back to his company to day. The left me without a Bunk Mate but I V Bates moved in with me. . . . No orders to move yet. No news of importance. I wish we would move. I am tired of lying here. There is nothing but the regular routine of camp life. I would prefer campaigning and the attendent excitement. I[t] gives more life and keeps us vigorous and seams more like wipeing out the Johnies. Inactivity in the life of a Soldier makes him lazy and he grumbles more than in active campaign.

TUESDAY JAN [FEB] 9TH

This is a beautifull day. The train was late. I received a Glee Book called the Bugle Call from Kate Keagle but no letters from home.[17] Major Connoly returned to day. I was over to the Regiment this Evening. I was writing nearly all day. . . .

WEDNESDAY JAN [FEB] 10TH

. . . No mail. I was over to the company this eve. No news.

THURSDAY FEB 11TH

I have plenty of writing to do to day. We received orders to prepare our Books so as to move Saturday and rumor says we are bound for Knoxville. The camps are all astir and the Boys elated over the prospect of moving. I visited my Regiment this evening and they have the same orders. . . . Nothing new.

FRIDAY FEB 12TH

I worked on Furloughs all day. . . . Report that our move is postponed untill Monday.

SATURDAY FEB 13TH

The indications point strongly to a move. The Ambulance Train was organized and "Correlled" which looks like buisiness. . . . Some of my company Boys come and invited me to come and eat oysters but I did not go. I took a "Bath" in preference.

SUNDAY FEB 14TH

This is a rainy day. . . . It is rumored that we will move to morrow. There was about thirty Recruits came to the 74th Indiana. They look very nice and clean in their new clothes compared with us. I was over to the Regiment this eve. But came back before night and the report to night is that our move is put off again untill Tuesday. I thought we would be marching before this but I presume our Generals know what they are about and will let us know when they are ready to move.

Monday Feb 15th

We did not receive marching orders and it is a wonder for it was a very wet and disagreeable day and that is the kind of days we generally move. . . . Genl Shermans Corps come up and went into camp South of Lookout Creek. They are from Vicksburgh and now we have an army of about Eighty Thousand men here. We campaigned over the mountains against "Bragg" with a little over half that many and we have force enough to push Johnston to the wall. When we move the "Bark" ["]will fly." There will be Something done and the Rebel Army will have to get out of the way Sure. I dont care how soon it comes. I suppose Shermans men are to remain in this Department and Rumor says that Genl Grant will command us in person.

Tuesday Feby 16th

Genl Shermans men the 15th and 17th Army Corps are moveing now and we have no orders yet but are Still in readiness to move. The weather is cold and very blustery and disagreeable. I received a letter from Jim and Magg Spake but did not answer it. They are at Indianapolis and Jim has a "soft" time Soldiering. But I prefer being here as there. If I have to soldier at all. I dont like this "Paper Coller" Service. Let those have that who enjoy it. . . . I did not have much writing to do in the office but remained at Head Quarters all day.

Wednesday Feb 17th

. . . It is very cold. I visited the Regiment this evening. We did not receive marching orders yet. No news of importance.

Thursday Feby 18th

General Steadman took command of the Department of the Ettewa with Head Quarters here which now relieves us for active service.[18] It is still cold. I did not get any mail. We are Still in readiness to move when we get the orders. I cant think it is a general move now for the roads would be terible. We may be going to Knoxville to relieve our forces but will not Start on an active campaign this season of the year.

Friday Feby 19th

I was writing all day on Inspection Reports. . . . No news.

SATURDAY FEB 20TH

My "Three Years or during the war" is just half up to day and to look back and see what I have passed through and imagine what is comeing yet it almost discourages me. But I hope the war may close long before my time expires. . . . This is a nice day.

SUNDAY FEB 21ST

This is a nice day. . . . Orders came this evening to be ready to move in the morning at Seven Oclock. Report says now we are going to try Dalton. That is the point occupied by the Rebels and is said to be strongly fortified. It may be only a feeler to see what they have in the way of defence. There is always more or less false moves and preliminary Skirmishes to bring on a General engagement. Boath parties Strive for advantage in the begining and then to hold it. But only time can tell what the result of our move will be. Some think Johnston will not retreat as Bragg did but try to hold his ground.

MONDAY FEB 22ND

The aniversary of the birth of Genl Washington finds us all on the move. Genl Baird gave orders for Head Quarters to remain here so that vetoes my going. I dont like that but must obey orders. Reports to night that there has been Some fighting in front but nothing reliable. I presume of course there will be some Skirmishing as our Troops would not have to go far untill they would find Rebels and I will not be Surprised to hear of an engagement at any time. It keeps me anxious all the time as to the result. . . . I was over to the old camp and find the Tents are Still Standing and some of the Boys there. That looks more like a feint move and circumstances will govern a permanent move. If our forces drive the Rebels we will move to hold all the advantage. I picked up a round fancy Stone on Hospittal Hill as I came back and put this date on it and where found and will take it home with me if I dont loose it.

TUESDAY FEB 23RD

The news from the front is very favorable and the Johnies are falling back and our Army advanceing. . . . I will not have much to do now untill we move or Head Quarters returns only guard the property left in my care. I would much rather be along and see what is going on in the front.

WEDNESDAY FEB 24TH

There is all kinds of rumers afloat. There is undoubtedly fighting going on. Our forces are reported near Dalton and still advanceing.[19] But what our losses are we cant learn. . . . I visited the Boys in camp and was down to see the 16th U.S. collord Rigiment on Dress Parade. They put on lots of Style and go through the manuel of Arms very nicely. Their officers are very tyranicle and they dont know any better than to obey. I dont know how they would Stand in Battle but I am willing to try them by giveing them the advance.

THURSDAY FEB 25TH

I had some work to do to day and carried some papers to the 35th Ohio. Some of the wounded came to day and a large Ambulance Train went to the front. I was at the Depot and Seen about a hundred Rebel prisoners on the train. They are being sent north. The report is current that our forces occupy Dalton. I was over to camp. The wind is blowing almost a hericane. The reports from the front are favorable and Shows that our Boys are standing up to the work and makeing it hot for the Johnies. I hope we may be able to drive them to the wall. The Confederacy is on its last legs any way. Their cause is lost and they certainly know they must surrender sooner or later. But they would not be worthy to be called Americans if they were not brave men.

FRIDAY FEB 26TH

. . . There is a very Sad report in circulation to day and that is that Genl Baird is mortally wounded and Capt Johnston of Staff Slightly. I do hope it will prove untrue for Genl Baird is a man we cant spare very well. He is among the most energetic men and one of the best Division commanders we have. His men all like him. Major McCole of my Regiment is reported to be wounded and if so our Boys have been where duty calls again and added more "Laurels to their Brows." The wounded are comeing in but I have not seen any of our Boys or any one whom I knew. Capt Karns came over and we took a long walk. I wrote to Nett. We cannot get any reliable word but the camps are full of all kinds of rumors. Some are that our men fell back to Tunnel Hill. I Stayed all night with Capt Karns. He did not go out but Lieut Starbuck is in command of the

company. We had some oysters. Lieut Dick of Division returned for
more Amunition in charge of the Ordinance Train.[20] He says they have
had some heavy Skirmishing but no pitched Battle yet.

SATURDAY FEBY 27TH

. . . This is a nice day. I had some Photos taken. They cost only $4.00
for six. Capt Johnston of Staff who was reported to be wounded returned
from the front and reports Genl Baird as all right and I feel to rejoice.
He says our men are now at Ringold. The loss of our Division is about
a hundred and principly from the 11th Ohio. Some of the wounded
were burned to death by the woods takeing fire. That is horible for men
to be disabled so they cant escape and be roasted alive.

SUNDAY FEB 28TH

. . . It is all quiet in front now as our advance has ended for the preasent.
. . . I was working on Abstracts. Major Connolly is still at the front but
I took the responsibility to make out the abstracts for this month.

MONDAY FEB 29TH

This is a rainy cold and disagreeable day and we got orders to move Head
Quarters to Ringold to morrow. . . . I finished my abstracts. . . . I will have
to ride a mule as I am still lame and cant march. I got one to day.

TUESDAY MAR 1ST

This is a rainy morning but we Struck Tents and I packed our Office furniture and put them on the wagon and mounted my mule and we started
for Ringold. We kept ahead of our Wagon Train. We crossed Chickamauga Creek at Lower Bridge and about 4 Oclock we were informed that
the Train had gone into camp. We had no Rations and had to go back
about three miles. It rained all day and turned cold this evening and I
could not get my Blankets and Brown Bates Mevis Meir Nailor and myself
passed the night sitting around the fire. We had plenty of nice dry rails
but the night was cold and we had a hard night of it. There is an old house
near us but no roof on it. Mevis got some whisky and was drunk enough
to be quarrelsom and concluded he would lick me and the only way I
could get rid of him was to slap his ears a little and I accommodated him

accordingly. He then layed down and went to sleep. I was drenched with rain and I thought some times I would freeze. I did not Sleep a wink. We are camped near Chickamauga Creek about two miles from the Battle Field. The roads are bad and I think is rather a rough introduction to a campaign. There is no news and no mail came up. We did not see nor hear of any Rebs as our Army have driven them all away.

WEDNESDAY MAR 2ND
[RINGGOLD, GEORGIA]

We started in advance of the train and arrived at Ringold about noon and the Train did not get in for a couple of hours but I got my Tent up and Bunk arranged and I am comfortable and I am very tired and think I will Sleep well. This has been quite a town but severel of the Buildings was burned by Genl Hookers men. Taylors Ridge South of Town is quite a mountain and is a splendid line of defense. Severel of our Boys under Hooker lost their lives on the summit a few days ago. Our men were under fire all the time after leaveing Chattanooga but drove the Rebels before them. They are now at Rockyface or Tunnel Hill only Six miles from here and report says they are Strongly posted and I presume we will amuse our selves the rest of the winter by paying them accasional visits. . . .

THURSDAY MAR 3RD

I put a floor in my tent this morning. Major Connolly returned to Chattanooga. I had plenty of work to do to day as a move always damages camp and Garrison equipage and then the Inspector condemns it and it has to be accounted for in this Department and makes work for me. I did not receive any mail but wrote to Nett.

FRIDAY MARCH 4TH

I had some work on hands to day. . . . It is all quiet here and the Johnies dont bother us. I was over to see the Boys. I found them all right. There was no body hurt in my Regiment. Major McCole was not hurt as reported.

SATURDAY MAR 5TH

. . . Some talk that the Rebels have got in our rear. If that is so they [will] want help to get out again. . . . Some excitement in camp over the escape of the 39th Indiana who came very near being captured and we may have to Skeedaddle from Ringold. We are somewhat exposed here but the only way they could get us out would be to flank us and sever our Rail Road So that we could not get supplies. By that kind of a move they have to[o] much to risk. They could not live off the country through which we passed and could not get Supplies otherwise than to haul them along and that would make their trains so large it would require to[o] many men to guard them and retard their moveing.

SUNDAY MAR 6TH

I supposed from indications yesterday that we would be retreating to day but we are still. The Rebels fell back over the ridge and it dont look as much like trouble as it did. They have concluded to let us remain for a few days yet at least. They know better than to bring on a general engagement now with us fighting on the defensive. We would punnish them teribly. . . .

MONDAY MAR 7TH

Every thing quiet in front. . . . I was over to the Regiment this evening. I dont have quite so far to go as I did at Chattanooga but it is quite a walk. Genl Baird has his Head Quarters in a house and the Staff have their Tents in the yard. My Tent is in the rear of [the] Inspectors.

TUESDAY MAR 8TH

I received Six months pay to day and Sent Nett Forty dollars by Alotment Roll. . . . I was writing all day except the time I was out for pay. There was some Cavalry fighting South of Taylors Ridge but not very heavy. I suppose it was between Scouting parties. We are only about six miles from the "Johnies" now but I dont think there will be any thing of importance for a while as the weather and roads are to[o] bad to move now.

WEDNESDAY MAR 9TH

I built a Chimney to my Tent as it is to[o] cold to write without fire. . . . It is all quiet in front. I did not hear a Shot to day.

THURSDAY MAR 10TH

. . . A Rebel Flag of Truce came to our lines and Col Vandaver with Escort went out to confer with them but I did not learn what it was for.[21] I went over to the Regiment and Settled up with the Boys. Some of them was owing me. I had plenty of work in the office.

FRIDAY MAR 11TH

I was writing all day. . . . I was working on Monthly Reports and did not go to bed untill about eleven Oclock. No news.

SATURDAY MAR 12TH

. . . I was writing all day. This is a nice day and warm and pleasent as spring in Indiana. The papers have nothing new and it was quiet along our front and the regular Camp routine was the order of the day.

SUNDAY MAR 13TH

I V Bates and I took a Field Glass and went up on Taylors Ridge to view the country. It is splendid. We could See the Rebel Pickets and Smoke from their camps and Rocky Face Gap. We also seen the graves of our men who were killed in the gap Nov 27th 1863 when our Army was pursueing the Rebels from Missionary and Genl Hooker pressed them to[o] hard and they made a Stand here. They are nearly on the summit of the Ridge. . . .

MONDAY MAR 14TH

Genl Baird sent out a Flag of Truce and I had a desire to go and one of the Mounted Escort kindly tenderd me his horse and place and I went. When we approached the Rebel line Col Lowrey hoisted a white cloth and Soon Some mounted Rebels came toward us displaying the same token of friendship.[22] We all dismounted and our Officers and the Rebel officers then advanced and met between us and the Rebel Escort leaveing us to hold their horses and to take care of their arms as they dare not cary any Arms with them. We could not hear what we was there for. But the officers seamed to enjoy it as they laughed heartily occasionally and passed their Canteens which contained water (I suppose) but it was remarkable what effect it had on our officers for when the[y] returned to us some of them could not mount their horses without assistance and with Shame I tell it one of them was so drunk he could not even ride without an orderly on either side of him. I dont know what the object of our trip was unless it was for a spree. It is a disgrace to the Army to be officerd by such men. It is bad enough for a private Soldier to get drunk. Much more an officer on duty. . . .

TUESDAY MAR 15TH

. . . I [was] makeing out Monthly and Semi-Monthly Reports and in Inventory and Inspection Reports of my Regiment. There is no news. I had so much to do I did not visit the Company. No Rebels Showed themselves but all was quiet on the Picket Lines.

WEDNESDAY MAR 16TH

The Air is cold and disagreeable. I finished my Reports and wrote to Nett but did not receive any mail. . . . I got the Wells County Union a paper from Home. No news.

THURSDAY MAR 17TH

This is a nice day. . . .

FRIDAY MAR 18TH

There was some Skirmishing on our right but I did not learn the cause but I presume it is Scouting parties. I did not get any mail nor write any. The train run up to our Picket line to day from Chattanooga. . . . An order transfering Jim Spake to the Vetran Reserve Corps passed through the office to day and I expect I will be relieved from duty here and will return to the company. But as I am Still lame I dont know whether I could Stand the march. I am willing to try so I can get back to the Regiment. There was some heavy Skirmishing this evening and a detail was sent out from the command to see what it meant.

SATURDAY MAR 19TH

I had but little work to do to day and did not get any mail. . . . The Skirmishing last night was caused by the Rebels Scouting around our Picket line. The[y] wanted to see how we are Situated and what our line of defense is. They may find out to their sorrow if the[y] fool around.

SUNDAY MAR 20TH

I am Sick haveing an attack of Dioreah. . . . I was over to the Regiment but they are on Picket. Genls Thomas and Palmer with their Staffs came up. The Train run into the Depot for the first time since we have been here.

MONDAY MAR 21ST

It is cloudy and rainy to day. . . . It snowed some this evening. No news of importance.

TUESDAY MAR 22ND

Five inches of Snow this morning and it lay very heavy on the Tents. It give things the appearance of Indiana. It [is] a very unusual accurrence for this country.[23] It was cold all day and froze some to night. . . . We had lots of fun Snow Balling to day. My duty was light and I got a copy of Mary Queen of Scotts and read it.[24]

WEDNESDAY MAR 23RD

It is cold this morning but the sun come out bright. . . . Another Flag of Truce came to our lines but I did not learn what for. The reason why they all come here is because we are the advance of our Army and all communications come to us.

THURSDAY MAR 24TH

I did not get any Letters. It snowed some again to night but not very much. I was writing all day.

Friday Mar 25th

This is a rainy day. I received Netts letter of the 17th and answered. The roads are terible muddy as the snow has all disappeard. I finished reading "Mary Queen of Scotts."

Saturday Mar 26th

. . . I expected to return to my company ere this but I guess they will let me remain for a while yet. If the Army Should move in all proba-bility I would be relieved at once.

Sunday Mar 27th

This is a beautiful day but I did not go away from Head Quarters. I did not have much to do but spent the day mostly reading. . . .

Monday Mar 28th

. . . This is a cold rainy day.

Tuesday Mar 29th

I was makeing out monthly abstracts all day. I answerd Lou Townsends Letter. The train did not come through So we did not get any mail. I dont know what is the matter but suppose the Rail Road is threatened by the Johnies Some place. It is surely a long line of Road to guard from here to Louisville and it seams like almost an impossibility to keep it in running order. The citizens would obstruct the track if the Rebel Soldiers did not.

Wednesday Mar 30th

We received orders to be ready to move at a moments warning but I guess it is only to feel of the Rebels and circumstances will govern a general move. If the Johnies Should run[?] as usual we may move our quarters South.

Thursday Mar 31st

Capt Karns was over and from him I learned of the death of Patrick Boyle a member of my company who died the 28th inst. I dont know where he died. He also told me I was a Sergeant to date from the 1st of this month. I feel very proud of a promotion as it convinces me that my superiors appretiate my services. I have tried to do my duty in any and all places I have been called to work and if I have not it is an error of the head and not of the heart. . . .

FRIDAY APRIL 1ST

This is a wet and dreary day and almost makes me feel homesick. . . . I was over to the company and came back after dark and it was as dark as a "Stack of black cats" and terible muddy.

SATURDAY APR 2ND

. . . The orders to move has not arrived yet.

SUNDAY APR 3RD

. . . It rained nearly all night and we have no marching orders. There may be Some move on hands and we are only held in readiness to Support in case we should be required.

MONDAY APR 4TH

Made out our monthly reports for Febuary. I did not get any mail. My Bunk Mate Bates went to Greysville and did not return this evening so I Slept by myself. I went to the company to draw a pair of Shoes but found them all on Picket. All quiet to day.

TUESDAY APR 5TH

Nice day. . . . No marching orders yet and every thing quiet.

WEDNESDAY APR 6TH

Our Division are prepareing for Grand Review to morrow. This is a nice day. I answerd Netts letters to night. Bates Walbridge and myself was out for a walk to the Grave Yard this evening. I met Eli Blackburn for the first time since I was at Hospittal in Gallatin Tennissee. He is looking well and I am always glad to meet an old Soldier acquaintance and Shake their hand.

Thursday Apr 7th

Our Division moved out for Review about 10 Oclock a.m and Genls
Thomas & Palmer arrived soon after. I Should liked very much to been
along but had no buisiness to go and remained in Quarters. I have been
worried about my wounded leg to day as it has been paining me and I
am afraid it is not properly healed and will break out in another place
and lay me up. I went to the Regiment and Dr Arthur gave me a lini-
ment for it. He thinks it will be all right in a few days and I sincerely
hope he is right.[25] I did not get any mail. The Troops returned to camp
this evening and we have no marching orders yet.

Friday Apr 8th

My Leg is very lame and Sore and Swollen considerably and makes me
restless and uneasy about it. I dont see what causes it as I have been
very carefull about it and I dont remember of hurting it any way. There
is talk that our Corps (The 14th) as going to the Army of the Potomac
but only a rumor.[26]

Saturday Apr 9th

My Leg is still very painfull and Dr Bogue looked at it and said I better
apply for a discharge as I cant never do duty again with my company
but I will wait awhile yet. . . . It commenced raining this p.m. I did not
do much to day as I have caught up with my writing. There was some
Cavalry fighting and the Rebel Pickets was driven in but our men withdrew after takeing some prisoners.

Sunday Apr 10th

. . . I was over to the company and went to the funeral of a Soldier out
of the 10th Indiana who died in camp.[27]. . .

Monday Apr 11th

I got no mail. Some Rebel Cavalry came up and fired into our Pickets
and wounded one man in the leg and it had to be Amputated but our
Boys made it to[o] warm for them and they retired after fireing a few
rounds.

TUESDAY APR 12TH

... A Flag of Truce was sent out to pass a woman through the lines but the Rebels refused to respond and the Lady came back to town. She is Said to come from Cincinnati Ohio and what She is going South for I cant imagine. We have no orders to move yet but there is Strong talk of moveing on Dalton.

WEDNESDAY APR 13TH

One of our Pickets was wounded to day by a Rebel and it seams they are getting bold about it. We will have to give them another Shakeing up to learn them to behave themselves. I was writing all day. I did not get any mail.

THURSDAY APR 14TH

I was writing all day [and] did not get any mail. Rumors of a move but no orders. The[y] will let us know when the time comes.

FRIDAY APR 15TH

I had work all day and untill after dark. . . .

SATURDAY APR 16TH

... This is a very nice day. Some talk of a move but no orders yet. Report that Columbus Ky was captured by the Rebels but only a rumor and not reliable.

SUNDAY APR 17TH

The Capture of Columbus Ky not confirmed. . . . I visited the Regiment camp but they are on Picket.

MONDAY APR 18TH

I was writing all day. . . . No news and no move yet.

TUESDAY APR 19TH

My Bunkmate Bates Smoked a pipe which was very anoying to me in the Tent and almost suffocated me and I proposed to him if he would quit Smoking I would quit chewing Tobacco and made the penalty for violating the pledge five dollars and consequently this is a "blue day" to me. I never knew what a desire for tobacco was untill I find I cant use it. But I am going to Stick to it. . . . We expected some Recruits to day but they did not come. They will get a rough introduction to Soldiering when they do come.

WEDNESDAY APR 20TH

Nine of our Recruits came up on the Train this morning. They are all from near Bluffton and I knew all but one or two. . . .

THURSDAY APR 21TH

The First Division of the 14th Ccrps have order[s] for thirty days rations on the wagons and be ready to move. That looks like buisiness. We have no orders yet but are expecting to get them. . . . Very Strong talk of a move this evening.

FRIDAY APR 22ND

This was the warmest day yet this Spring and I was in the office all day. Our orders to move have not come yet. . . .

SATURDAY APR 23RD

Our Cavalry Pickets at Nick-A-Jack Gap were attacted and nearly all captured. Our loss was five killed ten wounded and thirteen captured. They must have been asleep or very careless to let the Johnies get away with them that way. . . .

SUNDAY APR 24TH

Our lines in front was attacted this morning and it got up quite an excitement and Troops were hurried to their assistence and drove the Johnies. There was considerable Shooting done while it lasted. I did not learn what the casualities were. . . . There was some girls made their appearance on Taylors Ridge and I was looking at them through a Field Glass from the Provost Marshalls Tent. It is a nice view through a glass to gaze along the Ridge running East and west.

MONDAY APR 25TH

Severel of our men were found at Nick A Jack Gap to day who were murderd by the Rebels after surrendering. That is the kind of War they are worthy of conducting. Their cause Should sink to perdition and them with it.

TUESDAY APR 26TH

This was a very warm day. . . . No news and all quiet.

WEDNESDAY APR 27TH

This is a warm day and makes me begin to realize we are in a warm climate. The Rebels put in an appearance in our front but kept at a respect-full distance and there was no fighting. . . .

THURSDAY APR 28TH

I was in the office all day untill evening and Bates and I was over to the 101st Indiana. No mail.

FRIDAY APR 29TH

Genl Killpatricks Cavalry passed out this morning to stir up the Johnies and he done it handsomely.[28] I went up on the Ridge with a Glass to see the fight and had a nice view. Our men made a dash at the Rebels and they received them with a voley and then run. Our Boys charged them once and then held their position untill about ten Oclock when the Johnies concentrated their forces and troted out Infantry when our men fell back into the Gap and the fighting ceased. Our loss was two men killed a[nd] severel wounded. I received Netts letter of the 21st.

SATURDAY APR 30TH

I did not get any mail. There was no demonstration in our front untill towards evening when the Rebs advanced their lines and our Troops were pushed out to our Picket line to meet any emergency that might arise. The Rebels are mad over yesterdays move and want to retalliate. But we are prepared to meet them. We expected an attack but the night passed without any move on their part. The[y] seen we were ready and concluded very wisely to let us alone.

SUNDAY MAY 1ST

This is a cloudy [day] and all quiet along the lines. Our Troops returned
to Camp. . . . I was over to the Regiment this evening and they have
orders to move to the front any moment as the Johnies are restless and
Seam to want a fight. Our Troops moved out through the Gap after dark
but there was no fireing. Everything was conducted with caution and
with as little noise as possible. The object is to not let the Rebels know
but we are only protected by our Pickets and if they attack they will get
a warm reception and will find more than they expect. There was considerable excitement in camp but I could not learn any thing only
rumors as to the advance of the Johnies.

MONDAY MAY 2ND

I was awakend this morning by Cavalry passing and I found the entire
division ready to move. We also got the report that the "Rebs" had
retreated toward Dalton. Our forces followed to Tunnel Hill where they
commenced Skirmishing and the Rebels pushed a heavy force to the
front and there was considerable fireing. I was on the Ridge where I had
a good view of a portion of the fight. The Rebels was to[o] Strong and
our forces had to retire with a loss of four men Killed and seven
Wounded. It was cavalry fighting and the Infantry supporting.[29] Corps
Head Quarters came up and Genl Davises Division and camped near
town. Johnstons Division will come tomorrow which indicates a move
before many days.[30] There is all kinds of rumors afloat about moveing
but nothing reliable. I got Netts letter of the 24th. The Rebels occupy
a Strong position at Rocky face or Buzzard Roost and will hold it if possible and there will be some fighting there. Our entire Army is now
under Genl Sherman and have marching orders. Every available man
will be put into the field and when we move the "fir will fly."

TUESDAY MAY 3RD

With to day I commence a new Diary and to this time I have marched
Two thousand Five Hundred and Sixty Eight miles since I enlisted. Genl
Palmer and Johnstons Division came up. There was no Skirmishing to
day but I am now Satisfied there is a move on hand. And what we will
have [to] encounter it is hard telling. But let it come and we will do as
we have always done meet it manfully. Our Army is in Splendid

condition and composed of the 14th 15th 17th & 20th Army Corps and Kilpatricks Cavalry Amounting to near Eighty thousand men. I dont know what the Rebel force is. But they have a great advantage by fighting on the defensive. They have fortifications to protect them while we have the open field. . . .

WEDNESDAY MAY 4TH

This is a beautiful morning and there is considerable moveing but none to the front. Genl Thomas' Head Quarters came up and camped about a mile east of Town. There is rumors that we will move to morrow. . . . I was in the office all day expecting to move.

THURSDAY MAY 5TH

The Troops are moveing through the gap this morning and have been since daylight. Our men drove in the Rebel Pickets Killing three who were left on the field. Our advance is about four miles from here. The third Division did not move. Genl Sherman came up. Genl Hookers men have the advance to day but after passing the Gap they will be deployed to the right and left and advance from different points. The position occupied by the Rebels is a gap or pass through the mountains and will be driven out by a flank movement. It could not be carried by a direct assault from the front. Genl Hookers right is about three miles from here east. He will cross the Ridge at that point I presume. . . .

FRIDAY MAY 6TH

I got no mail to day. I was surprised to see Genl Hookers men come up and lay in line of Battle all day. The Rebels advanced their lines within about a half mile of our advance and remained during the day and are there to night. Our men are all under marching orders to start at daylight in the morning. The positions now occupied by the two armies will be the cause of much anxiety during the next few hours for now a move by either may bring on a pitched Battle and we have orders to move and I cant think we will retreat so it is probable the Battle will be fought to morrow or the Rebels will have to "Skedaddle" as usual. But they will certainly make some kind of an effort to hold their position. I got orders from Genl Baird to remain with a detail and take charge of the Head Quarter Baggage untill further orders and I suppose that will stop my going along to morrow. The Office Desks cannot be taken as the officers are not allcwed even a Tent. Only a "Fly."[31] . . . So the day ends wondering how it will be to morrow.

SATURDAY MAY 7TH

I was up before day light and the Troops moved early. Genl Johnstons Division moved out first and the 3rd followed about Nine Oclock. Mevis and [I] went on top of the Ridge and I witnessed a grand sight. The valey in our front is coverd with soldiers for miles. We could see nearly the whole Army lying before us all "Bivuacked" for dinner. We could See our advance and the Rebel position. Our men are near Rocky face.[32] There is some fireing along the lines but no advance was made by either. The[y] seam to be measureing the strength of either. I met Major Widmer but merely Spoke to him while passing. Our forces camp[ed] for the night with orders to move at three Oclock a.m.

SUNDAY MAY 8TH

The Troops immediately in our front did no[t] move to day but lay in line of Battle. Some of our forces are reported as near Dalton. They are flanking the Rebel position and enless driven back will compell them to evacuate Buzzard Roost. I was on the Ridge a part of the day to see the fight if it come off. . . . The town is full of Patroll Guards to night to gather up straglers but my order lets me go any place I wish to. I visited the cemetary this evening.

MONDAY MAY 9TH

We could hear the Boom of Cannon at intervols all day and occasionally musketry. I was down in Town to see some wounded men who come in but did not see any one I knew as they were principly Hookers men. There is all kinds of rumors and flying Reports. The mail was not put off here but carried through to the front. It rained very hard all night and was cold and disagreeable. Report this evening says the Rebels have evacuated Tunnel Hill and retreated to Dalton and that Genl Hooker occupies a position near Dalton. But we have a poor chance to get any thing reliable as we have to depend on wounded men and prisoners passing through.

TUESDAY MAY 10TH

I finished my letter to Nett and Mevis and I done our washing. This was a hot day and I was working on leaves of Absence. Some heavy Skirmishing in front but no general engagement as yet. Rumors are plenty and some are favorable and some are unfavorable.

WEDNESDAY MAY 11TH

I was down to the Depot to see them load the Hospital train with wounded but did not find any of my Regiment. Our Forces are moving to the right. Heavy Skirmishing all day. A number of wounded were brought in this evening but I did not find any acquaintances. . . . There is a flank movement going on and the Johnies will have to Skip or our men will sever their communication or cut their "Cracker Line."[33] I dont see how they can make a Stand against the force we are putting against them. Then our Army is in Splendid condition while theirs is poorly clad and Short of rations.

THURSDAY MAY 12TH

The wagon train of the 4th Corps was moveing to the left through Town early this morning. Fifty one prisoners was brought in who were captured on the Rail Road South of Dalton. Our forces are flanking and the 14th Corps is moveing to the right to night. Some more wounded was brought in this evening and passed through. I did not get any mail but John Hale came up and brought me some things from home. He was at home on furlough.

FRIDAY MAY 13TH

Our Forces enterd Dalton this morning and the Cars run through to night. The Rebels left Buzzard Roose and are retreating towards Atlanta and our men following up. We got a report there was a Battle in Virginia but no particulars.[34] The Train came this evening from Dalton and they Say there has been heavy fighting all day. The Rebels did not make much of a fight at Dalton as our men was getting in their rear. I was at the Depot when the train came from the front but did not meet any acquaintances. Our Teams were loading supplies for 20th Corps. . . . I have no orders to move yet. I have a detail of ten men with me and my duties is to see that a guard or two is mounted each morning to protect the Baggage and I loaf around the ballance of the time.

SATURDAY MAY 14TH

There is glorious Reports but I fear to[o] good to be true for they Say we captured Rasaca and Thirty five thousand Rebels but that is to[o] many prisoners. The Rebs are falling back and our men pressing them closely and keeping up the fight. The report is confirmed of the evacuation of Rasaca by the Rebels. The 5th Indiana Cavalry passed through here this morning and I followed them to our Picket line to see some acquaintances but could not get out and did not see them. . . .

SUNDAY MAY 15TH

The capture of Rasaca contradicted but our men are a Short distance only from there and still pressing the Rebs closely. Almost continuous Skirmishing and some times might be almost called a battle. I was up on the Ridge with John Hale. Some more wounded and Sick men passed here on the cars. The cars run into dalton to day. There was a number of prisoners came to day.

MONDAY MAY 16TH

Report that the great Battle between the two Armies commenced this morning early and continued throughout the day and that our men are gradually driveing the Johnies. Some prisoners came in but they were not captured in the fight and cant tell any thing about it. The Battle when it does come will determine the fate of Atlanta and if our men are Successfull I dont know where the Rebels can make another stand and will surely sue for a cessation of hostilities. I[t] looks as though their defeat at this time would [be] very disastrious to their cause.

TUESDAY MAY 17TH

One of the mounted Orderlies came in from the front and he says the Battles around Rasacca was fought Saturday & Sunday instead of yesterday and that our men occupy Rasacca and that the Rebels are retreating. A number of wounded come up also but I could not find any of our Boys among the croud. The news if reliable is good but there is so many

"Grape Vines" afloat. I did not receive any letters nor write any. The weather is warm. I did not receive any orders to leave here yet. . . .

WEDNESDAY MAY 18TH

I finished my Reports of Absentees to day. A number of of wounded came in and some from our Division but I did not see any from my Regiment. Our forces are Said to be at Kingston and still pushing forward toward Atlanta. The news from the Army of the Potomac is good and Lee is on the run as well as the Rebels here. I wrote to Nett but did not get any mail as it all passes through. I must have plenty of mail there some place.

THURSDAY MAY 19TH

The News is still very favorable. A number of our wounded came up to day but no one that I knew. . . . No orders to go to the front yet. I am getting tired loafing around here.

FRIDAY MAY 20TH

Mevis and I traded some hard Bread for milk and Butter. The citizens begin to come in now and I seen severel in town to day. They trade with our Boys for Coffee and other rations as they are hard up and we have plenty and can Spare some. There was some wounded came in but I found none from my command. This was a very hot day.

SATURDAY MAY 21ST

I seen a number of citizens in town to day. Mevis and I was out in the country about three miles. We went out south through the gap. We rode in on the Train by climbing on when it was running. There was Six hundred Rebel prisoners on the train. I talked with some of them and they say the war is nearly over. But I suppose they think so because they cant do any more dirt for a while or untill exchanged. The[y] was captured near Resacca and Say we have a complete victory and their loss was heavy.

SUNDAY MAY 22ND

I wrote a letter to Nett to day. The old Nineth Ohio came in from the front as they are going home. Their time haveing expired they are to

Seventy-fifth Indiana Monument on the Chickamauga Battlefield.

William Bluffton Miller.
A 1937 painting by Si
Baller, from a photograph
in the *Bluffton (Ind.)
Evening News,* May 31,
1918. Courtesy of the
Wells County (Indiana)
Historical Society.

William Roland Miller,
Miller's son, who died
at the age of nineteen
months, in August 1863.

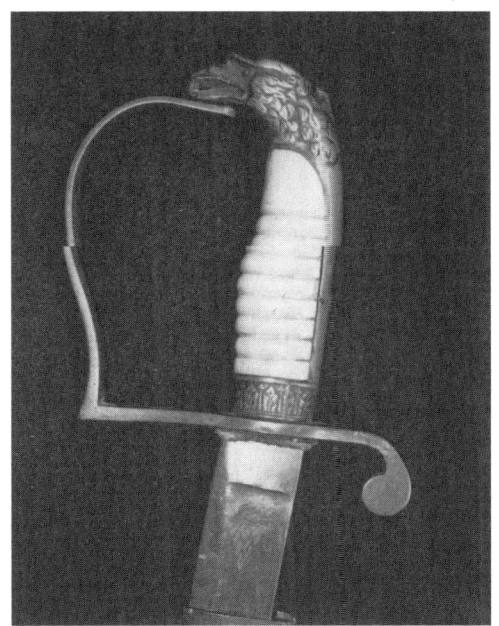

Close-up of hilt of pre–Civil War sword brought home by William Bluffton Miller.

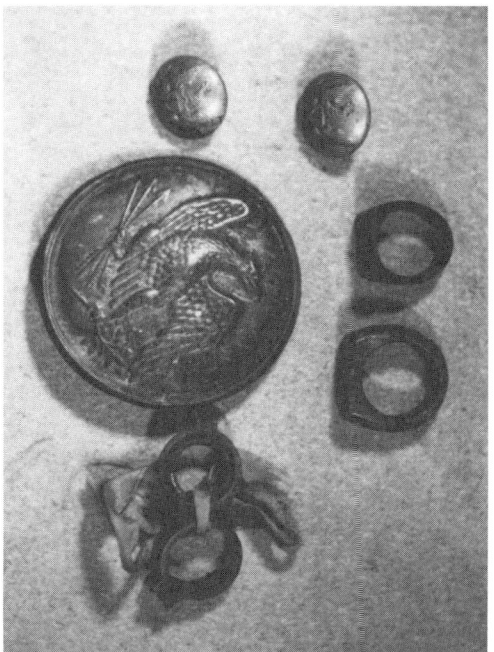

Wooden rings, uniform buttons, and cartridge box sling plate brought home by William Bluffton Miller.

Pvt. Ezariah Steffey, Company K, Seventy-fifth Indiana
Volunteer Infantry.

Melissa Jeannette "Nett" Miller (*left*), wife of William Bluffton Miller, and one of
W. B. Miller's sisters, most likely Mary Jane Miller.

Wooden book (*left*) and granite book (*upper right*), carved by William Bluffton
Miller, and a piece of a door of Libby Prison in Richmond brought home by Miller.

Pvt. Cornelius Reaser,
Company K, Seventy-fifth
Indiana Volunteer Infantry.

Maj. Gen. Joseph J.
Reynolds. From *The Soldier
of Indiana in the War for the
Union* (1866).

Souvenir items made by Miller during his Civil War service, including a granite book and wooden rings. The laurel root ring (center) was made by Miller for his son William Roland.

Pvt. Jeptha Hart, Company K, Seventy-fifth Indiana Volunteer Infantry.

Pvt. Elijah Lewark, Company G,
Seventy-fifth Indiana Volunteer Infantry.

Sgt. John T. Cartwright, Company K,
Seventy-fifth Indiana Volunteer
Infantry.

Confederate tin
"drum" canteen
brought home by
William Bluffton
Miller.

be musterd out of the service. They are all germans and most of them served in the old country and they have done a noble work in the last three years as their depleted ranks Show. The few who are left may well be proud of the record of the old nineth. The 14th Kentukey vetrans passed through to the front haveing been at home on furlough. The[y] have a number of recruits and look fine. There is Severel old Regiments whos term of Service expires soon and will be musterd out. Our Army did not move to day but will start to morrow.

MONDAY MAY 23RD

Mevis went to Dalton and met Chet Walbridge comeing in and we received orders to return to Chattanooga. . . . Our orders was only verbal to go to Chattanooga with the Baggage with Walbridge and I refused to obey untill further orders. I tellegraphed accordingly to Lieut Sanderson.[35] We packed up to be ready when the order comes. Some of the men with me were very anxious to go but I told them I did not obey "Second hand" verbal military orders. It may be all right but it is not safe as my orders written says "remain here untill further Orders" and I shall do so.

TUESDAY MAY 24TH

Our orders came by Tellegram to go to Chattanooga but I did not move as it is raining very hard. Some of my men seam to be in a hurry as they think it a little dangerous here as the Rebels have been around here for a day or two. Some more prisoners were brought in to day. Our Army Is again moveing South and seam to be invinceable and the Rebels have to get out of the way or suffer the consequences.

WEDNESDAY MAY 25TH

I got on the train and run up to Greysville for a ride and got a cinder in my eye and I sufferd teribly all day and kept a wet cloth on my eye all night. I answerd Netts letters. Our Army is still moveing and there is more or less fighting all the time. There is strong talk of Rebel Cavalry in our vacinity but we have not seen them yet. We moved our things into the house formly Genl Bairds Quarters and have good comfortable quarters. Sergent Price of the 18th Regulars took supper with us. Some of my men are still anxious to move to Chattanooga but I am not in a hurry. It rained some this eveining. I have a severe head-ache and I am about Sick. The news is very good to night.

THURSDAY MAY 26TH

I procured a team and moved our Baggage to the Depot this morning but could not get a car as every thing is loaded either with prisoners or wounded men. We layed around the Depot all day and we quarterd in the house to night. The news is about the same and our army is Still driveing the enemy before them. . . .

FRIDAY MAY 27TH

We layed around the Depot untill after noon before we got a Car to load our Baggage into. But we fineally got all aboard. Some more wounded passed through and the 14th Michigan Infantry went through to the front from home. Our Army is still advanceing and the Rebels opposeing every foot of ground and many poor men are Sacrificed. Hundreds have passed through here wounded which Shows what is doeing at the front. We are expecting every day will bring the great Battle. But it seams we have force Sufficient to Surround them if they make a fight and we drive them by threatening their rear and would capture the principle part of their Army if they make a Stand. They know that and will not fight unless they are Sure of victory. It would be very foolish for them to risk a Battle. We did not get away and slept in the Depot house untill two Oclock a.m. when they concluded we could go.

SATURDAY MAY 28TH

[CHATTANOOGA, TENNESSEE]

We got to Chattanooga about day light this morning. We unloaded our car and moved to the ground occupied by the other detachments of our Division and pitched our Tents and stored the goods all in. We are near the Freight House and on a low level piece of ground. Some of our things we did not get over untill Evening. . . . There was some wounded men on [the] same train we come on but none of our Boys. . . . There was a great many wounded came in to day. News all right yet. There is detachments from every Brigade and Division and the plane is coverd with Tents containing Baggage and Stores that could not be moved with the army.

SUNDAY MAY 29TH

O H Mevis and I went down to the river and I found Uncle Will Miller who has been exchange[d] haveing ben in Camp Chase Ohio since he was captured and wounded at the Battle of Chickamauga. There is a number of other men with him. He came up to quarters with me and we walked out to O[r]chard Knob to the Soldiers Cemetry. They have laid out a nice Cemetry and has been cleaned[?] off by the Soldiers and the men killed in the Battles around here are to be removed to this place. There will be a monument erected to their memory and I think it a tribute that the Nation ows to i[t]s brave defenders who lost their lives in defense of their country. This is a beautiful place for it. It is a high elevation and round at the base and cone Shaped and there is roads layed out circeling round it. The forest trees[?] are left Standing and makes it look nice. There is a rumor that our forces have Atlanta but I dont believe it as they would nct have had time to get there without any opposition. . . .

MONDAY MAY 3[0]TH

. . . I remained about our Tents about all day and wrote to Nett or rather finished my letter of yesterday and mailed it. The news was rather meager but our men are keeping close to the Johnies. I heard a Rebel prisoner express the campaign to [me] by Saying that Genl Sherman was a very Sociable man as when they moved away from him in the morning he would move up and Sit down beside them in the evening. They say he is commanding boath Armies for when he moves he moves the Rebels also. That is all right. I only hope he will move them out of existance and wind up the war on this campaign. . . .

TUESDAY MAY 31ST

Mevis and Walbridge went to Ringold after noon and I had to sleep by myself. Some Wounded and Prisoners came in and a host of Refugees from Rome. They Say they cant live there as everything is distroyed and nothing to eat. They look as though they had seen hard times. They are a poor ignorant Set of people. The[y] belong to the poorer class and are glad to get away from there. Scme of them pretend to be loyal but I presume it is the presence of the Yankees makes them so. The news is good to day and the campaign has been a success so far without any reverses and surely is telling on the Rebels. This was a very warm day.

Wednesday June 1st

The word come around to day that our men had taken Atlanta with five thousand prisoners but that is to[o] good to be true I fear. I hope it may prove correct and that we will get orders to move Soon. Some more wounded came in from Dallas. Mevis did not come back from Ringold to day. I wrote to Nett but got no mail as it all goes through to the front. I will not get [it] untill I go up or some one comes in from there. I dont like that very well but will have to Submit as I dont know how long I may remain here and I will not write to them to Send it here.

Thursday June 2nd

. . . It rained very hard and the water backed up by the Fortifications caused me to move the Tents in the rain and Some of our Desks were almost afloat before we knew it and Some of the papers got wet and we are in a nice predicament. There was four Trains loaded with Sick and wounded came in but I could not see any [of] our Boys. The[y] were wounded near Dallas. Uncle Will came over to see me. Mevis come in after I had went to bed from Ringold. It is Still raining and was so wet we got up and raised our bed off the ground for fear we would float away.

Friday June 3rd

It is still raining. I went down and drew Rations from Post Quarter Master for our detail. We moved all our Tents up on the hill near where our old Head Quarters whe[n] we were here before. We had a Wet and Muddy time moveing and some of the Desks was very wet and I fear some of the papers are ruined. A number of wounded come in to day and the hospittals are getting full here and there is some Tents up now. It rained all night hard. Some of our Blankets are wringing Wet. There is all kinds of rumors from our Army but we cant learn any thing reliable. It is singular that among all the wounded I have seen I did not find any of my Regiment. There must certainly [be] some in town and I Shal visit the Hospittals and Search for them as Soon as I get our quarters arranged and I can get off. . . . I wish Genl Baird would send orders for me to go to the front.

SATURDAY JUNE 4TH

This is my twenty-fifth birth day. But wont put down the Rebellion. It still rains and the mud is getting deep. I visited the Barracks to see the Boys as they have not been sent to the front yet. They cant get transportation as every train is loaded with supplies and there is plenty of trains passing over the road. I did not see any wounded come in to day. . . .

SUNDAY JUNE 5TH

I wrote to Nett and went to the Barracks to see the Boys but they Started to the front this morning. It cleared away to-wards evening and perhaps we will have a chance to dry some of our Blankets and clotheing. I did not get any mail. There is no news that is reliable from the front.

MONDAY JUNE 6TH

I went to Post Quarter Master and drew a pair of Shoes and two pairs of Drawers. The Hospittal Train from the front was loaded with wounded Officers principally but there from the 20th Army Corps. It was clear and very hot but it rained all night. . . .

TUESDAY JUNE 7TH

It is cloudy and cool with some indications of clearing away. . . . It is a hot day. . . . The Hospittal Train going South and a Freight going North colided near Dalton but I did not get the cause or particulars. I did not get any mail. The Army has been lying still for a few days but will move to morrow.

WEDNESDAY JUNE 8TH

The Army started to move again this morning with Nine days Rations. They are near Kennesaw Mountain and that is another strong hold. . . . I intended to go on Lookout to day but the rain prevented. I wrote to Nett.

THURSDAY JUNE 9TH

It has the appearence of rain this morning. Bates my Old Bunk Mate came in from the front So I understand but I did not get to see him. He is on his way home as his term of enlistment has expired. He did not bring my mail. Our Army is not moveing now for some reason. But they have had a hard campaign and move but a few miles a day as the Rebels do their utmost to harras them and only retreat when they are compelled to. But gradually and surely they must get back and Atlanta must be ours in spite of them.

FRIDAY JUNE 10TH

They have a large Vegetable Garden here attended to by Convalescents and they raise vegetables for the Hospittals. I went out there to day for our detail and we got onions and Radishes and as it was a change we appreciated them. It rained very hard this afternoon. Bates come to my Tent and he says our Army will not move for a few days. I found J. V. Kenagy in the Medical Directors Office. He is the first man I have seen from my company Since they left Ringold. Bates stayed all night with me. It almost makes me homesick to See Bates going home. But I have nearly a year yet to serve if I am lucky enough to get home at all and I Sometimes wonder to myself if I will ever get back to "Gods country."

SATURDAY JUNE 11TH

. . . Bates bid me "goodbye" and Started for Nashville on the 8 40 pm train. It seams like parting from a brother to see him leave. He is a good "Boy" and has Served his time honorably and I sincerely hope he will reach home and friends Safe and have a good time. He has not been at home since he enlisted and seamed very happy to get away. . . .

SUNDAY JUNE 12TH

I went to Genl Steadmans Head Quarters to get my Ration Requisition approved and to the Post Office. . . . We did not get any startling news from the front to day.

MONDAY JUNE 13TH

I succeeded in getting my Requisition for Rations approved to day and drew Rations from Post Commissary and I went to a Barber shop and got my hair cut and Shaved. I did not get any mail nor write any letters. The news from the front not very interesting or exciteing as our Army is laying Still and takeing a rest.

TUESDAY JUNE 14TH

This is the fourth anniversary of my marrage and I would like to be at home to celebrate it but I am a long ways from there. Sergt Godard of the 18th Regulars and myself was going on Point Lookout but no Trains left for Stevenson and we did not go. The news came that the Rebel Genl Morgan was defeated in Kentucky and was getting out of the State. No news from the front of interest. I got no mail. This is a nice warm day and it almost makes me homesick. I was thinking if I was at home they would kill the "fatted Calf" in honor of the return of the Prodigal Son.

WEDNESDAY JUNE 15TH

. . . There is a rumor that my Division done some heavy fighting on Monday and lost heavy but I cant learn any particulars as to where or what the casualities are. There was a number of Rebel Prisoners brought in but the news is not very reliable from the front. The Army has not made any demonstration for severel days but are getting a good [and] ready and will move again Shortly. I dont know where our advance is now but some place in the neighborhood of Kennesaw Mountain or Marietta.

THURSDAY JUNE 16TH

It is nice and clear this morning. I received five letters by the kindness of the Post Master of first Division viz Netts of the 3rd & 5th Mollies of the 5th Lou Townsends of the 5th and one from Jim Spake of the 5th and I spent the day very pleasantly peruseing them and answering Lous & Mollies. I sent Lou a Book made from Laurel Root from Look Out mountain where Genl Hooker made him self immortal by his "Battle behing the clouds." Some of our wounded men came in but I did not get to see them to know whether any of my company was among them. I got the report that my Captain (Karns) was killed. . . . But it appears our Boys have been fighting and I am anxious to learn who has been hurt. The news is very meager.

FRIDAY JUNE 17TH

Sergt Gordon and myself stole a ride down to Whiteside to pass the day. We craweled into an empty car. We was run out onto the Bridge and stood there some time. It is nearly a hundred and fifty feet high and made me dizzy to look down into the valley. We got back about Sun down and Spent the day very pleasantly. The report confirmed that our Division was in the Battle on Tuesday but I could not learn any particulars. I seen some Pontoons on the Train going to the front. I dont know why it is we dont get more reliable news from the front unless it is suppressed and not allowed to be published.

SATURDAY JUNE 18TH

. . . There was severel hundred prisoners come in and some wounded. . . .

SUNDAY JUNE 19TH

It rained some this morning. I wrote to Nett. Kenagy and I visited the Field Hospital and found James Hurst of my company but none others. He is sick. There was a Train load of Rebel Prisoners Shipped north from the military prison to day as they was getting "to[o] thick to thrive." . . . There is so many Sick and wounded here it is almost impossible to find our Boys that are here. The only way to find them would be to go through the Hospital wards and see every man which would take a long time and then they are comeing in and going out so that it would be almost impossible to do so.

MONDAY JUNE 20TH

I had to go to Head Quarters with Ration Requisition this morning to get it approved. . . . I was in town all day. It rained some this evening. No news of importance from the front.

TUESDAY JUNE 21ST

I drew Rations for our Detachment this morning. Some of my men are sick and I sent them to the Hospittal. It rained some to day. The report is that Genl Grant has captured Petersburgh with four thousand Prisoners but it is only a rumor. I hope he will not get it untill we capture Atlanta as they might then send Troops here to assist Bragg and as it is they cant do so. I was at the Tent all day. No mail for me.

WEDNESDAY JUNE 22ND

We rigged a Trot Line to catch some fish to day. We thought it would help us pass the time and be some amusement for us. We are haveing rather a "Soft time" Compared with the Boys on campaign but I would prefer being there as here as there is more excitement and not so lonesome & menotonus.

THURSDAY JUNE 23RD

I went with one of my Boys about daylight to visit our Line in the River but our Float sunk and we did not get any fish but we re-set it. We took a "Swim." The report is that the Johnies are again retreating and crossing the Chattahoochie River and our Army pushing on South. Some heavy fighting to day but no particulars. No mail for me.

FRIDAY JUNE 24TH

This is a very hot day. I found Lieut Todd a[nd] James Cutter from Pioneers. Todd is recruiting and has been promoted to First Lieutenant of U S Engineers. They are from the front but dont know any more than we do about my company. I helped take up the Trot Line and we caught some fish. . . . News not very exciteing.

SATURDAY JUNE 25TH

I received a letter from Lide Bulger[36] of the 12th and Six from Nett dated May 17th & 25th and June 1st 9th 11th & 13th but did not write any as it took me nearly all day to read and digest them. Brown of the 17th Ohio and Meir of 2nd Minnisota came from Head Quarters in the front. They brought my mail. Lieut Sanderson mustering Officer of our Division is comeing in to muster some of the Boys whos time is out and they are to do the writing.

SUNDAY JUNE 26TH

I answerd Netts Letter received with the Photograph and Album. . . . This was a hot day and I did not get any mail. . . .

MONDAY JUNE 27TH

I met Sergt Geo Riley of the 101st and he told me Capt Studabaker and Lieut Barlow of that Regiment were wounded and that Barlow was brought here. I also learned that our Regiment lost Eighty men but no particulars. I think some times every Soldier makes his own news and tells it to see how it sounds for I can hear all kinds of reports and have concluded not to rely on any but what I know myself to be true. . . . It rained some this evening.

TUESDAY JUNE 28TH

. . . The Quarter Masters clerk came from the front for some Desks & Tents but did not bring any orders for me to move. But I hope I will get orders before many days to go to the front. No mail. It rained Some.

WEDNESDAY JUNE 29TH

The Third Division of the 15th Army Corps passed through to the front from Huntsville Allabama. They have been on Garrison duty there. I visited the Pioneers again to day. I dont hardly know what to do with myself some times I get so lonesome. . . .

THURSDAY JUNE 30TH

It is cloudy and looks some for rain. Jesse Davis of the 21st Indiana the man who nursed me while at Murfreesboro passed through suffering from a wound in the hand.[37] I told him I guessed I had better go and nurse him as one good turn deserved another. But I cant leave here now. The Clerk who came for the Desks left this morning and we are left to await orders. Lieut Saunders of Division Staff came in and orderd me to move over near the river east of Town where he will establish [h]is office to muster out the men of the Division whos time has expired.[38]

CHAPTER 8

On to Atlanta

Despite the bloodbath on Kennesaw Mountain, the Army of the Tennessee was able to move again around Johnston's left, and the Confederates evacuated Kennesaw Mountain and fell back to Smyrna. The Seventy-fifth was detached to garrison the nearby town of Marietta, undoubtedly a welcome relief from the grueling "trench warfare." There they were charged with preserving public and private property, preventing plundering and pillaging, arresting deserters and stragglers from both sides, seizing cotton belonging to the Confederacy, and assisting Union citizens trying to move north. Sadly, after a few days of "fine weather, comfortable camps in a beautiful town, plenty of rations, and no fighting," the regiment rejoined the army in time to face Johnston at his next defensive line.[1]

The Confederates attempted a stand on the north bank of the Chattahoochee River, the last natural obstacle before Atlanta and only a few miles from the city's outskirts. Nonetheless, they were again outflanked, this time by the Army of the Ohio, which crossed the river on Johnston's right, and were forced to withdraw to the south bank, then even closer to Atlanta behind Peachtree Creek. The Seventy-fifth followed, moving to Vining's Station, then across the Chattahoochee and the Peachtree, where the regiment halted and dug earthworks.

A change in the Confederate command signaled an end to all the retreating. John Bell Hood replaced Joseph Johnston on July 17, and Hood made plans to attack the Federals in force. (Ironically, William Bluffton Miller arrived at the front the same day, although still a part of Gen. Absalom Baird's staff.) A few days later, Hood sent part of his army north of the city to meet the Army of the Cumberland. The new commander hoped to catch the Federals after they crossed Peachtree Creek, with the water at their backs but before they could entrench. Unfortunately for the Rebels, their commands either got lost, were stopped by respectable Union earthworks, or were forced to retreat by superior numbers of the enemy. Although the fighting was fierce, it did not result in the decisive victory Hood longed for. The Seventy-fifth was not directly engaged in the action but did come under Confederate artillery fire, which disabled Lieutenant Colonel O'Brien. Maj. Cyrus McCole then assumed command of the regiment.

Hood was not finished with his assaults, however. He struck the Army of the Tennessee east of Atlanta on July 22. The largest battle of the campaign ended that night with the Federal army still intact. Casualties were heavy in the vicious fighting, with Federal losses of four thousand and fifty-five hundred Confederates killed, wounded, or captured. The Army of the Cumberland and the Hoosiers remained in their earthworks north of the city during the action, trading sharpshooters' bullets and artillery rounds with the enemy.

With Hood temporarily rebuffed but a direct assault on the strong defenses of Atlanta out of the question, Sherman sought to capture the two remaining railroad lines (the Atlanta–West Point and the Macon-Western) into the city. Sherman shifted the Army of the Tennessee from a position east of the city to the west, then south to cut the Macon and Western Railroad. This movement afforded Hood another opportunity to attack. As the Federals moved to Ezra Church, Hood struck the Army of the Tennessee on July 28, and after savage fighting he was again defeated. Nevertheless, his railroads, defenses, and hold on the city remained intact.

Sherman was undeterred. In early August, the Seventy-fifth and General Palmer's Fourteenth Corps moved to the extreme right of the Union forces and entrenched along Utoy Creek, southwest of Atlanta, moving ever closer to severing Hood's rail lines. On August 4, General Palmer ordered the Seventy-fifth's brigade to make a reconnaissance of the Confederate works in front of them, determine their strength, and capture them if possible.

The brigade entered an open field in front of the enemy, in a "most magnificent display," and came under fire. They advanced on the entrenchments, determined them too strong to carry, then retired, with the Hoosiers losing only one man wounded. The following day, the entire division attempted another reconnaissance. Coming again to the Rebels' main line, within "short musket range," the Federals began to entrench under artillery fire and held their ground under a "galling musketry fire."[2] The fighting was brutal, but when it ended, the main lines of the opposing sides were a mere four hundred yards apart. Mercifully, again casualties were light—only six wounded in the Seventy-fifth, two of which were mortal.

For practically the remainder of the month of August, the Hoosiers endured a routine but potentially deadly existence in their trenches. "We were too near the rebel intrenched battle line for good health or a peaceful mind," wrote a member of the 101st Indiana.[3] The stalemate and siege continued even as Union artillery batteries hurled thousands of rounds into Atlanta itself. The popping of musketry along the Hoosiers' line finally gave way to a truce agreed to by both sides, with no firing except in the case of an advance, and as a result Confederate deserters came into the Union lines. In front of the Seventy-fifth, a ravine filled with water served as an area for both sides to fraternize. For a few days, the Hoosiers aided potential Rebel deserters by leaving Federal coats and trousers at the watering hole for the Rebels to use when they accompanied water parties back into the Union lines. On one occasion, a member of the 101st Indiana brought back seventeen Confederate deserters.[4]

On August 27, Sherman set in motion his final moves to capture Atlanta. After a Union cavalry raid failed to disrupt Hood's railroads, Sherman ordered all three of his armies to swing westward around the city, hoping a concentration of nearly his entire force would be able to decisively capture the two remaining rail lines. The Army of the Cumberland was ordered to hit Red Oak station on the Atlanta and West Point Railroad, then head east for a few miles to the Macon and Western Railroad. The Seventy-fifth withdrew from their Utoy

Creek entrenchments under Confederate artillery fire, but suffered no casualties in the process, and moved to destroy the West Point line. By the evening of the thirty-first, the unit had also helped seize and destroy a part of the Macon Railroad, and built fortifications to hold it, thereby guaranteeing the fall of Atlanta.

Hood was not out of fight yet, however. As the Army of the Tennessee completed their arcing march and moved toward the Macon and Western at Jonesboro, the Confederates launched two army corps against the Federals, with little success. The Rebels then switched to a defensive posture in order to meet the expected Federal counterattack. On the afternoon of September 1, the Seventy-fifth's brigade and the rest of the Army of the Cumberland moved toward Jonesboro to aid their comrades, and the Hoosiers arrived just in time to support a grand bayonet charge by part of the Army of the Cumberland against the Rebel positions. The late afternoon attack drove the Confederates from the field. The Seventy-fifth's brigade lost only one man killed and seven wounded. "Although not engaged with the enemy in the grand and successful assault," explained brigade commander Col. Newell Gleason, "my command kept well closed up in support under a heavy fire of artillery, and did all as a supporting column that was required. Officers and enlisted men all behaved splendidly."[5] After the battle, men from the 101st Indiana and others looked at the awful carnage of the battlefield. "The vision that was so deeply impressed upon our minds as we gazed upon the fallen . . . will never be erased as long as we have our reason," Levi P. Fodrea wrote.[6] Hood's army evacuated Atlanta that evening, and the Confederates beaten at Jonesboro joined him in a retreat that ended at Lovejoy's Station, south of Atlanta.[7]

A few days after Hood's evacuation, the Hoosiers entered their prize, the city of Atlanta, which had demanded so many lives and so much effort. During the difficult campaign, the regiment could point to the fact that their loss of life had been slight—a mere thirty-two casualties. Gen. George Thomas congratulated his army on their "tenacity of purpose, unmurmuring endurance, cheerful obedience, brilliant heroism, and all those high qualities which you have displayed to an eminent degree."

Although it had not taken part in any grand battles during the campaign, the drive for Atlanta was certainly the most severe test the regiment endured during the war. Frequent small, fierce fights and the miserable existence in the entrenchments had taken their toll. "During the night we slept on our arms and built our fortifications and during the day we fought behind our works and lived in our gopher holes," summarized one Hoosier veteran.[8] Although the regiment had started the campaign with 431 men, by September 2, just 321 soldiers remained in the ranks.[9]

Friday July 1st

I drew Rations and got some Teams and moved according to Lieut Sanders Orders and got a collored family to cook for us. They are very glad to do our cooking for the extra rations as they have no other way of procureing any thing to eat and the Rations issued to them is Short. I draw for the entire detail yet but some of my men are away Sick and that gives us more than we can use. . . . We are camped on the Bank of the River on a high Bluff and have a Splendid view up the river and it is a beautiful place.

Saturday July 2nd

I went down town early this morning and visited Lieut Barlow. He is wounded by a piece of Shell in the Shin Bone and it is a terible wound and very painful and he is very much discouraged and I fear will loose his leg if not his life. I would not be surprised if it kills him. He appeard to be very glad to see me and I advised him not to loose courage or it might be bad for him. I talked with him quite a while and he made me promise to come again. But "red tape" has it arranged so that no visitors are not allowed in any of the Hospittals without a pass from the Medical Director and he will only give a certain number each day. I suppose they were bothered some by visitors but it seams outrageous that they should issue such orders and debar the wounded and sick from seeing their friends. . . . Brown and I went to see Bishops Minstrels this evening. The[y] are performing in a Tent and dont amount to much only to gobble up Soldiers money. It rained hard as we were comeing to camp.

SUNDAY JULY 3RD

Meir and Mevis are musterd out and expected to Start for home to day but did not get off. This is a nice day. I See the Colored Soldiers are pulling a large Seige gun up Cammeron Hill to the fort preparatory for to morrow to celebrate the Independence day. I answerd Netts letter and was at the Depot when the Hospital Train run in and watched to see if there was any of our Boys but did not see one I knew. No news from the front of importance.

MONDAY JULY 4TH

The old gun on Cammeron Hill belched fourth at daylight and proclaimed that the Indipendence day of America had again rolled around and to remind us soldiers of the cause for which we are battleing. The severel Forts here responded and there was quite a cannonadeing. It dont seam so dangerouse where they are fireing for fun as during an engagement but still it is no music for me. Some of the officers who have their wives here had a Picnic on Lookout but there was nothing unusual occured with me and I dident celebrate very much. There is a rumor that Atlanta is captured also Petersburgh but I dont believe either. . . . Well this day passed rather on the dull style with me but I presume better than with the Boys who are standing between me and danger. The[y] no doubt are seeing rough times.

TUESDAY JULY 5TH

Meir and Mevis took another Start and succeeded in getting on the Train and are now on their way rejoiceing. I was down in town this p.m. News from the front good but the reported capture of Petersburgh is not confirmed. . . . I was lonesom after Meir and Mevis Started and I thought what a good time awaited them at home. I dont wish them deficiency in their pleasures but would like to enjoy Such a time myself. I am very tired of staying here and I wish our forces would get to some other point where they could use me and let me go to the front.

WEDNESDAY JULY 6TH

I see the name of Samuel Buckmaster of my company announced as haveing died here in Hospittal yesterday of Fever. Poor Boy I left you a Short time ago in the prime of manhood and always lively and the last man I would have expected to die here. But the[re] again reminds me that we dont know at what moment death may come. . . . Reported that Merietta is now in the hands of the Yankees and if so it will include Kennesaw mountain. I seen about five hundred Prisoners right from the front. They look hard and dirty as though the Rebels was on their last legs. Some of them say the war is nearly over and give it up while others claim they will Succed yet. They are poorly clad and look like they were half Starved and they are all coverd with red clay as they are kept in the Rifle pits all the time. . . .

THURSDAY JULY 7TH

Some of the Mustering Officers was on a drunk and got very boisterous but they can do so and are not molested but let a private do so and he will be put in the Guard house as soon as a guard can get to him. . . .

FRIDAY JULY 8TH

Nice morning. Another lot of prisoners was brought in and lodged in the Prison Pen. Our Army is on the Chattahoochie and the Rebels have left Marietta and our forces are but a few miles from Atlanta but those few miles may be the worst part of it. The Johnies will no doubt make some effort to hold the city. I think there will yet be some hard fighting around Atlanta and I may have to remain here untill She surrenders. . . .

SATURDAY JULY 9TH

I was told to day that my Regiment was on duty at the town of Marietta. A number of prisoners was brought in. The Army is still moveing but very Slow and they are gradually driveing the Rebels from one position to another and the doomed city is being approached and the Rebs are doeing all they can to resist but they will have to abandon the city of Atlanta as sure as fate. It may be some time yet but it will come. And it will be just so with the return of peace. Their Confederacy must crumble and fall and the[y] must submit to the "powers that be" and return to their allegiance to the Federal Government and the laws. They may keep up the fight a while after the fall of Atlanta for our army will have to stop for reorganization and resting up as this has been a hard campaign on men.

SUNDAY JULY 10TH

. . . There was about five hundred more prisoners brought in. This was a very hot day. I remained in my Tent nearly all day. There was a dispatch come from Corps Head Quarters Saying they were South of the Chattahoochie River. So there is no doubt of that and conforms the evacuation of Marietta and Kennesaw mountain where the fighting [was] the last few days and now the maneuvering for Atlanta will soon commence and if we meet with no reverse it will not be long untill that will also Succumb to the mighty Army Sent against it and then the next question will be where will they make another Stand. We will then be so as to opporate in conjunction with almost either of our other Armies. We will then be in the heart of the Confederacy.

MONDAY JULY 11TH

Major Steele of the 101st Indiana and Adjutant Medsker of my Regiment were here on their way to Bridgeport for Reigimental Baggage. They Say our men are in good Spirits and doeing a "big job." They spoke of the campaign as unprecidented during the war. That it has been allmost a continuous fight ever since they left Ringold and the Rebels have opposed our Army in every way. But they also Say they are very much discouraged and deserters come into our lines by hundreds.[10] Their ranks are depleted and they are on Short Rations and See very hard times while our men seam to Stand it very well and are elated with the success of the Campaign.

TUESDAY JULY 12TH

. . . There was no important news from Genl Sherman to day and not even any "Grape vines" of a Startling character which is very remarkable as we can generally hear any kind of news. But perhaps the Army is laying. There was no prisoners brought in nor any wounded. Takeing it all together this was not a very Stiring day. But we must not hurry it to[o] much but make it Sure is much the best plan.

WEDNESDAY JULY 13TH

Brown and I went to Ringold on buisiness for Lieutenant Sanderson and Stayed all night with Cisson who we found still Tellegraph Opperator.[11] The place looks natural yet only Cisson says it is comparetively dead since the army moved. There is no Soldiers here now only a small Garrison force to protect the Rail Road.

THURSDAY JULY 14TH

We returned to Chattanooga to day and I received Netts letters of June 14th 15th & 26th Mollies of the 14th and one from Uncle Saml Miller of the 27th which gave me pleasent employment to read them. How much pleasure it is to receive a kind letter after waiting so long for it. That is the great reason why I dont like to be here I cant get my mail regular. There is nothing that gives a Soldier more pleasure than to write and receive letters. If I could not read and write I dont know how I would feel for it gives me a medium by which I can converse with friends although we are Separated many miles and a few days brings the word from them and then how eagerly it is perused to find out whether they are Sick or well and if sick how impatient I get before another letter comes and how glad and thankful I feel when the word comes they are well again.

FRIDAY JULY 15TH

I answerd Uncle Samuels letter and about noon Capt Moulton arrived from the front and orderd me to be ready to go to the front.[12] . . . I am glad of it for I am heartily Sick of Chattanooga and want to get away.

SATURDAY JULY 16TH

I am still under orders to move and I hope they will not be contremanded before we get Started. We took the train at 2 35 p.m. from Chattanooga passed Ringold about four and arrived at Kingston in the early part of the night. I did not get any mail. We remained at Kingston all night as it is not safe to run after night. The country is rough and rocky and the soil very poor and mostly Red clay and the timber small and Scrubby and we passed a great many lines of breast works and lines of defense and it being warm we rode on "Car Deck" and had a good opportunity to See the country. We passed a large train loaded with Refugees or citizens going north to where they can live untill the war is over. They are a poor ignorant Set.

Sunday July 17th

Our train pulled out of Kingston about daylight and run very slow. We passed the celebrated Kennesaw Mountain before we arrived at Marietta. The country is mountainous and rocky and dont look like it was worth contending for. We arrived at Marietta at 11 Oclock a.m. This is a handsom Town. It is a summer resort for the Aristocracy and the mountains and fine Springs in the neighborhood makes it very healthy. Marietta is quite a city. The Streets are wide and nicely Shaded and some very fine Buildings. The Hotels are large and commodius and the southern Nabobs come here to spend the hot weather during the summer. I took a Strole around the town and we left here with wagon Train as this is as far as the cars run now. We went about six miles and camped with Head Quarter Provost Guard. I heard some heavy cannonadeing which reminded me that I am getting in the neighborhood of the Johnies again. There was quite a Battle fought yesterday near here and Wm Brown of my company was killed and Phill Stiffy wounded. Col OBrien of my Regiment was also wounded.

Monday July 18th
[Near Atlanta, Georgia]

We started about nine Oclock a.m. and crossed the river where the Battle was fought last night. There was some marks of the fight but the dead was all buried and wounded Sent to the rear. I found my Regiment South of the river only a Short distance and I was glad to see the Boys but I miss severel familiar faces. There is some Cannonadeing this evening but not fighting. I found Head Quarters about three miles South of the river about sun Set. I dont miss any body from Head Quarters yet. The officers are all here yet. There may be some of the orderlies missing but I have not seen them yet. We are severel miles from Atlanta yet.

Tuesday July 19th

Our Troops moved early and we were left in camp untill about noon. There was considerable musketry all day. Our Division went to the front and crossed Peach Tree Creek and as our Boys was throwing up a line of Breast Works Battery "F" 4th Ohio Artillery or "Leather Breeches" Battery[13] as the Boys call it came up to our lines and Shotted their guns and went out on "Double quick" or on the gallop and took a position in our front on an elevation and opend up on the Johnies and they returned the fire and a terific Artillery fight was kept up untill dark put a Stop to it. The Battery Sufferd considerably. One gun was knocked of[f] the Carriage and a number of horses and men killed. We could not see the Johnies but their Shot and Shell done some harm to us. My company had one man killed and one wounded and Severel in the Regiment was hurt. I never heard Shell make such a noise. It almost made my hair stand on end. We are said to be only four miles from Atlanta.

WEDNESDAY JULY 20TH

Genl Baird and Staff mounted and went to the front about daylight. The Rebels charged Genl Hooker the p.m. and were repulsed with heavy loss after a fight of three hours. I was on a hill where I could see a part of the Battle and our Boys Stood their ground manfully and punnished the Rebels Severely. The[y] made severel charges and was repulsed with great Slaughter. The musketry was terific. Head Quarters moved only about a mile to the creek and I returned there about dusk. I had no buisiness in front but I wanted to see what was going on and there was nothing for me to do at Head Quarters So I went to the front. It keeps me in hot water all the time when laying in the rear and listen[ing] [to] the fireing when I cant see what is going on and expecting every moment the Rebels will pounce on me. But if up where I can See and hear I know what to depend on.

THURSDAY JULY 21ST

Head Quarters did not move to day but our lines advanced and encounterd the enemy and had some heavy fighting to hold their position but they repulsed the Johnies and Fortified to night. We had one man killed and one wounded Slightly in my company. The cannonadeing was terific and some Sharp Musketry. There was fighting all along our front to the right and left. My opinion is that the next few days will be warm ones for us. The Johnies Seam determined to keep us back and they meet us at every Step and we are getting so close to the city that we will soon be able to throw shot into it. I wonder what can be the feelings of the inhabitants when they hear the Boom of cannon and know that it is a warning of the impending doom of their city and know that they are powerless to prevent it.

FRIDAY JULY 22ND

The Rebels have left our front this morning and our Division advanced. We moved about two miles and settled down within easy range of the Rebel works. We had some fighting for position but now "hold the Fort." We passed the Fortifications where the Rebs was posted last evening and gave the Ohio Battery and us such a terible Shelling. It is a "four Square["] "Bull Pen" our Boys call it and is large enough for about four Regiments of Infantry and they must [have] had severel pieces of Artillery in there. But our Batteries done terible execution as the timber and Fortifications Show. To look at it and see the marks of Shot and Shell I dont see how any person could live in there during the Bombardment but the killed and wounded have all been removed. The fighting to our left was very hard all day. It is the 15th and 17th Corps to our left and they have had a terible Battle. The Rebel Genl Hood took command of their Army yesterday and they say now we will get all the fighting we want. He has made a good Start sure. They pushed out a heavy Skirmishline in our front before dark and we thought they were comeing for us and we opend up on them and the fireing was quite Sharp for an hour when they withdrew to their old position. They threw Severel Shell[s] over us but done us no injury. Report that Genl McPherson was killed and I hope it will prove untrue for we cant spare such men as him now when the best ability is required.[14]

SATURDAY JULY 23RD

The Rebs are still in our front and Shelled us at intervals all day and some times I thought it would result in a Battle but they seamed content with Shelling us. A piece of Shell Struck near Capt Moulton of Division Staff. The Rebs come out of their works and formed two lines of Battle and advanced towards us and we thought they were going to try the same game on us they did on our left yesterday but we opend up on them and they retired behind their works. Perhaps they thought we were asleep and wanted to wake us up but we were ready and would have enjoyed the fun for them to Storm our line of works. I was along our front and thought I was going to see the fun. But they all disappeared and it is all quiet now. The death of Genl McPherson is confirmed and it casts a gloom over the entire Army. He was an officer like[d] by his men as yesterdays Battle will tell by the dead and wounded who fell with him. The fight was near Stone Mountain and Some of the time our men was between two fires but the Rebels lost heavy. The men say they made severel charges and was repulsed with great Slaughter. . . .

Sunday July 24th

I wrote to Nett this morning early so as to be ready for any case of emergency that might arise during the day. The distant Cannonadeing sounded like it might be in the rear of Atlanta but I dont think our men got so far yet. The Rebels came out once to day as though they were going to charge our works and we lay in terible suspense for them to come. It was nearly dark and we supposed we would have a Battle at night. They threw forward their Skirmishers and there was some heavy Skirmishing but only lasted a Short time. They retired behind their works and quiet prevailed. Our men Sleep in the Trenches with one Eye open as the saying is as it requires the greatest vigilance as we dont know what moment they may pounce on us and if they should surprise us and break our lines it might prove very disastrious and cause us to do all our work over if there would be enough of us left to tell the story. We are in a precarious situation and the least mistake would cause blood to flow like water. But implicit confidence in our commanding officers and the vetrans composeing the Army works wonders and we Shall succeed. I visited our Boys in the Trenches and went out to the Rifle Pits after dark and was in a "Stones Throw" of the Rebel line and could hear them in common Conversation.

Monday July 25th

The Rebel position is still unchanged in our fron[t] and the Skirmishing was kept up all day only when an Armistice was agreed upon by the Pickets then they crawl out of the Rifle Pits and converse together about the war. There is all kinds of rumors afloat about the Rebels attacking us but they cant spare the men they would lose in a move of that kind. They threw Severel large Shell[s] over but done us no harm. There was heavy fireing on our left this p.m[.] At the commencement of the war the Skirmishing that we do every day would be called Battles but we have become so accustomed to it we would hardly know what to be at if we was not shooting at some thing all the time. But what tells the most on the men is the continual excitement and being deprived of the needed rest at night. When we lay down we dont know what moment the order may come to fall in and perhaps put in the night in the Trenches. The best men we have physically are worn out.

Tuesday July 26th

I done my washing this morning and it has been very quiet along the lines to day. The Rebels have a Seige gun mounted in our front that throws a Sixty four pound Shell (Camp Kettles the Boys call them) and about every fifteen minutes they send one over.[15] It is about one mile to the gun and it is amuseing to be at the Trenches and See our men. The works will be strung full of men Sitting on top of them when we will see the smoke raise and then they will Jump off behind the works untill the Shell passes over and then they will climb up again untill another Shot is fired and so it goes all day. Their aim is bad and they cut their Fuze to[o] long and the Shells mostly pass over us. We count when we first see the Smok and it requires about ten Seconds for the Shell to reach us. . . . It rained Some to night. The Johnies seam disposed to let us rest.

Wednesday July 27th

Our lines advanced Some this morning and we had some heavy Skirmishing. The Army of the Tennisee moved passed us to the right which indicates going around the city in that direction. They were moveing all day and Some fighting for position. I think the music will commence again Shortly now as Hood seams to be spoiling for a fight and we will give it to him if we can draw him out of his Fortifications and when we threaten his rear he will have to come [out] or we will cut his "Cracker Line." We have cut one Rail Road now and the moves to day is for the others and I apprehend he will try to drive is back. But I cant tell when or where he will Strike first. But my guess is there is warm times brueing for us.

THURSDAY JULY 28TH

The 15th 16th and 17th Army Corps on our right advanced this morning and Hood hurled a heavy force against them and there was a terible Battle. The Rebels made charge after charge and was Severel Battallions deep but our Boys Stood their ground manfully and the Slaughter was terible. My Division moved to the right to support them but did not become engaged very heavy. The loss was heavy on boath Sides but the Rebels lost three to our one as we fought on the defensive. They were perfectly frantic and their men that was captured acted like they were drunk and some of them said whiskey was issued to them befor the Battle. There was quite an Artillery duel in our front and the Johnies send over severel twelve pound Solid Shot into our quarters and after I returned from the right where I went with our Staff I was takeing the Bridle off my horse when a Shot came crashing through the timber and I concluded it was comeing near me and I dropped down on the ground and it passed over me so close I felt the Sucction of the air. My falling and the Ball Strikeing almost similtaneously caused our Wagon Master (Strickner) to exclaim there Miller is hit and the men came rushing to me and I got up and John says "Miller are you hurt.["] I replied no but I was teribly Scared. The Artillery fireing was kept up untill dark when as the saying "there is always a calm after a Storm["] it Settled and become quiet and we rested well. . . .

FRIDAY JULY 29TH

It is remarkably quiet to day but I guess the drubbing they received yesterday has satisfied them. Our forces did not move but burried the dead. The Johnies sent a Camp Kettle over to our quarters at the usual intervals to day and that kept us awake. There was a little Skirmishing on our right but no fighting. I did not get any mail and there is to[o] much excitement for me to write any letters.

SATURDAY JULY 30TH

There was severel men wounded in 23rd Missouri by one of those large Shells. Jim Whetsil and I rode over and visited the Battlefield of the 28th. It was an awful Sight. Some places the dead Rebels lay almost in heaps. It is some hilly and one place our men occupied a hill and in their front was a deep gully or Ravine and about three or four hundred yards across it there was another hill. The Rebels run up a Battery and then their Infantry charged through the Ravine and up the hill to drive our men from their Breast Works. There is quite a growth of Small timber in the Ravine and it was all Shot off. Some Saplings Six inches in diameter are Shot off with Bullets and the ground is Strewen with the dead. Our men are engaged in burying the dead. It Seams their object was to turn our flanks and get an infaladeing fire on us but they found it an impossibility. Genl Logan advanced his lines while we was there and we watched the skirmishers.[16] The[y] had some Sharp fighting for a Short time but the Johnies soon gave away. We returned to find it comparatively quiet in our front. Our Small Cannon cannot reach the old Seige gun from here but they better take it away. We can go to the rear of our lines on a hill and see the spires and Smoke Stacks in Atlanta. We have a Battery there and they throw Shell into the city. They are building a Furnace to heat Shot to throw and they will set fire where they strike. Our Artillerymen aim at a large Smoke Stack in town supposed to be near the Depot. . . .

SUNDAY JULY 31ST

A very heavy rain passed around to the north and cooled off the air. I wrote to Nett. The Johnies sent over a few camp Kettles to see us but done us no damage. They cant get the range and their Shells mostly pass over us. Occasionally the[y] burst pretty close to us. There was no fighting to day.

MONDAY AUG 1ST

There was some very heavy Cannonadeing this afternoon and severel of our men was wounded in the Trenches. One Shell killed two mules and wounded two horses in the 7th Indiana Battery Capt Hannon.[17] There was a number of large Shell[s] came over. . . .

TUESDAY AUG 2ND

. . . The 23rd Army Corps moved by us to the right and took position without any fighting. The Rebel Genl Hood dont seam to be so keen for a fight as he was. He made a good start and a few more such Battles and he will have to recruit his ranks or he wont have any Army to command. Report says since he took command he has lost in killed wounded and prisoners about thirty five thousand men. I know he has lost heavy and the[y] have accomplished nothing but looseing ground all the time. Some talk of us moveing to morrow to the right. I see the move is to go around Atlanta on the west side.

Wednesday Aug 3rd

We received orders to move this morning and the 20th Corps relieved us from the Trenches. We moved South west about five miles and took a position on our extreme right after driveing the Johnies from it. We had heavy Skirmishing and I thought some times there would be a general engagement but the Rebels gave way and we are now fortifying our position. The Head Quarter Train was correlled near Genl Scofields Head Quarters and we did not camp untill after night and it was raining very hard. The Cavalry started on a Raid and the news from them is very Statisfactory. We are near one of the Rail Roads and it is reported to be torn up. We are camped on a hill and our Battery in front keeps up a fusilade and the Johnies reply and they send them in here pretty close. As the 10th Indiana was passing here there was a Shell lit in their ranks and killed and wounded severel men and one Mule. It was within a few steps of Head Quarters and Severel other shot and Shell come So close that there must be some mistake about our orders to camp here. I think we are out side of our lines to the right but we will remain here untill orderd out. The country is generally hilly. Soil Sandy. Timber mostly Pine. Water good and Wholesome. . . .

Thursday Aug 4th

The Johnies opend up on Head Quarters about day light and as I thought last night we had camped out side the lines and we thought once we would have to abandon our Tents but we Struck Tents under a heavy fire and moved to the rear Somewhat demoralized. There was severel of our Boys hurt but they missed me. But we moved every thing away and Genl Baird complimented us by saying "He was not afraid of the Johnies captureing his Head Quarters as long as we had charge of it.["] But three of our Boys paid the penalty of carelessness with their lives. We moved back about a mile and remained the rest of the day and night. I dont know how it came about but presume the Adjutant did not understand the order where to establish Head Quarters. I met John Morehead of the 130th Indiana. There was heavy fireing this pm and our men advanced and made them pull out the Guns that gave us such a shelling this morning.

FRIDAY AUG 5TH

We mounted early this morning and went out to the front and our Division charged the Rebel Rifle Pits and so completely surprised them that we captured a hundred and Seventy five of them and reversed the Pits and held them all day. The Skirmishers is very close now to the Rebel Fortifications. Things are getting very interesting on this part of the line. It seams to be the policy now to push a Division at a time to the right and gradually Surround the city and beseige it or compel its evacuation. Some of the prisoners we captured are very saucy. Our loss was about fifty killed & wounded. My Regiment lost some men. Cos E & G & K done the chargeing. One place we found a Reb Captain and Eleven men and they Said they would surrender and when our men approached the Pit one of them shot a Boy of Co G wounding him badly but the Rebel was Shot dead in an instant and it was hard work to keep our boys from killing every Reb in the "Pit." The Captain refused to Surrender to Sergt McMahan of Co G because he was below him in rank but he was pursuaded to give up his Sword when told if he did not immediately get out of his belt some of us would Shoot him out. It was no time to parley about rank with a Rebel and he concluded that discretion was the better part of valor and gave up his sword and was sent to the rear. While our Boys was at the Rebel Rifle Pits they kept up a heavy fire from their main line and that is where we lost so many men. Head Quarters came up this evening and located near where we were when we had to move in such a hurry yesterday morning. They send a Shell over here occasionally now but our lines are some distance out now and they cant see us but when the shot comes over the works we get it here. We did not go on Skirmish Line mounted this a.m and I have concluded it would rather go that way during a fight.

SATURDAY AUG 6TH

. . . The Rebels Shelled us more or less all day but their range was bad and did not do us much damage only causeing us to dodge occasionally.

There is really more scare than any thing els about artillery. The Artillery all along the lines kept up a Booming all day. There was some fighting on our right caused by Troops changeing their lines and takeing new positions. The Rebels are holding on like "grim death" and it seams as though this is about their last ditch that they blow so much about.[18] I cant imagine where they will go to from here. But we are gradually going around them and when we once Stop if only for a Short time we fortify and in one nights time they could not take any of our positions by Storm and their losses in the recent Battles has certainly weakend them considerable.

Sunday Aug 7th

I went back to supply train to get my horse Shod and as I passed a position of one of our Batteries they were Sheling the Johnies and fired a gun as I was passing close to it and it seamed to hurt my horses head for he did not recover from the effects for some time. I got back just in time to See Genl Johnstons Division charge the Rebel Pits in their front.[19] It was a gallant charge and our Boys drove the Rebels out and some parts of our line captured the main line of works but could not hold them. The fight was terific and along the works almost hand to hand. The Johnies Stood their ground manfully but our Boys held their Rifle pits and some of they lay up on the Rebel works and the Johnies dare not Show themselves. Our loss was heavy. A great many prisoners was brought in and sent to the rear. I tried to write a letter home this evening after the Battle but I found it a poor time to write after passing through such a Battle and dont know at what minute they may undertake to capture our Boys so close to them or drive us back and then the same awfull scenes will be enacted over again. We are so close to them we dare not expose ourselves in the least. We remained in that position untill after dark when we withdrew to our old position.

Monday Aug 8th

As it was comparatively quiet I finished my letter to Nett while in the Trenches. We like to write to our friends for we dont know what moment a Bullet may reach the vital Spot in our bodies and then our last is written. It is awfull to think of and I dont think I am brave and often wonder how it ever come that I have not run away from such a

Battle as yesterday or how I ever escaped without a scratch. Perhaps I got my dose at Chicamauga.[20] . . . There was about the usual amount of Cannonadeing to day but no move on our part and consequently no fighting. It rained hard nearly all day. . . .

TUESDAY AUG 9TH

Two years ago to day I left home for the war and when I look back and think over the hardships and exposeure with the Battles and marches I have passed through it seams more like a dream than a reallity. The thousands of men I have Seen lying on the Battlefield dead and dieing with the wounded and maimed for life it makes me think a kind providence has taken extra care of me.[21] When I look back two long weary years to the morning I left my native town and many friends and relatives I think the many escapes I have had is an assurance that I Shall return to them again and I will be proud to tell my Story of what I have seen and the part I have taken in this great war. I dont think any body can blame a Soldier for wanting to fight his battles over or claim all the honor due him. Money would be no incentive to me to ever enlist. The government never made money enough to ever hire me to pass even one such a Battle as the 7th inst which is nothing to a Chickamauga. But pure love of country free and indipendent untramelled by a Second confederacy divided against its self will induce men to leave their homes and endure what money could never do. I have seen many times when I did not expect to ever be permitted to enjoy it again but if I fall I would only be a "drop in the bucket" in comparison to what has gone before for the same glorious cause. . . .

WEDNESDAY AUG 10TH

Still raining and we did not change position and there was no fighting. . . . I commenced messing with the mounted orderlies. Report in camp that Genl Stonemans raiding party has been captured after doeing them considerable damage but I hope it will prove to be only a rumor. But if they have captured them they cant capture the force that is gradually crawling around them and their city like a serpent and they must move out.[22]

THURSDAY AUG 11TH

There is a report that Mobile is in the possession of the Yankees and if so that is another feather on the back of the now overloaded confederacy. They talk now so much about "dieing in the last ditch" and I think perhaps they will dig the ditch before long. They are discouraged as their deserters testify. They come over by dozens and some days by hundreds. There is a Spring in our front and our Boys go there to trade for Tobacco and the Rebs come there too. They persuade our Boys to exchange clotheing so they can come over without being fired on by their men. It is singular but true that often the pickets cease fireing and sit out on the "Gopher Holes" and talk back and fourth. And get water from the same spring and then return to their commands and Shoot each other. The Officers of the pickets come along and order the men on either Side to "keep up the fireing" but neither Side will violate the truce without first notifying the other. If the Rebels get the order they will sing out "*Lay down Yank for we have orders to fire*" and if we get orders we Say "*hunt your hole Johnie*" and then the show goes on. Many funny little incidents occur such as Shooting Ram Rods out of the guns &c and all kinds of Jests and Slang phrases are hurled at each other from the Pickets. But when the Battle begins all Jesting ends and we realize it in its worst feature. No mail today.

FRIDAY AUG 12TH

. . . There was some talk of moveing Head Quarters nearer the front. The pickets have not done much Shooting to day and I did not hear any important news. This was a nice day and we did not get any mail. There was a lot of deserters came over and was sent to the rear. They look hard and seame to be glad to get out of the scrape. They say the war is virtually over.

SATURDAY AUG 13TH

. . . I learned to day that Major Connolley had tenderd his resignation. All I can Say if my approval is only required he may go home. We could Spare some more such officers and then they can get their rations of whiskey more regular. Forty two deserters came into our lines and it is reported about three hundred came over at once and that the Rebs gave

them a parting Salute by opening up their Artillery on them. I cant
vouch for the truth of it but I do know that their men are deserting by
hundreds. . . .

SUNDAY AUG 14TH

. . . It was remarkably quiet along the Trenches. I started to find where
my Regiment is and rode along the lines some distance but did not find
them. I have not seen any of the Boys for severel days. There was no
deserters came in to our lines to day. . . . We did not move as anticipated. It rained some and was very warm.

MONDAY AUG 15TH

. . . I seen severel deserters to day. They Say we have Captured the city
of Mobile and also confirm the capture of Genl Stoneman in command
of our Cavalry and they gobbled his entire force. That is not very good
news. They also cla[i]m Longstreet has come from the Army of Virginia
with thirty thousand reinforcements and say we will have some warm
times. I begin to think they would soon need help or there wont be
Johnies enough here to fight any thing soon. But I dont believe they
have many to spare from there or they may loose their capital. They
have about all they can attend to every where. . . .

TUESDAY AUG 16TH

I answerd Jim Spakes letter. Twenty two deserters came over during the
night and were brought here this morning. I found my Regiment this
evening and visited the Boys in the Trences and found those who are
left well. The ranks have become very much depleted on this campaign.
I was tenderd the Orderly Seargeant promotion if I would go back to
the company and I concluded if I could stand it to march I would rather
be with the Boys. Then I would not get into all the Skirmishing of the
Divivision. Since I came up and followed the Staff I have been under
fire nearly every day and mounted at that the most of the time. I have
a nice position and I have a horse to ride but I am tired of it. The Rail
Road it cut near Dalton and no Trains came through to day but it will
soon be repaired and in running order again.

Wednesday Aug 17th

I answerd Netts letter of the 6th. I was to go to the Regiment again to night to report my acceptance of the Orderly Sergeant but I did not get my work done in time and did not go. The break in the Rail Road not repaired yet and no trains came through. Col Walker of the first Brigade reported to Genl Baird that indications in front pointed to an attack on our lines.[23] That the Rebels was prepareing for a move of Some kind and he thought an advance. The necissary precautions was taken and the men instructed to be vigilant and preparations made to give them a warm reception. But the day passed without any demonstration of that kind. There was some fireing but no heavy fighting to day. There is only a few deserters who came in and they confirm the reports of reinforcements from the east and they may give us a warming up some of these days. But we have a splendid line of defense and if they want it let them come and take it.

Thursday Aug 18th

Some talk of moveing this morning and that the Rebels have left our front. The cannonadeing Sounds as though it was nearly directly South of us and a long distance off. But the day passed without a move on our part and the Johnies seam to be plenty yet. I went over to the Regiment and Capt Karns being officer of the Picket I went with him out on the skirmis Line to See some Johnies come in as some was reported to be comeing but they failed to come. While we were sitting in a Rifle Pit the Johnies commenced moveing around and it was so dark we could not see what they were doeing and we waited untill we heard the command "Forward guide center Double quick" and I did not wait for the command march but Skipped out for our works. They came on and drove in our Skirmishers and by the time I reached the works they were a blaze of fire. They did not try to storm the works but held our Rifle Pits untill a line of battle was thrown out and drove them out. The fight lasted about an hour but only a few men hurt. There was heavy cannonadeing to our right and a report that the Rebels charged our men four times and was repulsed with heavy loss but it is only a rumor. There was only five deserters came in to day. I returned to Head Quarters at ten Oclock and had a dark ride of it.

FRIDAY AUG 19TH

Revelie Sounded at four Oclock this morning for a move and two Brigades went to the right but Head Quarters was orderd to pack up and be ready to move at any moment. But our men returned this evening to their old quarters and I did not even learn where the[y] was or what object they had in view. One thing I do know some of the S[t]aff Officers came back terible drunk. Some of them did not get into quarters untill very late at night. This was my cooking day for the mess. . . . It rained some and was very warm.

SATURDAY AUG 20TH

Two years ago to day I was musterd into the United States Service at Indianapolis. I received Netts Letters of 9th and 12th Mollies of the 7th and one from Joe Spake of the 9th. I did not answer any of them as the Division went to support Genl Killpatricks Cavalry in a movement but did not get into any trouble. We returned this evening. It rained very hard and we was completely soaked when we returned.

SUNDAY AUG 21ST

I answerd Netts letters. I visited the Regiment this evening. It rained very hard. Reported that our men cut the Rail Road and our Cracker Line was severed again and we did not get any mail. Some cannonadeing in our front and about the usual amount of Shooting. I talked to Levi Keagle about the Orderly Sergeant and he advised me to accept it although it is a leap over him. . . .

MONDAY AUG 22ND

Six Rebel deserters came in and claim that Killpatrick is gobbled up and that their Rail Road is not cut. But I dont believe it. . . .

TUESDAY AUG 23RD

Some heavy cannonadeing this morning. I only Seen one deserter to day. News from our Raiders is good and they were not captured. . . . Genl Killpatrick returned from his raid in the rear of Atlanta this evening and reports haveing acomplished all he went for having cut boath the Rail Roads running to the city and Stird up the Rebs generally. . . . It is all quiet now in front. No news of importance.

WEDNESDAY AUG 24TH

I learned the name of the creek here to be Eutoy. I made out the Monthly Reports which was a Small job this time. . . . There is talk of us stopping here untill we are pa.d off. But I dont believe Genl Sherman will stop now for any thing untill we have captured Atlanta. I dont think it would be policy as every day we give the Rebels the stronger they will make their defences and they are strong enough now.

THURSDAY AUG 25TH

There is a move of Some kind on hands for Genl Shermans Head Quarters moved to the right. The 20th Corps on our left fell back to the River. Genl Thomas passed us about noon going to the left which indicate some kind of a move Soon. Whe[re] our Troops fell back is the mistery. Reported that the Rebel general Forest had captured Memphis and Three Brigades of our Cavalry but not confirmed. It rained some to day. There is not much Shooting in our front. . . .

FRIDAY AUG 26TH

Seven Rebel deserters came in from a Kentucky Brigade in our front. They Say Killpatricks Raid was a complete success. . . . We struck Tents about three Oclock pm and parked the Train about 10 Oclock but did not unhitch the teams. The night is very dark and I remained with the Genl and Staff. We muffled the Artillery Wheels and the Troops moved very quietly to the rear of the works to a road and the Rebels began to Shell our works and yelled like Indians. Their Shells caused considerable uneasiness as we was afraid they would charge and take our old line of fortifications and fineally our men run some cannon back to the works and opend up on the Johnies and they concluded our previous silence was a ruse. They quieted down and then we moved on. We were marching nearly all night and the roads were very bad and we moved Slow. We only moved about four miles. The Rebels discoverd our evacuation some time during the night and began to move supposeing we was retreating and followed us up. The entire Army seams to be moveing. We passed Genl Sherman during the night in the Saddle. I did not Sleep any at all. From the direction we are moveing we are going around Atlanta as near as I can guess in a terible dark night. I got with Head Quarter Train during the night correlled but the mules hitched to the wagons and drivers mounted. We followed a Bye-Road and through the woods all night.

Saturday Aug 27th

Genl Baird and Staff was in the Saddle all night and come to us after daylight and fed their horses and got something to eat and orderd us to move out as the Rebels was pursueing and would Shell us. We moved about three miles and Stopped for dinner. We are following what the citizens call the Sand Town Road. We did not move after noon but we could see the Rebels moveing to the right to try to counteract our move. I followed Genl Baird and was with the Troops. The Rebels threw some shell into our Division and hurt severel men but none in my Regiment. There has been heavy Skirmishing the most of the day and we were expecting a fight but the race seams to be who can make some important point first but what point is the question.

Sunday Aug 28th

We were on the Alert at four oclock this morning. The Orders was for one wagon and Two Ambulances to follow the General and Staff and the rest of the wagons to follow Capt Seelys train and I was orderd to remain with the Train.[24] The orders indicate a Battle and I dont care to remain here. We moved about five miles and stopped for dinner and after noon only about one mile and stopped untill nearly dark and then mo[v]ed about seven miles and camped near the track of the Atlanta and Mongomery Rail Road about Eleven oclock at night. There was some Skirmishing but no battle. We have possession of one of the Two principle lines of Supplies and I think the move now is to sever the other and compell them to evacuate. This is a grand move and Hood has been beaten badly maneuvering as the result will Show hereafter.

Monday Aug 29th

The 9th Michigan is destroying the Rail Road by tearing up the Track pileing of the Ties and laying the Iron across and heating them which heats them hot enough so they twist them around Trees and Tellegraph Polls. Some of our orderlies went a Short distance from the Train and were fired into by Bushwhackers. The mounted Escort lost four horses and one man wounded. Some of the Boys even run away from their hats.

One Brigade of Infantry and Some Cavalry was sent out and captured four Rebels. That Shows that it is not very safe to leave the command as they are all around us. The prisoners say they cant understand what Sherman is driveing at and they thought we had got scared and was retreating when we cut loose but here we are away South of Atlanta instead of going North we are going South. But they will learn all about it when they have to evacuate the city and it will be to[o] late. We are Said to be only seven miles from the Macon Rail Road. We did not move to day. No mail came to us.

Tuesday Aug 30th

We pulled out about Six Oclock this morning but our moveing was impeded by trains ahead of us. I started about daylight to find Genl Bairds Head Quarters but rode severel Milles and did not find it. The troops are moveing and continuous Skirmishing along the lines. . . . I seen a number of prisoners. I returned to the Train after noon and they moved slow and did no[t] correll untill 12 Oclock at night. The country is generally level and the Soil Sandy and we have plenty of good water. I was very tired and Sore from being in the Saddle so continuously for the last three days and nights. The Johnies are in a terible fix and are moveing and maneuvering to keep us back but their cake is dough. I think about one Battle more and Atlanta will be ours and that will be near the other Rail Road and that before many days.

Wednesday Aug 31st

The first gun (Cannon) was fired about Seven Oclock this morning. I rode out to the front and our men Struck the Rail Road and the Second Brigade (mine) proceeded to build a Fort or a square Bull pen as the men call it on the track. The Army of the Tennisee had some fighting but we took possession of rail road with very little fighting. We are a few miles from Jonesboro and the Rebels are there in force under Rebel Genl Hardee and we are now between him and Hood and they must drive us out or Hood must evacuate Atlanta and they will either fight or run tomorrow as Ammunition was issued to the men to night and every thing indicates a move on their line of works in the morning and right here the thing will be decided. I returned to the Train to night with orders for them to camp and they did so about ten Oclock at night.

The first Division of our Corps went to the rear to guard our train in case of a Battle to morrow. Genl Baird and Staff did not come to Train but remained with the troops. I Shall return to the front in the morning to see the fight if there is any. The Rebels are fortified about a mile this side of town and have a Strong position but they will have to move out to morrow for we want it.

THURSDAY SEPT 1ST

The Battle commenced about daylight on our right and our Boys drove the Johnies before them untill noon. Then Genl Rousaus men the Regular Brigade charged along the Rail Road and drove them back to their main line which is on a ridge in the woods and for nearly a mile in their front there is an open field and decends gradually to the East to another strip of Timber. The Regulars re-formed in this timber with our Division to support them. We discoverd that here the day was to be decided. When the Bugle sounded the charge the Regulars Started on the Double quick across the field. The Rebels reserved their fire for short range and when our men got within about two or three hundred yards of their line they fired a volley and our line layed down but many of them never to rise again. The Bugle sounded the charge again but the Regulars refused to go. Genl Baird and others tried to get the men to go but they would not even get up. In the mean time the Rebels reinforced the works at this point. Finding they could not pursuad the Regulars to charge the third Brigade of our Division was formed in front line and the Ballance of the Division Supporting and the Bugle sounded the charge and we went in on Double quick with fixed Bayonetts.[25] They awaited our charge as they did before and we had passed the Regulars line before they opend up on us and when they did our Boys melted like Snow under a Summer sun. But they let us get to[o] close and when the second charge was sounded our Boys Started for their works and their fire being expended we was on to them before they could reload and our Boys Scalled their Redoubts and then came our chance and then a Slaughter commenced the like of which I never witnessed before and I pray I may never see again. A great many of the Rebels threw away their Arms and proposed to surrender but the next instant they were Shot down or received a Bayonett and the Bugle sounded to "cease fireing" three times before our boys gave any quarter.

Just about the time we passed the Regulars in the charge Genl Bairds horse (Old Barney) was Shot and the Genl dismounted and let him go and mounted an orderlies horse and only a few minutes after that horse received a Shot in the head an[d] fell dead under him. When I seen the Genl on the ground I supposed he was killed but he mounted again and remained with us during the rest of the fight cheering his men by his voice and presence. Many acts of heroism was displayed on the field by officers and men and none deserves more praise than Genl Baird in leading the charge in person. Capt McClurg and Capt Atchison of Staff was wounded Severely and some of the other officers Slightly.[26] The escort lost Eleven men in killed and wounded. The troops lost severely and some of our best officers bit the dust. Among the[m] Col Choat of the 38th Ohio a gallant officer was mortally wounded. The 14th Ohio lost all of her line officers but three. But we hold the Rebel works with twelve pieces of Artillery and Eight hundred prisoners out of Pat Clayborns Division.[27] We have met this Division Severel times before in Battle and here we wind up its career as we killed and wounded the greater part of it. The third Brigade lost about five hundred men. My Brigade lost some but not so heavy. But the prisoners was marched out in the field under guard and they was very saucy and called the guard all kinds of hard names and they tollerated it as long as possible and finely "forbearance ceased to be a virtue" and they pitched into the Johnies and but for genl Baird there would have been none of them left. Genl Baird rode up to the Rebel Brigadier Genl and Said to him to "mount that Stump and tell his men unless they conducted them selves as prisoners Should he would not be responsible for their lives.["] Mr Rebel done as requested and told his men they were now prisoners of war and captured by Vetran Soldiers and they would be treated right if they kept their tongues and if not they must suffer the consequences.[28] We had no more trouble with them. If the Regulars hade done as the volunteers did and drove ahead after receiveing the volley we would [have] Saved half of our men but I find it dont do to depend on them. I rode over the field after the fight and our Boys lay thick and along the line of works the dead Johnies tell the tale. The 17th N.Y Zouaves lost heavy as the number lying on the field Shows.[29] They are composed of Irish mostly and they stripped to the Skin as I seen severel dead without any Shirts on. They done good work. Well I had a very good opportunity to see the

Battle but I dont like this thing of being mounted in a fight as it makes us to[o] conspicuous. I have not seen any of my company and dont know who is hurt. I helped prepare places for some of our wounded Escort and Orderlies and when the Hospittal comes up they will be removed to it. I returned to our train this evening with orders to move to Jonesboro. The prisoners was all marched there as the town is ours. We camped about dark in the Town. The wounded was taken to a house and to morrow the dead will be burried. The citizens say Hardee has gone to Pine mountain about Sixty miles from here. We will probably pursue him a part of the way. But he is teribly crippled and cant make a Stand. The fighting to our right was not so heavy and losses light. This has been a terible day and as I Sit by the fire to write my Diary I miss severel familliar faces who are among the Dead and wounded. Some are lying Still on the Battlefield. I wonder some times how any of us are here to tell the story when I think of the terific storm of Shot & Shell we encounterd from the Rebel lines. There was a heavy cannonadeing in the direction of Atlanta where Hood is with all the Malitia and some think they are blowing up the works and from the reports I think so myself as some of them almost Shake the Earth. It is to[o] heavy for cannonadeing.

FRIDAY SEPT 2ND

We moved the Train into Jonesboro where we had the Battle of yesterday. I was over the Battlefield but could see nothing but dead Rebels as our men have all been burried. I did not see any of my company but learned that Beardsley was wounded on the hand. The word came in that Hood Evacuated Atlanta after Blowing up the works and distroying all the ordinance Stores as he had no way to remove them as we have possession of the last Rail Road leading from the city. The Rebels are still on the retreat and our forces are lying around the town. The 14th Army Corps was relieved from the front and sent to guard the wagon Train. Our men tore up the Rail Road and town generally. There was some fighting in front to day but I did not learn the particulars or what command it is but presume it is only Skirmishing with the rear guard of Hardee. We remaind in Town all day and I got a good rest as I was orderd to remain with [the] Train. The Genl and Staff are in the front and did not come in to night. We are about thirty miles from Atlanta.

Saturday Sept 3rd

I rode down in town to look at it. I find it considerably damaged from Shot and Shell. It was once a pretty little place. But a few of the inhabitants remain and they was not here during the Battle. The evacuation of Atlanta was confirmend and a wagon Train was sent there for supplies. The Heavy Ordinance along the Fortifications fell into our hands as they had no way to remove it. Genl Baird Sent for one of the Teams but I got no orders. I rode out over the Battlefield this pm and found "Old Barny" (Genl Bairds horse). He run about a quarter of a mile from where he was shot. The Ball Struck him in the Breast and ranged back and lay in his flank under the Skin and I cut it out and removed the Saddle and holsters and brought them in. They were all right not haveing been molested. I could hardly help shedding tears over the faithfull old horse as he was a favorite at Head Quarters. He was a "bright bay" and a fine animal. But he will not even receive a burial for all the service he has done. Severel wagon loads of wounded was brought to town to day from yesterdays fighting. It rained very hard. . . . There is talk that we will return to Atlanta in a few days.

Sunday Sept 4th

I done my washing. A large Wagon Train started for Atlanta and Coppage our Division Post Master [is] going home as his time is out. We was orderd up to Head Quarters and I had the pleasure of presenting Genl Baird with his Saddle and Holsters. He thanked me very kindly and was very much surprised to get them. He asked me Severel questions about Old Barney. The Army of the Tennessee returned from Pine Bluff and passed through town after night going toward Atlanta. I went and hunted up my Regiment and found Capt Karns very Sick. I also visited the 101st. I found the boys all right. It rained very hard to night.

Monday Sept 5th

. . . I moved quarters. The 15th 16th and 17th Army Corps fell back towards Atlanta. Our men burned about three hundred Bales of Cotton in the street to day and made other arrangements to return to Atlanta as we have orders to move in the morning. There was some fireing along the front.

TUESDAY SEPT 6TH

I got up at three Oclock this morning as I had to get Breakfast for our mess. We were packed up ready to move by day light but did not move untill nearly noon and haulted about three pm for dinner. The Rebel Cavalry hung on our flanks and there was some Sharp Skirmishing and our Cavalry captured about fifty of them in our front. It rained very hard this afternoon.

WEDNESDAY SEPT 7TH

Our Brigade coverd the rear to day but the Johnies kept at a respectable distance and the Skirmishing was light. We moved about ten miles and passed a little station called Rough and Ready. Genl Sherman and Thomas with their escorts passed us on the march. . . . This day makes four months Since our Army left Ringold on the Atlanta Campaign. . . . The report is John Morgan the Gurilla was killed and his command defeated.[30] I received two papers from home. I rode over to the camps of the 75th and 101st Indiana to see the Boys and found them feeling good over the result of the campaign. We have torn up the Rail Road from Jonesboro so the Johnies cant use it.

THURSDAY SEPT 8TH

We arrived at Atlanta after marching Six miles. We camped in a field South of the city about two miles. Some of the Staff and orderlies went to Town. The Rebel Works are the best I ever seen and it would be impossible to have taken them by storm.[31] We received President Lincolns and Genl Grants congratulatory orders and they were read to the Troops. We went into regular camp and made preparations to Stay for the preasent. I got no mail as the Rail Road is cut and no trains came through. . . . Every thing is quiet along the lines.

FRIDAY SEPT 9TH

. . . We could get no word from the north. An application to relieve me from duty to return to my company as Orderly Sergeant from Major McCole came to Head Quarters to day but I did not get orders to report there myself. . . . The country here is rolling and the soil Sandy and it all Shows the effects of the terible Battles that have occurred around the city.

Saturday Sept 10th

. . . Report that the Rebel Genl Wheeler has fortified a position on our Rail Road near Tullahoma Tennissee and that is cause of our mail not comeing through but I dont believe the report. I was over to the Regiment this evening. They built a Bower in front of Head Quarters and every thing looks like remaining here a while. There is not even any talk [of] moveing closer to town.

Sunday Sept 11th

I procured a pass for Levi Keagle and myself to the city and we visited some of the Fortifications and also the place where the Ordinance Stores was destroyed. It appears they were loaded on the Cars ready to move off but when we severd the Rail Road the only chance for them was to destroy them or they would fall into our hands. The Cars was burned and There is a little of almost every kind of Iron in the heap and there must have been severel Hundred Car loads. The Magazines was all blown up and some of the buildings is badly damaged from our Shellings. I noticed Solid Shot Sticking around in the houses. Atlanta is quite a city and there is some very fine buildings. The city is full of citizens especially women as there is a great many who do not live here. When we evacuated our works north of the city Hood supposed we was retreating and issued his proclamation that the Yankees was retreating and asking the citizens to come to the city to celebrate the occasion by bringing in all the good things available to eat and the consequence is the women came in by hundreds on the Rail Roads and when we cut them they could not get out and we are haveing an Armistice for ten days and passing them out by wagons. It is quite a joke on them that the Yankees come to their grand Pic-nic and their friends had to move out. Some of them are very Saucy and indipendent and it hurts their feelings to be hauled out in a wagon with a Yankee driver. Now that Atlanta is ours a recapitulation of the campaign with the final results would be proper. Our Army started on the 7th day of May and four months we have been under fire nearly every day and never out of hearing of Skirmishing and the following pitched Battles was fought viz. Dalton Rasaca Burnt Hickory Altoona Kennesaw Mountain Stone Mountain and the battle on July 28th and Jonesboro. The grand move on 26th of August resulting in the capture of Atlanta terminateing with the Battle of Jonesboro on Sept 1st was certainly a great achievement. It was hazzardous as we severd all communication and moved into the heart of the confederacy and risked it all. If we had met with a reverse we had no place to get supplies from. We abandoned our Breast works and the Rebels took possession of them and there certainly is great credit due our Generals for the way they have conducted the campaign. It was hard on the men and our ranks are greatly depleted but we find Rebel Field Hospittals scatterd all around here filled with their Sick and wounded which tells how much they sufferd. We have another advantage and that is we can recruit our ranks while they have nearly all their men now in the field. From this position we can opporate in conjunction with our other Armies and they will be abstructed in all their moves. I think the city of Atlanta to day is of vast more importance than the city of Richmond is to either party. . . .

MONDAY SEPT 12TH

I was relieved from duty at Head Quarters and returned to my company and enterd on my duty as Orderly Sergeant and was surprised to find my promotion dates from July 1st. . . . I went to messing with the Capt & Lieut. This was a very warm day. . . . I had to return to Head Quarters this evening to see the Boys as I have some good friends among them. I was there about nine months and it will soon be a year since I was wounded.

TUESDAY SEPT 13TH

. . . We have a splendid camp and plenty of good water with full Rations and a few days rest will make is ready for another lick at the *Corn thieveracy*. They are getting sick of their contract and some think we will get home. But they are gritty and may hold out some time yet. There is not so many deserters comeing in now as their chances to get away are not so good as when we lay right by them all the time. I expect they are as well satisfied as if we were after them again. They dont molest us now and we are haveing easy times again. But I dont know how long it may last. A few days or weeks is all the rest required to reorganize and recruit up the Army.

WEDNESDAY SEPT 14TH

There is talk that all the Indiana Soldiers will be Sent home to vote as we cant vote in the field. I dont think we Should be disfranchised be cause we are Soldiers but Some of our Democratic friends in the North think we Should as they know we would not vote their ticket. We received orders to prepare for inspection at five Oclock p.m. The Army in the East must be resting too as we get no news from them and we are not stiring up the Johnies and it seams rather dull and monotinous after such a campaign just over. . . . This was a nice day.

THURSDAY SEPT 15TH

. . . I remained in camp all day as there is considerable writing to do. No news of importance from any part of our Army. Some appeerence of rain and the weather is cool and blustery.

FRIDAY SEPT 16TH

Henry Wagner and myself started out to hunt some lumber and was down in the edge of the city. Our Company Baggage and Books came up to day. I answerd Uncle Saml Millers letter but no Mail came through as the Rail Road is cut again by the Rebels. It seams almost impossible to keep them off our Cracker line. It is done by their Cavalry Scouts.

SATURDAY SEPT 17TH

It looks very much like rain this morning. The mail came from Chattanooga. I was working all day adjusting Company Books and clotheing accounts. It rained all night. No news.

SUNDAY SEPT 18TH

This was a rainy day. Orders for company inspection at 11 Oclock. . . . It kept raining about all day. . . .

MONDAY SEPT 19TH

We got our quarters fixed up in good Shape and have quite a house to live in now. We was working on the company accounts this afternoon. . . . One year ago to day I was wounded.

TUESDAY SEPT 20TH

There is quite a Sensation in camp caused by the report that Valandingham was killed by a Soldier. I think if it is so the Soldier should be placed on the retired list and a good pension given him during life. I dont think half as much of Such men as I do of a Rebel in our front. A man who will utter the treason and live in a northern state the he has Should be tried by a court marshall and if found guilty be hung. The Regiment will go on Picket to morrow morning at Six Oclock. It rained all night.

WEDNESDAY SEPT 21ST

The Regiment went on picket but as I have no gun and so much writing to do I was excused. It rained very hard all day. . . . The Armistice between Genl Sherman and Hood expired by limitation at daylight this a.m and was celebrated by a cavalry fight and I suppose from this time on we will have warm times again.

THURSDAY SEPT 22ND

There is a rumor of a Cavalry fight near Sand Town yesterday but no particulars. There is still talk of us "Hoosiers" going home to vote. I was working all day on monthly Returns for June & July. . . . I am nearly sick this evening.

FRIDAY SEPT 23RD

The talk to day about going home is very Strong and all kinds of rumors are afloat but nothing certain. I think we should have a chance to say who shall be our rulers as well as those who Stay at home but it seams our Democratic Legislature thinks because we are fighting their friends we should not be allowed to vote. There is also a "Grape Vine" going that Genl Sheridan defeated the Rebels under Early in the Shannandoah Valley with heavy loss. It looks to me as though the Rebellion is about on its last legs as they have sufferd defeat after defeat this last year. They have not even Sustained any move they have made and they certainly See their country is being devastated and their cause hopeless.

Saturday Sept 24th

An Official dispatch was read to the Troops to day confirming the defeat of Early in the Shannandoah Valley which was received with cheers and made us all feel to rejoice and I hear the cheering all around us.[32] I finished my monthly Returns up to August 31st. We had Inspection twice to day to prepare for General Inspection to morrow. Our Rail Road is cut again and we got no mail. I did not write any letters. It rained nearly all day and it turned cold and very disagreeable this evening.

Sunday Sept 25th

. . . The report is the Johnies captured the mail Train at Big Shanty to day and tore up the Rail Road again. The General Inspection was postponed untill to morrow.

Monday Sept 26th

We was inspected by Major Connolly and Capt Moulton and Genl Baird was in camp. I finished my Returns and wrote a letter of advice and mailed them to Washington City. . . . I visited the 101st Indiana and found them with orders to march tomorrow but we have no orders yet. They may be only going on a Scout.

Tuesday Sept 27th

There is a report to day that Richmond was evacuated but I dont believe it. I would rejoice as much as any body if it proves to be so. But I fear it is to[o] good to be true. The 101st Ind Started out for forage but returned to camp as the Johnies was to[o] plenty and they was orderd back. . . .

Wednesday Sept 28th

Our Wagon Train brought in Some of our Boys who have been prisoners and was exchanged. Some of them was Starved nearly to death. To look at the poor naked and Starveing men it makes my blood boil. Any Set of men who will deliberately Starve prisoners guilty of no crime but fighting for freedom when they have no way to protect themselves it seams to me there is no punnishment severe enough on earth to do them Justice and if there is a Purgatory hereafter that is the place for them. The Prisoners tell some horable Stories of their cruel treatment. Their appearance confirms their Stories. . . .

Thursday Sept 29th

There is a rumor that the Rebel Genl Forest captured Huntesville Allabama but not reliable. . . . All quiet as far as heard from.

CHAPTER 9

Chasing Hood

After resting in Atlanta for the rest of September, the Hoosiers faced a new threat from John Bell Hood's still-lethal Army of Tennessee. The Confederates moved north of Atlanta, intending to destroy Sherman's lines of supply and communication and draw the Union armies away from the city. In early October, the Seventy-fifth set off in pursuit of Hood, moving back through the towns of Acworth, Cartersville, Kingston, Rome, and Resaca. The regiment ended up in Gaylesville, Alabama, near the Georgia border, but there gave up the pursuit.

In late October, the Indiana men returned to Rome, Georgia, then on to Kingston, where an informal presidential vote was taken, as the regiment was not allowed to leave the front and vote back in Indiana. The result confirmed the men's faith in the Republican Party and its leader, for nearly all the votes cast were for Lincoln and Andrew Johnson. The Hoosiers marched back to Atlanta, destroying part of the Western and Atlantic Railroad on their way, severing their communications with the North for the next major campaign.

FRIDAY SEPT 30TH

Some of our Troops are moveing north or to the rear to day and it is rumored that the Johnies are playing the Same game on us that we did on them viz getting in our rear.[1] One report is they are in heavy force between Nashville and Chattanooga and the rumor that Richmond was evacuated was confirmed and I dont see but an object in that and that would be to gobble us by cutting us off by moveing west from there but I guess Genl Grant will look after Lee. But they must be getting desperate and will make their last kick soon and if they make that it will be the death sure. They might cut off our supplies for a while but we would soon get out. I believe they will make a move of that kind. I made out my monthly Return and vouchers for September with Invoices. . . .

SATURDAY OCT 1ST

We was reviewed at 2 Oclock pm by Genl Baird and was detailed for Picket to morrow. I wrote to Nett but our mail failed to get through as it seams the Johnies are getting pretty thick north of us. There is a move of some kind on hand by them but what it is time will only tell.

SUNDAY OCT 2ND

We relieved the picket line this morning and we did not have a very nice day as it rained about all day and night and word came to us that we would move to morrow but which direction is the question. There are all kinds of rumors in camp. Some claim Hood has started north and that we are going to follow him. I hope he has for it will make our Rail Road Shorter and I dont see how he can subsist his Army and he will get a terible drubbing and wish he was back before he gets very far. We did not see any Rebels on Picket and nothing of importance occurred.

MONDAY OCT 3RD

We was not relieved from Picket untill about Eleven Oclock this a.m. on account of marching orders and when we returned to camp we found every thing torn up and ready to leave here. We did not get started untill three Oclock p.m and marched very hard untill about ten Oclock and then only haulted in the road without orders to camp. But our Wagon Train kept us back. We had marched about ten miles. It rained very hard nearly all night. I spread my "Poncho" on the ground and layed down and pulled it around me and Slept some but it nearly drownded me and when I got up I was laying in a hole in the sand and what I did not occupy was filled up with water. I was terible tired and lame by not being used to marching. Hood is ahead of us and pushing north as fast as possible. But our men are all laughing at the idea of this move and anxious to come up to him and compelling him to fight for when that occurs there wont be many of the Johnies left to tell the tale. They will be pressed so hard they cant fortify and we will have an equal chance with them.

TUESDAY OCT 4TH

We started about daylight leaveing Merietta to our right and after march-ing about seven miles halted for dinner. There has been Skirmishing nearly all day in our front. We expected to remain all night but about five Oclock p.m. we pulled out again marching about five miles and camped for the night. The Skirmishing was quite brisk this evening and perhaps Hood will give us a drubbing to morrow if we dont let him alone. But we will "tickle his rear" while he is going to the Ohio river as that is where he Says he is going before he stops. Perhaps he will cross into Indiana and that will let us home to vote. He knows we want to go home and he is going as an escort. It is still raining. There was a report come back that Genl Jeff C Davis and escort had been fired into but no body hurt. Our Camp to night is Sixteen miles from Marietta.

WEDNESDAY OCT 5TH
[MARIETTA, GEORGIA]

We left camp about Nine Oclock a.m. and marched towards Marietta and halted for dinner about three p.m. It was dark when we reached Marietta and we was orderd on to Pine Mountain but the orders was countramanded and we camped near Kennesaw Mountain. The Rebels tore up considerable Rail Road but we pushed them so hard they have about all they can do to keep out of our way. There was some Sharp Skirmishing to day but mostly with the Cavalry. Reported that we cap-tured Eight hundred Rebels near Big Shanty. The Rebs are steering for Ackworth and tearing up the Rail Road as they go.

THURSDAY OCT 6TH

We got out in a heavy rain about four Oclock am and have orders to march at daylight. We started as soon as we could see the road and it rained continually untill after noon and the roads are terible and the country so mountainous that we only moved about five miles and camped along an old line of Breast Works built by the Rebels on the campaign South. We keep up to them and harras them and pick up their Straglers and the prisoners say their Army is in poor condition to Stand the march-ing and dont know where they are going to. If they should get a position they cant hold it on account of haveing no way to procure supplies.

FRIDAY OCT 7TH

We got orders to move early and went to lost mountain to reconoiter. We had some Skirmishing but no fighting. We had a splendid view from the mountain. We could see Kennesaw Pine and Black Hickory Mountains. We formed a line of Battle and drove the Johnies away. Threw out Pickets and got our dinners and then started to return to our old camp. I presume this move was a feeler and the design was to ascertain what the Rebel force was there. Some times we anticipate a Battle on going into camp but the next morning the Johnies Skip out and our generals let them go and then we follow them up and settle down beside them at night. Our Boys Swear about it but I presume Genl Sherman knows what he is doeing and I leave it all to him. I think he wants Hood to get as far North as possible before he attacks him and then he will annihilate the entire Rebel Army. I apprehend that he will command a much smaller force when he returns than he has now. We arrived at our old camp about dark very tired.

SATURDAY OCT 8TH
[ACKWORTH, GEORGIA]

We lay in camp all day untill about five Oclock pm when we struck Tents and started towards Ackworth. We did not see any Rebels and camped about Eight Oclock about three miles from that renowned city. I was sick all day but marched with the company. It was a hard tramp for me. It was cold and windy all day and very disagreeable. No news. I learned of the Battle of Altoona Pass to day which was fought on the fifth. It took nearly the entire Rebel Army to capture the little garrison and they lost very heavy. But our gallant little band had to surrender to superior numbers after doeing good work and they are now prisoners of war in the hands of the Rebels.

SUNDAY OCT 9TH

. . . Genl Shermans congratulatory order to the garrison at Altoona was read to us. The Rebel loss was about Six hundred and the Garrison was not captured as reported but repulsed the Rebels and Genl Sherman Signaled them that he was comeing to their relief and they refused to surrender and the Johnies had no time to spare and moved on and left them. The Rebels burned up some supplies with the Freight house at

Altoona and tore up the Rail Road but furnished their own music to the tune of Six hundred dead Rebels. . . .

MONDAY OCT 10TH

We lay in camp all day and untill five Oclock this evening and marched all night and crossed the Ettewa River. We passed Altoona and the Battlefield of the fifth but could not see many of the marks as it was about midnight but I noticed some dead horses lying around. My Boots is about worn out and my feet is very Sore but I kept up with the Regiment. The Rebels are reported going towards Rome haveing left the Rail Road. They have demoralized the Road bad and it will take a long time to repair it. But if they will only keep on going north we Shant want it any more. It seams like a curious move in our Generals in letting Hood get so far north when we could compell him to fight any time and I know we have force enough to defeat him. But we lay still about every other day and let him paddle on and then march as far in one day or night as he does in two and run onto him and then let him move off again. But I think there is an object in view which time will tell. . . .

TUESDAY OCT 11TH
[KINGSTON, GEORGIA]

We halted for Breakfast about daylight and I got a very Short Sleep and then we started for Kingston and camped after dark after marching twelve miles to day. This is Election day for State officers in Ohio and the Ohio Troops voted but we have no say but I trust it will be all right and our Nation is to[o] wise to vote against the principles we are fighting for and I do pray Abraham Lincoln will be re-elected and that he will continue the war untill every Rebel North or South will r[e]cognize the supremacy of the government or annihilate the whole of them. The war cannot last another year and now to elect a Democrat is virtually saying we are wrong. But we Soldiers have faith that our friends at home will not refuse to endorse us by their votes. The result of the Election will have its effects. If Lincoln is elected we know what his policy has been and he will continue and if McClellan is elected we also know his record as a general in our Army and I really believe he would recognize the Rebel Government and they think so too. They so express themselves and "hurrah" for McClellan as loud as the Northern Democrats. The mail Train come through and that Shows the Rail Road is clear. The Rebels are reported near Rome. We passed through Kingston and camped near town on the Rome Road.

WEDNESDAY OCT 12TH

I received three Letters from Nett before we Started but we was on the march early and going towards Rome. We passed over a very hilly and mountainous country untill nearly dark when we Struck the main road about Eight miles from Rome. We camped about nine Oclock at a Steam Grist Mill three miles from town. The Rebels demanded the surrender of the Garrison but the reply was "If you want us come and take us" and they concluded they could get along without Rome and passed on. We found some wheat and corn in the mill and as our rations was Short we ground it and appropriated [it] to our use. We had wheat Straw for beds and rested splendidly. It rained and was very hard marching and my company only Stached fifteen guns on going into camp. The weather is cool and a good nights rest will be a great benefit to us.

THURSDAY OCT 13TH

We lay in camp all day again untill nearly dark and the[n] drew three days rations and about Nine Oclock to night Started back towards Calhoun and went into camp after marching about Eight miles. The Rebels are reported on our Rail Road line near Dalton. We passed some nice farms and plantations. The country is rolling and not mountainous. The Soil some Sandy and it is the best country we have seen lately. I think the main part of the Rebel Army has left the direct north course and are going towards Stephenson and Nashville. They will probably cut the Road again and cross the Cumberland Mountains along that line.

FRIDAY OCT 14TH
[RESACA, GEORGIA]

We started early and marched very Steady passed Calhoun this afternoon and then Struck north and camped for the night near Rasaca. We had a hard camp. I drew Shoes for the company from supply train. Some of us was nearly barefooted and my feet is very Sore from tramping over the Rocky roads. We passed one place where the Rebels have torn up the Rail Road. There is a report that the[y] captured Dalton which was garrisoned by Collored Troops. I dont believe it for Genl Sherman is watching them and will not sacrifice any Garrisons when he can avoid it. We are getting nearly back to where we Started from in May.

SATURDAY OCT 15TH

We left Rasaca early and took a north west direction and there was some heavy Skirmishing on our left but did not last long. We traveled very Slow untill afternoon and we Struck of[f] lively and struck the mountains about dark and commenced to climb them and had no road and some places it was very Steep. But we kept going untill about Nine oclock when we haulted but was not allowed to build any fires or [?] make any noise. The place where we stoped is on the side of the mountain and so steep that we placed a poll from one Sapling to another so as to place our feet against it while we slept. It was not exactly sleeping Standing but it was very near it. I found myself severel times in the night doubled up like a pocket knife. We could not get any water without going back to the foot of the mountain and as I was very tired I "went dry" or in other words done without. It rained some and put it all together this is a camp that I will long remember as the worst one I have found yet. There is some body going to be surprised is my guess about to morrow morning but who is it?

SUNDAY OCT 16TH

We started up the mountain again at daylight and soon reached the summit and passing along a narrow ridge we decended into Snake Creek Gap and we discoverd what we were after. There was a Brigade of Johnies engaged in obstructing the Gap by cutting timber in it and we was trying to cut them off but we had our climb for nothing as they had skipped out. We passed the fourth Corps and followed the gap north untill we was into the valley and the fifteenth Corps passed us. We camped on a creek after marching ten miles. The Rebs are reported to have taken a stand north of White Oak Ridge which is in our front. There was considerable Skirmishing to day in the mountains but we done none of it. We learned where our old "Pap Thomas" (Genl Thomas) has gone by getting the report that he had defeated the Rebel Cavalry at Tunnel Hill and that he will organize and take command of a force large enough to meet hood and we will have an Army on boath sides of him. We run out of Rations but our Darky Andy captured a hog that had rebellious principles and we eat him. We also got some Sweat Potatoes and consequently fared pretty well.

MONDAY OCT 17TH

. . . The Rebels are reported to be moveing west towards the Allabama line. We drew rations and sent the sick to Ringold. . . . There was a large Wagon Train sent to Tunnel Hill for Rations. There was no Skirmishing to day. We have marching orders for to morrow morning.

TUESDAY OCT 18TH

We got ready to move early but did not get out of camp untill about ten Oclock as the fourth Army Corps passed us and we had to wait untill their agon train passed. We then crossed White Oak Ridge and took a South west direction. We had good roads untill dark when we left the main road and marched through a kind of mountain pass. We camped about Nine Oclock near Taylors Ridge but some distance from Ringold. We marched only twelve miles. No mail to day.

WEDNESDAY OCT 19TH
[SUMMERVILLE, GEORGIA]

We moved out early and passed the fourth Corps and moved towards Summerville. The Johnies are on the run and Said to be one day ahead of us and the citizens say they are going to Blue Mountain Alabama. Some of them say they have taken a position only eight miles from here and if that is so we will find them to day. They are barefooted and nothing to eat and very much discouraged. We marched ten miles and camped near Summerville and did not see a Johnie to day.

THURSDAY OCT 20TH
[ALABAMA]

We drew three days Rations and started for Galesville Allabama. We crossed the Allabama line. Marched very Steady and found no Johnies to impede our march and we traveled twenty three miles and camped on the Talladega River near Galesville. We had to cross a creek soon after dark which delayed us untill about Eleven Oclock at night before we camped. It was a hard days march but our train brought in plenty of forage. This country is in a better condition as there has not been so many Soldiers here. The citizens seam to have plenty to live on. The country is hilly and rocky but under a fair state of cultivation. The Rebels keep out of our way and our Cavalry can only keep up with them. The Skirmishing is all done by them.

FRIDAY OCT 21ST
[GAYLESVILLE, ALABAMA]

We moved to Galesville and camped on a hill on the East Side. This is a small town and there is not many of the inhabitants left. The town looks deserted. Our Boys [got] some old houses for Boards to fix up camp. The Rebels reported to have crossed the Coose River and going to Blue Mountain. We find plenty of forage in the valley and we help ourselves as we go and will make the people feel the effects of the war as they cant raise any thing now. But that is the way to wipe them out for as long as we protect their property just that long they will continue the war. But if we apply the torch to all we cant use and give them to understand they have no rights that we are bound to respect and they find their Army cannot protect them they will lay down their Arms and not before.[2]

SATURDAY OCT 22ND

Did not move to day but sent out a detail for forageing and they returned loaded with fresh meat and Sweat Potatoes So that we can live here a while at least and by moveing we will find plenty more as the citizens tell us on west we will Strik a rich farming country. . . .

SUNDAY OCT 23RD

We remained in camp all day and we are getting rested for another move. . . . No news as all is quiet.

MONDAY OCT 24TH

. . . Severel wounded Cavalry men was brought in who was wounded yesterday about twenty miles from here. They say the Rebels are Fortifying there. We received the news of Sheridans great victory over Early and Longstreet in the Shanncndoa valley.[3] Reported capture of twelve pieces of Artillery and Seven thousand prisoners. Some Rebel Cavalry appeard at the river and fired into a forageing party but did not hurt any body. The foragers brought in some nice pork and we are liveing fat. No fighting in our front.

TUESDAY OCT 25TH

The sun came out clear but the weather is cool. . . . I got new Chevrons and put them on my Blouse. Some more wounded Cavalry was brought in to day. Genl Baird Started home on leave of Absence. . . . There is some anxiety about the forageing party sent out to day for fear they have been captured by the Johnies. I was in camp all day.

WEDNESDAY OCT 26TH

Our foragers sent out yesterday did not return yet and we begin to think they have been captured. . . . It rained all night.

THURSDAY OCT 27TH

Capt Karns got permission to do some writing in a house near camp and we I made out our monthly returns for October. Orders came in to prepare for a long march but the place we are going to was not stated. There is no Rebs here and we may be going to follow them. Some think we are going to Richmond Verginia. Some think Mobile Allabama and Some others think to Savannah Georgia. It is cold to night.

FRIDAY OCT 28TH

I commenced makeing out Pay Rolls. We was musterd for Sept and October and had Inspection. We got orders to be ready to move at five Oclock in the morning. The first and Second divisions passed through town going to Rome and I presume we will follow them. Some say we will be paid there. But where is Hood. Has he returned to Atlanta and are we going back after him or is he going north and us south. These are questions that time only can answer.

SATURDAY OCT 29TH

We Started towards Rome at daylight and passed through Cooseeville and camped five miles from town. We marched twenty miles. I seen the list of drafted men from Wells county Indiana and see severel mens names I know. . . . It has the appearance of Rain. Nothing unusual accurred.

SUNDAY OCT 30TH
[ROME, GEORGIA]

We reached Rome and camped on the bank of the Oostonalla River. This is a pretty stream here and we have good water and a nice place to camp. . . . Rome is quite a town and Strongly fortified. It is the terminous of a Short Rail Road from Kingston. The country around here is good but we are getting back on the battle line and every thing has been distroyed. It is muddy from recent rains.

MONDAY OCT 31ST

I worked on our pay Rolls. The 101st Indiana drew their pay. The first and Second Division Started for Kingston and we are to follow Soon. We was not paid as expected but will perhaps get our money when we get to Kingston or some other place soon. We are entitled to Eight months pay.

TUESDAY NOV 1ST

We received Eight months pay and I drew $142.65/100. I sent Nett one hundred and twenty dollars. I went over to the Pay masters quarters and made out the Allotment Roll for my company and paid the money over to him. We received orders to be ready to march in the morning. It rained all night.

WEDNESDAY NOV 2ND
[KINGSTON, GEORGIA]

Still raining and we started at day light. It was very hard marching as the roads was slipery. We did not stop for dinner and reached Kingston about two Oclock p.m. It is fifteen miles. I went to see uncle Will and from a letter from Uncle Samuel Miller I learned that mother died Oct 24th. It was very unexpected as I did not know she was dangerously Sick. It is Sad news to me and the last time I seen her or heard her gentle voice rushes back to me and now to think I will never see her any more.

I received Netts letter of the 23rd Oct but She Said Mother was better. I returned to my company hopeing it may prove a mistake yet I have Sad forbodings. He finished the letter by saying "*we have just received the word that Louise is dead*" and nothing more. I do hope I will receive different word in my next letter. But still I can hardly think he could be mistaken and there is none other of that name and my heart sinks within me. Then if we should move from here before I get a letter I dread the terible suspense.

THURSDAY NOV 3RD

The wind blows cold this morning with a misting rain and very disagreeable. . . . I did not get any letter and I hardly know some times what to do I am so anxious to hear from home. But I will have to wait. I walked down to the Depot this evening and that is about all the town there is here. There is only about a dozen houses here. We got a report that there had been a fight in Tennisee but I did not learn where or the result. It rained all day and was very disagreeable.

FRIDAY NOV 4TH

Still cold and some rain. . . . We received notice that when we leave here that we neither have an opportunity to send or receive any mail for the next forty days. In other words we will cut loose from all communication. We also received orders to draw all the additional clotheing that we required for a long campaign. We made out our requisition accordingly and sent it in. Now where are we going is the question that is talked about and many surmises are offerd. But Genl Sherman knows and it is not necissary we should all know. I think we are going through the Confederacy but I dont suggest any point to come out at and I think we will be governed by circumstances. . . .

SATURDAY NOV 5TH

The sun come out nice and warm. I wrote to Sue and mailed it this evening and after dark I received one from Nett confirming mothers death. She died Oct 25th at twenty three minutes past twelve M. Now there is no doubt she has gone and Nettin Says she spoke of me and regretted she could not see me before she died. Oh! what anguish such an anouncement brings to me. If I could helped smooth her pillow or been preasent at her death it would not seam so hard to bear. But I trust She died with the conviction that although I was absent that I was trying to do my duty and Serveing my country. I feel Sad to night not only on account of the sad news but now we will soon be where we cannot even write to our friends and where we cannot tell. Then how many of us will live to reach the place we start for. But if it will crush the monster Rebellion I am ready to go immediately. I feel revengefull some times as I could be at home enjoying peace and happiness but for the war.

Sunday Nov 6th

. . . This was another rainy day and quite cold. We did not receive marching orders. I remained in camp all day.

Monday Nov 7th

. . . It rained some this morning but cleared away afternoon and is nice and warm. The Guirillas under Henderson captured two wagons from foragers near Cassville.[4] He has about three hundred cut throats with him and he needs a warming up. . . .

Tuesday Nov 8th

This is Presidential Election day but a Democratic Legislature has disfranchised us because we are fighting for liberty and to perrpetuate the privilage. But we could express our prefference and did so by takeing a vote with the following result viz Co "K" polled forty four votes and all for Lincoln & Hamlin not one single vote for McClellan & Pendleton.[5] The Regiment numberd Three Hundred and thirty one Rank and file and the vote was Three Hundred and Ten for Lincoln and Seven for McClellan and fourteen refused to vote. Now the northern Democrats say we are tired of the war. Does that look like it. The Rebels boasted once that if President Lincoln would give them a white piece of paper to write their own terms to come back into the Union they would not write them. Now we propose to write them for them and within another year if Lincoln is the next president they will sue for peace. If he should be defeated then I cant Say what the result will be. But he will be re-elected Sure for I have faith enough in our people to think they will sustain us by their votes and we will do the fighting.

WEDNESDAY NOV 9TH

One year ago to day I arrived at home and met my mother at the door of the old house and was welcomed by friends and relatives. How changed. I will never meet her again on this Earth. But if I am spared another year I will be at home again and meet many of my old friends. I was down to the Depot and seen a Train load of Conscripts but none whom I knew. Our Boys dont play fair with them they Steal their Knapsacks and guns and every thing els.[6] They will find out how to watch their things closer after they Soldier a year or two. Some talk of moveing in the morning but no orders came. It rained very hard this evening. The mail got through but I did not get any Letters. There is no news from Hood or his command and I dont know where they are.

THURSDAY NOV 10TH

This is a nice morning. I commenced our Pay Rolls So as to be ready for muster. . . . The 74th Indiana captured and brought in the Guirilla Henderson and some of his men and I am fearfull from the excitement among the soldiers that there will be trouble to keep them from hanging him. They got him near Cassville. The Depot is lined with citizens or Refugees on their way to "Gods country." They are mostly women and children and the men are in the Rebel Army. But they cant live here now and it would not be right to let them starve but I dont know but they should be punished some. They are of the poorer class of people and the few men that come in are ignorant and dooless fellows. Some of them look as though they had seen very hard times now.

FRIDAY NOV 11TH

. . . The excitement about Henderson got so high that thousands of Soldiers gathered around the house where they have him and demand[ed] him to be hung and there was a double guard placed around him and the men counciled to return to their severel camps. I thought they would over power the guard but they fineally dispersed. The outrages this man has perpetrated on union men and soldiers has made him a terror to the country and he should be executed without so much as a trial. Our boys would kill him on Sight. His gang are not satisfied by killing every soldier they catch but they mutilate the bodys and lay them along our line of march telling us we will all meet the same fate if caught and as we have the leader he should be served the same way. Our government must retalliate in some way. We received orders this evening to march to morrow morning and I suppose this is our last day here. There was a lot of Refugees come in from Rome to day. No word from Hood. We understand that Genl Thomas has force enough to look after him and that we will return to Atlanta from here.

SATURDAY NOV 12TH

We started on the march early and passed Cartersville and burned boath it and Kingston. The Rations stored at the latter place was issued out to the men and the Depot fired. We then moved on and crossed the Ettawa River and camped at the foot of the Altoona mountains for the night. We had plenty of Rails and good water. All the building[s] was burned along our line of march and the Rail Road distroyed and it looks as though we are going to devastate or burn out the confederacy. That has always been my policy. That we must make them feel our power and give the Rebel Soldiers to understand that we will not protect their famlies while they remain in the Army. It looks hard to see women and children driven out without shelter but it seams to be the only remedy that will cure the disease. When they learn that unless they submit their famlies will suffer for their folly the war will end. If we go across the country and destroy the property as we have to day there will be sufferin all over the south and I think forbearance has long ago ceased to be a virtue. The thousands of men who lay in Soldiers graves cry for vengence. The widows and orphans Scatterd all over our land and the hardships endured by those of us who are left in the field cry for vengence and now we will either wind up the war suddenly or make them suffer the consequences.

SUNDAY NOV 13TH

We started early and crossed the Altoona mountains and through the town or where the town was but it has all disappeard but a Rebel Hospittal full of sick and wounded. The rest was all burned. We marched six miles and commenced tearing up the Rail Road. This is the only part of the road I have seen that is not torn up. We camped at Big Shanty for the night without meeting with any opposition. Of course we dont receive any mail or news from the north as we have crawled into the hole and pulled the hole in after us. I suppose the Rebel papers will tell all kinds of stories about us but they cant bring force enough against us to do us any damage. But our friends in the north will be very anxious to hear from us.

MONDAY NOV 14TH

We was on the march early and passed through Marietta and the town was fired. All the Buildings but a few was burned and it was almost suffi-cateing with heat and smoke. Our men would have to break ranks and run out to get their breath while marching. The beautiful town is only a mass of ruins. We marched about twenty miles and camped on the Chattahoochie river. We got on the wrong road and had to counter-march. It caused us a march of about Eight miles extra and made us late into camp. We camped about Eight and if there is any body tired to night I think I am one. Good camp and good water.

CHAPTER 10

We Have Surely Done a Big Work: The March to the Sea

The 75th was destined to participate in what has become Sherman's most famous campaign: the "March to the Sea" from Atlanta to Savannah. For several weeks, more than sixty thousand men were ordered to plunge into enemy territory, bring the war to the civilian population, destroy the Confederacy's ability to make war, and live off the land as an independent force, with no contact with home. In preparation for such a move, the Hoosiers camped east of Atlanta, and on the night of November 15 they witnessed a great fire that destroyed part of the city, deliberately set by the Federals to destroy businesses and industrial sites. The regiment drew some clothing and rations out of the business buildings being used as government storehouses before they went up in flames and the next morning started on the march. The Seventy-fifth would remain with the Fourteenth Army Corps, now under the command of Bvt. Maj. Gen. Jefferson C. Davis, a fellow Hoosier. Their corps was part of a two corps "left wing" led by Maj. Gen. Henry W. Slocum.

The first target of the Fourteenth Corps was Milledgeville, the capital of Georgia. As they marched from Atlanta, a member of the Seventy-fifth noted, "It was a charming November morning. The Corps . . . with swinging, regular step, arms glistening in the sunlight, and colors unfurled to the balmy breezes, was as fine a picture as eyes ever saw." Sherman himself accompanied the left wing as far as the Georgia capital.

On their way south, the Seventy-fifth helped destroy part of the Georgia Railroad. One eyewitness noted that "on account of its frequent recurrence, it was a work of destruction in which we became proficient, and for which we became famed."[1] Foraging parties, soon nicknamed "Sherman's bummers," set out

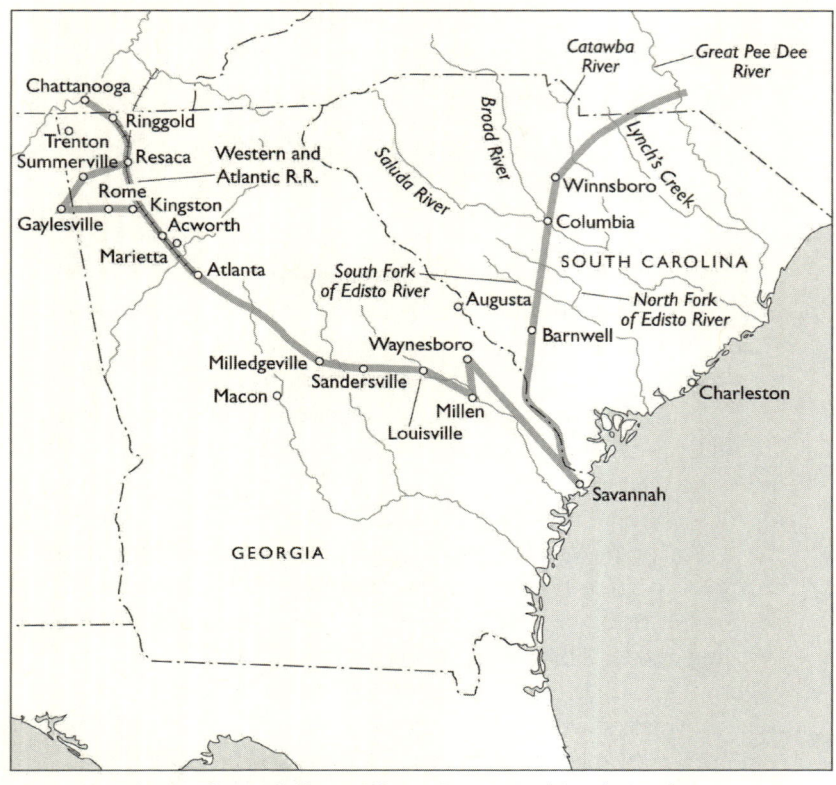

MAP 3. Travels of William Bluffton Miller in Georgia and South Carolina, 1864–1865.

to hunt for rations at local farms and plantations. It was "always considered a privilege" to be detailed on such expeditions, remembered a member of the regiment, as "there was such a fascination about it."[2]

With Milledgeville in Union hands on November 23, the next objective was the city of Millen, one hundred miles away. In the advance, the Hoosiers and the rest of their division were detailed to support Gen. Judson Kilpatrick's cavalry force. As they moved, the regiment continued to destroy railroads and forage off the land. Despite skirmishes with Rebel cavalry, obstructions of logs and felled trees, annoying rain, and scarce forage, the Seventy-fifth moved beyond Millen in early December and closed in around Savannah.

Settling in beyond the Rebel fortifications, the men enjoyed monotonous but abundant rations of rice. The regiment was soon sent out to forage for better fare, and the troops were successful in securing sweet potatoes and other provisions. While off on this expedition, General Sherman demanded the surrender of the city, a demand the Confederates refused. On December 20, the very day that the Seventy-fifth returned to the army, however, the Confederates withdrew from Savannah. The first objective of the conquering Hoosiers was the city's oyster beds, which they harvested for Christmas dinner.

After a review by General Sherman, the regiment rested until January 19, 1865, performing guard and picket duty and sightseeing around the city. One activity that broke the monotony of garrison life was the racing of thoroughbreds on the city track, a diversion that was continued until fistfights occurred and the races were canceled by the commanding general.

The March to the Sea had been a virtual holiday for the men of the Seventy-fifth. They had scarcely fired a round of ammunition, except at pigs and chickens, having encountered little enemy opposition. They had marched more than three hundred miles at a leisurely pace, lived off the land, and accomplished their mission of bringing devastation to Georgia, proving the impotence of the Confederate army in the region. Gen. Absalom Baird summarized a few of his division's achievements during the march as he rested in Savannah: "The amount of sweet potatoes, hogs, cattle, and poultry taken in the country and consumed by the troops cannot be estimated but it must have been very large, the men living well. The division destroyed quite effectually eighteen miles of railroad and two large bridges. . . . It destroyed, I feel quite sure, 1,000 bales of cotton. . . . The amount of forage and other minor articles consumed and destroyed cannot be estimated. The command foraged liberally. The number of drafted and saddle animals captured was about 597. . . . Negroes to the number of about 668 joined or followed our column on the march."[3]

So closed a very successful year for the Federal cause. Victory was in sight for Miller and his fellow soldiers.

Tuesday Nov 15th
[Atlanta, Georgia]

Moved out at daylight and arrived at Atlanta about Nine Oclock am. We stopped in the city untill after noon and then moved out on the Augusta Rail Road and camped on an elevation that overlooks the city. The city is fired in severel places and about dark the Torch was set into the Buisiness part. It was a grand sight from our camp to look down on the burning city. The night is dark and an accasional shell bursts and scatters things around promiscuously. Some of our Boys was down and got some clotheing from the burning buildings. The entire city was distroyed but a few accupied houses. It reminds me of the distruction of the city of Babalon as spoken of in the Bible whis was distroyed because of the wickedness of her people and that is the case with Atlanta. I feel Sorry for some of the people but a Soldier is not supposed to have any concience and must lay aside all scruples he may have. We drew some clotheing and Rations and have orders to move in the morning. With all the excitement and attending to duty I did not get any Sleep.

Wednesday Nov 16th

We Struck tents and formed Battallion on Collor line and Genl Sherma[n]s order was read to us. He says it has become necissary to change our base of opporation and that we will be required to march only fifteen miles a day unless circumstances should require more. He cautions us not to leave our commands unless to forage and then in partys large enough to protect our selves from Bushwhackers as they will follow us all the time. We left Atlanta about nine Oclock am and followed the Augusta Rail Road and passed through Decature and marched about fifteen miles. A Boy in Co E by name of Shull died to night Suddenly.[4] No one knew he was sick untill he was discovered dead. The country we passed to day is good some hilly but the Plantations in good shape.

Thursday Nov 17th

On the road early. Passed a small town called La Toona on the Rail Road. We put in part of the day tearing up the Rail Road. We marched fifteen miles and camped near Conyers Station. We find plenty of forage and live entirely off the country. Some of the old citizens complain teribly and claim to be Union men and have never been any thing els. Our Boys tell them if they are Union men they can afford to contribute some thing to help us cary on the war and if they are Rebels we will take it any way. In that way we manage to live. But if we was not here they would be all Rebels. They are loyal by compulsion only.

Friday Nov 18th

We pulled out early and marched hard. We tore up some more Rail Road. We passed near Oxford and through Covington boath nice towns. Some Bush Whackers attacked our foragers and wounded severel and Among them Capt Wilcox of the 105 Ohio. They hung some that they Captured which shows it will not be good for us to fall into their hands. They swear vengence on us for marching through their country but they have only got a taste to what they will get before we get through. We marched the usual fifteen miles and camped near Yellow River. This part of the country has never seen any Yankees only prisoners and the armies have not molested it and the citizens are well fixed and have plenty which makes it nice for us in levying contributions on them. We live like fighting cocks. There is a detail of two men from the company for forageing every morning makeing twenty from the Regiment under a Lieutenant and then they are organized by Divisions and swells the force to about two hundred me[n] which makes it perfectly safe. The Bush Whackers wont attack us unless in small parties.

Saturday Nov 19th

We was hurried out in the rain at daylight and the road was slipry which made it hard marching. We turned off the Rail Road to the right and went to Sand Town which we passed about dusk. We found plenty of forage such as Yams and Sweat Potatoes And Sorgum Molasses by the barrel. We could not use all that was brought in and it was distroyed. Some Bushwhackers hung on our flanks but kept at a safe distance. We camped after dark and had plenty of wood but water was scarce. It is raining some. We are on the Road direct to the capital Milledgeville. The Rebels reported in force at Jonesboro and ready for fight. But I dont think they have men enough to make a Breakfast Spell in this country. The country is generally level and Soil Sandy and the plantations under a good State of cultivation.

Sunday Nov 20th

We made the usual march of fifteen miles and nothing worthy of note transpired. The country is good and we found it well waterd. The principle products are Yams Sweat Potatoes Some corn and Pea Nutts. We dont find many men at home. They are either in the Rebel Armies or are called away about the time they learn we are comeing.

Monday Nov 21st

It rained all day and the roads are terible. We only marched about ten miles. We left Eatonton to our left. The soil here is mixed with Red clay and Icenglass and it is Slipery and sticks to the feet. It is hard on the teams and the mules travel very slow and the wagons did [dig] up the roads [and] makes work for the Pioneers and Darkies who are pressed into the service. We are still going towards Millidgeville. Forage plenty. Some of the citizens say the Johnies are waiting for us there and that we will get a whipping. Let them trot out their men.

Tuesday Nov 22nd

We started at daylight. It was quite cold but no rain. We Soon struck good roads and marched about fifteen miles and camped on Ex Gov Cobbs plantation.[5] He is now in command of Georgia State Malitia. We are eight miles from Millidgeville. We found plenty of Hogs Corn & Yams and supposed Gov Cobb would not want us to pass by his plantation when he had plenty w[i]thout asking him to contribute something for the *Union* we concluded to stay all night and as he was not at home we just helped ourselves to such as we found. It appears he had very urgent buisiness away from home when he heard we was comeing to see him. Pherhaps he thought we might want him to go along with us. But it is all right and we will excuse him. We was in the lead and camped about three Oclock p.m. Our troops have possession of the city and the Johnies have skipped out. Our quarters are full of all kinds of forage to night and we are happy. The wind blows hard and it is cold for this part of the country.

WEDNESDAY NOV 23RD
[MILLEDGEVILLE, GEORGIA]

All the principle Buildings was burned on the plantation to let the Ex Gov know we had been here and that it might be impressed on his mind so he would not forget it. Our quarters are coverd with Yams and they are frozen hard. The Darkies Say it was an unusualy cold night. This has been a pretty place and when we arrived here last night was in a good Shape but this morning we leave it stripped of its beauty and we start to Millidgeville. We camped in the edge of the city. It is a nice place. The Rebel Legislature was in Session but they adjourned as they had some other important buisiness on hand when the[y] heard Sherman was comeing. I was in the sennate chamber and our Boys held a Mock Legislature [im]personateing the Johnies and it was very amuseing to hear them. They kept it up nearly all the afternoon. They carried it on in regular Southren fire eating stile and was all armed with large knives captured from the Arsnell which is Situated in the same encloseure. The Arsnel contained Some Small arms and about four thousand Pikes and cutlasses for cutting up Yankees and now we are here for the sacrifice and the Butchers are not at home. The State papers was about all removed to Macon by the Rebels. The Arsnell was blown up to night and the state Prison was burned by the Rebels and all the prisoners liberated if they would join the Army. The men as usual are not at home and a great many citizens left the city. I noticed some fine buildings but the State House looks old and rusty. I was through the State prison building and it is badly damaged. I got one of the cutlasses and will endevour to cary it home as a curiosity. This was a cold frosty day. The 20th Army Corps has the advance and the[y] moved on to night and we are to follow in the morning. It is reported that our men had a fight at Macon to day but nothing reliable.

THURSDAY NOV 24TH

Unexpectedly we got no orders to move this morning. The weather is nice but still cool. Nice weather for marching. . . . Killpatricks Cavalry moved through the city. Our division will opperate on the left in conjunction with Killpatrick. We have a nice camping ground and good water and plenty of Rails.

Friday Nov 25th

We started from Millidgeville early this morning and marched about Eighteen miles and got into camp after night. We got into some swampy country and had bad roads. They differ from the swam[p]s in Indiana in this that they are quick Sand and are miery and Some times they are miles wide. The citizens say the farther we get south the more swamps. Our camp is about three miles from buffalo Creek.

Saturday Nov 26th

We took the advance this morning of the Division and we had the first skirmishing to day since we left Atlanta. This evening before we camped we had to drive the Rebel Cavalry away. We had one man killed and one wounded and found one dead Johnie and captured one. It did not last long. We drove them through a small town called Sandersonville. The Rebels said to be in force two miles ahead but they will be gone when we get there. We crossed severel Swamps and camped about three Oclock p.m.

Sunday Nov 27th

We started at daylight in advance and did not find any of the Johnies where they was reported. We marched twenty miles and camped about dusk. We passed a plantation where a Cotton Gin was burning and a large amount of Cotton was distroyed. We also found a Store House of wines and some of our Boys got gloriously drunk. They was run out here from Savannah when the Rebels thought the Yankees was comeing up the river. The proprietor was not at home haveing important buisiness to attend to when he heard Sherman would visit him. But it made no material difference as we helped ourselves as usual and made ourselves perfectly at home. The country is generally level and the soil Sandy and well waterd.

Monday Nov 28th

We have the advance again to day and started at day light and marched six miles to Blackrock Creek where we found the Bridge burned which detained us untill nearly night before we got it Bridged so as to cross. We then moved on a Short distance to Louisville which we found on fire. The report is a woman spit in a Yankees face and called him names

and he set the house on fire and it burned severel others and the
Regiment was orderd to put out the fire and protect the town against
any further damage. This is a county Seat of Jefferson county. My company quarterd in the court House. The town had about one thousand
inhabitants but the men are all gone and no body here but women and
children except very old men. The country about here is level and some
good farms. Rebels reported at Augusta in force. We find it hard marching in the Sand as it gives under our feet like Snow. Our men are scatterd over town as provost guards to protect the property. This is our last
day in advance as we only have it three days in Sucession.

TUESDAY NOV 29TH

The 20th Corps takes the advance and moved through town but we did
not move. We done provost duty. Genl Davis Sent to Capt Karns for a
Guard and I reported to him with two men and I was orderd to arrest a
Boy from the 20th Corps who had tried the Smoke house at His Head
quarters. The Genl orderd me to take him to our quarters and tie him
up and then go and get his Lieutenant at a Blacksmith Shop and bring
him to him. I done as orderd and Davis gave the Lieut a terible curseing and then orderd me to release them which I did. Genl Davis is a
good reliable Officer but very passionate and I concluded when I heard
him talking to that Lieut that it might do for him to curse some men
that way and I might have kept still if it had been my case but he has
no right to abuse a man simply because he out ranks him and I think I
should have cautioned him not to repeat it. I think every man should
show due respect for his officers but when the General or any officer
descends from his rank to curse and abuse the man below him he is not
entitled to any respect. Genl Davis took the life of Nelson at Louisville
for the same offense.[6] We was relieved from duty by Co H. at dark. Our
foragers had some Skirmishing with the Rebs and they also attacked
Train of the 20th A.C near Blackrock Creek Bridge but was repulsed.
Severel of our men was wounded. They undertook to capture the Train
but found more Yankees than they expected. We also have a report that
Genl Killpatrick was beaten near Millan but no particulars.[7]

WEDNESDAY NOV 30TH

No orders to move to day yet. There was some Skirmishing with
Bushwhackers and our forageing parties. I was down to town but could

find nothing amuseing or instructive and re[t]urned to camp. Nothing confirming the defeat of our Cavalry near Millan. We still have plenty of forage.

Thursday Dec 1st

We left town about nine Oclock and Joined the Brigade and camped for the night. The Cavalry and foragers done some Skirmishing and we formed a line of Battle and moved out about one mile but the Johnies Skipped out when they saw the old "flat foots["] comeing. Severel Cavalry was killed and wounded but we did not become engaged. I got hold of a Rebel paper to day and it is very amuseing to read their accounts of us. One item said Shermans men was Hungry and ragged and deserting by hundreds and he might possibly get out with a corporals Guard (two men) they would capture nearly his entire Army. They will have quite a number to gobble yet before they get us all. Our men are in the best of spirits and have plenty to eat and wear and think it fun. I learned to day that we left Kingston with ten days rations on the wagon and we have not drawn any since. So we are ten days ahead yet.[8] According to their papers we have been defeated severel times since we started. But I suppose the Democratic papers in the north will be glad to publish that kind of news and that will make our friends worry about us. But I will Say if the Johnies capture Sherman and his men they will want help to let us go. I dont believe one man has deserted on this march and I doubt if any does. The Rebel cavalry harrassing us only keeps our men together and they dont do us any harm and if they are not carefull they may get a warming up befor we reach our destination.

Friday Dec 2nd

We got marching orders and was on the road early and only marched ten miles. Wheeler and Hamptons Rebel Cavalry are keeping on our flanks.[9] We left Waynesboro to our left and they are reported to have a large force of Cavalry there. They are reported at so many places but when we go to them they are looking for us some place els. The[y] dont wait untill we come. But then it is safer for them.

Saturday Dec 3rd

We took the wrong road and marched twelve miles and was then only five miles from where we camped last night. We Struck the Augusta and Savannah Rail Road about two miles from Millan prison pen.[10] We tore up the track. Burned the Ties and crooked the Iron and camped along the Road. The Rebel Cavalry have been harrassing us all day and they have to[o] many for Killpatrick alone and we help him out when he gets into a bad scrape. They are near us to night.

Sunday Dec 4th

The Rebs run up a Howitzer and Shelled the 92nd Illinois and stampeeded a Cavalry Regiment before day light and we got into line quick. Genl Killpatrick formed and drove them off and followed towards Waynesboro where the[y] surroundid his command and they built a Barracade of Rails and we was orderd to support him. When we arrived they were haveing a lively time. We formed and E & K companies was thrown out as Skirmishers and they did not find out we was Infantry untill they discoverd our flag. We opend up on them they concluded they did not want Killpatrick. They had to retreat across a large swamp about a mile wide and the road was graded high and about wide enough for three or four men to ride abreast they was in such a hurry the[y] crouded each other off. Some of them undertook to ride through the Swamp and they mired down and was shot off their horses and quite a number lay along the road. We pushed on after our Cavalry into town and followed them some distance but they did not hault any more untill they put the river between them and us. We then returned to town. Gatherd up the guns and wounded left the dead to be buried by the citizens and started to catch up with the ballance of the Army. We did not get to camp untill after midnight and march[ed] over twenty miles. We camp at Alexandria. We run Wheeler away from his breakfast and came very near captureing him and his Staff. They was completely surprised at infantry getting there so soon and supposed we was at Millan. Our loss was about forty men altogether. We captured about a hundred prisoners and killed about thirty of them. It was fun for us to see them skip out. I seen one old Reb lying along the road (quite an old man) that had been a Saber stroke across his back and was not dead yet but mortally wounded and under other circumstances his grey hairs would have appealed to my heart for simpathy but we are not here to Simpathise with men who brought it on themselves. When we skirmished through the town we did not see any body but Rebel Cavalry but when we returned it was alive with women and children who had on their sunday clothes and it reminded me of home. They had hid in the cellars while the fight was going on and come out to see us.[11]

Monday Dec 5th

We was on the march early and marched twenty miles and camped near Jacksonboro. We had no Skirmishing to day as I guess they had all they wanted yesterday and will let us alone. This part of Georgia is very poor. The Soil is very Sandy and the timber mostly pine. I would not take the best plantation here as a gift and live on it. The citizens as a general thing have no education and are to[o] lazy or careless to work and have always depended on the Darkis to support them.

Tuesday Dec 6th

We had the lead to day and marched twenty miles. The Rebel cavalry put in an appearance again to day and kept popping away at us when ever they got a chance but they did not bother us much. I got a rebel paper and it is full of good news for them. It says Wheelers Cavalry cleaned out the 14th Corps and Killpatricks Cavalry Sunday at Waynesboro. If we had not been there I could believe it better. But if that is what they call a victory we will give them one every day. It also says Sherman is trying to get to Savannah and I am thankfull for the information as I did not know before where we are going. I noticed a Small item where the Tellegraph Opperator tellegraphed to Richmond from Millan Saying Sherman was within two miles of that place and he (The opporater) was about to bid it a hasty adiew and said they had not heard from him Since and the Editor supposed Sherman had Millan.

Wednesday Dec 7th

We marched twenty miles to day and camped and got our suppers when we received marching orders and started again about ten Oclock and moved five miles. The Cavalry coverd the rear and as they enterd a swamp charged them but our boys held their ground. The Rebels thought they would stampeed the Cavalry and play the same game we played on them at Waynesboro but they failed. We stopped about four Oclock am and got a little rest but we neaded it badly as we marched about twenty five miles Since Yesterday morning. It rained some during the night.

Thursday Dec 8th

Our Brigade had to take the rear and did not leave camp untill about Nine Oclock a.m. We had marched about Six miles when we haulted for dinner and the Rebels made a dash at us and we formed a line of Battle and moved out to meet them but they only come to our Picket line. There was a number of Shots fired and some men hurt. Some of our Boys was out in front of the picket line gathering pine Knots for fire when the Rebels [came] and we thought they were our own Cavalry. Among them was Capt Peter Studabaker of the 101st Indiana and when the charge was sounded he discoverd they were Johnies and he retreated on a "double quick" inside our lines. He had severel pine Knots in his arms but he left them for the "Johnies." I dont Say the Captain was scared but he done some pretty [keen?] running to get away. We lay in line untill midnight but they did not molest us any further and we then crossed Big Ebonezer River and the 75th coverd the rear and had orders to burn the Bridge which we did at day light. This stream runs through a swamp about three miles wide and the road is graded hight. It [was] to this time the Darkies have been following the Army from sections through which we passed and have accumulated to thousands of all Sizes and Sex and our orders is not let them cross the River. The Rebels shelled us some as we was leaveing but only wounded one man. Some say the shell came from a Gun Boat. There has been some heavy cannonadeing to day along our lines.

Friday Dec 9th

When we destroyed the Bridge across Big Ebonezer this morning the road as far as we could see north was lined with negroes who have followed us. It was really pitty full to see them and they are afraid of the Rebels and begged hard to get over. Some of them Swam the river but the women and children could not get over. I noticed women with two or three little children trudgeing along through the mud. Old white headed men who could hardly walk all trying to get away. They are very ignorant but they know on[e] thing and that is they want to be free.[12]

Thinking they could go with us they have gathered up their little effects and left their old homes. They are taught to believe that we were regular cut-throats by their masters but when we come they are ready to go with us. They know we are their friends and the mistery is how they know it. Some of them say they thought the Yankees had horns like an ox. I dont see how they can live in the country we have passed over for every thing was distroyed. Some Negro Huts are left but Smoke marked the advance of our Army and many of Shermans Monuments (as we call the chimneys) are standing in memory of the "March to the Sea." There was heavy cannonadeing to day and one place at the entrence to a Swamp the Johnies planted a Battery so as to rake the road and dismounted one of our Guns but it got to[o] hot for them and they pulled out. They killed a Lieutenant of one of our Batteries but I did not learn his name.[13] We had to go some out of our way on account of our wagon train and only moved about ten miles. Things look now like we should get through with a very Small loss and showes the Johnies did not make good their boasting of Captureing Sherman and his Army.

Saturday Dec 10th

We did not leave camp untill about ten Oclock a.m as we are still in the rear. The first Division drove the Rebels out of a small Fort and captured one gun. We struck the Charleston an[d] Savannah Rail Road about Eleven miles from the latter and near where it crosses the Savannah River. We tore up the Track and there is a long Trustle work through the Swamp leading to the Bridge and a detail was sent to fire it and the Bridge but the Rebs had a Gun Boat laying in the river and they Shelled us so we abandoned it. They made it "redd hot" for us. We camped for the night here and it rained very hard nearly all night. The Soil is yellow sand and the product of the country is principally Rice.

Sunday Dec 11th

The cannonadeing is heavy this morning in the direction of Savannah. It cleared away and we made another attempt to distroy the Trustleing and Bridge but the Swamp and Rebels prevented us. We moved about two miles across a Swamp and obstructed the road by cutting timber in. The Johnies made their appearence but did not attack us. It is reported that our fleet is lying at Fort Jackson below the city and will opporate in conjunction with us.[14] Wheeler made a dash on our pickets but he did not remain long.

Monday Dec 12th

We did not move to day. There was some Cannonadeing. The 20th Army Corps captured a Boat comeing down the river loaded with provission from Augusta. Our rations are getting Short and we dont get any hard Tack. Nothing but Coffee Beef & Rice and we have been liveing so well that it goes hard with us. Wheeler did not put in [an] appearence to day as he cannot cross the Swamp untill he cuts out the timber and we have a Battery Stationed to rake it and it would be very hazzar[d]ous. The weather is warm and I find one nice thing for us. That is no amount of rain can produce any mud. The sand when wet packs down solid and the water runs away.

Tuesday Dec 13th

We moved about Eight Oclock to the crossing of the Macon and Savannah Rail Road and took a position in rear of our wagon train as we front all around. We have Rebels in Savannah and Rebel behind us and dont know where they may attack us first. There was some heavy fighting on our right and it is reported that our men captured a Gun Boat in the river and that the Rebels are evacuating the city via the Gulf Rail Road and I think our lines must extend nearly all around the city on the north and south. We drew one quarter rations of hard Bread. But we have plenty of rice and we have to hull it in a tin cup with our Bayonett. It makes Rough feed as the Boys say but it does very well.

Wednesday Dec 14th

We remained in camp all day and the cannonadeing was kept up as usual but seams to be down the river from us and I suppose it is our fleet Shelling the city. We got the news of the capture of Fort McAllister on the Ogechee river and that we could now write our friends as that opend communication. I did not learn what our loss was but our men charged the fort from the land side carying it by storm captureing the entire Garrison.[15] This makes the thirty second day Since we left Kingston and Seventy one since we started north from Atlanta since which we have been moveing continuously and we have surely done a big work.

We have cut the confederacy in twain and destroyed the crops in the richest part of their country so as to cut off their supplies and now we are beseigeing one of their principle Seaport cites.

Thursday Dec 15th

I wrote a Letter to Nett to let her know that I am Still among the liveing and how many hearts will be made glad when our Letters get home to our friends many miles from us and who have looked anxiously for one word from us from day to day during our long march and how they will rejoice when the[y] know the victory gained over Treason and the prospect of a speedy close of the war. I am satisfied that unless the war closes that we will make more such Raids through their country and devastate their land entirely. They will begin to see that the Yankees are getting in earnest. Savannah must surrender soon and then we will make that a base of opporation. We got orders to go forageing to morrow morning. There was some Skirmishing to day. We did not get any mail.

Friday Dec 16th

Our entire Brigade started South west from camp for the purpose of forageing. We passed the prisoners captured at Fort McCallister and they are the worst looking Soldiers I ever Seen. They are little Boys and very old men not strong enough to be in the field. They were about played out marching. We took a good laugh at one of our men who was guarding a Boy quite small and they was behind the rest and the little fellow was about played [out] and one of our Boys suggested to the guard as we passed that if he could find a cow to let that *Babe* Suck. It sounded rediculous and caused considerable meriment. I see by these prisoners how the Rebels are pushed for Soldiers and convinces me that the war is nearly over. We marched about Twenty five miles and crossed the Ogechee river about dark and camped two miles from the river. Our rout was through a Swampy country and the land is mostly coverd with water. I started from Camp with four small crackers and a little Coffee and we found nothing but Rice on the march and I had to go to bed hungry to night but misery likes company and I console myself by thinking that nobody els has any more than I have. There was a mail Boat lying at the Wharf where we crossed the river. We did not see any Johnies. I am very tired and sore from marching.

Saturday Dec 17th

We started at day light and soon passed a long wagon train loaded with corn and they told us we would find plenty of forage. I had one little cracker and some Rice for breakfast. We passed a plantation in the evening where some Soldiers was cooking Sweet Potatoes and we inquired how far we would have to go before we would find forage and an old Darky said three miles and I almost felt as though I could never march it. But I did and we found plenty. This plantation belongs to an old Rebel by the name of Collins. I Shot a hog as the Regiment camped and Skind out a ham and Lieut Starbuck had some Yams and we got a square meal and we done it Justice. I thought I was hollow clear to my toes. We loaded our Wagons with corn during the night so as to return in the morning. We loade[d] Ninety one Wagons. We did not see any Johnies but they are reported to be at Rice ville a Short distance away. Some claim we are in the State of Florida. We marched twenty four miles to day.

Sunday Dec 18th

My Regiment with the 105th Ohio was Sent towards Riceville to see what was there in the Shape of Johnies. We went within about two miles of the Town and as they was gone we returned to the Train and we started back towards camp and marched ten miles and correlled the Train and camped for the night. We passed Station No 3 where we found about one hundred and fifty Barrells of Salt but the station house was burned. This is a terible country. It seams to be one continued swamp and the country coverd with water. They dont raise any thing but rice and alligators and there is plenty [of] boath. Our old Darky Andy is very fraid of the latter and I put up a little Job on him. When he went to the Swamp for wood about dark I followed and about the time he Shoulderd the wood I made a Splash in the water and he supposed it was an Allegator and dropped his wood and retreated in quick time to camp. The old fellow had a terible tale to relate when I came back about seeing an Allegator and how it tried to catch him and how he out run it. I tried to pursuade him to go back but he would not go and I had to go and get wood myself and I dont know whether the joke is on him or me.

MONDAY DEC 19TH

We started again at day light re-crossed the Ogechee and Stopped for the night near the 17th Corps. They say we will have to take another road than the one we come from here to camp. There was nothing unusual occured to day only we marched about twenty five miles. We heard some cannonadeing along the lines but no fighting of any consequence.

TUESDAY DEC 20TH

Started at day light and got on the wrong road and went a few miles out of our way. One place we had to pass within range of a Rebel Battery. The road was graded up and there is water on boath sides of it. It looked like a lake and the[y] have been shelling this part of the road and knocked Severel wagons off but our officers concluded rather than go around they would cross here. We was deployed at five paces and Started through and the Johnies opend up on us and the Shells would come skipping along on the surface of the water and strike in the road or pass over us. Our wagons was deployd and they pepered away at them but did not hurt a man or damage any of the wagons but all passed over safe and we went on to camp where I found four letters from Nett and one from Mollie with some Towells and a Handkerchief. The Letters was dated Nov 8th 12th 14th & 25th and being very tired I did not write any. We drew some Crackers. We brought in Some Rice haveing carried it fifty miles.

WEDNESDAY DEC 21ST

The report come into camp this morning the Rebels have evacuated Savannah. I wrote to Nett but did not mail it as the capture of the city was confirmed and we got orders to move to Town. The Rebels crossed the Savannah River near the city and went towards Charleston S.C. Where will they go now. They have no place to go that they can Stay for I think we will follow as soon as we rest a little and get supplies here. We did not move to day.

THURSDAY DEC 22ND
[SAVANNAH, GEORGIA]

We had orders to be ready to move at noon but did not leave camp untill about one Oclock. We camped in an old Brick Yard about a mile from the Depot but can see the city. Lieut Starbuck and I walked down to the Depot. The Rebels left the city without doeing any damage and their heavy Seige guns remain in the works. We passed severel of them and there is one mounted at the Depot to guard the Rail Road. They have all the flood gates closed is the reason the country is coverd with water. In raiseing Rice they have to Inundate and those gates are approached by Cannals and used for that purpose. We got only two hundred prisoners but found about thirty thousand Bales of cotton in the city. This is a cold day. We are camped near the Macon Rail Road Track.

Friday Dec 23rd

We spent the day in prepareing quarters and as we had plenty of Brick and Lumber we erected quite a house and we have a nice camp. The mail came in and brought me three Letters from Nett one from Mollie one from Sue and one from Jake Miller the latest was Dec 4th. Mollies letter contained a Lock of Mothers hair. I did not write any. We got the news that "Old Pap Thomas" had given hood a terible drubbing at or near Nashville Tenn and captured a great many of his men and Hood was retreating again.[16] This has been a year of Successes for the Union Army and now if Genl Grant will take Richmond we will soon go home. And if he cant do it let him send for us and we will go and help him. Genl Joe Johnston is commanding the Rebel Army here but I dont know where he has gone to. But we will soon hunt him up.[17] I believe we will go north from here to Charleston or some of those cities and if necissary on to Richmond. Perhaps Johnston will go there and the little difficulty be all settled at once. Let Hood come too with the few men he has left.

Saturday Dec 24th

James Reed of my company got badly hurt by the falling of a part of a Brick Kiln Wall. He got his foot crushed and the Boys carried him to camp. The news of Hoods defeat by Genl Thomas was confirmed and we say Glory. It let us out of a nice Scrape by comeing here. I finished my letter to Nett and mailed it. I got a copy of the Loyal Georgian published in the city and the first copy by the Yankees. Our Boys got on a Shooting Spree to night in honor of Christmas. The pickets fired the heavy guns along the works and our Boys fired their guns and they are haveing lots of fun. It sounds like a Battle. It is quite cold.

Sunday Dec 25th

Christmas and Sunday finds us in quarters in the old Brick Yard with no orders only Inspection at 2 Oclock pm and orders for grand review Tuesday. . . . This is a cloudy day with appearence of Rain. . . . We sent a detail to the Oyster Beds for Oysters but they did not get back. I visited the city and find a nice place. The Streets are wide and nicely Shaded with Live Oak Trees. Some of the houses are very old. One objection to the town is the mixture of different nations of people. I believe nearly every nation is represented here. The city has not been damaged any by the war. We can Stand on the Wharf and See Ft Jackson and our fleet lying near there. The channel has not been cleaned out yet of the Torpedoes so vessells can come up yet but it will be all right in a few days as they are flagging it now.

Monday Dec 26th

This is a very cold morning haveing rained all night. News from Genl Thomas getting better. Reported capture of fifty pieces of Artillery. Our Brigade was reviewed by Col Gleason and Staff this pm to prepare for to morrow. We are out of rations and we all went to bed hungry as there is none to draw untill to morrow.

Tuesday Dec 27th

We formed at Eight Oclock am and marched to the city and was reviewed by Genls Sherman Slocum Davis and Baird and returned to camp afternoon and drew Rations and got our dinners and we needed it.[18] We got a report to day that the Arch Traitor Davis was dead but only rumored.[19] But I hope that it will prove true. I commenced a letter to Nett but did not finish it.

Wednesday Dec 28th

Still raining. I was makeing out our Clotheing returns and was in camp all [day]. Some of our Boys caugh[t] an alligator and brought him into camp and they had lots of sport with it. . . .

Thursday Dec 29th

It cleared off and was cold. We built a chimney to our Shanty with a fire place. I was makeing out muster and Pay Rolls and was writing all day. There is some talk that the 3rd Division 14th Corps will be left on duty in Savannah as Garrison but nothing certain. I dont care this time of year but I dont believe I would want to be here during the summer seeson. I think it would be sickly. The camp is drying off nicely and this is a beautiful evening. Almost like Spring.

Friday Dec 30th

I completed the muster and pay Rolls for November and December and we received orders to be ready for muster at 12 Oclock M tomorrow. . . . No news of importance from any of our Armies.

Saturday Dec 31st

We was musterd in the rain to day. It turned cold and very windy. The Boys put in the evening Shooting the old year out and the new on[e] in. The Rebel guns in the fortifications was brought into use again and they Shelled the Swamps. I notice some rocket signaling going on to night. There was a vessell came into port to night and stopped at the wharf loaded with supplies for the Rebels and the captan and Crew did not know the Yanks had captured the city. They supposed they had run the Blockade and what was their surprise on finding they had run into the Yankees hands. We draw only quarter rations now and it is hardly enough for good Stout men. This day closes up this very eventful year of 1864. Last year at this time we was at Chattanooga and Ringold and when I think back over the year and see what we have done to[o] much credit [can]not be given to our Generals for the able manner they have conducted the severel campaigns. I will guess ere another New Year rolls around that we will all be at home enjoying the fruits of our labor and peace will reign throughout our beautifull land and our Goverment will all be under the Old Flag.

CHAPTER 11

South Carolina: A God Forsaken Region

As 1865 began, Sherman planned to march his sixty thousand men north through the Carolinas toward Petersburg, Virginia, where they could assist Ulysses S. Grant's forces in destroying Lee's Army of Northern Virginia. Miller and his fellow Hoosiers left Savannah on January 20 and moved into South Carolina in early February, then advanced with some difficulty through swamps toward the capital at Columbia. Enemy opposition was again practically nonexistent, and Sherman captured Columbia on February 17, forcing the Confederates to evacuate Charleston as well. With this leg of the march completed, Sherman's next objective was Fayetteville, North Carolina.

SUNDAY JAN 1ST
[SAVANNAH, GEORGIA]

The weather is cold it haveing frozen some last night. . . . The news from our Army under Genl Thomas is that he captured Eighteen thousand prisoners and Sixty pieces of Artillery and that there is an Armistice of fifty days to arrange terms of peace.[1] I dont think our rulers would be so foolish as to enter into any Such an arrangement as that. It would only give the Rebels [time] to recruit and reorganize their Shattered Armies and prolong the war. Our government tried to coax them back once and went into the war reluctantly and now I believe in pushing to a termination that will be lasting and compell them to allow us to fix the terms of surrender. They have forfeited all their rights. Some cannonadeing in the direction of Charleston. We got orders not to tear up any more Rail Road as they was going to repair it. . . . We had fried Oysters. . . . New Years day passed without any unusual occurrence and I[t] turned out to be a nice evening.

Monday Jan 2nd

. . . I was writing all day. The night is clear and Star light. It had the appearence of rain but cleared away. . . .

Tuesday Jany 3rd

I detailed fifteen men to work on the fortifications in the city. I finished our Monthly returns and ballanced the Books. This was a nice warm day and I was in Camp all day. . . .

Wednesday Jan 4th

Captain Karns and I went to the city to see the Cavalry review but it was postponed. We visited the Pulaski Monument erected to the Poland General who fell near here during the War of the Revolution.[2] We was also at the Wharf. Only one vessel came up while we was there as it is dangerous for them comeing up the river on account of the Torpedoes. We could look north over miles and miles of Rice Stubble and see Ships running up the rivers and they looked like they was sailing in the fields as we could not see the water. There is an old cannon planted in a small fort at the Wharf that was placed there a great many years ago and is preserved as a relic of the former War. There is severel Historical places here and I want to visit them before we leave. We returned to camp in time for Brigade drill which lasted three hours. I wrote to Nett this evening but go[t] no mail.

Thursday Jan 5th

The Regiment went on Picket but I had to remain in camp and finish our Pay Rolls. I sent to Nett to make me a pair of Chevrons as I wanted a pair of her make as we Soldiers take great pride in wearing any thing made by those we reverence and love. Nothing will make the heart of a Soldier glader than to receive some little token from home no difference how Small. It rained some to night. The news from Genl Thomas good and getting better.

Friday Jan 6th

Still raining this morning. The Regiment came in from Picket duty and we drew and issued to the men Some Clotheing and some of us needed it very much and we did not draw enough to go around. I was in camp all day.

SATURDAY JAN 7TH

This is a nice day. No drilling. . . . News from Genl Thomas is that he is still after Hood. Reported the Genl Butlers expedition has returned to Fortress Monroe and Porters fleet Still lying off Wilmington.[3] There is talk to night of our Regiment moveing into the city for Provost Duty but no orders and I tell the Boys we will never go there as our experience makes us to[o] good Soldiers for Garrison duty. There is plenty of commands that can do that kind of duty as well as we could and they could not fill our place on a campaign. I dont think it would be [good] policy to put experienced Soldiers in garrison and the "Gree[n] Horns" in the field and then I prefer the active service as the time passes quicker and is not so monotinous as laying in camp. Then there is so much "Red Tape" and drilling to be done and it is not so healthy as campaigning. I made out some ordinance Returns for Inspection.

SUNDAY JAN 8TH

Captain Karns and I visited the celebrated Jasper Spring to day. Here is where Sergt Jasper rescued the prisoners from the Brittish during the Revolutionary War Spoken of in the History of "Genl Marions" campaign.[4] It is Situated near a large Swamp and has a nice fence around it and the top of the spring has a large Stone cut out and layed around it. I got a bunch of Spanish Moss that hung over the spring to send home. I dipped up a canteen full of water and carried it to camp. We had Inspection at Nine Oclock a.m. . . . News that Genl Thomas has captured Hoods entire Army. The 15th A.C have orders to march at Seven am in the morning and I presume we will go in a few days at farthest.

MONDAY JAN 9TH

It is raining this morning. No mail. We received Orders to be ready to move in the morning with two days cooked rations in our haversacks. Now the question is where are we going. Some say Charleston & Richmond and others say Mobile. Time will tell. Some of our Boys feel disappointed because we are not going to remain here but I am Satisfied to go.

Tuesday Jan 10th

We moved at Seven Oclock following the same road north that we came in on and marched about Eight miles and relieved a Brigade of our Division on an "out post." It rained very hard this afternoon and we had no Shelter but Pine Brush which is not very much protection. No Rebels made their appearance and nothing unusual occurred. I dont understand this move whether it is a permanent move or whether we will return to Savannah and are only here on a kind of Picket duty by [but] my guess is that we will go on north and capture some of the Seaport Towns and form another Base. We can hold any of them with a small force when once captured.

Wednesday Jan 11th

My company was sent out to reconoiter about two miles from camp but found no Johnies and returned to camp. It is all quiet in our front. It is clear and cold. . . .

Thursday Jan 12th

There has been heavy cannonadeing towards Charleston to day. We was relieved by the 1st Brigade of the 1st Division of our Corps (14th) and we returned to camp at Savannah where I received Netts letter of the 30th Dec. Thirteen men and one Non Commissioned Officer was detailed to work on the Fortifications to morrow. [?] was in our camp. No news of importance.

Friday Jan 13th

We did not drill any to day. . . . I was in camp all day. Capt Studabaker spent the evening with us and we had a good old fashoend visit. No News. It is still cold.

Saturday Jany 14th

Genl Shermans congratulotery order was read to the Army to day in which he compliments the us very highly and Says we have accomplished all that was intended. That he anticipates a speedy close of the war. It turned very cold after noon and I was in camp all day. . . . There does not seam to be any move on our part now and there is no Rebels close here only a few cavalry. Our Brigade can go any place and the Johnies dont molest them.

SUNDAY JAN 15TH

. . . Lieut Starbuck and I went to the city to preaching at the First Baptist church. It is a splendid Edifice and they have a it nicely finished. It was crouded with Soldiers and seeing the women there reminds me of home. It is the first time in two and a half years I have heard the voice of the fairer Sex Singing and I thought of times gone by.

MONDAY JAN 16TH

Company "K" worked on the fortifications. . . . We had some sport with the camp Peddlers. The Soil is so sandy that we spade it as deep as the Trenches and our men would undermine the Ditches around the Forts and get it ready to cave in and then call a peddler and have them come over the trap and the moment they Step on the edge they come in to the Ditch on a "Sand Slide" and they get terible mad but cant get out without assistance and then the Boys torment them. Reported move Wednesday. . . . Lieut Starbuck and I went to the Theater to night and was Sold beautifully. It was no Snow at all. We have orders to go on Picket at Nine Oclock in the morning. This was a pleasent day.

TUESDAY JAN 17TH

We went on Picket and had a nice day only it was cold to night. There was nothing unusual occured and we had an easy time of it. There is no danger Picketing here. The times seam dull after being so long under excitements of an Active Campaign. No news.

WEDNESDAY JAN 18TH

We was relieved from Picket by the 14th Ohio Col Estie and returned to camp. I remained in camp the rest of the day. We have no orders to move to morrow and I guess it is only a Grape vine.

THURSDAY JAN 19TH

It has been raining about all day. I wrote to Nett and we received the news of the capture of Fort Fisher near Wilmington N.C. with the entire

Garrison of Seventeen hundred prisoners and Seventy two pieces of Artillery.[5] That is another grand success of our Arms and it Seams that we meet with victory at every move and they must know that it is foolishness to prolong the Struggle. There is talk of a move to morrow. We got orders at midnight to move at seven in the morning. I dont know whether it is realy a move or only a reconoisance in force.

Friday Jan 20th

We left camp and moved every thing early but only marched about Eight miles. We took the road leading North West up the Savannah River. It rained all night and we come very near floating away. It was cold and disagreeable. I received Netts Letter of Nov 18th/64. It has been on the road over two months. The reported capture of Wilmington contradicted. I have seven months from to day yet to soldier if I serve my full time but I believe we will be at home before that time. It looks like a long time and there will undoubtedly be some Stiring times. We could march a long distance and see a great many things in that time.

Saturday Jan 21st

My Regiment received orders to move and we went to the Savannah River about two miles and took up quarters in the negro Shanties on the Potter Plantation. This has been a beautiful place. The Dwelling has been burned but the Rice mill is in good order. When we first came here going to Savannah there was about thir[ty] thousand busshels of Rice in Ricks here but it has all disappeard. The Darkies here say there was at one time nearly a thousand working hands (Slaves) here and he must have been wealthy from the way the plantation is fixed now. The proprietor is dead. I seen Some of the oldest people here I ever seen. An old Collored man one hundred and Eight and his wife one hundred and Six years old. There was a darkie funeral here to day. There is a larg[e] grove of Live Oaks here which makes a splendid park. Still it rains but we have good quarters. I had a good laugh at our cook "Andy" and "Jack" of Company "E." The darkies are all very anxious to learn to read. Jack had an alphabet primer and Andy was learning him to spell and at each letter was a Short word commenceing with the letter. He spelled down untill he came to the letter T and it was illustrated with a tub and Jack spelled T-U-B and seeing the picture pronounced it Box.

The darkies being old men it sounded funny to me. But I have noticed that nearly every darky with the Army has some kind of a Book and put in their leasure hours trying to read. They was not allowed to have books when in Slavery and they enjoy the oppertunity. . . . There is a rumor that the Rebels cut the Levee on the opposite Side of the river and flooded the country and drounded some of our men and Mules but I cant vouch for the truth of it.

SUNDAY JAN 22ND

We did not receive any orders to move to day and I am glad of it for it is still raining. The cutting of the Levee is confirmed but our loss was small. But that seams to me to be the last resort. But desperate cases require desperate remedies and a man that is mean enough to be a Rebel it seams to cover all the rest of the Catalogue of crime and he is ready to do any thing els. The[y] dont care how they murder us so they succeed. We drew two days rations. We have a nice view across the river here. This was a gloomy and lonesome day.

MONDAY JAN 23RD

It is still raining. . . . I was with some of the Boys Fishing but we did not have very good luck as fish seamed to be scarce. No news and no marching orders.

TUESDAY JAN 24TH

. . . It is clear and cold but there is an consolation it has stopped raining. We have orders to be ready to march at Six Oclock in the morning and I suppose we will have to leave our good quarters and tramp again. But that is Soldiering. About the time we are getting fixed comfortable we get marching orders.

WEDNESDAY JAN 25TH

The Regiment left camt at Six a.m. and we caught up with the rest of the Brigade on the Ebonezer road ard we left it soon and traveled nearly west and camped in a lumber Yard where the Rebels had a lot of Sawed pine timber for Bridges which made rouseing camp fires for us and we made ourselves comfortable. It is quite cold and the Timber was dry and burned nicely.

Thursday Jan 26th

We was on the march early and went towards Springfield where there was some Rebel Cavalry but they run and we camped near town. We marched ten miles. We was delayed some cutting timber out of the road. We found plenty of Swamps and we burn pine knots and the smoke settles on our faces and whiskers and gives us a healthy collor. It is hard telling whether we are darkies or white men. It is cold and froze some. We seen no Johnies to day.

Friday Jan 27th

It is still cold and we did not move untill after noon and then only about two miles and crossed Big Ebonezer River. We passed through Springfield which is only a very Small Town although it is a county Seat. The inhabitants were all gone but a few. We seam to be following the Savannah River and I presume now we will cross it at some point into south Carolina. I think we will go north but some think we are only makeing a feint movement to dupe the Johnies and will then go to Mobile Alabama but I cant see as we need to fool them as they have nothing to hinder us.

Saturday Jan 28th

We moved about twelve miles to Switzers Ferry on the Savannah River. It is still cold. There is a report that Jeff Davis and the rest of the Rebel goverment have left Richmond and I think it is about time for if we get there and occupy a position South with the Army of the Potomac on the north it would be to[o] late for them to move and I will not be surprised to hear of them evacuateing Richmond any day.[6] The[y] are on the jump all the time and dont hardly know when they are safe now.

Sunday Jan 29th

We did not move. . . . Henry Cartwright of my company was Slightly wounded while on Picket. He did not know whither it was a Yankee shot at a hog or a Rebel who done the mischief as he did not see him. There is a gun Boat laying in the River near our camp. It is an Iron Clad and is a formidable looking affair. We will cross the river here as we are building a road through the swamp north of the river.

Monday Jan 30th

We did not move to day. I was at the Boat Landing. There is one Gun Boat and two Transports lying here. The Gun Boat run up the river on a reconnisance. I seen them selling Apples three for twenty five cents and there is Beer aboard of one of the Transports from the number of officers visiting it. Reported capture of Branchville and some fighting by the 15th and 20th Army corps. I did not learn any particulars or what the casualities were.

Tuesday Jan 31st

This is a nice day. I am not feeling well haveing taken a severe cold. We policed our quarters. . . . The Rebels planted the road across the river full of Torpedoes and we have to build a new road. One of them exploded to day and killed and wounded three men out of the first Brigade of our Division.

Wednesday Feby 1st

Beautiful day. . . . The Mail Boy of [the] 58th Indiana was apprehended for robbing the mail going out and was placed under guard. I was down to the Landing this after noon. There was only one Boat up and it was loaded with forage. . . . Some of our foragers run into the Rebels but made their escape after they exchanged a few shots. No marching orders yet.

Thursday Feby 2nd

Cloudy and cold this morning. . . . One of my company was put under arrest for failing to report at the Landing for fatigue duty after being detailed. My letter from home Said some of our Butternut friends there was putting their property out of their hands so as to be ready to Skip to Cannada in the event they was drafted. I hope they will place it in the hands of some good friend who will keep it. Any man who does not think enough of this government that he looks to for protection to go like a man and defend it Should not own any property. No marching orders.

Friday Feby 3rd

The 101st Indiana went forageing this morning and returned this evening loaded. We have plenty of rations as the supplies come up the river and the Rebels cant cut it like they can the Rail Roads. This was a cloudy day. . . . The main point now Seams to be Branchville and some reports say we hold it and others claim the Rebels still occupy it. But I think we will Soon be ready to move and then I know we will have it.

SATURDAY FEB 4TH

. . . We have a report that there was five Blockade runners came into Wilmington and was captured. They supposed they was running the Yankee Blockade and getting into port when our vessels let them pass in. We can make us[e] of the supplies they are carying over and then it dont cost the goverment any thing. The Captains of vessels comeing in from sea are not posted and run into ports where they have been entering during the war and some how the[y] find Yankees in nearly all of them and they surrender like little men. . . . There is a rumor that we will move to morrow.

SUNDAY FEB 5TH

We got orders to move and the Bugle Sounded "Strike Tents["] about nine Oclock a.m. but we did not get across the river untill after noon. We found a terible road through the swamps for four miles it being new and nothing but timber or pole bridgeing and it makes it rough. We camp at the Upper Landing as it is colled and only marched four miles. There is a rumor that there is heavy fighting at Branchville and the[n] we are going to reinforce the garrison. But nothing reliable. We drew Some clotheing after night and it rained nearly all night.

MONDAY FEB 6TH

It is rainy and cold and as there was no orders to move I went to the Landing but was not there long when the Bugle Sounded "Strike Tents" and we hurried to camp but the order was contramanded and changed to move at Seven in the morning and a second change said at six am. I guess the fighting at Branchvill yesterday was a hoax or we would [not] have remained in camp all day.

TUESDAY FEB 7TH
[SOUTH CAROLINA]

We started early to cross the swamp. It was four miles through and the road almost impassible. We haulted after getting over and sent men back to repair the road and help the Wagon Train out. We then moved on and passed Robertsvill which is all burned. Not a house of any kind Standing. Our Commissary Sergeant fount one of our men dead who had been killed by Guirillas. We had no fighting although a large force of Rebels under Johnston is reported in front. We are now fairly in the State of South Carolina. The first state to Seceed and fired the first gun And we have all sworn vengence against it.[7] Our mess have resolved to eat no meat but Ham or Chicken while in the state. I dont know how it will pan out but that is the resolution. We marched ten miles.

WEDNESDAY FEB 8TH

We started early and marched twenty five miles. The roads was bad and we was in rear of the wagon Train. The country was level and swampy. We did not see a single house in the whole days marching and plenty of Chimneys are Standing as monuments of the march. There is some important move on hands from the distance we marched to day. We did not see any Johnies. . . . We found plenty of forage and Still have "*ham*."

THURSDAY FEBY 9TH

We made a good days march. The weather was cold and disagreeable. We found plenty of Sweat Potatoes and Bacon. The houses are all distroyed along our march and we can see smoke all around us and tell where the advance is by the Smoke. We find Rosin and Turpentine factories and none of them escape. The citizens all get up and run. We took dinner at Lawtons plantation which was a nice place.

FRIDAY FEB 10TH

We had the advance to day and marched Eight miles to Barnwell Court House. All the public building[s] was distroyed by our Cavalry. We found a few citizens yet in town. We have marched about Sixty miles in this state and here is the first houses I have seen standing. We have foraged off the country and what we could not use was distroyed. This has been quite a Town but it looks now like it was nearly worn out. The Cavalry had some Skirmishing in the Town and the citizens complain of the treatment they received but I cant simpathise with them very much. This is a fair country around here.

SATURDAY FEB 11TH

We did not move untill noon and marched fifteen miles and camped about midnight. The hurry is to help Killpatrick out of a Scrape near Aiken. The report is that he is in a Baracade and surrounded by Wheeler and Hamptons Cavalry. We heard some cannonadeing to day and I suppose it is the Cavalry. This is a Sandy country and poor soil and no water to be had. We was so tired I did not wait for any thing to eat but layed down and went to Sleep.

SUNDAY FEB 12TH

We started early and marched fifteen miles and Struck the Charleston and Augusta Rail Road between the 24 & 25 mile post from Augusta and 113 miles from Charleston. We found the Cavalry all right but considerably Scared. They had quite a fight but the Rebels skipped when they found out we was here. We tore up the Rail Road Track and then marched Six miles North East or nearly East. We could not get any water and we suffered teribly. I scouted the country to night but did not get a drop. Some of our Boys say they traviled five miles but came back as they went. This is the poorest country I ever seen. I would not live here for the best plantation here. The Timber is lettle Scrubby stuff and I cant See how the people live here. They are a poor ignorant class and have the same dialect that the Guinna Negros have and that is all the slaves they have. The Slaves here are more monkey than human. I cant understand half they say. I hope we will get out of this God Forsaken region before many days into a good country.

MONDAY FEB 13TH

We left camp without our usual cup of Coffee as we had no water. We suffered teribly all day. We went back about a mile and tore up the Rail Road and then marched to the South Edistoe River. The first water I found was in a dirty Pond and it had been stired in untill it was nearly thick but I dont think I ever drank with more relish in my life. We got our dinners at the river and then moved on to Davises Bridge where we camped for the night. The Reb Cavalry followed us up but kept out of our way. There was a few Shots fired after dark. Capt Karns was detailed for Picket. It turned cold and was a very disagreeable night.

Tuesday Feb 14th

It is Still cold this morning. We left camp about Eleven Oclock a.m. The 105th Ohio remained in line with one piece of Artillery to guard against a dash by the Rebels untill we crossed the swamp and River and then they distroyed the Bridge. We had a hard days march and camped about dark but soon after crossed a Creek and camped about Eleven Oclock at night near the Creek. It Sleeted and rained nearly all day and was a bad day for us. The Rebels have been following us all day but did not molest us and our men are out of patience and if they give us an opportunity we will give them a dressing in fine stile. This is Valuntine day but I did not receive any Valuntines.

Wednesday Feb 15th

We Started at day light and marched about 10 miles and came upon our Corps Wagon Train and haulted for supper and crossed Turkey creek after dark. We moved about two miles and camped for the night about ten Oclock with orders to move at Six in the morning. The Cavalry had some Skirmishing. Forage is very Scarce and we draw only one third rations. We burned a mill and cut out the Dam to flood the country. We are nine miles from Lexington and approaching the city of Columbia (The capital) where report says we will meet a large force of Rebels. If they can defend any place I would think it would be their capital but I dont think there will be any fighting but they will evacuate as they are better at that than any other military move now.

Thursday Feb 16th

We started at day light and passed the first and third Brigade and guarded our Corps Train. We arrived at Lexington about ten Oclock a.m and haulted in the edge to town for dinner. This is quite a town and the citizens are mostly gone and the town is badly torn up. There was some buisiness done here untill recently. Some of us got a large Jug full of some kind of preserves. It would hold Six or Eight gallons and we could not get the contents out and we concluded to cary it to camp and we carried it Six miles. It was more than we contracted for but we had plenty of preserves after we got to camp. We are now near Columbia and there was some cannonadeing to day. But I dont apprehend any very serious trouble here. There is a reported fight at Orangeville but no particulars. We did not see any Johnies to day. If there is a large force at Columbia we will go around it and cut the Rail Roads and pass on.

Friday Feb 17th

All kinds of rumors about Columbia. Some that our men hold the city and some that we are going around it. We got orders to move at Six a.m but our Train and the ballance of the Division passed us and we did not move untill after noon. We left Columbia to our right about four miles and crossed the Soloola river about dusk. We marched Eighteen miles and camped about midnight. The wind was high and the woods all fired and the smoke made it bad for us. Our forces enterd Columbia to day. I was present at the capture of the Lieut Col 15th South Carolina Infantry at Lexington and he got away from his command to[o] far and was captured by foragers and I have his sword.[8]

Saturday Feby 18th

A nice warm day. We was relieved from guarding Train[s] and done some Bridgeing. The 1st Division done some Skirmishing with the Johnies and one Brigade crossed Broad River. We moved about five miles and camped on the South bank of the river. We got plenty of forage. This part of the country is hilly and the soil is red clay and the roads is Slippery when wet. We find some nice plantations but their crops are generally Short as the soil is not very productive. The water is generally good. The roads are bad and our wagon train and Artillery cut them up bad. We captured Six wagons from the Johnies. They was sent out for forage and got lost and got to our lines instead of their own. Broad River is wide and deep but not navigable I believe. The Rebel Cavalry Still move with us and gather up our straglers.

SUNDAY FEBY 19TH

It is clear and cold. We left camp about Eight Oclock am and crossed Broad River. Our Brigade was in the advance. Our train was threatened and my Regiment & company was sent back near Alston to protect it but the Rebels did not make a dash on it and my company was sent on Picket. I went about two miles to a Tobacco house and got a Caddy of Tobacco. Our foragers brought in lots of forage but had Some Skirmishing with the Rebels. We marched Eight miles.

MONDAY FEB 20TH

We started early and commenced Skirmishing and kept it up untill we got to Little River. We could not Cross as the Bridge was burned. We marched six miles and Stopped about Eleven Oclock a.m. Plenty of forage.

TUESDAY FEB 21ST

We crossed the river on Pontoons and started towards Winnsboro and we had some Sharp Skirmishing before we enterd the Town about Eleven Oclock a.m. The 20th Corps beat us in a little. Our foragers and Some of Gearys Division had a fight over some forage.[9] Severel men was wounded. It Seams very foolish for our own men to fight among themselves but The Eastern and western men dont get along together and I dont know the reason. One difficulty is the Eastern men put on considerable Style and think that we are ignorant and are hardly fit for Soldiers. But when the time comes to Stand up in the Battle front there is no discount on either and one is anxious to have the other on hands.[10] We camped near town but I did not go into town at all. From where we are camped it looks like a nice place. Genl Beaureguard passed through on the Train a short time before we cut the Rail Road. He was going north. We moved on three miles this evening and camped for the night haveing marched Seventeen miles. There was two of our Soldiers killed and layed along the side of the Road and their bodys mutilated with a Board across their Breasts saying "we will serve all the Yankees we catch the same way." That does not make us feel any better towards the Rebels and our men talk vengence on men who perpetrate such outrages.

WEDNESDAY FEBY 22ND

It rained some and we Started early following the Rail Road towards Charlotte. We passed White Oak Station and burned the Rebel Store House at Youngs Point and tore up the Rail Road. We marched twelve miles.

THURSDAY FEBY 23RD

We was in the rear of the Division and did not move untill Seven Oclock a.m. We left the Rail Road and took the road towards Lancaster and left Chester Court House to our left and camped after marching Seventeen miles. We passed the Second Division on the road. Killpatrick hung Seven Bushwhackers in retalliation for some of his men we was murdered by them. It seams dreadfull to carry on that kind of a war but it will stop them when nothing els will. This is a rich country and the planters are wealthy and seam to know Something. The Soil is mostly red clay and it is hilly. The Soil is productive. It rained all night. We did not see any Johnies.

FRIDAY FEB 24TH

It is still raining. Reported evacuation of Charleston by the Rebels. We did not move as our Engineers had to Po[n]toon the Catawba River. It rained all night and the roads will be terible to move our Wagon Train.

SATURDAY FEB 25TH

Still raining. We could not move to day as the River is so high and such a stiff current that the Pontoon Anchors would not hold so as to keep the Bridge to its place. We have plenty of mud and the worst kind.

SUNDAY FEB 26TH

We got orders to move but when we got to the river two miles from camp the Pontoons had broken and we had to hault. It cleared away once but commenced raining again and kept it up all night. Forage is getting scarce and we must get out of here some way soon.

MONDAY FEB 27TH

Still it rains. Our Engineers worked faithfull all day and Genl Davis says
we must cross if we have to burn our wagons. It is getting desperate. We
was called out at ten Oclock at night in the rain to cross the river. The
Rebels came up to our line and we had a little Skirmishing but it did not
last long. We crossed during the night and climbed the hills and it was
daylight when we haulted on the north side. It was a terible night and
the roads are almost impassible and I dont hardly see how our wagons and
artillery will ever get up the hills as they are steep and rugged.

TUESDAY FEB 28TH

We moved about a miles from the River and was then sent back to help
the wagons up the hill. We had to push them and I felt sorry to see the
poor mules tugging at those heavy wagons but it was a hard time for us.
Genl Davis came along just when the driver was tying his broken hame
string and he cursed and swore around and gave our Lieutenant a terible
curseing and Showed himself in his usual Style. I do think our government is hard up when such men are allowed a command. I should not
[have] blamed Starbuck if he had shot him dead off his horse. I dont
believe I should have taken it. Our Train all got over about four Oclock
p.m and we then moved on about two miles and camped for the night.
It rained all night and the country is afloat. We will have terible roads to
morrow but we will have to move as we[?] our "grub" is getting scarce and
we cant subsist here very long. I hope we will have better weather.

WEDNESDAY MAR 1ST

Still ra[i]ning and we Started early. We had a hard day of it as we found
no forage and our rations are "played out." We marched fifteen miles
and camp near the Battlefield where Genl Gates was defeated in 1780.
There is no marks of the Struggle left.[11] The Rebels did not get over the
river consequently we were not molested. The roads are terible and are
almost impassible. But the Johnies say the Yankees do just whatever
they want to and we made the usual march. The country is very hilly
and not cultivated very extensively and the 20th Corps haveing crossed
severel days ago at another crossing have foraged the country and
stripped it. The soil is red clay and we have the appearance of Ground

hogs. I think we will get into some better country when we get away from the River.

THURSDAY MAR 2ND

It did not rain any to day and we feel very thankfull but forage is still scarce and we are getting very hungry and I hope we will find plenty to morrow. We marched thirty four miles and camped on Big Lynch creek. The people here are Suffering as well as ourselves for provissions. This is a poor country but we have a good camp to night and the prospects are more favorable. I was detailed for forageing to morrow in Lieut Starbucks place and it suits me. We are all very tired and hungry to night.

FRIDAY MAR 3RD

I started out with the foragers before the Regiment left camp. It was cloudy and misting rain and we got lost in the hills and heard a Rooster crow and went to the plantation and an old women sitting in the door was very much surprised [and] on looking up exclamed "*Aint Youens all Yankees.*" We politely informed her we was and enquired the road and she told us and we left her. We did not find any forage untill afternoon and we then found an old Grist mill and plenty of corn and ground Some corn meal and when we got to camp we had a wagon loaded with meal Bacon and a Barrel of Sorgum molasses and in addition had pressed four darkies into service and they was loaded so we had plenty to night. The Rebels made a dash on Some straglers in advance and killed one man and captured twenty two others and we found two of our Brigade Band hid in Brush nearly scared to death. An officer out of the 20th Corps undertook to take our forage away from us as we got onto the road they was marching on but we would not surrender it and after sauceing him a while we drove on and got onto the road that our own corps was on. We are on what the citizens call the Chesterfield road. The Army moved about Eighteen miles. But I dont know how many I did march but about thirty.

CHAPTER 12

Bentonville, Raleigh, and War's End

As they marched toward Fayetteville, North Carolina, Miller and the other Yankees found that the days were consumed by marching, waiting for the building of pontoon bridges to cross streams and rivers, destroying railroad lines, burning cotton gins, mills, factories, and towns, and foraging for rations. But often life on the march was even more difficult. On February 27, as the last regiment of the Fourteenth Corps to cross the Catawba River, the soldiers of the Seventy-fifth were called out at ten o'clock in the evening in a relentless rainstorm. The men waded in knee-deep mud and water for the remainder of the night, helping wagons ford the river.

The Hoosiers claimed the honor of being the first organized Union troops into Fayetteville on March 11, driving a Confederate rear guard ahead of them. After destroying the arsenal there, and taking a four-day rest, the Federals pushed on to Goldsboro, sixty miles away, where rail connections with the coast would allow refitting before moving on to Raleigh.

The only serious opposition of the entire campaign came at Bentonville, on the way to Goldsboro. Gen. Joseph E. Johnston, Sherman's old nemesis, recently returned to command the Army of Tennessee, along with all troops in the Department of South Carolina, Georgia and Florida, launched a surprise attack to destroy both corps of Sherman's left wing in detail. His first target was the Fourteenth Corps. The battle began on March 19, and the Seventy-fifth entered the fray the following morning. Miller and his comrades were involved in brisk skirmishing and came under Confederate artillery fire, but by late afternoon Johnston had retreated. On the twenty-second, the march to Goldsboro resumed, and the Hoosiers arrived in the city the following day.

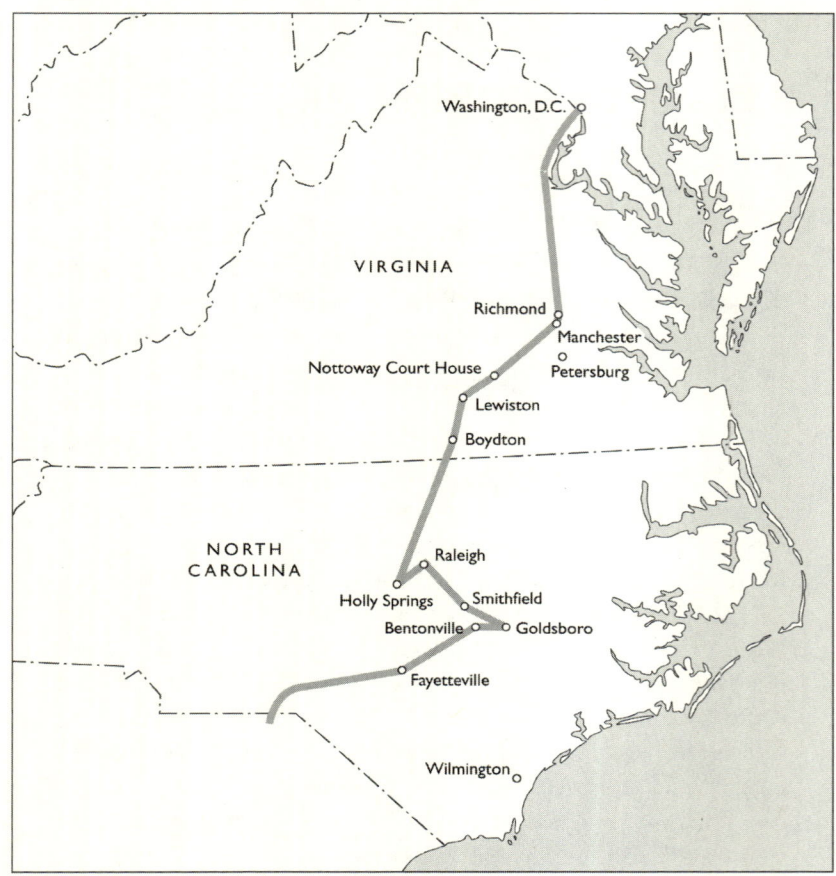

MAP 4. Travels of William Bluffton Miller in North Carolina and Virginia, 1865.

In Goldsboro, one observer described the tattered and ragged condition of Sherman's men after the long campaign: "Some of our men wore a boot on one foot and a shoe on the other, trousers with one leg of blue and the other of gray material; others wore caps, wool and straw hats." Sgt. David Floyd remembered that he was wearing butternut trousers, a plug hat, and a confiscated linen shirt. "Doubtless we were the most ragged soldiers in the United States Army," he wrote.[1]

By the time they reached Goldsboro, Sherman's troops had traveled nearly five hundred miles in sixty-three days, had crossed five large rivers, and had survived in large part by foraging rations from the barren and wasted countryside. Lt. Col. Thomas Doan, commanding the Second Brigade, Third Division, Fourteenth Corps, including the Seventy-fifth Indiana, paid tribute to his men at Goldsboro: "During the whole campaign, wherein we have . . . overcome difficulties perhaps without a parallel, the officers and men of this command, with scarcely an exception, have exhibited the most admirable and untiring patience, energy, and perseverance, and I am happy to tender them my most sincere thanks for the cheerful and hearty manner in which they have performed their whole duty."[2]

The army rested in Goldsboro until April 10, then began the final stage of their epic march, the fifty miles to the city of Raleigh. The Seventy-fifth led the army, and on their way they fought the last battle and suffered the last combat casualty of Sherman's masterful campaign. The regiment's skirmishers pushed the enemy before them and in a brisk fight captured the city of Smithfield on April 11. The Hoosier soldiers were paid a rare compliment there by wing commander Maj. Gen. Henry Slocum, for when Capt. Mahlon Floyd reported for duty with the Seventy-fifth's skirmishers outside Smithfield, General Slocum asked if they were part of the same regiment that had been the first to enter Fayetteville. When he was told that indeed they were, he replied, 'I want no better; I will risk those fellows with anything.'"[3]

The regiment entered Raleigh on the thirteenth, and on the way the troops were cheered by the news of Gen. Robert E. Lee's surrender at Appomattox Court House in Virginia. The Hoosiers then went into camp near the city. With the fall of Raleigh and the surrender of the Army of Northern Virginia, Joe Johnston decided to negotiate with Sherman. On April 26, the Confederate commander at last signed surrender documents at the Bennett Place near Durham's Station. For William Bluffton Miller, three years of war ended on a spectacular note—after marching hundreds of miles through enemy territory, he had helped force the capitulation of one of the last Confederate armies. Now the men could look forward to returning home.

SATURDAY MAR 4TH
[NORTH CAROLINA]

This is the day of Presidential Inauguration and Old Abe will still occupy the chair. The Rebels know what to expect from him and say they will not ask for any quarter nor give any but I think they will change their minds. Our Cavalry had some fighting on our left but we marched Eighteen miles and crossed into North Carolina about noon. We left Chesterfield on our right. We passed through a small town called Maysville. We are getting into a better country now and report says we are going to Fayetteville. It is on the Cape Fear River and that will open up communication again. The citizens claim that Johnston will meet us on the rout. But he cant muster men enough to make much of a fight unless he fights by detail and handles one corps at a time. But Genl Sherman will look after that.

SUNDAY MAR 5TH

We left camp in the rear of [the] Wagon Train and did not get started untill about Nine Oclock. We marched ten miles to the Yadkin river and camped about noon. This is the first clear day for Eight days. The roads are Sandy and very good. There was some cannonadeing in the direction of Cheraw but we did not see any Johnies. We are Train Guards and will be in the rear four days. I dont like it as we are always late starting in the morning and consequently late getting into camp at night. No news.

MONDAY MAR 6TH

The Yadkin is considerable of a Stream and will delay us a day or two to pontoon it. Cheraw Surrenderd to the 17th Army Corps to day. A large quantity of Stores and amunition fell into our hands and some of the Amunition was issued to us. There was a dense Smoke arose in that direction and one very heavy explosion and I suppose the Yankees are destroying the town. I was to the river to see the Engineers putting the Pontoon Bridge across and they will have it ready for us to cross in the morning. There is a report that there is a large force of Rebels over there but I dont believe it or they would not allow us to pass the river unmolested if it was so.

TUESDAY MAR 7TH

We crossed the river about noon but found no Johnies. We marched about ten miles and camped near a very large swamp. We passed over some good country and some nice Farms. The soil is sandy and productive. The men citizens are all gone and most of them are in the Rebel Army and have left the darkies and women to do the farming. Some of them are very destitute. The men are poor managers themselves and the women and Darkies dont know anything. Their crops was short last year and they have eat it all up. The women say we will get a "Licking" when we get a little further along.

WEDNESDAY MAR 8TH

It rained hard all day. We started early and marched twenty five miles. Our Brigade was in the advance and it was easier marching. We marched beside the 20th Corps Train a part of the day. We was passing them. We found plenty of forage. The country along our rout is thinly settled. We only passed two houses. But we was on a Byroad. The soil is not very good. No fighting to day.

THURSDAY MAR 9TH

We was on the road early. It commenced raining about three Oclock p.m and continued untill after night. Some of our Bummers[4] set a Large Rosin factory on fire and the melted resin run down across the road into a Creek and burned out the Bridge and when we got there the creek was on fire as far as we could see caused by the Rosin floating on top of the water and burning. We were detained a couple of hours to build a Bridge. We are following an old Plank Road and it is about worn out and very bad. We camped about ten oclock pm at the Seventeen mile post from Fayetteville after marching Nineteen miles. Some think we will have some fighting before we get Fayetteville. It is said to be considerable of a town. There is a government Arsnell located there.

FRIDAY MAR 10TH

We started early but only moved about four miles as the Rebels have burned some Bridges before us. There was heavy cannonadeing on our right supposed to be our Cavalry. The Johnies beat us to Fayetteville. It rained some. Word came into camp that Genl Killpatrick was surprised this morning by the Rebels cavalry. They dashed into his head quarters and captured his wagons but our Boys rallied and re-captured them after a spirited engagement.[5] I did not ascertain the loss. The Johnies are said to be in heavy force in our front. Major Steele of the 101st Indiana rode into the Rebel Pickets in mistake and captured Eleven Johnies and marched them off.[6]

SATURDAY MAR 11TH
[FAYETTEVILLE, NORTH CAROLINA]

We started at Six a.m. My regiment leading and marching "left in front." We did not find any Rebels untill we got to the Six mile post from Fayetteville where they had built a barracade in the road and near a Lumber River. The four left companies deployed. Two on either side of the road. Companies E & K on the right. We drove them into the swamp but could not wade the river and some of us had to cross a foot log and as I was on the right of the company I stepped on the log which raised me above the Bank on the north Side and a Cavalryman Shot at me and the Ball struck my Cartradge Box Belt and passed through it and the rest of my clotheing comeing out through my Waiste Belt and tore the corner out of my Cartridge Box Searing my Side. I thought when it Struck me I was Shot through. It made me very Sick but I soon got over it. It was a close call and I feel thankfull it was no worse. If I had been a little farther forward the Ball would undoubtedly have passed through me. After we got over and one of our Batteries was posted we charged their Barracade and drove them out. We found three dead Johnies in the Barracade. We did not have any other man hurt in my company. We Skirmished with them untill we enterd the town. When [we] got near the town we had to cross a deep Ravine and on the opposite side we could see the Arsnell and line of works. The 79th Pennsylvania was on our right and commenced to double quick to beat us into town and some of us on the right of the company Started on the run when Capt Karns "Sang out" hault! but we paid no attention to him and he Said "well then go to h—ll if you wont hault.["] The Johnies got frightend and left their works and some rode across the river on the Bridge when it was on fire. We was the first into town and have the name of captureing it.[7] I was sent by Adjutant

Medsker to guard a large Ware House that was stored full of Supplies and furniture. My orders was not to allow anything taken out and had a racket with a captain of the 17th Corps about a barrell of flour but I kept the flour all the same. There was scme poor women in the house and some of them had gotten some meat when we got there and I told them to take what they had. I thought it to[o] bad to deprive them when there was more than we could use. I was on guard untill after night when we was relieved and went to camp near town. Some of our Boys found some wine and got gloriously drunk. This town has about Eight Thousand inhabitants and there is some large cotton factories here. It is a pretty town. The men are all gone as usual. It is Situated on the Cape Fear river which is navigable to this place. This will open up communication and we may get some mail and hear from home. I dont know how long we may remain here but presume not long. Some Say we will go to Goldsboro from here.

SUNDAY MAR 12TH

. . . There is two small Transpors lying at the landing which come up last night. There was some canronadeing on the East. I was down to the Levee this evening and there was some of our men crossing the River. Companies A F & I went to Town for Provost duty. The citizens prophesy that Johnston will give us a fight before we reach Goldsboro and claim he has a large force to oppose us. But I know they havent enough men to give us Battle only by detail. This was a nice day.

MONDAY MAR 13TH

I went with Capt Karns to the Arsnel to see them battering it down. The[y] have Battering Rams made with Rail Road Iron and they demolish it very fast. The 20th Corps is crossing the River. Mail left to day but I did not write any. There is a report that a Fleet will come up to night with supplies. Severel of the citizens took the Boats going north. Some of them claim to be loyal but they dare not show it untill we come. They are very glad to get away some place where they can live without being in constant fear all the time. We was in a house where there was severel women and they was all b_tter Rebbells and one of them said her husband was with Johnston and she hoped he would meet me because [I] to talked saucy to her. I told her I would send her a lock of his hair if I met him. She said no wonder we whipped them for we were all big Stout fellows while their men are weakly. She is right for our army is in splendid condition and we are healthy and the marching keeps us so.

Tuesday Mar 14th

. . . The 15th Corps passed through town and crossed the River. All the Cotton Factories was all burned.[8] It looks like a pitty that the war necessitates the distruction of so much property. New York city papers of the 3rd gives the defeat of Early in the Shannondoah valley by Genl Sheridan and also confirms the occupation of Kingston by Genl Schofield so that we will have help to dress Johnston if we should need it.[9] Early is reported captured but the news is to[o] good to be true. I dont think we will Stay here many days but will soon go to Goldsboro and from there to Richmond and help Genl Grant. It looks darker every day for the Rebels and they meet with one disaster after another and will certainly give it up soon.

Wednesday Mar 15th

Rumors of a move and as the mail left this a.m I wrote to Nett and we left camp at ten Oclock and crossed the River. It commenced raining soon after we started and was Showery the rest of the day. We only marched about seven miles and camped. The roads was very bad. We are on the Raleigh plank Road. There is a rumor that the 15th Corps is orderd to reach Goldsboro in two days and a half for fear of an attack by Johnston on Genl Schofield but we have no such orders yet. But we may receive them any time. It would be a heavy march but we are good for it if it is necissary. It looks like we might have a little fight before many days as the Johnies are getting impertinent and the citizens say they have considerable of an Army in our front.

Thursday Mar 16th

We remained in camp untill the rest of the Division came up with our Wagon Train and did not move untill three pm and then only moved three miles and camped. Our Division was the last to leave Fayetteville and the[y] found a lot of Flour that was hid. One of the 105th Ohio

Boys was Shot by a citizen for insulting his daughter. I dont know but he was served right as we are not here for insulting women or makeing war on children although they suffer more or less in consequence of the war. There is a rumor that the 1st and 2nd Division with the Cavalry had a fight near Black River but no particulars. It rained all day.

FRIDAY MAR 17TH

This is a nice morning quite cold. We did not march untill after noon and then only moved about five miles. The roads are bad and it looks as though we might have a little fight to get through as we are moveing very careful. There is all kinds of rumors in refference to the fight yesterday. A portion of our wagon Train went for wounded. The roads are terible and our Wagon Train moves slow. We are camped three miles from Black River. We are guarding Train and it is the worst kind of soldiering. It makes us late starting and late into camp. Some times we are marched hard and then again we only play along. Johnston is in our front with considerable of an Army and he will watch an opportunity to Jump onto us when he can surprise us but I think our Generals will watch him. He cant do much with us unless we get to[o] far apart and cant concentrate quick enough.

SATURDAY MAR 18TH

We was in the rear of Train and it was late when we got on the road. We only moved about five miles. We crossed Black River. We cant get any particulars from the fight yesterday and I presume it did not amount to much. This was a nice day.

SUNDAY MAR 19TH
[BENTONVILLE, NORTH CAROLINA]

The fireing in our front commenced early and we soon received orders to pass the Train and go to the front. We marched about fifteen miles and came up with our advance about 4 Oclock. We found that the 1st and 2nd Division and the 20th Corps had been driven back. The Rebels are in force and fortified. They charged through a Swamp on our 1st Division and they were marching along the road in column and the General commanding had been cautioned but paid no attention to the warning and the result was our men being surprised Stampeded on the first charge but our 2nd Division stood the charge and the 1st reforming fineally made a stand after being driven about a mile. We found the[m] posted and glad to see us. The Rebels fought bravely as the[y] wanted to demolish the Old 14th Corps it being the "Left Wing" or whip one Corps at a time.[10] The movement was well planed and but for Genl Sherman haveing the Army well in hand might have met with a terible disaster but we took the advance and pushed on and drove the Johnies through the swamp to their fortifications and are to night about seven miles in advance of where the Battle was fought this morning and are fortifying. The fighting has lasted all day and the loss heavy on boath sides. Many of our brave Boys are lying on the battlefield in our rear Still in death which tell the Sad tale. But tonight we are concentrated and what tomorrow will bring fourth is yet to be seen.

MONDAY MAR 20TH

The Troops was on the move early and we occupied the 2nd line of battle. About noon we passed to the front and reconoiterd the Rebel line and had a sharp Skirmish when we withdrew a Short distance and built a line of fortifications and remained there untill after dark when we returned to the rear. My regiment lost a few men and the 2nd Minnisota some. The Rebel position is strong but they cant hold it long. Their time to do us much damage has gone by and if they remain Genl Sherman will surround them. But they know that and will get out. There was one Section of our Battery (two guns) which lost all their horses in the fight to day and was left on the field between the lines and we could not get them away nor the Johnies could not get them. Severel efforts was made by boath Sides to get them and after dark we pulled them off. The wheels was litterally shot to pieces by musket Balls.[11] Johnston is a Sharp old fellow and if he had the men might make us considerable trouble. He is one of the best Generals they have. He lays his plans well but has not got men enough to help him out.

TUESDAY MAR 21ST

I learned that they call this battle ground "Bentonville." I have not seen any Town or even a good place for on[e] as it seams to be all swamp here. We received orders early to be ready to move at a moments warning. There was heavy fireing all day on our right and the Rebels undertook to drive the 15th Corps out of their works and made severel charges. If they had succeeded in driveing them it would cut us off but the old 15th stood the charges and repulsed them with heavy loss. A Rebel Regiment of heavy Artillery from Charleston who had never been in Battle before and who was sent out from their fortifications fought desperately and their ranks will tell the tale to night. The[y] were dressed better than the Rebs are generally and was a "crack" Regiment. They are wiser to night than before as regards fighting. From the number to be seen lying around with their "Toes turned up" (as our Boys say) there cant be many left.[12] In on[e] charge the Collor Bearer set his Flag on our works but it remained there and he was riddled with bullets. We expected orders to charge their works all day but it was better for us to let them do the chargeing. . . . I am Sick to night.

WEDNESDAY MAR 22ND

This is a cold blustery day and we received orders to move at Nine am but as our Train did not get up we did not move untill after noon. The Johnies left our front during the night and we moved right over their works. This would have been the heavyest fighting if they had remained. I went over the Battlefield and seen a great many dead men unburried and lots of wounded Rebels one of which we took out of a pond of water and gave him a drink. He was wounded in the head and was delirious. But the water revived him and I enquired his name and he told me Francis White of the 4th Georgia and that his home was near Pond Spring.[13] Then he seamed to think we were Johnies and said "Boys if I could kill one more Yankee I would die happy" and we left him. The 15th Corps captured a Brigade of Mississipians at the crossing of the Tar River as the Bridge had been fired by the retreating Rebels and they could not cross and had to surrender. We marched ten miles towards Goldsboro and camped about ten Oclock. I was about played out.

THURSDAY MAR 23RD
[GOLDSBORO, NORTH CAROLINA]

We started early for Goldsboro and passed Genl Terrys command the 24th & 25th Corps composed of Collored Soldiers at the river and the road was lined with Negroes for miles on either Side.[14] I suppose they

will stop Rebel Bullets as well as a white man. We also met some of the
130th Ind among others Lieut W H Covert who was sitting on the fence
waiting for us to come up. We are considerable of a curiosity to the
Troops here as our reputation has preceeded us. They call us "Shermans
Bummers." We marched in review on entering Goldsboro. Genl
Sherman I presume desired to see the noble condition of his army. But
now to contrast the army with the day we left Ringold Georgia. Then
our Boys wore the "Blue" entirely and was in a splendid condition and
thought to be invinceble. But since that time we have broken the back
of the Rebel Elephant and passed over a year in active campaigning and
we enter here with ranks depleted and hardly two men dressed alike.
We see men wearing the immortal "plug hat" and all collors of clotheing. They are ragged but fat and Saucy and their experience has taught
them to look out for themselves and expecting to remain here severel
days they have layed in S[u]pplies accordingly. Some are carying hams
of meat Some chickens and others a sack of Black Peas with Frying Pans
tied on their guns and very many laughable things occur and I have no
doubt Genl Sherman himself feels proud of the men who have made
themselves immortal in "The March to the Sea." We have left many of
our Boys behind us but the men who are left will make it warm for the
Johnies if the war continues for they have carried their lives in their
hands as it were for the last year and are very reckless. We passed
through town to the north side crossed Little River and camped on the
north Side. Goldsboro is a small town but a county Seat. There is some
nice houses and some of the citizens remain. This was a cold blustry day
and very disagreeable.

Friday Mar 24th

The Darkies perpetrated a joke on some Rebel Cavalry to day. A Brigade
of them was sent out and Skirmished with them and the Johnies claim
the Negroes wont fight and when one of the collored Regiments
retreated they followed them up and the result was they was surrounded
by Darkies and had to surrender or do worse. The[y] gobbled five hundred Johnies. The Rebs Say they dont care only they was captured by
the — "niggers." It was fun for us to hollow at them when they was
marched into camp and the darkies riding their horses. "The collored
Troops fought nobly." . . .

SATURDAY MAR 25TH

We changed our camp a Short distance and put up "Shanties" and have a nice camp now. The 23rd Corps moved out of town. I seen severel Indiana Conscripts to day but none that I knew. There was two companies from each Regiment in our Brigade was detailed to run the Grist Mills near here of which there is a number. This is a good country. The soil is some Sandy and very productive. Our men seam to be well supplied with Buggies and Carriages and put on lots of Stile. The road by camp is full nearly all the time. I suppose the Boys borrowed them from the citizens while on the march. The[y] have broken severel with their reckless driveing and running tcgether. While in town I noticed some very fine Carriages comeing in but they was generally loaded with Bacon or some kind of forage. I was diverted at a Band Drummer who was dressed in a Swallow Tailed coat and Plug hat and one of the new Colonels enquired of him what Regiment was passing. He replied "*The same old regiment in new clothes.*" I presume the answer was satisfactory as the colonel did not ask any more questions.

SUNDAY MAR 26TH

I received four Letters from Nett. . . . Also a package of Letter paper and my Orderly Sergeant Cheverons from Nett. . . . I feel very proud of my cheverons and will wear them with great pleasure. We had company inspection at nine a.m. I remained in camp all day.

MONDAY MAR 27TH

Companies E & K was detailed to go with [the] forage train but the orders were countramanded and we did not go. A number of conscripts came to the 79th Pennsylvania and company A got three recruits. We drew and issued some clotheing. . . . There is rumors in camp of peace and that our government has sent commissioners to Richmond. I dont think the report can be true as I dont believe President Lincoln will now ask them to make peace but push them to make propositions. I would rather see them ask as our government propose to them. They will come to time soon.

Tuesday Mar 28th

It is very Smokey this morning. I was down in town and got two Northren papers and the news is very favorable for peace as the Johnies seam to be getting tired of the war. They begin to realize that the war is hurting them badly and we are getting them in a shape to distroy their entire Army for we will assist Genl Grant now at Richmond and the Surrender of Lee virtueally ends the strife. He cant get out nor Stay very well where he is. . . .

Wednesday Mar 29th

I commenced makeing pay Rolls and also made out Inspection reports. A Train of Sixty cars of "Hard Tack" came in and that looks like liveing again. There is all kinds of "Grape vines" in refference to peace negotiations in camp. . . .

Thursday Mar 30th

This is a rainy morning. I was down in town. Still plenty of rumors about the close of the war. . . .

Friday Mar 31st

This was a windy day. I was working on pay rolls when I heard "muffled drums" approaching and they passed camp and I inquired what was up and was informed that a man in the Ambulance a member of the 12th N Y Cavalry was to be Shot. I followed to the place of execution and learned his name was Prebble.[15] A Brigade of Infantry formed a "hollow square." He was brought in to the square and marched around it to where his grave was dug and a rough Coffin was sitting and he was then asked if he had anything to say and he then advised all present not to do as he had done but be good Soldiers that he regretted to have to die in the way he did on account of his mother and that he forgave all who had any thing to do with his trial and co[n]viction. He then knelt beside his coffin and a file of eight men was brought forward. There was severel Indians among them. Prebble was blindfolded and the commands given Ready! Aim!! Fire!!! and he fell forward on his coffin dead. His offense was attempting to outrage an old Lady over fifty years of age and it was the third offense. He was a fine looking young man and report says a good Soldier before. I dont approve of his conduct neither do I approve of the proceedings of the Court martial that imposed the sentence. His death did not make amends for the wrong he committed. But I call it murder in the first degree in takeing his life. I dont think I will ever witness another such a horror if I can get away from it. I have seen men Shot in Battle but never in cold blood before. He died brave like a soldier that he was. After he was burried the ground was leveled off and Sodded over so that no trace can ever be found of him. But that is military and was done to Scare the rest of us who are unfortunate enough to carry a gun in defense of our country. Then again it gives our superiors such a good opportunity to display what terible brave men they are. If they would lead out the man who sentenced poor Prebble and Shoot him for murder I would be tempted to go and see it done.[16] The news is rather meager and no moveing orders.

SATURDAY APR 1ST

This was a nice warm morning. I completed the Pay Rolls and wrote to Nett. We had company Inspection. I went down to town this afternoon. We have no orders to move and no news that is reliable although we get plenty of "Grape Vines."

SUNDAY APR 2ND

I was writing all day makeing out our monthly Reports. . . .

MONDAY APR 3RD

Rumors of a move soon in camp report says the 10th. Orders for grand Review to morrow. . . . We had Dress Parade this evening.

TUESDAY APR 4TH

The Division is being reviewed by Genls Schofield Slocum Davis and Baird. I did not go out as I have so much writeing to do to get the company Books Straitend up. Still a report that we will move on the 10th some say west and others north but nothing reliable. Nice day. No news.

WEDNESDAY APR 5TH

Cloudy morning. The Regiment went on Picket but I was writing all day in camp. Our supply train was loading which looks some like moveing but no orders. I think we will go from here to Ralleigh and stir up

the capital and let them know in that city that there is a civil war in
America if they have not found it out. It looks to me like we will soon
have to look for some place to go to as we are nearly once around. But
I have been here long enough.

THURSDAY APR 6TH

The Regiment came in from Picket duty about ten Oclock. . . . I finished the Clotheing returns and we are nearly read[y] to move.

FRIDAY APR 7TH

Richmond has fallen. The Shouting and cheering along our lines commenced at daylight announceing the Glorious news. We formed by
company in mass at Regimental Head Quarters and the Tellegram was
read to us. Reported capture of the entire Verginia Army but that is
to[o] good to be true. But there is no doubt but Richmond is ours with
Twenty five thousand prisoners. There is great rejoiceing throughout
our camps and have we not an occasion for rejoiceing over the good
prospect of getting home again and a cessation of the carnage and
bloo[d]shed that has been going on for nearly four long years. Now if
Lee and Johnston [don't] concentrate and Battle more [it] will surely
wind up the war. But Genl Grant will not stop in Richmond long if he
has driven Lee out of his stronghold but will follow him up to see that
they do not take advantage of some portion of our army and cause a disaster. We almost begin to think we can See home now but we may meet
with a reverse yet.

SATURDAY APR 8TH

News from Richmond is Still good and Genl Grant has gained a great
victory and he is following it up and pushing Lee to the wall. There is
a rumor that Lee and his Staff are prisoners but I must have some more
evidence before I can believe it. . . . Two men put on extra duty to day
for disobeying orders. We had dress parade this evening. Report in camp
that we will move monday and are going to intercept Lee. I believe that
will be the move but it is only guess work with me.

SUNDAY APR 9TH

. . . We drew Rations and received orders to move in the morning. The 23rd Corps moved up and camped near us this evening. I met severel of the Boys. Davis Griffin and Turner came up from the Hospittal to day. I still think our move will be to Ralleigh and perhaps will intercept Lee and if we do there will be a terible Battle but I think it will be the last one.

MONDAY APR 10TH

The second Division took the advance and we followed and started from camp early. The advance had some Skirmishing and lost fifteen men in killed and wounded. The Johnies kept falling back towards Smithfield. We marched about fifteen miles. It rained nearly all day and was bad marching. We will have the advance to morry and will have the skirmishing to do if any.

TUESDAY APR 11TH
[SMITHFIELD, NORTH CAROLINA]

Our Division took the advance and my Regiment in the lead with Companies E & K as skirmishers. We encounterd Rebel Cavalry soon after leaveing camp and drove them all day untill we enterd Smithfield about noon. We had three men wounded. One man in Co B was seriously wounded. We had a lively time and severel funny little things occurred. The Johnies would bu[i]ld Barricades of Rails and wait for us. The[y] was Cavalry and are Armed with Carbines and can only do execution at Short range while our guns do execution at Nine hundred yards. They would commence on us when we would come close and then our time would come when they left their Barricade and we would make it warm for them untill they would get out of range. I noticed a number of empty Saddles of the Rebels. Just before we enterd the Town they had a line of old Logs and we Skirmished for some time and while laying in an open field the man to my left Pine while loading his gun a Johnie shot at him from behind a red Smoke House and the Ball struck his knapsack and when he opend it up there was Twenty Seven holes in his Blanket cut by it being folded. We concentrated our fire (three or four of us) on that Smoke House and when we passed it the Johnie was lying on his back. Some of us had send a leaden messenger into his head and ended his earthly career. I noticed a Rebel officer who rode a white horse a number of times and nearly every man on the skirmish line Shot at him during the day but he was not hurt. He seams to have a charmed life.[17] But we drove them across the Neuse River and they burned the Bridge and we could not cross. We found a number of prisoners hid in town. Some of our Boys got into an Odd Fellows Lodge and got some masks and Long Gounds and scared some of the darkies nearly to death. Others found some Apple Jack and was drunk.[18] This is a small Town but a beautiful location and there are some Union citizens here. The Confederacy had some trouble to keep them in subjection and they can now enjoy their loyalty. We are going towards Ralliegh and I think that is our destination. Some of our men are doeing guard duty to night and we are camped on the west side of town.

Wednesday Apr 12th

We started in advance early and Skirmished all day untill about three Oclock pm when we enterd a town called Clinton or Tollings Station. About dark we was surprised to hear the Sharp Whistle of a Locomotive comeing from towards Ralleigh which run into the depot. But we soon learned that it brought the Governer of the state and other dignitaries to tender the surrender of the Capital of the state so that we would enter the city without injureing the city. But we received other good news and that was the surrender of Lee to Genl Grant and to night our camps ring with rejoiceing over the victories and the speedy close of the Rebellion that has caused so much misery in our land. Johnston is the only one left for us to defeat and he will get it soon if we can only catch him for our Boys are very anxious to meet him now and put the final stroke to the war. We formed in column at half distance and Lt Col OBrien read the official dispatch to us from General Sherman so there is no doubt about it. We had five men wounded to day and I dont look for any more fighting in this department as Johnston has nothing to fight for and will surrender before many days. He might Strike across the country but we have Armies to oppose him at every point. Genl Grant has no Rebels in his front. Hoods Army is demoralized and Johnston has not men enough to oppose Genl Sherman. The dark cloud that has hung on the horizon for nearly four years is receeding and the sun Shine of peace begins to peep out and there are many glad hearts here to night among the vetrans camped about this little Town and no doubt many pleasent dreams of happy homes will be had to night. To morrow we enter Ralleigh.

THURSDAY APR 13TH
[RALEIGH, NORTH CAROLINA]

Our troops began moveing at four a.m and the first Division had the advance and it was our turn in the rear as we served our third yester[day] in the advance. Some of our men enterd Ralleigh about Nine am but it was noon when we marched through the city. We marched in Collum by company and was reviewed by Genl Sherman. We beat the 20 Corps in and marched fifteen miles. We marched by the State House and camped on a hill near the Lunatic Assylum. I was down in the city this evening. It is a nice place and quite a city. It looks clean and nice and nothing was molested by our men. There are a great many citizens here who claim to be loyal. There was some fireing to our left but we did not learn any particulars. Now we have the all important city of this state and where will we go next. I presume Genl Sherman will push Johnston untill he surrenders but where is a question.

FRIDAY APR 14TH

We did not receive marching orders untill Eight Oclock am and left the city at ten. It was a beautiful morning. We had no skirmishing only what was done by the Cavalry. We took the Rail Road towards Hillsboro and followed it about ten miles when we filed off on the Fayetteville road and after marching Eighteen miles we camped. We passed two station Houses but I only learned the name of one Johnstons Station. It was very warm marching. The soil is sandy.

SATURDAY APR 15TH

It was raining this morning. We was relieved from the front and took charge of the train. There is a report that Johnston has surrenderd to Sheridan and Seams to be credited by our general Officers. We only moved Eight miles to Holly Springs. We had no fighting but some of our foragers was captured by Rebel Cavalry. The town of Holly Springs is a small place and nearly deserted. We passed some nice plantations but this is not a rich country.

SUNDAY APR 16TH

The rumor of Johnstons Surrender is not confirmed and I have some doubts about it as so important an event would not need confirmation so long. We marched only Six miles. We found a red clay Soil which made hard marching. We camped near Collinses Cross Roads. I was told that nothing of our men but the 14th Corps have left Ralleigh yet. I suppose we are thrown out to keep an eye on Johnstons movements. . . .

MONDAY APR 17TH

We did not move to day and we received orders from Genl Slocum to remain in camp and a rumor is afloat that there will be an Armistice of ten days. Our Pontooneers was orderd not to complete the Bridge across the river untill further orders. Takeing all the grape vines and circumstances surrounding it looks like there might be something in the reports. We dont see or hear any Johnies now. We [may] remain here severel days untill some arrangements of surrender are made but if this closes the war we will remain cheerfully.

TUESDAY APR 18TH

Nice morning. No marching orders. Still rumors of peace negotiations and a probability of Johnstons surrender.[19] There was a conference between Genl Sherman & Johnston between our lines. But with all our good news and glorious prospects for peace we was startled to day by the terible news of the assassination of President Lincoln. We was orderd to fall in and marched to head quarters and the dispatch read to us by the Adjutant. He was shot by Wilks Booth in the Theater at Washington City on the night of the 14th and at the same time Secretary Seward was stabed at his own house by an assassin. I have seen our Army driven from the field with great Slaughter and reverses but never did any thing I remember of ever cast such a gloom over our Army. It was decernable on every countinance. We feel that we have lost the best friend and Statesman America ever produced and then just when victory is about to perch on our Banners. He saved the nation but was not permitted to enjoy his laibor. Then to think a man was ever created so base as to commit such a crime in a public place where hundreds was assembled and he had come out to enjoy a few minutes of pleasure and was assassinated in cold blood. As I wonder around camp I hear the Sad news from every Soldier and then they express a desire to revenge his death and if a Battle should occur there would be but few prisoners taken and the best thing the Rebels can do is get out of the Scrape as best they can. But now every thing centers on Vice President Johnston will he follow in the footsteps of his illustrious predicessor or has he the abillity to do so. We hope he may. This was a rainy night.

WEDNESDAY APR 19TH

I passed out of our Picket lines to a house where I heard a "Southren Belle" sing some of their Rebel songs and play the Pianno. I returned to camp about noon. Some claim this is the last day of the Armistice as they say it was only to last five days instead of ten. There was a mail came but none for me. We have no chance to write. There was a rumor that the Dispatch in regard to the assassi[n]ation of President Lincoln was a forgery but alas it is confirmed this evening.

THURSDAY APR 20TH

No move to day. We received Genl Field Orders No 58 in regard to the peace negotiations which caused great rejoiceing throughout the camps.[20] Hostillities have virtueally ceased and the prospects are glorious. . . . There is talk that we will return to Holly Springs to morrow but no orders. This was a very hot[?] day but we have a pleasent camp.

FRIDAY APR 21ST

We received the word that "Jeff Davis" and family was captured. He was trying to escape in the disguise of an old woman but the Yankees was to[o] smart for him and identified him. It is a joke that the great "Southren Rebellions" "last ditch" that they blowed so much about should consist of a "womens Petticoat." But it seams to[o] absurd to believe unless confirmed by better testimony. The first and Second Divisions are moveing camp and we received the same orders afternoon and moved about four miles back towards Holly Springs.[21] It rained very hard this evening. We camped in a nice pine grove and a beautiful place.

SATURDAY APR 22ND

This was a hot day and we built good quarters out of Pine Poles and are comfortable now. There is a rumor that our Corps will march through to Harpers Ferry Virginia but we are not ready to go yet. The reported capture of Davis and famly is still going the rounds and may prove to be true.

SUNDAY APR 23RD

. . . There was Preaching in commemoration of the death of President Lincoln. The text was Second Samuel 3rd Chapter and 38th veise [verse] viz *"Know ye not there is a great man A Prince this day has fallen in Israel."* The remarks of the Chaplain was very appropriate and he dwelt considerable on the able manner in which he had conducted the war for the preservation of the Union and his many virtues and kindnesses extended to the Soldiers and it maks us feel as though we had lost a near and dear relative. He was the man for the times and his praise will be sung for generations to come. The entire Regiment attended. There is still rumors that we will go to Harpers Ferry and that we will Start Wednesday the 26th. We had company Inspection at Nine a.m.

MONDAY APR 24TH

Captain Karns and I to[ok] a ramble in the country and was at severel Houses among them we found the names of Collins Norris Widow Burt and Hunter. We found that the people are in a distressing condition and nothing left to eat. The army has appropriated all they had and they depend on our commissaries for supplies. We met Severel of Lees old soldiers and among them we met on horse back a major and a Lieutenant and had quite a talk with they. They say the war did not end as they would have liked it to but they said they must submit. They spoke very hig[h]ly of Genl Grant and one said if there was any more fighting to do he would fight for Grant. We find a Union man here accasionally and when we do find one he is very rank and feels elated over the result. But generally they are Rebels and have served in the Army three or four years.

TUESDAY APR 25TH

. . . I wrote to Nett in regard to what I heard through Uncle Will in reffernce [to] Pa going to be married. I feel as though it is hurrying mat-

ters some but presume he knows his own buisiness. I visited the 101st
Ind with Bob Davis and we had Dress Parade this evening. We also
received orders to move in the morning and I suppose we are going
home but we may have some work to do yet as I dont know that
Johnston has surrenderd yet. But we will soon ascertain.

WEDNESDAY APR 26TH

Revelie blowed at three oclock a.m and we got ready to move but the
order was countramanded and we got the report that the Army under
Johnston had surrenderd. . . . We have all kinds of rumers in camp but
nothing reliable. Genl Grant is reported to be at Ralleigh and confer-
ing with the Rebels.

THURSDAY APR 27TH

. . . This was a beautiful day and we have orders to move at day light
in the morning also a rumor that Johnston surrenderd at ten a.m to day.
But it is only a rumor. Some say we are going to Ralleigh from here. I
was down to the mill this evening and was in camp the rest of the day.
No mail for me.

FRIDAY APR 28TH

We were awakend this morning about two Oclock by very heavy cannonadeing and musketry on our left which kept up untill after day light.
We supposed Johnston was trying to cut loose and had attacked the 1st
Division. We soon got orders to Strike Tents and stacked arms on the
collor line and "cleared the Deck for action.["] We got our Breakfast
and about Six Oclock moved to the left to help the 1st Division out but
only went about a mile and haulted and soon after Genl Baird and Staff
came along and made the Joyfull anouncement that the *war is over* and
we "about faced" and with light hearts started towards Ralleigh. How
different we felt to what we did when we was expecting the Rebels a
short time before. The fireing was the Boys who had received the news
of the surrender and as we had nothing reliable we naturally supposed
it was a Battle. This day will long be rememberd as the day on which
we realized for the first time that our bloody work was over by drawing
off from the front and makeing the first move to go home. We have

longed for this day and to night for the first time in nearly three years we lay down with the assurance that to morrow will not bring fourth a bloody Battle and that our lives are owr own. We bid farewell to our less fortunate comrads who Sleep the sleep of the martyr to their country. We go home to lay down our arms and resume our places in the ranks of citizens and our severel occupations. Shouts resound throughout our command and I think we have reason to rejoice. We have accomplished the work we set out to do and I feel proud that I can say I was a soldier and recount to generations the adventures I have passed through. We met a number of Old Rebel Soldiers returning home but how different they will find it to what we will. Their homes are desolated and we return to land of plenty. Although I have met them on the Battlefield and helped lay waste their country my heart goes out to them in sympathy for them. They have Showen themselves to be worthy of Americans and brave men. We passed Holly Springs and camped near where we did the first night out from Ralleigh. We moved ten miles.

CHAPTER 13

Going Home

One last great march remained—this time north to Washington, D.C. The Hoosiers set out from Raleigh on April 30, ordered to make the first stage of the march to Richmond, Virginia, in a leisurely ten days. But competition was fierce among Sherman's troops to be the first to reach the Confederate capital, and the distance was covered in a mere seven days. "We actually did about the hardest marching after the war was over, and when there was no necessity for it," remembered Sergeant Floyd. A "foolish foot-race" ensued, and several lives were subsequently lost due to exhaustion.[1]

An unusual incident occurred on May 1 while the troops were passing through the town of Wilton, North Carolina. Here the Hoosiers saw the Stars and Stripes raised by Southern civilians for the first time during the war. They halted in the town for an hour, and while the Eighty-seventh Indiana's band struck up "Coming Through the Rye" (their brigade commander's favorite tune), some surrendered Confederate soldiers joined hands with the Union troops in a stag dance, probably one of the first fraternal unions of Blue and Gray following the end of the war.

Despite orders against entering Richmond without passes, many of Sherman's men could not restrain their curiosity and did so anyway, looking for something to eat and enjoying the sights. In more than one instance, a guard who tried to stop these veterans of the "March to the Sea" was knocked down and his musket taken from him.

Finally, the Fourteenth Corps completed the trek through Virginia and arrived near Washington on May 19. Five days later, Sherman's sixty-five thousand men passed up Pennsylvania Avenue in a grand review before President Andrew Johnson, members of his Cabinet and Congress, and the army's generals. Despite the scorching heat, the marching was perfect, as the

ranks of the Seventy-fifth filled the street from one side to the
other and swept the avenue. Military bands worked up the crowd
to the "highest pitch," and they enthusiastically cheered
Sherman's western men.

After the Grand Review, the Hoosiers visited Washington,
noting with regret the many buildings and monuments still
draped in black in memory of recently assassinated President
Lincoln. Another depressing scene occurred on June 3, when the
men of the Fourteenth Corps officially said goodbye to their old
commander, Gen. George Thomas, and "wept like children."[2]

The Seventy-fifth Indiana was officially mustered out of
United States service on June 8. The troops left Washington
by train the same day for Parkersburg, West Virginia. There
they embarked on a steamer for Lawrenceburg, Indiana, then
traveled by train again to Indianapolis, where they arrived on
June 14. Back in the state capital where they had begun their
journey nearly three years earlier, the members of the regiment
surrendered their muskets and equipment at the State Arsenal
then enjoyed a public reception on the capital grounds hosted
by Governor Oliver P. Morton. On June 16, the proud 468 survivors of the Seventy-fifth Indiana were given their discharges
and began the journey north to home. The editor of the *Howard
Tribune* witnessed the return of the Kokomo company and
proudly wrote that this "regiment of gallant and heroic men"
bore "unmistakable evidence of having seen severe service."[3]

The Seventy-fifth Indiana Volunteer Infantry took part in
practically every important Civil War campaign in Tennessee,
Georgia, and the Carolinas. From their initial bloodletting at
Chickamauga to the final major battle at Bentonville, William
Bluffton Miller and his fellow soldiers in the ranks took great
pride in the fact that they had performed as well, if not better,
than most volunteer soldiers in the Union army and had contributed greatly to the preservation of the Union.

SATURDAY APR 29TH

We started early and went to Joneses Station on the Rail Road and
camped and got the Ralleigh Progress with Genl Shermans order send-

ing us north. He compliments the Army highly for the work they have accomplished and advises us to return to our homes and be as good citizens as Soldiers. We are to Start on Monday for Richmond Virginia One hundred and ninety four miles. I made out muster Rolls for March and April and about dark orders came to march in the morning and I answerd Netts letter and sent her three Papers and by mistake I enclosed some letter paper. A good Joke on the paper.

SUNDAY APR 30TH

We Started early and marched about Eighteen miles nearly North East leaveing Ralleigh to our right. Some of our Boys went to the city yesterday and have not come up yet. We passed the 1st Division still in camp. We passed one small station on the Rail Road but I did not learn the name of it. We camped three miles from the nuse river and have a good camp and good water. We passed some nice Plantations and they have not been damaged by the war as there never was any Yankees here before. We met Severel old Rebel Soldiers and the citizens came out to see us. Our Boys would hollow at the Johnies and ask them How the war was. Some said nothing and others would laugh and Say the "*Wa is done played out.*" Some of them are very crest fallen.

MONDAY MAY 1ST

Another gloom was cast over our men by seeing the censure against Genl Sherman about the peace negotiations and they think it was an error of the head and not of the heart as they all stand by Sherman. We are sorry he made a mistake but all are liable to err. The goverment repudiated the proposition and made it better.[4] Our Regiment led to day and we started at daylight. It has been our custom for some time when we moved to throw out Skirmishers but we had none to day. There was lots of citizens along the road to look at "Shermans Bummers." We crossed the Nuse river about eleven Oclock a.m. When we arrived a[t] Wilton Post office the loyal citizens had erected a pole and had a flag on it which was said has been hid during the war and was dug out to day. There was a number of citizens and old Rebel soldiers preasent and all Seemed happy to know the war is over. There was lots of loyal citizens through this section. One old Lady Shouted when we came up. Our Band played severel pieces and we rested a short time and then resumed the march towards Oxford Court House. We haulted at

Tar River for dinner after marching twenty miles. We marched Six miles after dinner and camped near Oxford where we found the 1st Division had passed us by another road and we found out there was a race for Richmond and we have the start of the 20th Corps. But from this on we will have heavy marching. We passed some nice country but the soil is not very good. The Plantations are nicely fixed up. Good buildings and the Planters are regular Nabobs and lived in style before the war. But how they will get along without the Slaves is a question.

TUESDAY MAY 2ND

We had to take the rear to day and did not leave camp untill about seven Oclock. We passed through Oxford and followed the road to Boydston through Midway Williamsboro and we camped near Lineville after marching twenty two miles. Oxford is a county Seat and quite a nice little town. Midway was composed of one little Store house. Williamsboro is a small place. We passed some splendid Plantations and some nice country. The citizens look very cross and are not very sociable. . . .

WEDNESDAY MAY 3RD
[VIRGINIA]

We passed Lineville to the right and kept the main road to Boyedton which we passed in the eveing and camped two miles from Town. It is a small place but very pretty and is a county seat. Mecklinburgh college is located here. We crossed the Roanoke river to day and was detained severel hours on account of pontooning. This is Mecklinburgh county Verginia as we crossed the state line about ten Oclock a.m. We met a number of Rebel Soldiers on the road. This is a beautifull country and we passed a number of fine plantations. Darkies was plenty and very merry. One place an Old Darky had an old tin Bucket drumming on it and severel little ones was danceing. If they keep it up untill the entire Army passes they will get very tired. Nice camp and good water. We marched Sixteen miles.

THURSDAY MAY 4TH

Our Brigade had the advance and we moved at five Oclock a.m. We was detained by crossing severel Small Streams. We marched twenty two miles and camped near Lewistown on Reedy creek. It rained some and the roads was not as good as for the last few days. We crossed the Moherin River Buck creek and Reedy creek. The country is good and the Plantations have been well cultivated and the people in good circumstances before the war. The men dont know how to work and have depended on the Slaves to do the work and I dont know how they will make it now. The darkies begin to realize their freedom.

FRIDAY MAY 5TH

The advance started early. We passed through Lewistown or Lunan Court House and some beautiful country. We had good roads. We passed through Nottoway Court Hous this evening and camped five miles from the latter. Our lame was sent from Nottoway to Richmond by Rail Road and [the] Captain left us with them. Some of our Boys are getting smart and start out ahead of the command in the morning and get through easier. We marched thirty miles and are said to be ten miles in advance of the 20th Corps. I have concluded this is a very foolish piece of buisiness but it is Eastern men against the Western and I suppose they will keep it up untill we reach Richmond. Men become over heated and drink so much water that the[y] cant stand it. The companies are mere corporals guards and when we stop to rest we drop down in the road and dont stack arms. They are simply killing themselves and the officers are letting them. If it was necissary I would no[t] care but it is useless and not necissary.

SATURDAY MAY 6

We marched twenty five miles to day. Our Brigade was in the center and my Regiment lead the Brigade. We did not pass any town of importance. It was very hot and severel men was Sun Struck. We are still ahead but must make the Apomatox river before we are sure of coming out ahead. We stopped for dinner at Nottoway falls. It is a beautiful place. The roads was nice and I stood the march very well. One man drank a tin cup of water when very hot and dropped dead in an instant.

SUNDAY MAY 7TH
[RICHMOND, VIRGINIA]

Our Brigade had the advance and we marched twenty five miles and camped about a mile from Manchester on the James River and oposite Richmond. Our Corps is about played out. I guess they are scatterd from here to Ralleigh. We have marched one hundred and ninety five miles in Eight days. An average of twenty four miles a day. A man can walk it easy enough but marching is another thing. It provokes me when I think what a foolish piece of buisiness it is. But we are here and I shall take my time to it from this on. . . . This was a very warm day. We are camped in a thicket of Small Oaks near a line of old Rebel fortifications. It tried [?] to rain.

Monday May 8th

As we did not move I wrote to Nett. It rained some this evening and was a very hot day. I dont know how long we will remain here but suppose only a day or two. There is a rumor that we will move in the morning. My feet are very Sore from the marching and some of our men are nearly ruined. The more I think of the foolishness of such marching the less I think of our General Officers for allowing it. The war being over they thought what few of us was left they would kill on the road home. If our men was not made of Iron there would not be many of us left. But here we are at Richmond the capital of the great boasted Confederacy and the war cry for nearly four years past and I shall procure a pass and visit the great city to morrow.

Tuesday May 9th

I procured a pass for myself and four men and went to Richmond through Manchester. The latter is quite a Town and I noticed about every other house was occupied by some kind of a Suttler. We visited the Capital Building and the late residences of Jeff Davis and Genl Lee the latter is now in the city. We were also in the Rebel prisons Libby and Castle Thunder. Here the union Soldiers were Starved to death by the Rebel government. The[y] have been cleaned out and white washed and yet they are dismal looking places. Libby is now occupied by some Rebels and among them the old Turn key under the Rebels. The city is located on the James River and it is quite hilly. A number of buisiness houses was distroyed by the Rebels and the city generally shows the effects of the war. There is a number of large cotton Factories here. There is some nice buildings here and the city is full of Sutle[r]s and prices very high. The statue of Genl Washington on horse back in the State house yard is draped in mourning in memory of President Lincoln.

It rained very hard soon after we got to Town. We met a number of Rebel officers Still wearing the Uniform and now draw rations from Uncle Samuels cupboard. We got a good view of the city and returned to camp and found they have orders to march at Six am in the morning and pass in review through the city. We are in a nice condition for review and I suppose the[y] want to see how nice we look. The citizens are very afraid of us. They cal[l] us Shermans Bummers and I presume they have occasion to be afraid from the experience they have had.

Wednesday May 10th

All our men who are not able to march was sent with Capt Karns to [the] Rail Road for transportation to City Point and we struck tents preparatory to a move but the order was contremanted. It is cool and has the appearence of rain. There is a rumor in camp that on the arrival of Genl Sherman he put Genl Slocum under arrest for marching us so hard recently. But I dont think it is reliable. I was to the camp of the 23rd Indiana to see Dan Miller and as I came back through Manchester the 14th and 17th Corps was clearing out the Sutlers and Provost Guards. They was haveing considerable of a time but succeed remarkably well. I seen some of our Boys loaded with Sutlers stores. Some of the Sutlers have been skinning our Boys ever since the war commenced and now they have no money to buy with and are retalliateing. There is not many Sutlers left on this side of the James River and what are here have been more or less damaged. The Cripples and Captain did not get off and returned to camp this Evening.

Thursday May 11th

Our sick left camp again this morning again at 3 Oclock a.m. and we again struck Tents ant at Seven we Started on the march. The Provost Guards were all out in line as we marched through Manchester. We crossed the James on Pontoon[s] into Richmond via Libby Prison and Castle Thunder at a *rout Step* and did not march in review but Cavalry Guards was stationed all along the line of march through the city to keep our men in the Ranks and the side walks was lined with Soldiers and Citizens to gaze on *Shermans Bummers*. We seam to be a terror to the *Secesh* here I presume from the notoriety of our "March to the Sea." We took the road toward Hanover Court House. When Genl Sherman arrived he vetoed Genl Hallecks orders on the Review. They are bad friends and Sherman concluded his men was not there for a Show for Halleck. We haulted for Dinner on Brook Creek and near the church by that name. We passed severel strong lines of fortifications as we left Richmond. They were considered impregnable but fineally succumbed to "Yankee" Strategy. We crossed the Chickahomany this pm. and camped Six miles from Hanover. We passed some nice country and the best improvements I have seen yet. The old Planters live in fine style and have beautiful places. But still it showes the ravages of the war as there are no fences left. Wood was very Scarce at noon. It is very Swampy about the Chickahomany and looks some like portions of country we found farther south. It rained and hailed nearly all night. We got the Richmond papers this evening but they contained no news. They discribed the appearance of and march of Shermans Army through Richmond.[5]

FRIDAY MAY 12TH

It is quite cool and we did not resume the march untill about Nine Oclock a.m. We passed Hanover C.H and Genl Shermans Head Quarters. The roads are bad from last nights rains. We stoped on the Pamonky River for dinner. We crossed the South Ann river and passed Concord church and camped on a Rebel Officers plantation for the night after marching only about twelve miles. There dont seam to be much of a rush since Genl Sherman has command in person. . . .

SATURDAY MAY 13TH

We started at 5 a.m. Our Brigade with the 2nd Minnisota in the lead. We haulted for dinner at some old Rebbel Breast works. We marched twenty miles. The mail came up but I did not get any letters. The Richmond Papers of today complain of the 14th Corps and I suppose they may have some cause as our Boys are reckless and when they want any think they dont wait for an invitation to help themselves. This was a warm day. We passed two small towns but I did not learn the name of either. The roads are bad in places.

SUNDAY MAY 14TH

We was on the march early. We followed a By road for severel miles and fineally struck the Culp[e]per road passing Andrews and Good Hope churches. We traveled Slow on account of our wagon train but we marched twenty miles. This is a beautifull country but the fences being all destroyed it resembles a vast prarie. The grazeing for the mules is good and I almost imagine I can see the old vetrans smile to know they have plenty to eat after the hardships and privations they have endured for some time. We have plenty of good water but wood is scarce and we have to cary it long distances. The soil is Sandy and the timber generally pine.

MONDAY MAY 15TH

We started early and made Raccoon ford on the Rapadan River for dinner. We passed through the Rapadan Valey. The country is good and well watered. We waded the river by takeing off our pants and S[t]rapping them with our Cartridge Boxes to the guns. We camped for the night at Stoney Mountain where the Army of the Potomac camped in the winter of 1863 & 64. I notice the citizens are planting Some corn and there is some wheat growing but not very much. I tried to buy some butter at one house but they was out of that article. This was a very warm day but we made the usual march of twenty miles. Our train was all night crossing the River. Wood scarce as usual.

TUESDAY MAY 16TH

Started at 5 Oclock am with our Brigade and the 105th Ohio in the advance. We marched to Georgetown on the Rapphannock and waded the river and haulted on the north Side untill four Oclock p.m to let the Second Division pass and then marched seven miles and camped for the night. We passed some beautifull country and the soil is rich and fertile. But the war has done its work. The timber is all destroyed and fences burned and there is scarcely any thing left. The stock has all been taken by one or the other Army. This section has been the Battle field for the last four years and the Planters could not raise any thing. I dont hardly see how they could manage to live. It will take severel years to make it what it was.

WEDNESDAY MAY 17TH

We had to take the rear this morning and did not get started untill Seven Oclock. We passed Catlets Station on the Rail Road. Marched twenty miles and camped on Broad Run. Passed severel old Stocades and lines of Breast Works of the Rebels. Some of the houses bear the marks of Shot and Shell. This was a very hot day and the roads are dusty. The land is destitute of timber or fences but the soil is good. We passed Brentsvill to the East of us. I was nearly played out when we camped. We drew three days Rations this morning. We are Still thirty miles from Alexandria. This is the Stomping ground of the old 12th Indiana in the spring of 1862.

THURSDAY MAY 18TH

We resumed the march early and passed Manassus or Bull Run Battle ground.[6] There is some old fortifications on the surrounding Hills. It is a very rough hilly country. We waded Bull Run about ten oclock am. The creek is very Shallow and a gravel Bottom. The hills on the South Side are fortified. We struck the pike at Centerville. There is only a few old houses left. We followed the line of the retreat of our Army. We passed Fairfax Court House after noon. It is quite a nice little town. But the towns and country all bear the marks of the war. There has been fighting all around here. We camped five miles from Fairfax after marching twenty miles. Water is plenty but it was almost impossible to get any wood. We will reach Alexandria to morrow opposite Washington city.

FRIDAY MAY 19TH
[ALEXANDRIA, VIRGINIA]

It is raining and the air is cool. We did not move untill Nine Oclock a.m. The 75th Lead the Division and we marched about eight miles and camped for the night near Arlington Heights near a small creek. It rained all day. . . . We are four miles from Alexandria and some of our Boys went down to the city. We are now nearly done marching I think and will travail by Rail Road. It is hilly here. There is plenty of pedlers here and lots to buy but we dont have any money. The 14th Corps is all camped in the valley. We got Washington City Papers and they anounce the capture of Jeff Davis in womens clotheing and it is singular that the long and bloody war should wind up with a farce and that the Rebels "last ditch" that they blowed so much about should be a "*petticoat.*" But I am gratified to know that it is over and we are on the eve of returning to our homes and loved ones.[7] I dont want to remain here long but it may be severel days before we are mustered out as there is no orders yet.[8]

BIOGRAPHICAL APPENDIX

A number of sources were used to assemble the following bio-graphical profiles of the soldiers and civilians mentioned in the Miller diary. Compiled military service records in the National Archives were consulted for each soldier, although this infor-mation was sometimes fragmentary and contradictory. Data from the 1860 federal census for Wells County was used to doc-ument civilians. Where possible, additional information has been added from published state adjutant general's reports, David B. Floyd's *History of the Seventy-Fifth Regiment of Indiana Infantry Volunteers*, and the Registers of Enlistments in the United States Army, 1798–1914, in the National Archives.

ARTHUR, CHRISTOPHER S.: SEVENTY-FIFTH INDIANA VOLUNTEER INFANTRY. Elected captain of Company F, August 2, 1862. Appointed regimental surgeon August 20, 1862, and transferred to field and staff. Residence: Pennville, Jay County, Indiana. Occupation: Physician. Place of birth: Jay County, Indiana. Age: 29. Captured at Chickamauga, Georgia, September 20, 1863, while treating the wounded. Imprisoned in Libby Prison, Richmond, Virginia. Resigned September 11, 1864, due to disability.

ASHBY, WILLIAM: COMPANY E, SEVENTY-SECOND INDIANA VOLUNTEER INFANTRY. Mustered into service July 19, 1862. Residence: Ladoga, Indiana. Occupation: Minister. Place of birth: Butler County, Ohio. Age: 42. Promoted to first duty sergeant November 29, 1862. Died at Hospital No. 5 in Gallatin, Tennessee, of rheumatism and typhoid pneumonia December 27, 1862. Buried in Nashville National Cemetery.

BARLOW, ANDREW J.: COMPANY B, 101ST INDIANA INFANTRY. Mustered into service September 5, 1862, as first lieutenant. Residence: Bluffton, Indiana. Occupation: Carpenter. Place of birth: Columbus, Ohio. Age: 24. Commissioned captain May 31, 1863, but not mustered as such. Wounded in left shoulder, November 25, 1863, at Missionary Ridge,

Tennessee. Died September 16, 1864, in division field hospital at Chattanooga, Tennessee, of wounds received in action at Kennesaw Mountain, Georgia, on June 23, 1864. Wounded in right leg by shell fragment, resulting in amputation of lower two-thirds of leg, followed by death. Buried in Chattanooga National Cemetery.

BARTLERMY, ADAM: COMPANY B, 101ST INDIANA VOLUNTEER INFANTRY. Mustered into service August 15, 1862. Residence: Bluffton, Indiana. Occupation: Farmer. Place of birth: Lebanon County, Pennsylvania. Age: 21. Mustered out as corporal June 24, 1865.

BASSETT, MATTHEW: CIVILIAN. Residence: Bluffton, Indiana. Occupation: Carpenter. Place of birth: New York. Age: 21. Value of real estate: $0. Value of personal estate: $50. Other members of his household: Sarah and one child. (1860 census.)

BATES, ISAIAH N.: COMPANY B, NINETEENTH ILLINOIS VOLUNTEER INFANTRY. Mustered into service June 17, 1861, as musician. Residence: Toulon, Stark County, Illinois. Occupation: Farmer. Age: 18. Hospital clerk from December 18, 1862 to April 5, 1864. Mustered out July 9, 1864.

BEAN, SOLOMON R.: COMPANY A, SEVENTY-FIFTH INDIANA VOLUNTEER INFANTRY. Mustered into service July 28, 1862. Residence: Wabash, Indiana. Occupation: Engineer. Place of birth: Franklin County, Pennsylvania. Age: 18. Sent to hospital at Gallatin, Tennessee, December 25, 1862. Returned to regiment March 27, 1863. Wounded September 19, 1863, at Chickamauga, Georgia, and sent to hospital. Returned December 21, 1863. Mustered out June 8, 1865.

BEARDSLEY, CALVIN W.: COMPANY K, SEVENTY-FIFTH INDIANA VOLUNTEER INFANTRY. Mustered into service July 25, 1862, as fifth corporal. Residence: Ossian, Indiana. Occupation: Mechanic/wagon maker. Place of birth: Licking County, Ohio. Age: 34. Mustered out June 8, 1865.

BLACKBURN, ELI J.: COMPANY A, NINETY-EIGHTH ILLINOIS INFANTRY. Enlisted August 5, 1862. Mustered into service September 3, 1862, as corporal. Residence: Flora, Illinois. Age: 29. On detached duty November 1862–February 1863. Reduced from corporal to the ranks at his own request December 14, 1864. Mustered out June 27, 1865, as a private.

BOGUE, ROSWELL G.: SURGEON, NINETEENTH ILLINOIS VOLUNTEER INFANTRY. Mustered into service August 14, 1861. Residence: Chicago, Illinois. Occupation: Physician. Place of birth: Louisville, St. Lawrence County, New York. Date of birth: May 3, 1832. Assigned as medical director, Second Division, Fourteenth Army Corps, March 31, 1863. Relieved October 16, 1863, assigned as medical director, Third Division, Fourteenth Army Corps, relieved and returned to duty with the regiment March 11, 1864. Mustered out July 9, 1864.

BOYDEN, ORVILLE B.: SEVENTY-FIFTH INDIANA VOLUNTEER INFANTRY. Enlisted as a private in Company E, August 1, 1862. Appointed regimental chaplain October 14, 1862. Residence: Muncie, Indiana. Occupation: Minister. Place of birth: Hardin County, Kentucky. Age: 42. Resigned February 15, 1863, and resignation accepted "for the good of the service."

BOYLE, PATRICK: COMPANY K, SEVENTY-FIFTH INDIANA VOLUNTEER INFANTRY. Mustered into service July 28, 1862. Residence: Bluffton, Indiana. Occupation: Farmer. Place of birth: Queens County, Ireland. Age: 35. Died March 29, 1864, in camp at Ringgold, Georgia, of lung fever.

BRICKLEY, ANDREW J.: COMPANY K, SEVENTY-FIFTH INDIANA VOLUNTEER INFANTRY. Mustered into service August 4, 1862. Residence: Bluffton, Indiana. Occupation: Farmer. Place of birth: Mahoning County, Ohio. Age 22. Wounded at Chickamauga, Georgia (toe shot off). Mustered out June 8, 1865.

BRIGGS, THOMAS: COMPANY G, SEVENTY-FIFTH INDIANA VOLUNTEER INFANTRY. Mustered into service August 4, 1862. Residence: Anderson, Indiana. Occupation: Farmer. Place of birth: Fleming County, Kentucky. Age: 38. Detailed November 29, 1862, as teamster. Promoted to sergeant July 13, 1863. Mustered out June 3, 1865.

BROWN, GEORGE H.: COMPANY G, SEVENTEENTH OHIO VOLUNTEER INFANTRY. Mustered into service September 15, 1861. Occupation: Carpenter. Age: 19. Mustered out October 27, 1864.

BROWN, WILLIAM: SECOND MINNESOTA VOLUNTEER INFANTRY. Commissioned assistant surgeon September 5, 1862. Mustered into service September 6, 1862. Residence: Red Wing, Minnesota. Place of birth: Ohio. Age: 35. Detailed to temporary duty at General Hospital Gallatin, Tennessee, January 27, 1863, then ordered to report to regiment April 4, 1863. Captured at the Battle of Chickamauga. Commissioned surgeon January 1, 1865, enrolled and mustered into service to date March 27, 1865. Mustered out July 11, 1865.

BROWN, WILLIAM: COMPANY K, SEVENTY-FIFTH INDIANA VOLUNTEER INFANTRY. Mustered into service July 30, 1862. Residence: Bluffton, Indiana. Occupation: Farmer. Place of birth: Wells County, Indiana. Age: 19. Died of wounds near Peachtree Creek, Georgia, July 20, 1864.

BUCKMASTER, RICHARD W.: COMPANY K, SEVENTY-FIFTH INDIANA VOLUNTEER INFANTRY. Mustered into service July 26, 1862. Residence: Decatur, Indiana. Occupation: Farmer. Place of birth: Wayne County, Ohio. Age: 22. Mustered out of service June 8, 1865.

BUCKMASTER, SAMUEL: COMPANY K, SEVENTY-FIFTH INDIANA VOLUNTEER INFANTRY. Mustered into service July 26, 1862. Appointed fourth sergeant. Residence: Decatur, Indiana. Occupation: Farmer. Place of birth: Wayne County, Ohio. Age: 20. Reduced to ranks January 22, 1863, by special order for leaving his company while on the march from Gallatin, Tennessee, to Glasgow, Kentucky, without leave and remaining absent for several days. Died July 2, 1864, at Chattanooga, Tennessee's General Hospital, of pneumonia.

BULGER, AFFIE: CIVILIAN. Residence: Bluffton, Indiana. Occupation: None. Place of birth: Ohio. Age: 43. Value of real estate: $0. Value of personal estate: $0. Listed as Apphia J. in household of Wilson M. Bulger. (1860 census.)

BURCH, CHARLES J.: COMPANY F, SEVENTY-SECOND INDIANA VOLUNTEER INFANTRY. Mustered into service July 28, 1862. Residence: Warren County, Indiana. Occupation: Farmer. Place of birth: Warren County, Ohio. Age: 26. Died January 20, 1863, at Gallatin, Tennessee, of fever.

BURWELL, JAMES: COMPANY K, SEVENTY-FIFTH INDIANA VOLUNTEER INFANTRY. Mustered into service July 25, 1862. Residence: Bluffton, Indiana. Occupation: Cooper. Place of birth: Westmoreland County, Pennsylvania. Age: 56. Died January 9, 1863, in hospital at Gallatin, Tennessee.

BURWELL, NEWTON: CIVILIAN. Residence: Bluffton, Indiana. Occupation: Attorney. Place of birth: Ohio. Age: 23. Value of real estate: $0. Value of personal estate: $300. Listed in the household of James Burwell, a cooper, age 54, born in New York, and mother, one brother, and one sister. (1860 census.)

CARR, SAMUEL H.: COMPANY G, SEVENTY-FIFTH INDIANA VOLUNTEER INFANTRY. Mustered into service July 30, 1862. Residence: Ogden, Indiana. Occupation: Carpenter. Place of birth: Wayne County, Indiana. Age: 41. Mustered in as second lieutenant January 8, 1863. Resigned May 29, 1863, because of disability.

CARTWRIGHT, HENRY J.: COMPANY K, SEVENTY-FIFTH INDIANA VOLUNTEER INFANTRY. Mustered into service July 25, 1862. Residence: Ossian, Indiana. Occupation: Farmer. Place of birth: Trumbull County, Ohio. Age: 18. Promoted to seventh corporal January 1, 1863. Slightly wounded January 28, 1865, by accident while on picket. Mustered out June 8, 1865.

CARTWRIGHT, JOHN T.: COMPANY K, SEVENTY-FIFTH INDIANA VOLUNTEER INFANTRY. Mustered into service August 4, 1862, as fifth sergeant. Residence: Ossian, Indiana. Occupation: Farmer. Place of birth: Trumbull County, Ohio. Age: 19. Transferred to Engineer Corps December 10, 1862. Died October 22, 1863, at General Hospital No. 14, Nashville, Tennessee, of erysipelas. Buried in Nashville City Cemetery. Also a member of Company G, Twelfth Indiana Volunteer Infantry.

CASE, HAMILTON: COMPANY K, SEVENTY-FIFTH INDIANA VOLUNTEER INFANTRY. Mustered into service August 20, 1862. Residence: Bluffton, Indiana. Occupation: Farmer. Place of birth: Bluffton, Indiana. Age: 18. Appointed principal musician of the regiment January 1, 1864. Mustered out June 8, 1865.

CASSEY, JOHN: COMPANY A, SEVENTY-FIFTH INDIANA VOLUNTEER INFANTRY. Mustered into service July 23, 1862. Residence: Lagro, Indiana. Occupation: Blacksmith. Place of birth: Canada. Age: 19. Appointed corporal August 20, 1862. Reduced to ranks September 20, 1862. Mustered out June 8, 1865.

CHAMNESS, JOHN W.: COMPANY G, SEVENTY-FIFTH INDIANA VOLUNTEER INFANTRY. Mustered into service July 30, 1862 as sergeant. Residence: Somerset, Indiana. Occupation: Farmer. Place of birth: Madison County, Indiana. Age: 23. Promoted to first sergeant January 8, 1863. Commissioned second lieutenant May 30, 1863. Mustered in as first lieutenant September 6, 1863. Resigned March 31, 1864, because of disability from wound to the arm received September 19, 1863, at Chickamauga, Georgia.

CHOATE, WILLIAM A.: THIRTY-EIGHTH OHIO VOLUNTEER INFANTRY. Mustered into service August 12, 1861. Elected captain of Company B August 12, 1861. Promoted to lieutenant colonel February 6, 1862. Promoted to colonel November 25, 1863. Died on the evening of September 12, 1864, "from wounds received while gallantly leading his regiment in the assault upon the Rebel stronghold near Jonesboro, Georgia, September 1, 1864."

CLARK, JOHN S.: COMPANY B, 101ST INDIANA VOLUNTEER INFANTRY. Mustered into service August 15, 1862. Residence: Bluffton, Indiana. Occupation: Farmer. Place of birth: Allegany County, New York. Age: 28. Died November 4, 1863 at Chattanooga, Tennessee, of wounds received September 20, 1863, at Chickamauga, Georgia.

COMMONS, ROBERT B.: COMPANY I, SEVENTY-FIFTH INDIANA VOLUNTEER INFANTRY. Mustered into service July 14, 1862. Residence: Clarksville, Indiana. Occupation: Farmer. Place of birth: Randolph County, North

Carolina. Age: 25. Drowned September 1, 1863, in Tennessee River near Shellmound, Tennessee. Miller refers to this man as "Cummings."

CONKLIN, ANTHONY: COMPANY D, SEVENTY-FIFTH INDIANA VOLUNTEER INFANTRY. Mustered into service July 25, 1862. Residence: Noblesville, Indiana. Occupation: Soldier. Place of birth: Clark County, Ohio. Age: 21. Appointed sergeant August 12, 1862. Promoted to first sergeant September 28, 1862. Commissioned second lieutenant December 23, 1862. Mustered into service as such January 24, 1863. Promoted to first lieutenant March 18, 1865. Mustered into service as such April 1, 1865. Mustered out June 8, 1865.

COOLBAUGH, CHARLES W.: COMPANIES C AND D, EIGHTEENTH UNITED STATES INFANTRY. Mustered into service December 10, 1861. Occupation: Farmer. Place of birth: Bradford County, Pennsylvania. Age: 21. Discharged January 20, 1863. Died January 29, 1863, of typhoid pneumonia at Gallatin, Tennessee, after discharge.

COVERT, WILLIAM H.: COMPANY F, 130TH INDIANA INFANTRY. Mustered into service January 28, 1864. Residence: Harrison Township, Wells County, Indiana. Occupation: Gunsmith. Place of birth: Wells County, Indiana. Age: 23. Mustered in as first lieutenant March 12, 1864. Absent at brigade headquarters September 25, 1864. Acting aide-de-camp, First Brigade, Second Division, Twenty-third Army Corps October 1864. Acting topographical engineer, First Brigade, Second Division, Twenty-third Army Corps, November 1864. Relieved as topographical engineer January 1865. Detailed at brigade headquarters February 1, 1865. Assigned to Second Brigade, First Division, Twenty-third Army Corps as acting assistant adjutant general February 16, 1865. Mustered in as captain to date from November 10, 1865. Mustered out as captain December 2, 1865.

COVERT, WILLIAM H. J.: CIVILIAN. Residence: Bluffton, Indiana. Occupation: Hotel keeper. Place of birth: Ohio. Age: 44. Value of real estate: $2,000. Value of personal estate: $1,100. Other members of his household: Elisa, age 44, born in Ohio, three children, plus numerous employees and others. (1860 census.)

CUTTER, JAMES E.: COMPANY K, SEVENTY-FIFTH INDIANA VOLUNTEER INFANTRY. Mustered into service July 30, 1862. Residence: Bluffton, Indiana. Occupation: Farmer/wagon maker. Age: 28. Detailed to engineers December 10, 1862, then transferred to Engineer Corps July 29, 1864.

DAVIS, JESSE: COMPANY A, THIRTY-FIRST INDIANA VOLUNTEER INFANTRY. Mustered into service August 25, 1862. Residence: Armiesburg, Indiana. Occupation: Farmer. Place of birth: Pickaway County, Ohio. Age: 21. Sent to Murfreesboro, Tennessee, sick, May 21, 1863. Patient at Hospital No. 1, Murfreesboro, Tennessee, September 1863–February, 1864. Suffered gunshot wound to little finger of right hand (fractured metacarpal), finger amputated by Minié ball at Kennesaw Mountain, Georgia, June 27, 1864. Admitted to Jeffersonville, Indiana's General Hospital July 16, 1864. Mustered out June 21, 1865.

DAVIS, ROBERT W.: COMPANY K, SEVENTY-FIFTH INDIANA VOLUNTEER INFANTRY. Mustered into service August 4, 1862. Residence: Farmington, Missouri. Occupation: Tailor. Place of birth: Westmoreland County, Pennsylvania. Age: 30. Mustered out June 8, 1865.

DEAM, WILLIAM SHANNON (ALSO KNOWN AS WILSON S. DRAIN): COMPANY I, TWENTY-SECOND INDIANA VOLUNTEER INFANTRY. Mustered into service August 15, 1861. Residence: Bluffton, Indiana. Occupation: Farmer. Place of birth: Montgomery County, Ohio. Age: 21. Promoted to second lieutenant February 4, 1865. Mustered out July 24, 1865.

DUFFEY, SEELY: COMPANY K, SEVENTY-FIFTH INDIANA VOLUNTEER INFANTRY. Mustered into service August 6, 1862. Residence: Montpelier, Indiana. Occupation: Farmer. Place of birth: Blackford County, Indiana. Age: 21. Mustered out June 8, 1865.

DUMOND, JOHN B.: COMPANY K, SEVENTY-FIFTH INDIANA VOLUNTEER INFANTRY. Mustered into service July 26, 1862. Residence: Bluffton, Indiana. Occupation: Farmer. Place of birth: Licking County, Ohio. Age: 24. Died December 13, 1863, in hospital at Gallatin, Tennessee, of typhoid fever.

ESTE, GEORGE P.: FOURTEENTH OHIO VOLUNTEER INFANTRY. Enlisted August 16, 1861, as lieutenant colonel. Age 31. Promoted to colonel to take effect from August 17, 1862. Commanded Third Brigade, Third Division, Fourteenth Army Corps, April 1–October 25,1864, and November 16, 1864–March 29, 1865. Mustered out July 7, 1865.

FARLEY, GEORGE E.: COMPANY H, FOURTEENTH OHIO VOLUNTEER INFANTRY. Mustered into service September 1, 1861, as corporal. Occupation: Farmer. Age: 19. Reduced from corporal April 5, 1863. Mustered out September 12, 1864.

FIELDS, ISAAC: COMPANY K, SEVENTY-FIFTH INDIANA VOLUNTEER INFANTRY. Mustered into service July 25, 1862. Residence: Bluffton, Indiana. Occupation: Engineer. Place of birth: Fulton County, Ohio. Age: 19. Wounded at Chickamauga, Georgia, September 19, 1863. Sent to hospital at Murfreesboro, Tennessee. Returned to the regiment January 22, 1864. Mustered out June 8, 1865.

FONCANNON, HARRISON: COMPANY B, 101ST INDIANA VOLUNTEER INFANTRY. Mustered into service August 15, 1862. Residence: Fort Wayne, Indiana. Occupation: Grocer. Place of birth: Seneca County, Ohio. Age: 25. Appointed second sergeant September 5, 1862. Died February 12, 1863, at Gallatin, Tennessee, of disease.

FULTON, NELSON G.: COMPANY I, TWENTY-SECOND INDIANA VOLUNTEER INFANTRY. Mustered into service August 15, 1861. Residence: Bluffton, Indiana. Occupation: Farmer. Place of birth: Westmoreland County, Pennsylvania. Age: 22. Killed May 17, 1864, at Rome, Georgia, in a skirmish with the enemy.

GINGER, LEWIS: COMPANY F, SEVENTY-FIFTH INDIANA VOLUNTEER INFANTRY. Mustered into service July 21, 1862. Residence: Pennville, Indiana. Occupation: Farmer. Place of birth: Preble County, Ohio. Age: 18. On detached service October 25, 1863, orderly at brigade headquarters. Mustered out June 8, 1865.

GLEASON, NEWELL: EIGHTY-SEVENTH INDIANA VOLUNTEER INFANTRY. Mustered into service September 2, 1862, as lieutenant colonel. Residence: Laporte. Age: 38. Promoted to colonel March 22, 1863. Commanded Second Brigade, Third Division, Fourteenth Army Corps from June 27, 1864, to end of the war. Brevetted brigadier general to date from March 13, 1865. Mustered out June 10, 1865.

GODDARD, CHARLES F.: EIGHTEENTH UNITED STATES INFANTRY. Mustered into service August 22, 1861. Appointed quartermaster sergeant, Eighteenth Infantry. Mustered out August 22, 1864.

GODFREY, JAMES: COMPANY K, SEVENTY-FIFTH INDIANA VOLUNTEER INFANTRY. Mustered into service August 8, 1862. Residence: Bluffton, Indiana. Occupation: Farmer. Place of birth: Madison, Indiana. Age: 23. Deserted from the regiment near Scottsville, Kentucky, December 27, 1862. Returned to the regiment February 15, 1863. Wounded in skirmish at Hoover's Gap, Tennessee, and Chickamauga, Georgia. In hospital at Nashville, Tennessee. Returned to the regiment February 6, 1864. Mustered out June 8, 1865.

GRIFFIN, EMANUEL: COMPANY K, SEVENTY-FIFTH INDIANA VOLUNTEER INFANTRY. Mustered into service July 25, 1862. Residence: Bluffton, Indiana. Occupation: Farmer. Place of birth: Wells County, Indiana. Age: 19. Mustered out June 8, 1865.

HAINES, ADAM: COMPANY K, SEVENTY-FIFTH INDIANA VOLUNTEER INFANTRY. Mustered into service August 4, 1862, as eighth corporal. Residence: Bluffton, Indiana. Occupation: Farmer. Place of birth: Fairfield County, Ohio. Age: 24. Reduced to ranks by his own request. Appointed teamster February 1, 1863. Detailed as teamster at brigade headquarters. Mustered out June 8, 1865.

HALE, JOHN D.: COMPANY B, 101ST INDIANA VOLUNTEER INFANTRY. Mustered into service August 15, 1862. Residence: Bluffton, Indiana. Occupation: Farmer. Place of birth: Wells County, Indiana. Age: 19. Appointed corporal September 5, 1862. Mustered out June 24, 1865.

Hall, Albert S.: 105th Ohio Volunteer Infantry. Mustered into service June 3, 1861, as captain of Company F, Twenty-fourth Ohio Volunteer Infantry. Promoted to major December 20, 1861. Promoted to lieutenant colonel May 14, 1862. Promoted to colonel of 105th Ohio Volunteer Infantry August 11, 1862. Age: 31. Died July 10, 1863, at Murfreesboro, Tennessee, of disease.

Hall, Stanley: Company A, Fourth Indiana Cavalry. Mustered into service July 29, 1862, as private. Promoted to regimental commissary sergeant August 10, 1862. Residence: Hendricks County, Indiana. Occupation: Merchant. Place of birth: Canfield, Ohio. Age: 25. Mustered in as first lieutenant July 5, 1864. Mustered out June 29, 1865.

Harris, Samuel J.: Nineteenth Battery Indiana Light Artillery. Mustered into service July 23, 1862, as second lieutenant. Residence: Columbus, Indiana. Age: 43. Appointed captain August 15, 1862. Wounded at Chickamauga, Georgia, September 19, 1863, "disabled by a contusion from an artillery shell." Absent sick on November 18, 1863, and relinquished command November 22, 1863. Discharged June 3, 1864, for physical disability from wounds received in action at Dalton, Georgia, February 25, 1864.

Harter, Andrew J.: Company K, Seventy-fifth Indiana Volunteer Infantry. Mustered into service July 25, 1862. Residence: Ossian, Indiana. Occupation: Farmer. Place of birth: Beaver County, Pennsylvania. Age: 20. Mortally wounded September 19, 1863, at Chickamauga, Georgia.

Hurst, James: Company K, Seventy-fifth Indiana Volunteer Infantry. Mustered into service March 7, 1864. Residence: Bluffton, Indiana. Occupation: Mechanic. Place of birth: Shelby County, Ohio. Age: 21. Transferred to Forty-second Indiana Volunteer Infantry, June 8, 1865.

Hurt, George: Company K, Seventy-fifth Indiana Volunteer Infantry. Mustered into service July 25, 1862. Residence: Bluffton, Indiana. Occupation: Engineer. Place of birth: Shelby County, Ohio.

Age: 26. Discharged February 23, 1863, at Murfreesboro, Tennessee, for disability.

JACOBY, BENJAMIN F.: COMPANY F, THIRTY-FIFTH OHIO VOLUNTEER INFANTRY. Enlisted September 5, 1861. Age: 19. Died February 1, 1863, in hospital at Gallatin, Tennessee.

KARNS, CALVIN F.: COMPANY H, FORTY-SEVENTH INDIANA VOLUNTEER INFANTRY. Mustered into service December 13, 1861. Residence: Bluffton, Indiana. Occupation: Wagon maker. Place of birth: Muskingum County, Ohio. Age: 31. Appointed corporal. Transferred to Invalid Corps.

KARNS, SANDFORD A.: COMPANY K, SEVENTY-FIFTH INDIANA VOLUNTEER INFANTRY. Mustered into service July 25, 1862. Residence: Bluffton, Indiana. Occupation: Farmer. Place of birth: Muskingum County, Ohio. Age: 18. Detached October 15, 1863, on guard at division headquarters. Mustered out June 8, 1865.

KARNS, SANFORD R.: COMPANY K, SEVENTY-FIFTH INDIANA VOLUNTEER INFANTRY. Mustered into service July 25, 1862, as a private. Residence: Bluffton, Indiana. Occupation: Wagon maker. Place of birth: Muskingum County, Ohio. Age: 49. Commissioned captain August 8, 1862. Mustered into service August 19, 1862. Wounded at Chickamauga, Georgia, September 19–20, 1863 (contusion to left leg). Mustered out June 8, 1865. Died in Bluffton in May 1881.

KEAGLE, LEVI: COMPANY K, SEVENTY-FIFTH INDIANA VOLUNTEER INFANTRY. Mustered into service July 25, 1862. Residence: Bluffton, Indiana. Occupation: Farmer. Place of birth: Wayne County, Ohio. Age: 25. Appointed third corporal August 11, 1862. Promoted to fourth sergeant January 23, 1863. Promoted to third sergeant December 31, 1864. Mustered out June 8, 1865.

KENAGY, JACOB V.: COMPANY K, SEVENTY-FIFTH INDIANA VOLUNTEER INFANTRY. Mustered into service July 25, 1862. Residence: Bluffton, Indiana. Occupation: Farmer. Place of birth: Wayne County, Ohio. Age: 26. Appointed second sergeant August 11, 1862. Reduced to ranks January 1, 1863, for absence in hospital, returned to sergeant November 16, 1863. Detailed as clerk in office of surgeon M. S. Messick, medical director at Chattanooga, on January 4, 1864. Mustered out June 8, 1865.

KING, EDWARD A.: SIXTY-EIGHTH INDIANA VOLUNTEER INFANTRY. Mustered into service August 19, 1862, as colonel from lieutenant colonel, Nineteenth U.S. Infantry. Residence: Indianapolis, Indiana. Place of birth: Cambridge, New York. Age: 46. Captured at Munfordville, Kentucky, September 17, 1862. Killed September 20, 1863, at Chickamauga, Georgia, while commanding Second Brigade, Fourth Division, Fourteenth Army Corps. Shot through the head by Confederate sharpshooter.

LEW, CHRISTIAN: COMPANY K, SEVENTY-FIFTH INDIANA VOLUNTEER INFANTRY. Mustered into service August 5, 1862. Residence: Markle, Indiana. Occupation: Farmer. Place of birth: Bern, Switzerland. Age: 22. Appointed corporal December 1, 1863. Mustered out June 8, 1865.

LINK, JOHN E.: TWENTY-FIRST ILLINOIS VOLUNTEER INFANTRY. Mustered into service November 26, 1862, as second assistant surgeon, to take effect November 5, 1862. Residence: Paris, Illinois. Age: 22. On detached service at General Hospital, Murfreesboro, Tennessee, April 17, 1863, and detailed again for hospital duty at Murfreesboro June 24, 1863. Mustered out July 5, 1864. Also a member of the Twelfth Illinois Volunteer Infantry and hospital steward, Sixty-eighth Illinois Volunteer Infantry.

LOWENSBURY, LEVI W.: COMPANY H, FOURTEENTH OHIO VOLUNTEER INFANTRY. Mustered into service September 1, 1861, as corporal. Occupation: Clerk. Place of birth: Lucas County, Ohio. Age: 19. Detached as clerk at division headquarters (inspector's office) August 14, 1863. Reenlisted as a veteran volunteer December 15, 1863, and mustered in December 26, 1863. Mustered out July 14, 1865. Miller refers to this man as "Lousbury."

LUCAS, JACKSON: COMPANY C, TENTH INDIANA VOLUNTEER INFANTRY. Mustered into service September 13, 1861. Residence: Clinton County,

Indiana. Occupation: Farmer. Place of birth: Indiana. Age: 20. Absent sick at Gallatin, Tennessee, January 1863. Mustered out September 19, 1864.

MAIR, SAMUEL S.: COMPANY D, SECOND MINNESOTA VOLUNTEER INFANTRY. Mustered in July 5, 1861. Age: 26. Detached to adjutant general's office, Third Division, Fourteenth Army Corps, January 5, 1864, as clerk. Mustered out July 5, 1864.

MARKLEY, JOHN: COMPANY B, 101ST INDIANA VOLUNTEER INFANTRY. Mustered into service August 15, 1862. Residence: Bluffton, Indiana. Occupation: Farmer. Place of birth: Wells County, Indiana. Age: 19. Promoted to corporal March 1, 1863. Mustered out June 24, 1865.

MCAFEE, JAMES W.: COMPANY I, TWENTY-SECOND INDIANA VOLUNTEER INFANTRY. Mustered into service August 15, 1861. Residence: Bluffton, Indiana. Occupation: Farmer. Place of birth: Wooster, Ohio. Age: 19. Mustered out July 24, 1865 as sergeant.

MCCOLE, CYRUS J.: SEVENTY-FIFTH INDIANA VOLUNTEER INFANTRY. Mustered into service August 19, 1862, as captain of Company D. Residence: Noblesville, Indiana. Age: 28. Appointed major August 20, 1862. Wounded in hip near Rocky Face Ridge, Georgia, February 25, 1864, and wounded again at Kennesaw Mountain, Georgia, date not specified. Mustered out June 8, 1865. Appointed lieutenant colonel by brevet, August 22, 1865, to date from March 13, 1865, for gallant and meritorious service during the war.

MCMAHAN, JOEL W.: COMPANY G, SEVENTY-FIFTH INDIANA VOLUNTEER INFANTRY. Mustered into service July 26, 1862. Residence: Forest Hill, Indiana. Occupation: Teacher. Place of birth: Madison County, Indiana. Age: 21. Promoted to fourth sergeant August 8, 1862. Wounded September 20, 1863, at Chickamauga, Georgia, on right side of head and face. Promoted to first sergeant April 27, 1864. Mustered out June 8, 1865.

MEDSKER, JAMES CARSON: COMPANY C, SEVENTY-FIFTH INDIANA VOLUNTEER INFANTRY. Mustered into service July 31, 1862, as first lieutenant.

Residence: Kokomo, Indiana. Age: 24. Promoted to adjutant August 20, 1862. Mustered out June 8, 1865.

MEVIS, OLIVER H., JR.: COMPANY D, SECOND MINNESOTA VOLUNTEER INFANTRY. Mustered into service July 5, 1861. Age: 25. Detached at Chattanooga with commissary of musters, Third Division, Fourteenth Army Corps from January 5, 1864. Mustered out July 5, 1864.

MILLER, ABRAM O.: SEVENTY-SECOND INDIANA VOLUNTEER INFANTRY. Appointed colonel August 13, 1862. Mustered in August 24, 1862. Residence: Jeffersonville, Indiana. Age: 35. Wounded in leg at Selma, Alabama, April 2, 1865. Mustered out June 26, 1865. Also lieutenant colonel, Tenth Indiana Infantry.

MILLER, CHARLES: COMPANY B, 101ST INDIANA VOLUNTEER INFANTRY. Mustered into service August 15, 1862. Residence: Bluffton, Indiana. Occupation: Farmer. Place of birth: Baltimore, Maryland. Age: 35. Appointed sergeant September 7, 1862. Died May 2, 1863, in camp near Murfreesboro, Tennessee, of disease.

MILLER, DANIEL: COMPANY F, TWENTY-THIRD INDIANA VOLUNTEER INFANTRY. Mustered into service October 13, 1864. Residence: Murray, Indiana. Occupation: Farmer. Place of birth: Rush County, Indiana. Age: 34. Mustered out July 23, 1865.

MILLER, JACOB: COMPANY K, SEVENTY-FIFTH INDIANA VOLUNTEER INFANTRY. Mustered into service August 6, 1862. Residence: Bluffton, Indiana. Occupation: Farmer. Place of birth: Fairfield County, Ohio. Age: 25. Sent to convalescent barracks at Murfreesboro, Tennessee, June 23, 1863. Returned to the regiment February 3, 1864. Mustered out June 8, 1865.

MILLER, JAMES B.: COMPANY B, 101ST INDIANA VOLUNTEER INFANTRY. Mustered into service August 16, 1862. Residence: Bluffton, Indiana. Occupation: Carpenter. Place of birth: Maryland. Age: 32. Discharged July 29, 1863, at Nashville, Tennessee, by surgeon's order on account of disability occasioned by wounds.

MILLER, MELISSA JEANNETTE KARNES (KARNS): CIVILIAN. Wife of William Bluffton Miller. Residence: Bluffton, Indiana. Occupation: Seamstress. Place of birth: Ohio. Age: 21. Listed in the household of Michael Karnes (Karns). (1860 census.)

MILLER, MICHAEL: CIVILIAN. Father of William Bluffton Miller. Residence: Bluffton, Indiana. Occupation: Sheriff. Place of birth: Pennsylvania. Age: 50. Value of real estate: $2,400. Value of personal estate: $300. Other members of his household: Louisa, age 45, William B., age 21, Mary Jane, age 18, Susan C., age 12. (1860 census.)

MILLER, MOLLIE (ALSO KNOWN AS MARY JANE MILLER): CIVILIAN. Sister of William Bluffton Miller. Residence: Bluffton, Indiana. Place of birth: Indiana. Age: 18. Listed in the household of Michael Miller. (1860 census.)

MILLER, SAMUEL R.: CIVILIAN. Residence: Rock Creek Township, Wells County, Indiana. Occupation: Farmer. Place of birth: Ohio. Age: 47. Value of real estate: $2,000. Value of personal estate $1,000. Other members of his household: wife Mary A., age 35, born in Ohio, and six children. (1860 census.)

MILLER, SUSAN C.: CIVILIAN. Sister of William Bluffton Miller. Residence: Bluffton, Indiana. Place of birth: Indiana. Age: 12. Listed in the household of Michael Miller. (1860 census.)

MILLER, WILLIAM: COMPANY B, 101ST INDIANA VOLUNTEER INFANTRY. Mustered into service August 15, 1862. Residence: Bluffton, Indiana. Occupation: Farmer. Place of birth: Baltimore, Maryland. Age: 37. Appointed first sergeant September 5, 1862. Commissioned but not mustered as second and first lieutenant. Mustered out June 24, 1865.

MILLER, WILLIAM ROLAND: Son of William Bluffton Miller and Melissa Jeannette Karns Miller. Died August 4, 1863.

MILLIKEN, JOHN C.: COMPANY K, SEVENTY-FIFTH INDIANA VOLUNTEER INFANTRY. Mustered into service July 30, 1862. Residence: Ossian,

Indiana. Occupation: Farmer. Place of birth: Trumbull County, Ohio. Age: 20. Mustered out June 8, 1865.

MOREHEAD, JONATHAN F.: COMPANY F, 130TH INDIANA VOLUNTEER INFANTRY. Mustered into service January 28, 1864. Residence: Bluffton, Indiana. Occupation: Mechanic/carpenter. Place of birth: Hocking County, Ohio. Age: 30. Deserted November 26, 1865 at Charlotte, North Carolina.

MORGAN, JAMES L.: COMPANY B, 101ST INDIANA VOLUNTEER INFANTRY. Mustered into service August 16, 1862. Residence: Bluffton, Indiana. Occupation: Lumberman. Place of birth: Fairfield County, Ohio. Age: 25. Appointed fourth sergeant September 5, 1862. Missing in action September 19, 1863, at Chickamauga, Georgia. Died September 25, 1863, of wounds received at Chickamauga, Georgia.

MOSURE, ABNER: COMPANY K, SEVENTY-FIFTH INDIANA VOLUNTEER INFANTRY. Mustered into service July 26, 1862. Residence: Decatur, Indiana. Occupation: Farmer. Place of birth: Ashland County, Ohio. Age: 18. Mustered out June 8, 1865.

MOUNT, BENJAMIN F.: COMPANY G, SEVENTY-FIFTH INDIANA VOLUNTEER INFANTRY. Mustered into service August 20, 1862. Occupation: Blacksmith. Place of birth: Oxtown, Ohio. Age: 19. Detailed to Thirteenth Indiana Battery September 13, 1862. Captured at Hartsville, Tennessee, December 7, 1862. Paroled and exchanged then sent back to company February 6, 1863. Mustered out July 8, 1865.

NAYLOR, JAMES B.: COMPANY H. 105TH OHIO VOLUNTEER INFANTRY. Mustered into service August 6, 1862. Residence: Goshen, Ohio. Occupation: Laborer. Place of birth: Mahoning County, Ohio. Age 20. Mustered out June 3, 1865.

NEVINS, GEORGE: COMPANY E, SEVENTY-FIFTH INDIANA VOLUNTEER INFANTRY. Mustered into service August 1, 1862. Residence: Huntington, Indiana. Died October 29, 1863, at Chattanooga, Tennessee, of wounds.

Nevins, James: Company K, Seventy-fifth Indiana Volunteer Infantry. Mustered into service July 30, 1862. Residence: Bluffton, Indiana. Occupation: Farmer. Place of birth: Jay County, Indiana. Age: 21. Discharged February 25, 1863, at hospital in Gallatin, Tennessee, for disability.

O'Brien, William: Seventy-fifth Indiana Volunteer Infantry. Mustered into service August 20, 1862, as lieutenant colonel. Residence: Noblesville, Indiana. Age: 23. Wounded slightly in arm at Chickamauga, Georgia, September 20, 1863. Commissioned colonel April 1, 1864, but not mustered as such. Lost two middle fingers from artillery fragment July 20, 1864, at Peach Tree Creek, Georgia. Reported absent without leave from September 4, 1864, to November 1, 1864, and from November 11, 1864, to April 10, 1865, when in fact in hospital. Appointed brevet colonel March 13, 1865, "for gallantry and good conduct as commander of his regiment" and special gallantry at the Battle of Peach Tree Creek, Georgia, July 20, 1864. Mustered out June 8, 1865.

Parker, Henry J.: Company A, Eighty-seventh Indiana Volunteer Infantry. Mustered into service August 11, 1862, as a corporal. Residence: Pleasant Grove, Indiana. Occupation: Farmer. Place of birth: Champaign County, Ohio. Age: 21. Died October 26, 1863, at Murfreesboro, Tennessee.

Perry, Adam: Company K, Seventy-fifth Indiana Volunteer Infantry. Mustered into service August 8, 1862. Residence: Bluffton, Indiana. Occupation: Farmer. Place of birth: Harrison County, Ohio. Age: 23. Died February 5, 1863 at Gallatin, Tennessee, of typhus fever.

Perry, William W.: Civilian. Residence: Lancaster Township, Wells County, Indiana. Occupation: Farmer. Place of birth: Ohio. Age: 24. Value of real estate: $0. Value of personal estate: $300. Other members of his household: wife Mary, born in Ohio, age 21. (1860 census.)

Pine, Hiram: Company K, Seventy-fifth Indiana Volunteer Infantry. Mustered into service August 6, 1862. Residence: Bluffton,

Indiana. Occupation: Farmer. Place of birth: Perry County, Ohio. Age: 21. Deserted December 27, 1862, at Scottsville, Kentucky. Returned to the regiment on his own April 20, 1863. Mustered out June 8, 1865.

PRICE, JOHN W.: EIGHTEENTH UNITED STATES INFANTRY. Mustered into service August 22, 1861. Occupation: Soldier. Place of birth: Buffalo, New York. Age: 29. Appointed quartermaster sergeant, Eighteenth Infantry. Mustered out August 14, 1864.

REED, JAMES: COMPANY K, SEVENTY-FIFTH INDIANA VOLUNTEER INFANTRY. Mustered into service July 28, 1862. Residence: Ossian, Indiana. Occupation: Farmer. Place of birth: Portage County, Ohio. Age: 18. Detached to Ambulance Corps August 13, 1864. Mustered out June 8, 1865.

RHINE, JOHN (ALSO KNOWN AS JOHN RYAN): COMPANY K, SEVENTY-FIFTH INDIANA VOLUNTEER INFANTRY. Mustered into service August 6, 1862. Residence: Montpelier, Indiana. Occupation: Farmer. Place of birth: Jay County, Indiana. Age: 29. Appointed third sergeant August 11, 1862. Promoted to second sergeant January 1, 1863. Wounded slightly in head at Chickamauga, Georgia, September 20, 1863, and taken prisoner. Mustered out June 8, 1865.

RICHEY, JOSEPH: CIVILIAN. Residence: Bluffton, Indiana. Occupation: Laborer. Place of birth: Ohio. Age: 48. Value of real estate: $0. Value of personal estate: $50. Other members of his household: wife and seven children. (1860 census.)

RICHEY, THOMAS: COMPANY K, SEVENTY-FIFTH INDIANA VOLUNTEER INFANTRY. Mustered into service July 26, 1862. Residence: Bluffton, Indiana. Occupation: Farmer. Place of birth: Wayne County, Indiana. Age: 26. Discharged April 4, 1865, by surgeon's certificate at New York.

RILEY, GEORGE W.: COMPANY K, 101ST INDIANA VOLUNTEER INFANTRY. Mustered into service December 12, 1862. Residence: Bluffton, Indiana. Occupation: Farmer. Place of birth: Clark County, Ohio. Age: 23. Mustered out June 24, 1865.

ROBINSON, MILTON S.: SEVENTY-FIFTH INDIANA VOLUNTEER INFANTRY. Commissioned colonel October 21, 1862. Mustered into service November 3, 1862. Residence: Kokomo, Indiana. Occupation: Carpenter. Place of birth: Hiland, Indiana. Age: 44. Resigned March 29, 1864, due to sickness in family.

SHAFFER, ABNER H.: SEVENTY-FIFTH INDIANA VOLUNTEER INFANTRY. Mustered into service June 23, 1863, as first assistant surgeon. Residence: Huntington, Indiana. Occupation: Physician. Place of birth: Huntington County, Indiana. Age: 31. Captured at Chickamauga, Georgia, September 20, 1863, while treating the wounded. Paroled at City Point, Virginia, November 24, 1863. Mustered in as regimental surgeon November 16, 1864. Mustered out June 8, 1865.

SHINN, SILAS N.: COMPANY K, SEVENTY-FIFTH INDIANA VOLUNTEER INFANTRY. Mustered into service August 6, 1862. Residence: Montpelier, Indiana. Occupation: Farmer. Place of birth: Blackford County, Indiana. Age: 18. Died December 30, 1862 at Gallatin, Tennessee, of fever.

SHULL, JOHN S.: COMPANY E, SEVENTY-FIFTH INDIANA VOLUNTEER INFANTRY. Mustered into service January 27, 1864. Residence: Huntington, Indiana. Died of chronic diarrhea near Stone Mountain, Georgia, November 17, 1864.

SISSON, ORIN: COMPANY G, EIGHTY-EIGHTH INDIANA VOLUNTEER INFANTRY. Mustered into service August 29, 1862. Residence: LaGrange County, Indiana. Occupation: Farmer. Age: 19. Wounded September 19, 1863, at Chickamauga, Georgia. Mustered out May 26, 1865.

SPAKE, JAMES W.: COMPANY K, SEVENTY-FIFTH INDIANA VOLUNTEER INFANTRY. Mustered into service July 25, 1862, as sixth corporal. Residence: Bluffton, Indiana. Occupation: Carpenter. Place of birth: Guernsey County, Ohio. Age: 29. Promoted to sergeant January 1, 1863. Transferred November 1, 1863, to Veteran Reserve Corps and served in Indianapolis.

SPAKE, JOSEPH: CIVILIAN. Residence: Lancaster Township, Wells County, Indiana. Occupation: Shoemaker. Place of birth: Ohio. Age:

21. Listed in the household of William Spake, age 58, a farmer, his mother, and six siblings. (1860 census.)

SPAKE, MAGG (ALSO KNOWN AS MARGARET A.): CIVILIAN. Wife of James W. Spake. Residence: Bluffton, Indiana. Place of birth: Ohio. Age: 23. Listed in the household of James W. Spake. (1860 census.)

STARBUCK, JAMES A.: COMPANY K, SEVENTY-FIFTH INDIANA VOLUNTEER INFANTRY. Mustered into service July 25, 1862, as a private. Elected and commissioned first lieutenant August 8, 1862. Mustered into service as first lieutenant August 19, 1862. Residence: Bluffton, Indiana. Occupation: Mason. Place of birth: Logan County, Ohio. Age: 23. Mustered out June 8, 1865. Also a member of Company G, Twelfth Indiana Infantry. Died near Pennville, Indiana, in June 1914.

STARR, WILLIAM W.: COMPANY K, SEVENTY-FIFTH INDIANA VOLUNTEER INFANTRY. Mustered into service August 2, 1862. Residence: Bluffton, Indiana. Occupation: Farmer. Place of birth: Wells County, Indiana. Age: 19. Mustered out June 8, 1865.

STEELE, GEORGE WASHINGTON: 101ST INDIANA VOLUNTEER INFANTRY. Appointed first lieutenant of Company I August 17, 1862. Mustered into service September 6, 1862, as captain. Residence: Marion, Indiana. Age: 22. Promoted to major January 27, 1863. Promoted to lieutenant colonel May 31, 1863. Mustered out June 24, 1865.

STEFFEY, EZARIAH: COMPANY K SEVENTY-FIFTH INDIANA VOLUNTEER INFANTRY. Mustered into service August 8, 1862. Residence: Bluffton, Indiana. Occupation: Farmer. Place of birth: Westmoreland County, Pennsylvania. Age: 28. Mustered out June 8, 1865.

STEFFEY, PHILIP A.: COMPANY K, SEVENTY-FIFTH INDIANA VOLUNTEER INFANTRY. Mustered into service March 7, 1864. Residence: Bluffton, Indiana. Occupation: Laborer. Place of birth: Westmoreland County, Pennsylvania. Age: 18. Discharged November 10, 1864, for disability from a wound received on July 19, 1864, at Peach Tree Creek, Georgia.

STUDABAKER, PETER: COMPANY B, 101ST INDIANA VOLUNTEER INFANTRY. Mustered into service as captain September 5, 1862. Residence: Bluffton, Indiana. Occupation: Farmer. Place of birth: Darke County, Ohio. Age: 30. Commissioned major May 31, 1863, and mustered in June 1, 1863. Mustered out of service June 24, 1865.

SWANEY, JAMES W.: COMPANY A, SEVENTY-FIFTH INDIANA VOLUNTEER INFANTRY. Mustered into service July 22, 1862. Residence: New Holland, Indiana. Occupation: Farmer. Place of birth: Noble County, Indiana. Age: 19. Appointed second sergeant January 22, 1863. Reduced to ranks May 14, 1863. Restored to sergeant November 4, 1863. Appointed first sergeant May 1, 1864. Mustered out June 8, 1865.

SWEET, HENRY C.: COMPANIES I AND K, 105TH OHIO VOLUNTEER INFANTRY. Mustered into service July 16, 1862, as first lieutenant in Company K. Age: 21. Promoted to captain of Company I October 8, 1862. Dishonorably dismissed from the service March 12, 1863.

THOMAS, MORGAN: COMPANY E, SEVENTY-FIFTH INDIANA VOLUNTEER INFANTRY. Mustered into service August 1, 1862. Residence: Warren, Indiana. Occupation: Farmer. Place of birth: Union County, Indiana. Age: 22. Mustered out June 8, 1865.

THORP, WILLIAM W.: COMPANY F, SEVENTY-FIFTH INDIANA VOLUNTEER INFANTRY. Mustered into service August 6, 1862. Residence: Bluffton, Indiana. Occupation: Farmer. Place of birth: Campbell County, Kentucky. Age: 19. Mustered out June 8, 1865.

TODD, URIAH: COMPANY K, SEVENTY-FIFTH INDIANA VOLUNTEER INFANTRY. Mustered into service August 19, 1862, as second lieutenant. Residence: Bluffton, Indiana. Age: 26. Appointed first lieutenant in Company H, First U.S. Veteran Volunteer Engineers. Mustered into service November 19, 1864. Resigned February 24, 1865.

TOWNSEND, AMOS. CIVILIAN. Residence: Bluffton, Indiana. Occupation: Merchant. Place of birth: Ohio. Age: 43. Value of real estate: $1,200. Value of personal estate: $2,000. Other members of his household: wife

Mary, age 40, born in Ohio, Adelade L., age 19, born in Indiana, and four siblings. (1860 census.)

TOWNSEND, LOU: CIVILIAN. Probably Adalade L. Townsend. Residence: Bluffton, Indiana. Place of birth: Indiana. Age: 19. Listed in the household of Amos Townsend. (1860 census.)

TRUSDALL, DAVID: COMPANY G, 101ST INDIANA VOLUNTEER INFANTRY. Appointed captain August 16, 1862. Mustered into service September 6, 1862. Age: 22. Resigned February 13, 1864 (date resignation accepted), for disability (chronic diarrhea, debility, and emaciation).

TUMBLESON, FRANCIS M.: COMPANY H, SEVENTY-FIFTH INDIANA VOLUNTEER INFANTRY. Mustered into service August 6, 1862. Residence: Roanoke, Indiana. Occupation: Physician. Place of birth: Preble County, Ohio. Age: 31. On duty as hospital steward in regimental hospital. Mustered out June 8, 1865.

TURNER, MARK C.: COMPANY K, SEVENTY-FIFTH INDIANA VOLUNTEER INFANTRY. Mustered into service August 6, 1862. Residence: Montpelier, Indiana. Occupation: Farmer. Place of birth: Fayette County, Indiana. Age: 25. Deserted October 27, 1862, while on the march from Frankfort to Bowling Green, Kentucky. Returned to the regiment August 26, 1863. Detached November 1, 1863 to Fourth U.S. Artillery. Mustered out June 8, 1865.

URTON, PETER: COMPANY K, SEVENTY-FIFTH INDIANA VOLUNTEER INFANTRY. Mustered into service August 4, 1862. Residence: Bluffton, Indiana. Occupation: Farmer. Place of birth: Warren County, Ohio. Age: 25. Deserted March 16, 1863, at Murfreesboro, Tennessee. Arrested October 2, 1863, by order of Captain C. Cowgill, provost marshal, Eleventh District. Escaped from guards at Nashville, Tennessee, and never heard from again.

WAGONER, HENRY: COMPANY K, SEVENTY-FIFTH INDIANA VOLUNTEER INFANTRY. Mustered into service August 4, 1862. Residence: Bluffton, Indiana. Occupation: Farmer. Place of birth: Meigs County, Ohio. Age:

24. Detailed as brigade teamster May 14, 1863. Promoted to corporal March 3, 1865. Mustered out June 8, 1865.

WALBRIDGE, CHARLES H.: COMPANY A, FOURTEENTH OHIO VOLUNTEER INFANTRY. Mustered into service August 17, 1862. Occupation: Carpenter. Age: 30. Killed (murdered) September 13, 1864, at Atlanta, Georgia.

WALTON, ALBERT (ALSO KNOWN AS ALBERT B. BENEWAY): COMPANY C, SEVENTY-FIFTH INDIANA VOLUNTEER INFANTRY. Mustered into service September 1, 1862. Occupation: Peddler. Place of birth: New York, New York. Age: 15. Taken prisoner at Chickamauga, Georgia, September 20, 1863. Exchanged and mustered out June 8, 1865. Also an unofficial musician in the Nineteenth Indiana Volunteer Infantry and Sixtieth Indiana Volunteer Infantry.

WALTON, JOHN B.: COMPANY B, SEVENTIETH INDIANA VOLUNTEER INFANTRY. Mustered into service July 18, 1862. Residence: Shelbyville, Indiana. Died in Gallatin, Tennessee, December 15, 1862.

WANDELL, JOHN WASHINGTON: COMPANY I, TWENTY-SECOND INDIANA VOLUNTEER INFANTRY. Mustered into service August 15, 1861. Residence: Bluffton, Indiana. Occupation: Farmer. Place of birth: Hancock County, Indiana. Age: 19. Mustered out of service July 24, 1865.

WENTZ, SILAS H.: COMPANY K, SEVENTY-FIFTH INDIANA VOLUNTEER INFANTRY. Mustered into service August 2, 1862. Residence: Bluffton, Indiana. Occupation: Farmer. Place of birth: Wells County, Indiana. Age: 18. Attached to brigade headquarters as guard October 21, 1863. Mustered out June 8, 1865.

WHEELER, HENRY HARRISON: COMPANY A, SEVENTY-FIFTH INDIANA VOLUNTEER INFANTRY. Mustered into service July 25, 1862. Age: 23. Commissioned first lieutenant July 25, 1862. Mustered into service as such August 19, 1862. Resigned December 6, 1863.

WHETSEL, JAMES: COMPANY F, THIRTY-FIFTH OHIO VOLUNTEER INFANTRY. Mustered into service September 5, 1861. Age: 20. Detailed as orderly for division surgeon May 16, 1863. Mustered out September 8, 1864.

WHITESTINE, GEORGE M.: COMPANY E, SEVENTY-FIFTH INDIANA VOLUN-
TEER INFANTRY. Mustered into service August 1, 1862. Residence: Huntington, Indiana. Occupation: Laborer. Place of birth: Huntington County,
Indiana. Age: 18. Died July 21, 1863, of injuries received by falling from
a tree at Camp Winfred, Tennessee.

WIDMER, JOHN H.: 104TH ILLINOIS VOLUNTEER INFANTRY. Mustered into
service August 20, 1861, as private in Company I, Eleventh Illinois
Volunteer Infantry. Residence: Ottawa, Illinois. Age: 26. Promoted to
first lieutenant September 1, 1861. Promoted to captain April 24, 1862.
Promoted to major, 104th Illinois Volunteer Infantry September 25,
1862. Captured at Hartsville, Tennessee, December 7, 1862. Paroled
April 23, 1863. Mustered out June 6, 1865. Also a member of Company
I, Eleventh Illinois Volunteer Infantry (three months).

WILCOX, ALFRED G.: COMPANY F, 105TH OHIO VOLUNTEER INFANTRY.
Mustered into service August 21, 1862. Promoted from first lieutenant
to captain January 18, 1863. Residence: Madison County, Ohio. Age:
21. Mustered out June 3, 1865.

WILEY, BENJAMIN FRANKLIN: COMPANY K, SEVENTY-FIFTH INDIANA
VOLUNTEER INFANTRY. Mustered into service August 8, 1862. Residence:
Bluffton, Indiana. Occupation: Mason/plasterer. Place of birth: Darke
County, Ohio. Age: 31. Appointed first sergeant August 11, 1862.
Detailed to report to Governor Oliver P. Morton in Indianapolis for
recruiting. Listed as a deserter December 31, 1863. Commissioned cap-
tain of Company E, 153d Indiana Volunteer Infantry February 21, 1865.
Mustered out September 4, 1865.

WILLIAMSON, ALFRED: COMPANY E, NINETEENTH UNITED STATES
INFANTRY. Enlisted January 20, 1862. Occupation: Laborer. Place of
birth: Stark County, Ohio. Age: 26. Discharged January 20, 1865, by
expiration of term of service at Lookout Mountain, Tennessee.

WILSON, ABRAHAM T.: COMPANY K, SEVENTY-FIFTH INDIANA VOLUNTEER
INFANTRY. Mustered into service August 4, 1862. Residence: Bluffton,
Indiana. Place of birth: Fayette County, Pennsylvania. Age: 24. Mustered
out June 8, 1865.

WILSON, EDWARD K.: CIVILIAN. Residence: Bluffton, Indiana. Occupation: Attorney. Place of birth: Ohio. Age: 30. Value of real estate: $3,850. Value of personal estate: $450. Other members of his household: wife and three children. (1860 census.)

WILSON, JOHN S.: COMPANY K, SEVENTY-FIFTH INDIANA VOLUNTEER INFANTRY. Mustered into service August 5, 1862. Residence: Bluffton, Indiana. Occupation: Blacksmith. Place of birth: Decatur County, Indiana. Age: 23. Died July 4, 1863, at Tullahoma, Tennessee, of disease.

WILSON, LORENZO D.: COMPANY G, 101ST INDIANA VOLUNTEER INFANTRY. Mustered into service August 21, 1862, as second sergeant. Residence: Fort Wayne, Indiana. Occupation: Lawyer. Place of birth: Fairfax County, Virginia. Age: 28. Promoted to first sergeant December 12, 1862. Wounded December 31, 1862, at Stones River, Tennessee, by artillery shell lacerating left thigh. Mustered in as second lieutenant March 4, 1863. Mustered in as first lieutenant March 10, 1863. Wounded March 20, 1863 in battle at Milton, Tennessee, by gunshot to left leg. Wounded September 20, 1863, at Chickamauga, Georgia. Promoted to captain February 14, 1864. Wounded August 21, 1864, at Atlanta, Georgia, and sent to hospital. Mustered out June 24, 1865.

ZERSE, AUGUSTUS: COMPANY H, SEVENTY-SECOND INDIANA VOLUNTEER INFANTRY. Mustered into service July 16, 1862. Residence: Fountain County, Indiana. Occupation: Clerk. Place of birth: New York, New York. Age: 21. Discharged February 4, 1863, at Gallatin, Tennessee, for disability.

NOTES

INTRODUCTION

1. Census Bureau, *Eighth Census of the United States, 1860, Population Schedules for City of Bluffton, Wells County, Indiana*, Microcopy 653, Reel 309, NA; pension file of William Bluffton Miller, Pension Records of Volunteer Soldiers Who Served in Organizations from the State of Indiana, RG 15, NA (hereafter cited as William Bluffton Miller file). Michael Miller was the son of Frederick and Susan (Paulus) Miller and was born in York County, Pennsylvania, about 1810. About 1825, the family moved to Baltimore County, Maryland, then to Fairfield County, Ohio, about 1829. Although his parents bought land in Wells County, Indiana, in 1836, they remained in Ohio. Some sources state that Michael moved to Wells County in the fall of 1837 with his brother Jacob and purchased land there the following year. He served as county sheriff from 1853 to 1857 and again from 1859 to 1861. His thirteen siblings were Jacob, William, Samuel, Benjamin, George, Lena, Catherine, Eliza, Mary Ann, John, Charles, Susan, and Henry. Jacob, William, John, Charles, and Susan lived in Wells County, Indiana. Lewis Publishing, *Biographical and Historical Record of Adams and Wells Counties, Indiana* (Chicago: Lewis Publishing, 1887), 563–64, 577, 937–38, 970–71, 1002.

2. William Bluffton Miller diary, August 21, 1862, Robert J. Willey Collection.

3. Miller was living in Ossian, Indiana, by 1879, Fort Wayne by 1888, and Marion by 1900. William Bluffton Miller file.

4. *Bluffton (Ind.) Evening News*, May 31, 1918; *Charleston (Ill.) Daily Courier*, May 31, 1918; William Bluffton Miller file.

CHAPTER 1

1. William H. H. Terrell, *Report of the Adjutant General of the State of Indiana*, 8 vols. (Indianapolis: Alexander H. Conner, W. R. Holloway and Samuel M. Douglass, 1865–69), 1:333–34.

2. Rev. David B. Floyd, *History of the Seventy-Fifth Regiment of Indiana Infantry Volunteers, Its Organization, Campaigns and Battles, 1862–65* (Philadelphia: Lutheran Publication Society, 1893), 12.

3. Theodore T. Scribner, *Indiana's Roll of Honor*, 2 vols. (Indianapolis: A. D. Streight, 1866), 2:552.

4. Miller often wrote about the concept of "duty" in his diary. Many soldiers on both sides agreed with Miller that duty required them to serve. For further examples, see Miller's entries of August 21 and September 11, 1862, and November 9, 1863, along with James M. McPherson, *For Cause and Comrades: Why Men Fought in the Civil War* (New York: Oxford Univ. Press, 1997), 22–23, 168–69.

5. Possibly Henry Banta of Decatur, soon to be commissioned captain of Company I, Eighty-ninth Indiana Volunteer Infantry. Terrell, *Report of the Adjutant General* 3:97.

6. Miller's wife and son.

7. A War Department order was issued on July 2, 1862, calling for three hundred thousand men to serve for three years. The Seventy-fifth Indiana Volunteer Infantry, Miller's regiment, was recruited under this order. Francis A. Lord, *They Fought for the Union* (Harrisburg, Pa.: Stackpole, 1960), 3.

8. According to one source, forty men were enrolled in the company by this date. Compiled Service Record of James A. Starbuck, Company K, Seventy-fifth Indiana Volunteer Infantry, RG 94, NA.

9. Jacob Eversole and Dwight Klinck have not been identified.

10. Possibly Andrew J. Barlow of Bluffton, who enlisted a few days later in Company B, 101st Indiana Infantry, rose to the rank of first lieutenant, and died in 1864. See biographical appendix.

11. Possibly the home of Jacob Stahl, a thirty-five-year-old carpenter and resident of nearby Liberty Township, Wells County. Stahl and his wife Mary had two children and real estate valued at fifteen hundred dollars. Census Bureau, *Eighth Census of the United States, 1860, Population Schedules for Wells County, Indiana*, Microcopy 653, Reel 309, NA.

12. A note in Capt. Sanford Karns's compiled military service record states that eighty men were enrolled in Company K by this date. Compiled Service Record of Sanford Karns, Company K, Seventy-fifth Indiana Volunteer Infantry, RG 94, NA.

13. Uriah Todd, one of the candidates mentioned, would have been the most qualified. He had already served in Company H, Fourteenth Ohio Volunteer Infantry from April to August 1861. Following his service as a second lieutenant with the Seventy-fifth Indiana, Todd was a first lieutenant in Company H, First U.S. Veteran Volunteer Engineers until his resignation in February 1865. Ohio Adjutant General, *Official Roster of the Soldiers of the State of Ohio in the War of the Rebellion, 1861–1866*, 12 vols. (Akron, Ohio: Werner, 1886–95), 1:311; U.S. Adjutant General's Office, *Official Army Register of the Volunteer Force of the United States Army*, 8 vols. (Washington, D.C.: Adjutant General's Office, 1865), 8:120; Terrell, *Report of the Adjutant General* 8:399.

14. Undoubtedly Miller's sister Mary Jane, whom he continually referred to as "Molly." She was a frequent correspondent with her brother throughout his time in the army. See biographical appendix.

15. Miller refers to the Sibley tent, invented prior to the war by Henry Hopkins Sibley for use by the U.S. Army. A conical tent with a central pole, resembling an Indian tepee, it could comfortably accommodate about fifteen soldiers with a fire or stove in the center. The tent saw a good deal of use in the field by Union forces early in the war then was relegated to permanent camps. Mark Mayo Boatner III, *The Civil War Dictionary* (New York: David McKay, 1988), 760.

16. A reference to the army bread ration, known officially as "hardtack" or "hard bread." The large, hard crackers were a staple of the army diet. Nine or ten were issued daily. "Sowbelly" was a slang term for salt pork, part of a soldier's meat ration. John D. Billings, *Hardtack and Coffee: The Unwritten Story of Army Life* (Boston: George M. Smith, 1888; reprint, Chicago: R. R. Donnelley & Sons, 1960), 114–37.

17. The regiment's departure was more complicated than Miller admits. Although all the men were in place at the depot at 10:00 a.m., the railroad refused to

issue the required number of cars on short notice. Colonel Pettit then ordered two companies to take control of the railroad and soon had sufficient cars to transport his men. *Wabash (Ind.) Plain Dealer,* Aug. 22, 1862.

18. Miller's acquaintance with these men stems from the fact that Bluffton's 1860 population was only 760. Joseph C. G. Kennedy, *Population of the United States in 1860; Compiled from the Original Returns of the Eighth Census, under the Direction of the Secretary of the Interior* (Washington, D.C.: GPO, 1864), 128.

19. On August 30, 1862, the Twelfth Indiana was severely mauled at the Battle of Richmond, Kentucky, losing 173 men killed and wounded. D. Warren Lambert, *When the Ripe Pears Fell: The Battle of Richmond, Kentucky* (Richmond, Ky.: Madison County Historical Society, 1995), 236.

20. A slang term referring to liquor.

21. Henry Beebee Carrington (1824–1912) was commissioned a colonel in the Regular Army in 1861. The following year, as a brigadier general of volunteers, Carrington supervised the organization of thousands of Hoosier recruits. Ezra J. Warner, *Generals in Blue: Lives of the Union Commanders* (Baton Rouge: Louisiana State Univ. Press, 1964), 72–73.

CHAPTER 2

1. *Indianapolis Daily Journal,* as quoted in the *Wabash (Ind.) Plain Dealer,* Aug. 29, 1862; Floyd, *History of the Seventy-Fifth Regiment,* 34.

2. Floyd, *History of the Seventy-Fifth Regiment,* 36.

3. Ibid., 47–48.

4. Ibid., 47–49; Scribner, *Indiana's Roll of Honor* 2:552; *Wabash (Ind.) Plain Dealer,* Nov. 28, 1862.

5. *Howard Tribune* (Kokomo, Ind.), Nov. 20, 1862.

6. In 1860, Louisville had a population of 68,033 people living in eight wards and was the largest city in Kentucky. Kennedy, *Population of the United States in 1860,* 182.

7. Miller did not have the same impression of Lebanon as his comrade E. W. Freeman, who thought that there was "not a more stinking, nasty, dirty, secesh town in the State of Kentucky" than Lebanon, with business men even staying open on Sunday to take advantage of Union soldiers. *Howard Tribune* (Kokomo, Ind.), Sept. 11, 1862. According to the 1860 census, the town contained a population of 953. Kennedy, *Population of the United States in 1860,* 182.

8. Ebenezer Dumont (1814–1871) served as colonel of the Seventh Indiana Infantry in western Virginia before being promoted to brigadier general of volunteers. Early in 1862, he was named to command a brigade of the Army of the Ohio then led a division in that army during Braxton Bragg's invasion of Kentucky. Warner, *Generals in Blue,* 132–33.

9. Despite Miller's unfavorable first impression of Dumont, the general did attempt to win over the Hoosiers. In a speech to the regiment in mid-September, Dumont said that "no better regiment ever left the State of Indiana than the 75th." *Howard Tribune* (Kokomo, Ind.), Sept. 25, 1862.

10. A "picket" was an advance guard placed around a camp. "Secesh" was a slang term referring to Confederate sympathizers.

11. According to regulations, a dress parade was required to be held once a day, with all men not "especially excused" to be in attendance. U.S. War Department, *Revised Regulations for the Army of the United States, 1861* (Philadelphia: J. G. L. Brown, 1861), 51–53.

12. Throughout his diary, Miller refers to Confederate troops as "Johnies," "Rebs," or "Rebels." Miller and his comrades were like thousands of new recruits on both sides who were eager for their first taste of combat. For other examples, see McPherson, *For Cause and Comrades,* 30–33.

13. The Union army occasionally organized informal "Pioneer" detachments, composed of troops detached from their regular units to clear roads, erect and repair bridges, and build fortifications. In November 1862, a formal Pioneer Corps was organized in the new Army of the Cumberland. Patricia L. Faust, ed., *Historical Times Illustrated Encyclopedia of the Civil War* (New York: Harper Collins, 1986), 586–87.

14. As Miller indicates, mail (or a lack thereof) had an enormous impact on a soldier's morale. Because letters were the crucial link between a soldier and his family and friends, many men grew impatient when those at home failed to write frequently or in great detail. McPherson, *For Cause and Comrades,* 132.

15. The haversack was a tarred cloth bag suspended from a shoulder strap in which a soldier carried his food ration.

16. Braxton Bragg (1817–1876), a graduate of West Point, was named a brigadier general in March 1861. Promoted to major general, he led a corps at the Battle of Shiloh. Raised to full general, he assumed command the Army of the Mississippi in June 1862. In cooperation with a force under Gen. Edmund Kirby Smith, Bragg moved from Tennessee in late August to invade Kentucky. He captured Munfordville's garrison on September 17 and won a tactical victory against Union forces under Maj. Gen. Don Carlos Buell at the Battle of Perryville on October 8, 1862. Following the battle, Bragg left the field and retreated to Tennessee. Boatner, *Civil War Dictionary,* 78–80; Ezra J. Warner, *Generals in Gray: Lives of the Confederate Commanders* (Baton Rouge: Louisiana State Univ. Press, 1959), 30–31. For a full account of the Bragg-Smith campaign, see Kenneth W. Noe, *Perryville: This Grand Havoc of Battle* (Lexington: Univ. Press of Kentucky, 2001).

17. John T. Wilder, a resident of Greensburg, Indiana, and colonel of the Seventeenth Indiana Volunteer Infantry, overcame the stigma of surrender at Munfordville through his service as commander of "Wilder's Lightning Brigade," a collection of mounted infantry regiments famous for resolute fighting at Hoover's Gap, Tennessee, and Chickamauga, Georgia. See Miller's June 24, 1863, entry.

18. Don Carlos Buell (1818–1898) graduated from West Point in 1841. Commissioned a brigadier general of volunteers in May 1861, Buell led his Army of the Ohio in the capture of Nashville, Tennessee, and helped save Ulysses S. Grant's forces on the second day of the Battle of Shiloh. Promoted to major general, Buell led the Army of the Ohio to oppose the Confederate invasion of Kentucky. Because of his slow pursuit of Bragg following the Battle of Perryville, he was relieved of command on October 24, 1862. Warner, *Generals in Blue,* 51–52.

19. A reference to Jacob Geary. Although Miller frequently wrote to the Geary family, they could not be located in the 1860 census for Ohio.

20. Miller was correct, as Shelbyville had a population of 811 in 1860. Kennedy, *Population of the United States in 1860,* 183.

21. On October 4, 1862, Richard Hawes was inaugurated in Frankfort as Kentucky's Confederate governor. Unfortunately for Hawes, Federal troops were nearing the capital. According to one source, Union artillery fire actually interrupted his speech and the new governor and his supporters were forced to evacuate the city. Other sources state only that cannon fire could be heard in Frankfort following the governor's post-inauguration dinner. Frankfort fell to Federal forces two days later. James Lee McDonough, *War in Kentucky: From Shiloh to Perryville* (Knoxville: Univ. of Tennessee Press, 1994), 200; Earl J. Hess, *Banners to the Breeze: The Kentucky Campaign, Corinth, and Stones River* (Lincoln: Univ. of Nebraska Press, 2000), 83.

22. E. W. Freeman of the Seventy-fifth expected to find a city of "wealth and beauty" but instead found not more than twenty-five hundred inhabitants, "few nice buildings," public buildings that could not compare with those in Indiana, and business suspended. "Everything looks desolate and it seems as if we were away in the backwoods," Freeman believed. S. W. Payne agreed that there was "little appearance of thrift or business about the place," and the only interesting thing was the city cemetery. *Howard Tribune* (Kokomo, Ind.), Oct. 30, Nov. 20, 1862. Including a large slave population, Frankfort contained 3,702 people in 1860. Kennedy, *Population of the United States in 1860,* 182.

23. Versailles actually had a population of 1,142 in 1860. Kennedy, *Population of the United States in 1860,* 183.

24. According to regulations, regiments were required to maintain extensive records, including company descriptive books that listed detailed personal information about every soldier and morning reports, which accounted for the presence or absence of every soldier in a company. August V. Kautz, *The Company Clerk* (Philadelphia: Lippincott, 1865), 12–13, 30–32.

25. William Thomas Ward (1808–1878), a former congressman from Kentucky, was commissioned a brigadier general of volunteers in September 1861. After a stint as a brigade commander in the Army of the Ohio, Ward was made post commander at Gallatin, Tennessee, in November 1862. Warner, *Generals in Blue,* 538–39.

26. E. W. Freeman of the regiment wrote in mid-October that he thought the Seventy-fifth had done more marching as raw troops in the previous three weeks than any other regiment from Indiana. *Howard Tribune* (Kokomo, Ind.), Oct. 30, 1862.

27. One of Miller's comrades agreed, describing Kentucky as "nothing but rocks and yellow mud, and once in a while a persimmon or chestnut tree." *Howard Tribune* (Kokomo, Ind.), Nov. 27, 1862.

28. Munfordville had a population of 192 in 1860. Kennedy, *Population of the United States in 1860,* 182.

29. William Starke Rosecrans (1819–1898) graduated in the West Point class of 1842. Promoted to brigadier general in the Regular Army in 1861, Rosecrans won glory fighting Confederates in western Virginia that summer and at the Battles of Corinth and Iuka, Mississippi, in 1862. Appointed a major general of volunteers, he assumed command of Buell's Army of the Ohio, reorganized as the Fourteenth Army Corps (later the Army of the Cumberland) on October 30, 1862. Boatner, *Civil War*

Dictionary, 708; Warner, *Generals in Blue*, 410–11. Miller consistently misspelled this general's name throughout his diary.

30. According to one soldier, Rosecrans remarked to Lieutenant Colonel O'Brien that he commanded a "crack regiment." Due to the lack of clothing in the unit, O'Brien had no doubt that when Rosecrans rode in the rear of the Seventy-fifth, "the general would be fully convinced of the correctness of his impression." *Howard Tribune* (Kokomo, Ind.), Nov. 20, 1862.

CHAPTER 3

1. Scribner, *Indiana's Roll of Honor* 2:555.

2. Floyd, *History of the Seventy-Fifth Regiment*, 51, 54.

3. A newspaper reporter noted that of the three thousand inhabitants of Gallatin, there was "but one true Union man." He also reported that the town's extensive cotton manufactory had produced a large quantity of excellent "heavy brown domestics, tent duck and cotton goods of a coarse texture" for the Confederate army. The Gallatin area also showed signs of war, including "uncultivated fields, dilapidated outhouses, vacant residences, empty school-houses, wasted farm lands, and neglected children." *New York Times*, Nov. 24, 1862.

4. E. W. Freeman shared Miller's enthusiasm for battle. "All we want is to give the rebels a trial," he wrote. S. W. Payne agreed, writing, "We have come to accomplish a certain work and the sentiment of every soldier is 'let's at it and get done.'" *Howard Tribune* (Kokomo, Ind.), Nov. 20, 1862.

5. In this entry, Miller seems to describe the culmination of a process that historian Reid Mitchell calls "hardening." Weeks of hard marching and few comforts had transformed him from civilian to soldier, allowing him to "forage" food without remorse. The final step in the "hardening" process took place on December 6, when Miller saw his first battlefield. His entries describing the carnage of battle later in the war do not contain similar statements regretting the loss of human life. Mitchell, *The Vacant Chair: The Northern Soldier Leaves Home* (New York: Oxford Univ. Press, 1993), 7–11.

6. Another soldier failed to see anything attractive about the spring. Although a "noted watering place," "Private" described it as small "but great in scent." He did admit that the camp site was rather pleasant. *Wabash (Ind.) Plain Dealer*, Dec. 19, 1862.

7. Instead of drawing rations as enlisted men did, officers were allowed a cash allowance, according to rank, in order to purchase food from the brigade commissary. A captain, for instance, was allowed four rations worth thirty-six dollars. Since officers were to purchase rations for their own use, Miller and his comrades were not required by regulation to furnish food to them. Billings, *Hardtack and Coffee*, 113; War Department, *Revised Regulations for the Army of the United States, 1861*, 245.

8. Because volunteer units like the Seventy-fifth Indiana were raised locally, most Civil War enlisted men and officers enjoyed a unique relationship. Enlisted men generally knew their officers before the war and believed that there were actually few differences between them. In addition, officers were expected to care for their men in a "fatherly" manner, with kind and fair treatment and a minimum of discipline, always looking out for their best interests. Obviously Miller's officers vio-

lated this unwritten contract by "stealing" food from the enlisted men. Mitchell, *Vacant Chair*, 42–54; Gerald F. Linderman, *Embattled Courage: The Experience of Combat in the American Civil War* (New York: Free Press, 1987), 50–56; McPherson, *For Cause and Comrades*, 57–58. For another of Miller's unpleasant encounters with officers, see his April 22, 1863, entry.

9. Eyewitnesses reported that the "*traveling* 75th was on a dead run, making good time." *Wabash (Ind.) Plain Dealer*, Dec. 19, 1862.

10. John Hunt Morgan (1825–1864) was appointed colonel of the Second Kentucky Cavalry in April 1862 and a brigadier general that December. By the time of the Battle of Hartsville, Morgan was famous for leading successful cavalry strikes against Federal forces in Kentucky in July and August 1862. Warner, *Generals in Gray*, 220–21.

11. Further information about the Hartsville action may be found in War Department, *The War of the Rebellion: A Compilation of the Official Records of the Union and Confederate Armies*, 128 vols. (Washington, D.C.: GPO, 1880–1901), ser. 1, vol. 20, pt. 1, pp. 40–72 (hereafter cited as *Official Records*, followed by series, volume, part, and page numbers). Also see James A. Ramage's *Rebel Raider: The Life of General John Hunt Morgan* (Lexington: Univ. Press of Kentucky, 1986), 128–32. Union losses in this action totaled more than two thousand in killed, wounded, captured, or missing.

12. Soldiers with little or no medical training were often detailed "from the ranks" to serve as hospital orderlies.

13. Dr. William Brown, assistant surgeon in the Second Minnesota Infantry. Minnesota Adjutant General, *Annual Report of the Adjutant General of the State of Minnesota* (St. Paul: Pioneer Printing, 1866), 50; State of Minnesota, *Minnesota in the Civil and Indian Wars, 1861–1865* (St. Paul: Pioneer Press, 1890), 123.

14. The First Presbyterian Church on West Main Street in Gallatin became Hospital Number 5 for sick and wounded Union soldiers.

15. The U.S. Sanitary Commission was organized as a civilian relief agency to help soldiers. Their duties included raising the hygienic standards of camps and hospitals, caring for the sick and wounded, and coordinating the raising and delivery of food and supplies to troops in the field. Boatner, *Civil War Dictionary*, 720.

16. "Gray backs" was a slang term for body lice.

17. Soldiers routinely sent letters home asking relatives and friends to mail boxes of personal items, food, and clothing to them at the front. The subject is covered in great detail in Billings, *Hardtack and Coffee*, 233–39.

18. John B. Walton of Company B, Seventieth Indiana Infantry. See biographical appendix.

19. Sgt. William Ashby of Ladoga, Indiana, was a member of Company E, Seventy-second Indiana Infantry. According to one source, he died at Gallatin on December 27, 1862, one day earlier than Miller indicates. He is buried in Nashville National Cemetery. Terrell, *Report of the Adjutant General* 6:170; 8:612. See biographical appendix.

20. On December 31, 1862, Gen. Braxton Bragg's Confederate Army of Tennessee launched a vicious attack on Rosecrans's Army of the Cumberland, then encamped along Stones River near Murfreesboro, Tennessee. Several desperate

holding actions by Union troops narrowly saved Rosecrans's force, and after a second Confederate attack failed on January 2, Bragg withdrew from the field. The Seventy-fifth Indiana Regiment was not involved in the battle. Boatner, *Civil War Dictionary*, 803–8.

Chapter 4

1. Floyd, *History of the Seventy-Fifth Regiment*, 65.
2. *Howard Tribune* (Kokomo, Ind.), Feb. 12, 1863.
3. Scribner, *Indiana's Roll of Honor* 2:556.
4. *Howard Tribune* (Kokomo, Ind.), Apr. 9, 1863.
5. A brief fight occurred between Confederate cavalry under Joseph Wheeler and Union cavalry and infantry led by Robert Minty and John Palmer near Lavergne on December 26. Miller was correct in his report that the town was subsequently destroyed. Peter Cozzens, *No Better Place to Die: The Battle of Stones River* (Urbana: Univ. of Illinois Press, 1990), 51–58.
6. One Indiana soldier described the laborious process by which sick men were discharged. First, the sick soldier's company commander and surgeon were required to give written opinions about the man's condition. These were then sent to the regiment's colonel, the general of the brigade, the commander of the post, the medical director of the post, the department medical director, then back through channels to the regimental adjutant, who was to draft a discharge. By the time all was in order, noted the writer, the sick soldier had been dead two or three weeks, thanks to "red tape." *Indianapolis Daily Journal*, Jan. 11, 1862.
7. Miller refers to being a supporter of Senator Stephen A. Douglas, the northern Democratic Party's nominee in the presidential campaign of 1860. A proponent of popular sovereignty (the notion that residents of new territories could decide for themselves whether or not to allow slavery within their boundaries), Douglas worked for a compromise between North and South during the secession crisis but firmly supported Lincoln after the war began. Boatner, *Civil War Dictionary*, 244–45.
8. Miller was clearly motivated by ideology. Throughout his service, he remained convinced that he was fighting for law, order, freedom and democratic government, and that those who started the war (even civilians, if necessary) should be punished. Committed to serving in the ranks until the Union was restored, he stood ready to give his life for the cause if necessary. He maintained his beliefs even after experiencing the horrors of combat. Surprisingly, even after terrible battlefield losses in 1863 and 1864, Union soldiers became even more ideological motivated and determined to fight on in order to justify the enormous cost in lives. Mitchell, *Vacant Chair*, 154–58; Earl J. Hess, *The Union Soldier in Battle: Enduring the Ordeal of Combat* (Lawrence: Univ. Press of Kansas, 1997), 98–101, 141; McPherson, *For Cause and Comrades*, 99–100, 111–12, 154, 168, 172–75.
9. Col. Frank Wolford and his First Kentucky Cavalry Regiment participated in a number of important battles early in the war, including Mill Springs and Perryville, Kentucky, and Shiloh and Stones River, Tennessee. *Report of the Adjutant General of the State of Kentucky*, 2 vols. (Frankfort, Ky.: John H. Harney, 1866), vol. 1:2, 47.

10. "Inst" is an abbreviation of "instant," meaning the present or, as here, the current month.

11. Possibly Landon C. H. Shipley, a private in Company C, First Kentucky Cavalry (U.S.). Shipley was mustered into service at Camp Dick Robinson, Kentucky, on October 28, 1861, but his later service is unknown. *Report of the Adjutant General of the State of Kentucky* 1:12.

12. "French furlough" is probably identical to the old term "French leave," meaning leave taken without permission or notice. Miller expressed a common feeling among both Union and Confederate troops. A soldier's morale usually suffered when he received word that a family member was ill or destitute, for it was rarely possible for him to leave his command to help at home. Mitchell, *Vacant Chair*, 29–30. Honor was an important concept to Miller and other Civil War soldiers as well, who believed that less than exemplary army service would damage their personal and family's reputation at home. McPherson, *For Cause and Comrades*, 23–25, 138–39, 169.

13. Lincoln's Emancipation Proclamation freed all slaves in those areas still in rebellion against the government on January 1, 1863. Miller was not alone in his opposition to the decree, but many Unionists who initially opposed the measure eventually accepted it as a military necessity. Reid Mitchell, *Civil War Soldiers: Their Expectations and Their Experiences* (New York: Viking Penguin, 1988), 126–27 and Mark Grimsley, *The Hard Hand of War: Union Military Policy Toward Southern Civilians, 1861–1865* (Cambridge: Cambridge Univ. Press, 1995), 137.

14. Likely candidates include two members of the 129th Illinois Infantry: George W. Randall, a private in Company B, or James H. Cornwell, a private in Company G. Both men died in Gallatin, Tennessee, on February 21, 1863. J. N. Reece, *Report of the Adjutant General of the State of Illinois*, 9 vols. (Springfield, Ill.: Phillips Brothers and the Journal Company, 1900–1902), 6:537, 546.

15. Miller and other soldiers on both sides found that the routine of army life provided much more leisure time than they were allowed at home. Reading for entertainment helped pass the time, and bored troops devoured cheap novels, both dull and sensational. For example, another Hoosier soldier purchased a copy of *Iron Cross* in Chattanooga for twenty-five cents. David Kaser, *Books and Libraries in Camp and Battle: The Civil War Experience* (Westport, Conn.: Greenwood Press, 1984), 35–38.

16. The hospital steward supervised the hospital staff (apart from the surgeons) and was responsible for the efficient operation of the facility, including the condition of the patients and the hygienic state of the rooms. George Worthington Adams, *Doctors in Blue: The Medical History of the Union Army in the Civil War* (New York: Henry Schuman, 1952), 160.

17. Miller's son William Roland.

18. During the Battle of Mill Springs Kentucky (January 19, 1862), Confederate brigadier general Felix Zollicoffer accidentally rode to meet Union colonel Speed S. Fry, whom he mistook for a Confederate officer. When one of Zollicoffer's aides opened fire on Fry, the Federal officer shot and killed Zollicoffer. Boatner, *Civil War Dictionary*, 487–89.

19. Miller's views on emancipation were apparently well known. On February 25, 1863, General Rosecrans issued Special Field Order 53, directing hospital steward

William Bluffton Miller to rejoin the Seventy-fifth Indiana "without delay." Col. Milton Robinson likewise ordered Miller to return on March 12, noting that he was "exceedingly desirous" of having Miller return from his duty as steward due to the "infamous letters" he had written. Robinson enclosed this extract from one of Miller's letters: "I am going to try and get home don't know how I can go but I shall try the Doctor for leave of absence and then work it through some way. . . . D—n the nigger proclamation. I did not come out to free the niggers and wont do it if I can help it." Miller then wrote "an allusion to the President too filthy" for Robinson to repeat. "If I had him back I could learn him the effect of his oath," the colonel concluded. Unbound Regimental Papers, 75th Indiana Infantry, RG 94, NA.

20. On March 18, 1863, Col. Albert S. Hall led a brigade of about fifteen hundred men from Murfreesboro to "reconnoiter the enemy." When he discovered that about twenty-two hundred Confederate cavalrymen under John Hunt Morgan were about to attack him, Hall took position at Vaught's Hill, near the town of Milton. On March 20, the Confederates launched several determined attacks, but Hall's men held firm and the Rebels withdrew. Hall suffered fifty-six casualties. Further details regarding this action may be found in *Official Records*, ser. 1, vol. 23, pt. 1, pp.152–60.

21. The only man with that surname in Company G was Benjamin F. Mount. See biographical appendix.

22. George Henry Thomas (1816–1870), one of the most famous Union generals, graduated from West Point in 1840 and saw service in the Mexican War. Thomas was made a brigadier general of volunteers in 1861 and a major general after his impressive victory at Mill Springs, Kentucky, on January 19, 1862. Thomas rendered valuable service at Perryville and Stones River and in the spring of 1863 commanded the Fourteenth Army Corps. Warner, *Generals in Blue*, 500–502. Joseph Jones Reynolds (1822–1899), a native of Kentucky, moved to Lafayette, Indiana, at an early age. A U.S. Military Academy graduate, Reynolds was appointed a brigadier general of volunteers when the Civil War began. He resigned in January 1862 but was commissioned again as a brigadier and major general later the same year. At the time Miller saw him, Reynolds was a division commander in the Fourteenth Army Corps. Warner, *Generals in Blue*, 397–98.

23. Probably a reference to the Sibley tent, still in use at this period of the war in established camps. The Sibley utilized an iron tripod supporting a center pole.

24. Apparently the Hoosiers damaged the building during their occupation. S. W. Payne wrote that the college did not "prosper much under military patronage, judging from the appearance of things about this building when we left it upon the following day." *Howard Tribune* (Kokomo, Ind.), Apr. 23, 1863.

25. Miller refers to the First Kentucky Cavalry Regiment (U.S.).

26. Apparently the local plantation owners sent their slaves and horses into the woods and hills to avoid losing them to the Federals, without much success. *Howard Tribune* (Kokomo, Ind.), Apr. 23, 1863.

27. Hoosier S. W. Payne agreed with Miller, writing that it was time for "butternuts" at home to "begin trying to redeem their depreciated characters before it is too late." He predicted a day of reckoning for them at war's end if they did not support the Union cause. *Howard Tribune* (Kokomo, Ind.), Apr. 23, 1863.

28. Bragg's army retreated from the Stones River battlefield on the night of January 2, 1863.

29. Lt. Samuel Carr of Company G and Pvt. George Nevins of Company E.

30. Article Eight of the Articles of War required that any officer or soldier who struck a superior or even threatened any violence against him could suffer death or any punishment inflicted by a court-martial. In addition, Article Twenty-four noted that no officer or soldier could use "reproachful or provoking speeches or gestures" to another without suffering arrest (if an officer) or confinement (if an enlisted man). Miller and quite likely Carr as well would have faced a court-martial for their actions that day. War Department, *Revised United States Army Regulations of 1861* (Washington, D.C.: GPO, 1863), 486, 489.

31. E. W. Freeman of the Seventy-fifth wrote that Sweet's men dressed in Rebel clothes and took the captain prisoner. Sweet told his "captors" all about the Army of the Cumberland and how it was positioned. Freeman believed that Sweet would be conducted to the Ohio River under guard. *Howard Tribune* (Kokomo, Ind.), May 28, 1863.

32. The leather cartridge box was normally suspended from a shoulder sling and contained tin dividers holding forty rounds of paper cartridge ammunition.

33. "Postmaster" of the Seventy-fifth shared Miller's sentiments. In a letter home, he wrote, "We are all getting tired of staying here." *Howard Tribune* (Kokomo, Ind.), June 11, 1863.

34. Possibly Edward George Earle Bulwer-Lytton's *Falkland, A Novel*, published by T. B. Peterson of Philadelphia in 1852.

35. Identified in the biographical appendix as Albert Walton.

36. This action is thoroughly documented in *Official Records*, ser. 1, vol. 23, pt. 1, pp. 359–62.

37. At this time, Vicksburg was under siege by Maj. Gen. Ulysses S. Grant's Army of the Tennessee.

38. "Column by company" meant that each of the regiment's companies, formed in two long ranks as if in battle, followed one behind the other in a column. Col. William Williams of Warsaw, Indiana, held meetings in the divisions and brigades of the Army of the Cumberland where Hoosiers were serving and addressed them "upon the topics of the war and the prospects and feelings of the people at home." According to Colonel Robinson of the Seventy-fifth, some two to four thousand soldiers turned out at these meetings and warmly received Williams. *Indianapolis Daily Journal*, June 19, 1863.

39. Cpl. Joseph Wyrick of Company A, Eleventh Ohio Volunteer Infantry, enlisted on June 20, 1861, at the age of twenty-six. He died of wounds received by the accidental explosion of a shell on July 21, 1863. Ohio Adjutant General, *Official Roster of the Soldiers of the State of Ohio* 2 322.

Chapter 5

1. The report of Maj. Gen. Joseph J. Reynolds on the action at Hoover's Gap is contained in *Official Records*, ser. 1, vol. 23, pt. 1, pp. 454–56.

2. Floyd, *History of the Seventy-Fifth Regiment*, 113.

3. Ibid., 122–23.

4. *Howard Tribune* (Kokomo, Ind.), Sept. 10, 17, 1863.

5. After the Battle of Stones River, Braxton Bragg moved his army to a position north of the Duck River in order to defend Chattanooga. After several months of preparation, Rosecrans left the Murfreesboro area, and his cavalry and infantry (including the Seventy-fifth Indiana) captured Hoover's Gap from the Confederates on June 24. This action helped turn Bragg's right flank and forced him to withdraw first to Tullahoma and eventually to Chattanooga. Boatner, *Civil War Dictionary*, 850–51.

6. Perhaps Maj. F. Claybrooke of the Twentieth Tennessee, who reportedly died of wounds received at Hoover's Gap. *Official Records*, ser. 1, vol. 23, pt. 1, p. 614.

7. E. W. Freeman of the regiment labeled this a "brisk artillery fight" and claimed that two or three Confederate guns were dismounted. *Howard Tribune* (Kokomo, Ind.), July 23, 1863.

8. Another Hoosier agreed with Miller and wrote, "I never saw it rain harder. The creeks raised so fast that we were obliged to wade up to our necks." That evening the men went into camp wet, weary, and cold, with no blankets, and were forced to build fires in order to dry the ground and create a place to sleep. *Howard Tribune* (Kokomo, Ind.), July 23, 1863.

9. Fellow soldier E. W. Freeman thought the area "a wilderness, with scrub-oak flats and few cleared farms." *Howard Tribune* (Kokomo, Ind.), July 23, 1863.

10. Miller meant Maj. Gen. Lovell Harrison Rousseau (1818–1869). As a brigadier general, Rousseau led a brigade at the Battle of Shiloh and a division at Perryville and Stones River, and in the summer of 1863 he was commander of the First Division, Fourteenth Corps, Army of the Cumberland. Boatner, *Civil War Dictionary*, 710; Warner, *Generals in Blue*, 412–13.

11. Some in the regiment apparently had plentiful rations. E. W. Freeman said that he had "fresh pork and beef in abundance. I think if we can get plenty of salt we can live better than at Murfreesboro." *Howard Tribune* (Kokomo, Ind.), July 23, 1863.

12. E. W. Freeman of the Seventy-fifth poetically wrote that Independence Day was consecrated to the marching of one hundred thousand men "whose measured tread is a death knell to traitors, Bragg, and his hosts of vagabonds." He noted that salute guns were fired, bands played, and the woods rang with shouts in honor of the Fourth of July and the victory at Gettysburg. Following a three-day battle (July 1–3, 1863), Robert E. Lee's Army of Northern Virginia began to retreat from Gettysburg, Pennsylvania, back to Virginia, leaving George Gordon Meade's Army of the Potomac in possession of the field. Apparently the erroneous rumor was circulating that Meade captured some twenty-five thousand Confederates. *Howard Tribune* (Kokomo, Ind.), July 23, 1863.

13. The men received orders on July 5 to write letters, the first time since leaving Murfreesboro. Strangely, Miller did not participate, but many other soldiers in the regiment did, as an incredible 579 letters were written that day. *Howard Tribune* (Kokomo, Ind.), July 23, 1863.

14. Apparently other Hoosiers secured many sheep and hogs as well. "I am surprised to see the destruction of property," wrote E. W. Freeman, "and how fast everything that is good to eat disappears. Whole orchards of unripe apples vanish like

snow flakes in the sun—all kinds of stock, chickens, turkeys &c., all killed and ate up in a night leaving scarce enough to feed a mosquito. Even the wheat, corn, hay &c., are used up to feed the numerous mules and horses of the army." *Howard Tribune* (Kokomo, Ind.), July 23, 1863.

15. The Confederate garrison at Vicksburg, Mississippi, commanded by John C. Pemberton, surrendered to Ulysses S. Grant on July 4, 1863.

16. E. W. Freeman of the regiment believed the camp rumors that several regiments of Bragg's army had been captured at Tullahoma, that his men were scattered, that Bragg himself was at Atlanta, and that there were no Confederates in Chattanooga. He also reported that Rebels were coming into camp to surrender and that the prisoners believed they would be killed by the Federals when they were found. *Howard Tribune* (Kokomo, Ind.), July 23, 1863.

17. See "Rhine, John" in the biographical appendix.

18. Although Miller's comment may appear to be entirely based on racism, historian Gerald Linderman notes that Union soldiers also believed that black men would share their fate, not be their substitutes. Linderman, *Embattled Courage*, 247–48. In addition, some soldiers believed that the organization of black regiments would help end the war more quickly. McPherson, *For Cause and Comrades*, 126–30.

19. Historian Mark Grimsley likewise found that 1863 was a "watershed" year for Union forces in which "large-scale destruction" was carried out "in fairly routine fashion, by large bodies of troops." Ironically, Miller's own division commander, Joseph J. Reynolds, had suggested that harsher measures be adopted toward "disloyal" civilians in Middle Tennessee. Union chief of staff Henry Halleck supported the idea in a March 1863 letter to Army of the Cumberland commander William Rosecrans. Grimsley, *Hard Hand of War*, 143–48.

20. Many soldiers like Miller gradually came to admire the bravery and fighting qualities of the enemy. Others never wavered in their hatred of the foe. Linderman, *Embattled Courage*, 66–67.

21. Philip Henry Sheridan (1831–1838) was named a brigadier general of volunteers in the fall of 1862. After fine performances at Perryville and Stones River, Sheridan was promoted to major general and commanded the Third Division, Twentieth Army Corps in the summer of 1863. Sheridan went on to greater glory as the Army of the Potomac's cavalry commander in 1864–65. Warner, *Generals in Blue*, 437–39. Alexander McDowell McCook (1831–1903), one of fourteen members of the "Fighting McCook" family involved in the Civil War, led the First Ohio Volunteer Infantry at Battle of First Bull Run then was made a brigadier general of volunteers. Promoted to major general, McCook fought at Perryville and Stones River and commanded the Twentieth Army Corps during the Tullahoma and Chickamauga campaigns. Warner, *Generals in Blue*, 294–95.

Chapter 6

1. Floyd, *History of the Seventy-Fifth Regiment*, 132.

2. *Noblesville (Ind.) Republican Ledger*, Oct. 9, 1885.

3. John M. Palmer, *Personal Recollections of John M. Palmer: The Story of an Earnest Life* (Cincinnati: Robert Clarke, 1901), 176. David B. Floyd, in his *History of*

the Seventy-Fifth Regiment, maintains the charge took place about 2:00 p.m. As with any battle, few sources agree as to the exact time any particular incident occurred.

4. Floyd, *History of the Seventy-Fifth Regiment*, 138. In his recollections, Palmer believed the regiment pushed the Confederates back "a quarter of a mile or more." Palmer, *Personal Recollections*, 176.

5. Palmer, *Personal Recollections*, 176.

6. Ibid., 178.

7. Floyd, *History of the Seventy-Fifth Regiment*, 143, 145.

8. Ibid., 151.

9. *Noblesville (Ind.) Republican Ledger*, Oct. 16, 1885.

10. *Official Records*, ser. 1, vol. 30, pt. 1, p. 442.

11. *Howard Tribune* (Kokomo, Ind.), Nov. 5, 1863.

12. Floyd, *History of the Seventy-Fifth Regiment*, 178.

13. *Noblesville (Ind.) Republican Ledger*, Oct. 16, 1885.

14. An excellent account of the Chickamauga campaign may be found in Peter Cozzens's *This Terrible Sound: The Battle of Chickamauga* (Urbana: Univ. of Illinois Press, 1992).

15. *Wabash (Ind.) Plain Dealer*, Oct. 23, 1863.

16. *Howard Tribune* (Kokomo, Ind.), Nov. 5, 1863.

17. *Indianapolis Daily Journal*, Nov. 24, 1863.

18. Floyd, *History of the Seventy-Fifth Regiment*, 233.

19. *Noblesville (Ind.) Republican Ledger*, Oct. 30, 1885.

20. Floyd, *History of the Seventy-Fifth Regiment*, 233.

21. *Official Records*, ser. 1, vol. 31, pt. 2, p. 528. Although there is some debate as to whether the Federals continued up the ridge *without* orders, E. W. Freeman of the Seventy-fifth wrote that orders were in fact given to advance to the top. *Howard Tribune* (Kokomo, Ind.), Dec. 10, 1863.

22. *Noblesville (Ind.) Republican Ledger*, Oct. 30, 1885.

23. *Noblesville (Ind.) Republican Ledger*, Oct. 30, 1885. E. W. Freeman of the Seventy-fifth claimed that the regiment captured nine artillery pieces and "a number of prisoners." *Howard Tribune* (Kokomo, Ind.), Dec. 10, 1863.

24. Floyd, *History of the Seventy-Fifth Regiment*, 246.

25. *Official Records*, ser. 1, vol. 31, pt. 2, p. 528. See also Peter Cozzens, *The Shipwreck of Their Hopes: The Battles for Chattanooga* (Urbana: Univ. of Illinois Press, 1994); Richard A. Baumgartner and Larry M. Strayer, *Echoes of Battle: The Struggle for Chattanooga* (Huntington, W.Va.: Blue Acorn Press, 1996); and Wiley Sword, *Mountains Touched with Fire: Chattanooga Besieged, 1863* (New York: St. Martin's Press, 1995).

26. Just as both unmarried and married soldiers worried about their parents back home (see Miller's February 20, 1863, entry, for example), married men had the additional worries of a wife and children. Soldiers on both sides had to reconcile their responsibilities as fathers and husbands with their soldierly duty. Although it pained Miller to learn of disease and death at home (as in his August 9, 1863, entry), he apparently never seriously contemplated shirking his duty and dishonoring himself and his family by deserting. McPherson, *For Cause and Comrades*, 133–40.

27. A U.S. artillery battery was normally divided into three two-gun sections.

28. S. B. and L. R. Wilder were privates in Company B, Forty-first Mississippi Volunteer Infantry. Both enlisted on April 15, 1862, in Verona, Mississippi. S. B. was sick from August to November 1862, then returned to duty with the company, while L. R. was ill from September 1862 to February 1863 before rejoining the unit. Unfortunately, no information survives regarding their capture in August 1863. Compiled Service Records of Confederate Soldiers Who Served in Organizations from the State of Mississippi, Microcopy 269, Reel 391, RG 109, NA; Janet B. Hewett, ed., *The Roster of Confederate Soldiers*, 16 vols. (Wilmington, N.C.: Broadfoot, 1996), 16:243–44. L. R. is also listed as a member of Company A, Ninth Mississippi Sharpshooters.

29. "Flavius" of the 101st Indiana noted that "six prisoners out of forty in the camp were taken, with eleven horses, some guns and camp equipage. Haversacks, with bacon and salt, were left behind " Despite the small number of Confederates captured, "there is a wild romance in adventures of this kind," the writer noted, as such expeditions were "a source of continued pleasantry . . . lightening the burden of a soldier's duty." *Indianapolis Daily Journal*, Sept. 7, 1863. Col. Edward A. King, Second Brigade commander, meticulously reported the capture of six men, eleven horses, seven saddles, twelve muskets, a bugle, and a surgeon's kit. *Official Records*, ser. 1, vol. 30, pt. 1, pp. 468–69.

30. This individual could not be identified. Perhaps he was a member of the Third Confederate Cavalry, a unit partially composed of Alabamians. Col. Edward King's men attacked one company of that regiment on August 28. *Official Records*, ser. 1, vol. 30, pt. 1, pp. 468–69. Two men named "Gage" (John and L. A.) were members of the Third Cavalry Regiment, in Companies A and G respectively. Hewett, *Roster of Confederate Soldiers* 6:180.

31. John Basil Turchin (Ivan Turchinoff), born in Russia in 1822, came to America in the 1850s. When the Civil War began, he became colonel of the Nineteenth Illinois Infantry but was recommended for dismissal the following year due to the unruly behavior of his troops. Commissioned a brigadier general instead, Turchin fought well as commander of the Third Brigade, Fourth Division, Fourteenth Army Corps. Warner, *Generals in Blue*, 511–12.

32. Further details on Cumming's death may be found in *Howard Tribune* (Kokomo, Ind.), Sept. 10, 1863.

33. The rumor was premature. Two divisions of Gen. James Longstreet's corps from the Army of Northern Virginia began to move west to reinforce Bragg's army on September 9, 1863, but the leading elements of the corps did not begin arriving near Ringgold, Georgia, until September 17. Peter Cozzens, *This Terrible Sound*, 59–60, 94–95.

34. James Scott Negley (1826–1901) was named a brigadier general in 1862 and commanded a division at the Battle of Stones River. Promoted to major general, he led the Second Division, Fourteenth Army Corps during the Chickamauga campaign. Warner, *Generals in Blue*, 341–42. Although Negley himself reported no fighting on September 8, his Second Brigade commander, Col. T. R. Stanley, reported that the Eleventh Michigan Infantry, "skirmishing briskly," drove the enemy off and occupied Stevens' Gap in Lookout Mountain. *Official Records*, ser. 1, vol. 30, pt. 1, pp. 326, 378.

35. John Milton Brannan (1819–1892), a brigadier general of volunteers, led the Third Division, Fourteenth Army Corps. Warner, *Generals in Blue*, 42–43.

36. Joseph Wheeler (1836–1906), served as an infantry colonel at the Battle of Shiloh but then became famous as a cavalry commander. Wheeler led the cavalry forces of Bragg's Army of Tennessee through the invasion of Kentucky and the Stones River, Chickamauga, and Chattanooga campaigns, rising to the rank of major general. He continued his cavalry service during the Atlanta campaign and Sherman's March to the Sea. Warner, *Generals in Gray*, 332–33.

37. John McCauley Palmer (1817–1900), a major general of volunteers by the spring of 1863, commanded a division at Stones River and led the Second Division of the Twenty-first Army Corps at Chickamauga. Warner, *Generals in Blue*, 358–59. Thomas Leonidas Crittenden (1819–1893) became a brigadier general in 1861 and was a division commander at Shiloh the following spring. As a major general, he headed the Twenty-first Army Corps in the Army of the Cumberland during the Chickamauga Campaign. Warner, *Generals in Gray*, 100–101.

38. Turchin's Third Brigade, Fourth Division, Fourteenth Army Corps guarded the western opening to Catlett's Gap in Pigeon Mountain from September 15 to 17 and skirmished daily with the enemy before being relieved by Miller and the rest of the Second Brigade. In reality, Bailey's Cross Roads was more than half a mile west of Turchin's position at the gap. *Official Records*, ser. 1, vol. 30, pt. 1, pp. 473, 476.

39. Here Miller refers to the Minié ball, the most commonly used small arms projectile of the Civil War. Designed by French army captain Claude Minié, the elongated bullet was formed with a hollow base. When the weapon was fired, gases from the powder charge filled the base and pushed the sides of the bullet into the weapon's rifling, ensuring greater accuracy. The large, soft, relatively slow moving bullet often caused horrific trauma when it struck a human target. Boatner, *Civil War Dictionary*, 552.

40. A tompion was a wooden or cork plug that could be inserted into a musket muzzle in order to keep dirt or water from entering the barrel.

41. Probably Surgeon Lucius J. Dixon of the First Wisconsin Infantry. A resident of Madison, Dixon entered the army on August 28, 1861. After being taken prisoner at Chickamauga, he was mustered out on October 13, 1864. Chandler P. Chapman, *Roster of Wisconsin Volunteers, War of the Rebellion, 1861–1865*, 2 vols. (Madison: Democrat Printing, 1886), 1:312.

42. Seven out of the ten Federal field hospitals were located at Crawfish Springs to take advantage of the abundant water supply. Unfortunately, the spring was located far on the Federal right flank (an average journey of three miles for the wounded) and far enough in the enemy's country to risk being overrun in case of a Federal retreat. The medical director of the Fourth Division, Fourteenth Army Corps tried to move his hospital from Crawfish Springs toward the Federal left flank but was prevented by the movement of troops and enemy fire. Louis C. Duncan, *The Medical Department of the United States Army in the Civil War* (N.p., n.d.; reprint, Gaithersburg, Md.: Olde Soldier Books, 1987), 288, 309, 311.

43. In his pension application, Miller claimed he "got back to the rear and laid there until about 10 oclock p.m. of said Sept. 19, 1863. Thence taken to field Hospital at Crawfish Springs." William Bluffton Miller file.

44. Miller did not know that his uncle William Miller, a member of Company B, 101st Indiana Infantry, had been wounded and captured during the battle. Lewis Publishing, *Biographical and Historical Record of Adams and Wells Counties*, 937–38.

45. Since the Twenty-sixth Indiana was not at Chickamauga, it was more likely men from the Thirty-sixth or Eighty-sixth Indiana Infantry. Fortunately for Miller, Federal cavalrymen covered the withdrawal of the walking wounded and ambulances. Duncan, *Medical Department*, 300.

46. Confederate major general Joseph Wheeler reported that about dark on September 20 he captured five large hospitals, with medicine, camp equipage, and "a great number of wounded prisoners," along with more than one hundred surgeons. *Official Records*, ser. 1, vol. 30, pt. 2, p. 521. The hospital of the Fourth Division, Fourteenth Army Corps was included in this number. Duncan, *Medical Department*, 300.

47. Miller was quite correct. Churches, public buildings, and private homes were seized for use as hospitals, as some seventy-five hundred wounded Federals had managed to escape the battlefield. Duncan, *Medical Department*, 301.

48. Possibly the fifteen-hundred-bed tent hospital established on September 21 and 22 at Stringer's Spring on the north side of the Tennessee River. Duncan, *Medical Department*, 302.

49. Miller probably had little actual contact with Jews in his civilian life or during his time in the army, although there were small Jewish congregations in a few Indiana cities, including Fort Wayne. Miller undoubtedly held the same anti-Semitic beliefs as most Americans at the time. Emma Lou Thornbrough, *Indiana in the Civil War Era, 1850–1880* (Indianapolis: Indiana Historical Society, 1965), 634.

50. Captain J. A. Pettigrew of the Twentieth Tennessee was reported killed at the Battle of Hoover's Gap. *Official Records*, ser. 1, vol. 23, pt. 1, p. 614.

51. Dr. Threlkeld could not be identified. It is possible he was an acting assistant surgeon, also known as a contract surgeon, and would therefore be absent from published state adjutant general's reports and U.S. Army registers of commissioned surgeons. More than fifty-five hundred contract surgeons served during the war, mainly in hospitals. Dr. Link is John E. Link from Paris, Illinois, second assistant surgeon with the Twenty-first Illinois Infantry. Reece, *Report of the Adjutant General of the State of Illinois* 2:186.

52. Actually, four divisions of the Eleventh and Twelfth Army Corps were detached from the Army of the Potomac to reinforce Chattanooga. The Forty-first Pennsylvania was not part of either corps.

53. Miller was not alone in his belief that Southern women were particularly ferocious. See Mitchell, *Vacant Chair*, 97.

54. Probably a preparation of bromine, which was used to treat hospital gangrene in a number of Union hospitals, including those in Murfreesboro. Extensive information on its use may be found in U.S. Surgeon General's Office, *The Medical and Surgical History of the War of the Rebellion*, 6 vols. (Washington, D.C.: GPO, 1870–1888), vol. 2, pt. 3 (Surgical History), 832–37.

55. According to U.S. Regulations, a medical purveyor was charged with "the selection and purchase of all medical supplies," including books, instruments,

hospital stores, furniture, and other articles needed by the sick and wounded. Exactly why this officer was needed to approve Miller's furlough is unclear. War Department, *Revised United States Army Regulations of 1861*, 531–32.

56. Even veterans such as Miller admitted that they were afraid on the battlefield. McPherson, *For Cause and Comrades*, 37.

57. Possibly John Stewart, born in New Hampshire and appointed to the Regular Army from Illinois. Stewart was commissioned a captain and assistant quartermaster of volunteers in February 1863 and later received a brevet major's promotion for his services during the Atlanta campaign and as depot quartermaster in Atlanta. Francis B. Heitman, *Historical Register and Dictionary of the United States Army*, 2 vols. (Washington, D.C.: GPO, 1903), 1:925.

58. Miller refers to Clement Laird Vallandigham, a Democratic veteran of the Ohio legislature and U.S. Congress who ran for governor of Ohio in 1863. An outspoken critic of President Lincoln and the Republican Party and vehemently opposed to the prosecution of the war, he was arrested and banished to the Confederacy by Lincoln. Boatner, *Civil War Dictionary*, 864–65.

59. By the end of 1863, Miller had undergone a remarkable transformation in his views on race. In his December 30, 1862, entry he referred to blacks as "niggers," and on March 13, 1863, he was hauled before his commanding officer for his strong criticism of the Emancipation Proclamation. By July 1863, he seemed willing to accept both the proclamation and the notion of blacks serving as soldiers. That fall he expressed relatively enlightened views of black Americans, and during 1864 and 1865, Miller continued to support the idea of black soldiers. For other examples, see entries of July 16 and September 24, 1863, February 24, 1864, and March 24, 1865. McPherson, *For Cause and Comrades*, 118–30.

60. Miller maintained his disdain for "draft dodgers" and anti-war Democrats throughout his service. For similar opinions by other soldiers, see Mitchell, *Civil War Soldiers*, 83–87; Mitchell, *Vacant Chair*, 32–33; Linderman, *Embattled Courage*, 222–23, and McPherson, *For Cause and Comrades*, 143–46.

61. In April 1863, the Union army established the Invalid Corps, later called the Veteran Reserve Corps, for those officers and men who were unable to serve in combat but could still be useful as guards, nurses, and cooks. Boatner, *Civil War Dictionary*, 870.

62. A camp for Confederate prisoners located on the western edge of Columbus, Ohio. Boatner, *Civil War Dictionary*, 117.

63. Joseph Hooker (1814–1879) commanded the Army of the Potomac during its defeat at Chancellorsville, Virginia, in May 1863. Sent west with four divisions of the Eleventh and Twelfth Army Corps, Hooker enjoyed much more success, as Miller notes, in capturing Lookout Mountain in November 1863, helping break the Confederate siege of Chattanooga, Tennessee. Warner, *Generals in Blue*, 233–35.

64. Probably a version of *Sweeney Todd, the Demon Barber*, originally written in short-story form by Thomas Peckett Prest and published in the *People's Periodical and Family Library* in 1846.

65. Miller could be referring to one of three documents. Possibly this was the Union government's December 8 amnesty proclamation, which called for a pardon for all those Confederates who took an oath to the United States (with numerous

exceptions). He might also have read Lincoln's annual message to Congress, dated December 8, or his call dated the day before for all loyal people to worship and thank God for recent Union successes in eastern Tennessee. Roy P. Basler, ed., *The Collected Works of Abraham Lincoln*, 9 vols. (New Brunswick: Rutgers Univ. Press, 1953), 7:35–56.

66. Chalmers is actually Chamness, and he is identified as such in the biographical appendix.

67. Mist and fog obscured the battle from Gen. Ulysses S. Grant's headquarters until finally it lifted briefly to reveal Union forces attacking the mountain. Brig. Gen. Montgomery Meigs coined the popular phrase when he spotted the Federal advance. Faust, *Historical Times Illustrated Encyclopedia*, 445–47.

68. Probably a reference to the message of President Jefferson Davis to the Confederate Congress, delivered on December 7, in which he stated that several Union forces had been defeated and insisted that those who fought for home, liberty, and independence had superior endurance and were able to triumph over those who would enslave them. Gen. Clement A. Evans, ed., *Confederate Military History, Extended Edition*, 17 vols. (Atlanta: Confederate Publishing, 1899; reprint, Wilmington, N.C.: Broadfoot, 1987–89), 1:500–501.

69. Companies were required by regulation to maintain clothing books in which a careful record was kept of clothing items that had been issued to each soldier. Kautz, *Company Clerk*, 17–24.

70. Longstreet was not killed in action but in fact survived the war. Miller was correct, however, in his belief that Longstreet's men were beaten. The Confederates suffered heavy casualties in an unsuccessful assault on Union-held Knoxville, Tennessee, on November 29, 1863. Boatner, *Civil War Dictionary*, 297–98.

71. Miller was mistaken about Ginger's rank. According to his compiled military service record, Ginger remained a private throughout his service.

72. Major Connolly echoed Miller's comments. In a letter to his wife on December 10, 1863, he wrote, "I am having the easiest time now I have ever had in the service." Apart from making sure that the pickets were properly posted and instructed each morning, Connolly had to inspect government property in the division. "I have a clerk who prepares all my official papers," he wrote, with a wall tent for his own use and one for the clerk's office. "All this is very nice," he continued, "but I don't feel that I am earning what the government pays me." Early in January 1864, Connolly received a furlough to go home and did not return to Chattanooga until early the following month. Paul M. Angle, ed., *Three Years in the Army of the Cumberland: The Letters and Diary of Major James A. Connolly* (Bloomington: Indiana Univ. Press, 1959), 161–65. Connolly then served as assistant inspector general for Brig. Gen. Absalom Baird's Third Division, Fourteenth Corps during the Atlanta campaign. *Official Records*, ser. 1, vol. 33, pt. 1, p. 755.

73. Absalom Baird (1824–1905) graduated from West Point in 1849. A veteran of the Battle of First Bull Run and the Peninsula campaign, Baird was appointed a brigadier general of volunteers in early 1862. He led the First Division, Fourteenth Corps during the Chickamauga campaign, then continued as a division commander in that corps during the Atlanta campaign. Warner, *Generals in Blue*, 15–16. One of Sherman's aides described Baird as "one of the most elegant officers of the army,"

"the ideal of a gentleman and a soldier." George W. Nichols, *The Story of the Great March* (New York: Harper & Bros., 1865), 46. Also see John A. Baird Jr., *Profile of a Hero: The Story of Absalom Baird, His Family, and the American Military Tradition* (Philadelphia: Dorrance, 1977).

CHAPTER 7

1. Floyd, *History of the Seventy-Fifth Regiment*, 290.
2. Ibid., 292–93; *Noblesville (Ind.) Republican Ledger*, Nov. 6, 1885.
3. *Noblesville (Ind.) Republican Ledger*, Nov. 13, 1885.
4. Floyd, *History of the Seventy-Fifth Regiment*, 296–97.
5. *Noblesville (Ind.) Republican Ledger*, Nov. 6, 1885.
6. *Noblesville (Ind.) Republican Ledger*, Nov. 13, 1885. Despite the lethal nature of artillery fire, some soldiers like Gen. Absalom Baird believed that at times the artillery duels "assumed a degree of magnificence." *Official Records*, ser. 1, vol. 38, pt. 1, p. 739.
7. *Noblesville (Ind.) Republican Ledger*, Nov. 13, 1885.
8. Floyd, *History of the Seventy-Fifth Regiment*, 296–97.
9. Originally meaning a native district ruler or a wealthy European in India.
10. Major Connolly undoubtedly would have disagreed with Miller. In a letter to his wife on February 14, 1864, Connolly explained he was "busy as a bee every day," inspecting and condemning government property, so much so that his office had "quite a formidable appearance of business and red tape." Angle, *Three Years in the Army of the Cumberland*, 166–69.
11. One member of the Seventy-fifth noted that the train whistle was cheered heartily by the soldiers. *Howard Tribune* (Kokomo, Ind.), Jan. 28, 1864.
12. Possibly *The White Lady: A Romance*, by Karoline von Woltmann, translated by James D. Haas and published in London in 1845. Other possibilities include *The White Lady and Undine*, another translation of von Woltmann, published in London in 1844, and *The White Lady*, a translation of the François Boieldieu opera published in Baltimore in 1831.
13. Jefferson Columbus Davis (1828–1879), a brigadier general, led a division at Pea Ridge, Stones River, and Chickamauga. During the Atlanta campaign, his division was part of the Fourteenth Army Corps, and in the closing days of the campaign he assumed command of the entire corps. Davis continued to lead the Fourteenth Corps during Sherman's March to the Sea and the Carolinas campaign. Warner, *Generals in Blue*, 115–16. For further information on this colorful but controversial officer, see Nathaniel Cheairs Hughes Jr. and Gordon D. Whitney, *Jefferson Davis in Blue: The Life of Sherman's Relentless Warrior* (Baton Rouge: Louisiana State Univ. Press, 2002).
14. Miller's reference to the siege of Knoxville at this point in time is a mystery. James Longstreet's Confederate force ended their siege of the Union garrison there in early December 1863 and went into winter quarters nearly two months before this entry was written. Boatner, *Civil War Dictionary*, 466–68.
15. Possibly Robert Coppage, a member of Company B, Thirty-fifth Ohio Volunteer Infantry, a part of Gen. Absalom Baird's Third Division, Fourteenth Army

Corps, but more likely William R. Coppage of the same company, who was mustered out at Chattanooga on September 8, 1864. Ohio Adjutant General, *Official Roster of the Soldiers of the State of Ohio* 3:606.

16. Probably Lewis Johnson, a native of Germany, who enlisted as a private in the Tenth Indiana in 1861. He was promoted to first lieutenant later that year and to captain in 1862. He served as provost marshal of Absalom Baird's Third Division, Fourteenth Army Corps during the Chattanooga campaign and may have been serving in that capacity at this time. *Official Records*, ser. 1, vol. 31, pt. 2, p. 511.

17. Probably a relative of soldier Levi Keagle but otherwise unidentified.

18. James Blair Steedman (1817–1883) commanded a brigade at Perryville and Stones River. During the Chickamauga campaign he led the First Division, Reserve Corps and helped rescue the Union army there on the second day of the battle, but he performed rear echelon duty during Gen. William T. Sherman's drive for Atlanta. Warner, *Generals in Blue*, 473–74.

19. From February 24–26, a force that included Baird's division of the Fourteenth Corps "demonstrated" against the strong Confederate positions on Rocky Face Ridge. The Federals withdrew after suffering 345 casualties. *Official Records*, ser. 1, vol. 32, pt. 1, pp. 9–10, 419–21.

20. Probably Samuel J. Dick of Pennsylvania, commissioned a first lieutenant in the Eighteenth U.S. Infantry in June 1862. Dick served as mustering officer in the Third Division, Fourteenth Army Corps before his death in December 1864. Heitman, *Historical Register* 1:372; *Official Records*, ser. 1, vol. 31, pt. 2, p. 511.

21. Ferdinand Van Derveer initially commanded the Thirty-fifth Ohio Volunteer Infantry. In late 1862, he assumed brigade command and, with the rank of colonel, ably led his men through the Chickamauga, Chattanooga, and Atlanta campaigns. During the latter campaign, he directed the Second Brigade, Third Division, Fourteenth Army Corps. Whitelaw Reid, *Ohio in the War*, 2 vols. (Cincinnati: Moore, Wilstach & Baldwin, 1868), 1:890–93; Warner, *Generals in Blue*, 522.

22. Maj. James Anderson Lowrie was born in Pittsburgh, Pennsylvania, on January 23, 1833. He graduated from Miami University (Oxford, Ohio) in 1851 and was admitted to the bar in Pittsburgh. When the Civil War began, he served first as a private in the Thirteenth Pennsylvania (three months), then was appointed a captain and assistant adjutant general of volunteers in October 1861. Promoted to major in May 1863, Lowrie served as assistant adjutant general of Gen. Absalom Baird's Third Division, Fourteenth Army Corps during the Atlanta campaign. He resigned in October 1864 and died in 1886. *Official Records*, ser. 1, vol. 38, pt. 1, p. 755; Heitman, *Historical Register* 1:645; John Fitch, *Annals of the Army of the Cumberland* (Philadelphia: J. B. Lippincott, 1864), 111.

23. Hoosier S. W. Payne wrote that the oldest inhabitants of the area were astounded by the amount of snow that fell. *Howard Tribune* (Kokomo, Ind.), Apr. 7, 1864.

24. Possibly William Joseph Walter's *Mary, Queen of Scots; a Journal of Her Twenty Years' Captivity, Trial and Execution*, published by Carey & Hart of Philadelphia in 1840.

25. According to Company K's Lt. James Starbuck, Miller continued to complain about his wound after he rejoined the company and complained more during hard

marches. He quoted Miller as saying, "I expect it will always bother me." By 1900, Miller was lame in his right leg, dragged his foot while walking, and suffered pain from the wound. William Bluffton Miller file.

26. The Army of the Potomac was opposing Robert E. Lee's Army of Northern Virginia. Boatner, *Civil War Dictionary*, 664.

27. Probably Robert W. Hampton, a private in Company D, Tenth Indiana Volunteer Infantry. The Benton County, Indiana, resident was mustered into service on December 16, 1863, and died on April 9, 1864. Terrell, *Report of the Adjutant General* 4:161.

28. Hugh Judson Kilpatrick (1836–1881), a brigadier general of volunteers, had commanded a cavalry division in the Army of the Potomac before joining Sherman's army. He led a cavalry division in the Army of the Cumberland until seriously wounded at Resaca in May 1864. Returning to duty in July, Kilpatrick continued at the head of a cavalry division through the March to the Sea and the Carolinas campaign. Warner, *Generals in Blue*, 266–67. For more information on this controversial officer, see Samuel J. Martin, *Kill-Cavalry: The Life of Union General Hugh Judson Kilpatrick* (Mechanicsburg, Pa.: Stackpole Books, 2000).

29. On the morning of May 2, Brig. Gen. Absalom Baird sent Brig. Gen. Judson Kilpatrick's cavalry division and a brigade from his own division toward Tunnel Hill, just a few miles northwest of Dalton and Johnston's defensive position on Rocky Face Ridge. Kilpatrick engaged the enemy on Tunnel Hill Ridge then asked for Baird's help. Baird arrived on the scene with four of his regiments and withdrew the entire force, losing only ten men wounded. Baird's report on the action may be found in *Official Records*, ser. 1, vol. 38, pt. 1, p. 732.

30. Richard W. Johnson (1827–1897), commissioned a brigadier general in October 1861, missed the Battle of Shiloh due to illness then was captured by Confederate cavalryman John Hunt Morgan. After his exchange, he commanded a division of the Army of the Cumberland at Stones River, Chickamauga, and Chattanooga. During the initial phase of the Atlanta campaign he led the First Division, Fourteenth Army Corps. Badly wounded in late May, Johnson returned to duty commanding cavalry forces. Warner, *Generals in Blue*, 253–54.

31. Sherman ordered wagons to carry only food, ammunition and clothing. "Tents were forbidden to all save the sick and wounded," he later wrote, "and one tent only was allowed to each headquarters for use as an office." Although there were exceptions, Sherman's order certainly reduced the amount of excess baggage normally carried on campaign. William T. Sherman, *Memoirs of General William T. Sherman*, 2 vols. (New York: D. Appleton, 1875), 2:22.

32. The Fourteenth Army Corps, including most of Baird's division, advanced on Tunnel Hill on the morning of May 7. The Confederates withdrew to Rocky Face Ridge, part of their defensive line located west of Dalton. *Official Records*, ser. 1, vol. 38, pt. 1, p. 734.

33. Specifically, the "Cracker Line" was the name given to the water supply route opened from Bridgeport, Alabama, up the Tennessee River to near Chattanooga in late October and early November 1863. This supply system replaced an unreliable wagon route, provided rations to the starving Union soldiers in Chattanooga, and

helped weaken Confederate general Bragg's siege of the city. Faust, *Historical Times Illustrated Encyclopedia*, 189. Here Miller uses the name in more general terms, meaning simply a supply line.

34. On May 5 and 6, 1864, Ulysses S. Grant and the Army of the Potomac fought Robert E. Lee's Army of Northern Virginia in the Battle of the Wilderness near Fredericksburg, Virginia. The armies clashed again at Spotsylvania Courthouse from May 10 to 19. Miller was most likely referring to the latter battle.

35. Lt. George Kaiser Sanderson, a native of Pennsylvania, enlisted in the Fifteenth U.S. Infantry as a private in 1861 but was promoted to second lieutenant the same year and to first lieutenant in 1862. During the Atlanta campaign, he was assistant commissary of musters and acting aide-de-camp to Gen. Absalom Baird and was promoted to brevet captain for his services. *Official Records*, ser. 1, vol. 38, pt. 1, p. 755; Heitman, *Historical Register* 1:858.

36. Lide Bulger has not been positively identified, but she is probably either Lucena or Elisa Bulger, who were the daughters of Miller's Aunt "Affie" (Apphia).

37. Actually Davis was a member of the Thirty-first Indiana. See biographical appendix.

38. Either William P. Saunders of Ohio, a captain and commissary of subsistence of volunteers, or Thomas Jefferson Saunders of Iowa, an additional paymaster of volunteers. Heitman, *Historical Register* 1:861.

CHAPTER 8

1. Floyd, *History of the Seventy-Fifth Regiment*, 299.

2. Floyd, *History of the Seventy-Fifth Regiment*, 309–11; *Official Records*, ser. 1, vol. 38, pt. 1, p. 746.

3. *Noblesville (Ind.) Republican Ledger*, Nov. 13, 1885.

4. *Noblesville (Ind.) Republican Ledger*, Nov. 13, 1885. General Baird reported that most of the deserters were from Alabama regiments and "the most strenuous means were resorted to by the rebel officers" to prevent desertion. *Official Records*, ser. 1, vol. 38, pt. 1, p. 747. It should be noted that while truces prevailed on certain portions of the line, at other locations vicious skirmishing was maintained for days.

5. *Official Records*, ser. 1, vol. 38, pt. 1, pp. 792–94.

6. *Noblesville (Ind.) Republican Ledger*, Nov. 13, 1885.

7. For a thorough account of the campaign for Atlanta, see Albert Castel's *Decision in the West: The Atlanta Campaign of 1864* (Lawrence: Univ. Press of Kansas, 1992).

8. Floyd, *History of the Seventy-Fifth Regiment*, 330–31.

9. *Official Records*, ser. 1, vol. 38, pt. 1, pp. 733, 754, 795. Maj. Cyrus J. McCole of the Seventy-fifth Indiana gives slightly different figures. He reported that 424 officers and men were present on May 7, 1864, and 326 on September 9, with 27 detailed to guard medical supplies, 27 sick, 23 wounded, 9 killed, and 12 detached as hospital attendants.

10. Miller was correct about the large number of Rebel deserters that month, particularly from Georgia units. A total of 356 Georgia troops deserted during July 1864,

the highest number during any month of the Atlanta campaign (May–September). Mark A. Weitz, *A Higher Duty: Desertion among Georgia Troops during the Civil War* (Lincoln: Univ. of Nebraska Press, 2000), 67; Castel, *Decision in the West*, 350–51.

11. See "Sisson, Orin" in the biographical appendix.

12. Captain John Moulton, age twenty-five, was mustered into service as a sergeant of Company D, Second Minnesota Infantry in July 1861. He was promoted to second lieutenant in January 1862, first lieutenant in May, and captain that November. During the Atlanta campaign, he served as provost marshal on the staff of Gen. Absalom Baird. He was finally promoted to major in April 1865. State of Minnesota, *Minnesota in the Civil and Indian Wars*, 130; *Official Records*, ser. 1, vol. 38, pt. 1, p. 755.

13. Captain Hubert Dilger, a veteran of the army of the Grand Duchy of Baden, commanded Battery I, First Ohio Light Artillery. After service at Chancellorsville (where he won the Medal of Honor) and Gettysburg, Dilger took his battery west for the Chattanooga and Atlanta campaigns. Miller is in error referring to them as part of the Fourth Ohio Artillery. Fairfax Downey, *The Guns at Gettysburg* (New York: David McKay, 1958), 47–48, 253; Richard A. Baumgartner and Larry M. Strayer, *Kennesaw Mountain, June 1864: Bitter Standoff at the Gibraltar of Georgia* (Huntington, W.Va.: Blue Acorn Press, 1998), 77–79.

14. James Birdseye McPherson (1828–1864) led the Army of the Tennessee in the Atlanta campaign. He was indeed killed on July 22, 1864, at the Battle of Atlanta. As an army commander (brigadier general in the Regular Army and major general of volunteers), McPherson was the highest ranking Union officer killed in action during the war. Warner, *Generals in Blue*, 306–8.

15. General Baird noted that sixty-four-pound shells "from the 'old 32-pounder rifle,' came regularly into our camps, a weight of metal entirely out of proportion to our light field pieces." *Official Records*, ser. 1, vol. 38, pt. 1, p. 743. Levi P. Fodrea of the 101st Indiana wrote, "At first they seemed to strike the boys with a terror . . . and their coming roared like the mighty winds of a cyclone, and voices as hideous as the sounds of the lower regions." When they burst, they shook the earth and threw fragments from three to five hundred yards. Within twenty-four hours, Fodrea believed, the men learned to dodge them by lying flat on the ground; the fragments would then pass over them. "The large balls were the ones to scare," he added, "but the small ones those to fear." *Noblesville (Ind.) Republican Ledger*, Nov. 13, 1885.

16. Maj. Gen. John Alexander Logan (1826–1886) commanded the Fifteenth Army Corps in Sherman's campaign for Atlanta. After General McPherson's death on July 22, 1864, Logan temporarily commanded the Army of the Tennessee. Warner, *Generals in Blue*, 281–83.

17. Miller is mistaken in that Capt. Otho H. Morgan commanded the Seventh Indiana Battery at this time. Morgan did not report this incident, but since the battery was attached to Absalom Baird's Third Division, Fourteenth Army Corps, Miller may be correct regarding the losses the unit suffered. For Morgan's report of the Atlanta campaign, see *Official Records*, ser. 1, vol. 38, pt. 1, pp. 830–33.

18. A reference to the Confederate vow to "die in the last ditch" rather than surrender. See also Miller's August 11, 1864, entry. Gen. William T. Sherman referred

to the phrase as the Confederates' "common and popular clamor." Sherman, *Memoirs of General William T. Sherman* 2:112. An example of the use of this phrase in official correspondence may be found in *Official Records*, ser. 2, vol. 6, pp. 225–26.

19. Brig. Gen. Richard W. Johnson was named commander of the Fourteenth Army Corps on August 6, but as an ordinary infantryman Miller could not have known that fact. The First Division, Fourteenth Corps attacked the Confederate skirmish line on August 7, and Baird's Third Division supported the attack. *Official Records*, ser. 1, vol. 38, pt. 1, p. 747.

20. The fear of becoming a casualty was, in the words of historian Earl Hess, "one of a soldier's greatest fears," and many realized that eventually their luck might run out. Nevertheless, some soldiers comforted themselves with the belief that if they survived one terrible battle, perhaps they could actually make it through the war alive. Interestingly, in this passage, Miller indicates that despite his previous experience under fire, he did not think of himself as a brave soldier and believed there was a chance he might not stand firm in every battle. Other soldiers agreed that there were limits to courage and even a veteran might temporarily remove himself from combat. Miller also obviously hoped that perhaps his crippling Chickamauga wound had "earned" him the right to survive other battles unhurt. Hess, *Union Soldier in Battle*, 29, 75–86, 150.

21. The view that God controlled all things, including the time and place of death of individual soldiers, was a common one among the men of Civil War armies. Because death could come at any instant, some soldiers resigned themselves to their fate, while others took strength from the belief that God could keep them from harm as well. Apparently Miller did not spend considerable time pondering when and where he would meet his fate. Mitchell, *Vacant Chair*, 140; Hess, *Union Soldier in Battle*, 104, 140; McPherson, *For Cause and Comrades*, 64–66. Historian Gerald Linderman argues that as the war progressed, soldiers drifted away from the belief that God protected them and supported their cause. Miller's beliefs apparently remained intact, however, until the war ended. Linderman, *Embattled Courage*, 256–57.

22. On July 27, 1864, Maj. Gen. George Stoneman took about fifty-five hundred cavalrymen on a mission to ride from Decatur, east of Atlanta, south to Lovejoy's Station to cut the Macon and Western Railroad. After this was accomplished, he was to ride south and liberate Union prisoners from the Macon and Andersonville, Georgia, prison camps. Stoneman chose to perform the rescue mission first, and on July 31 he was surrounded and captured near Macon with seven hundred of his men. Faust, *Historical Times Illustrated Encyclopedia*, 721.

23. Col. Moses B. Walker was commissioned colonel of the Thirty-first Ohio Volunteer Infantry in August 1861. In the spring of 1862, he was elevated to brigade command, and despite being under arrest during the Chickamauga campaign, he performed well during the Army of the Cumberland's desperate stand on Horseshoe Ridge on the second day of the battle. He led the First Brigade, Third Division, Fourteenth Army Corps during the campaign for Atlanta. Reid, *Ohio in the War* 1:955.

24. Franklin Austin Seely, a native of Pennsylvania, was commissioned captain and assistant quartermaster of volunteers in 1862. Heitman, *Historical Register* 1:873. He also participated in General Sherman's campaign through the Carolinas. *Official Records*, ser. 1, vol. 53:45, 48.

25. In actuality, most of the initial Union attacking force halted after advancing only a short distance. The Regular Brigade (Second Brigade, First Division, Fourteenth Corps) then moved on alone and captured part of the Confederate forward line. When the enemy counterattacked, the Regulars withdrew and were soon pinned down, unable to advance or retreat. In his official report, Maj. John R. Edie, commander of the Regulars, did not state that his men refused to advance on the enemy earthworks. Instead, he explained that heavy losses and a lack of ammunition necessitated the withdrawal of his brigade. Corps commander Gen. Jefferson Davis then managed to get the rest of the line moving forward again and sent a brigade of Baird's division marching through the ranks of the halted Regulars to renew the assault. It may have appeared to Miller that the Regulars were *refusing* to advance. Edie lost a total of 167 killed, wounded, and missing out of the 917 men he led into the action. *Official Records*, ser. 1, vol. 38, pt. 1, pp. 558–59; Mark W. Johnson, *That Body of Brave Men: The U.S. Regular Infantry and The Civil War in the West* (Cambridge, Mass.: Da Capo Press, 2003), 534–45, 647–48. According to one source, General Baird gave a simple order: "Boys, pile your knapsacks, fix bayonets, and charge those works." Baird, *Profile of a Hero*, 1.

26. Baird clearly demonstrated that officers could inspire their soldiers and strengthen the bonds of loyalty with enlisted men when they exhibited personal bravery in combat. Hess, *Union Soldier in Battle*, 120–21. In 1896, General Baird was awarded the Medal of Honor for his heroism at Jonesboro. Capt. John W. Acheson (assistant adjutant general) and two orderlies accompanied Baird. Acheson was wounded in the charge. *Official Records*, ser. 1, vol. 38, pt. 1, pp. 751, 755. Miller's old superior Major Connolly accompanied the charge as well. His vivid account of the assault may be found in Angle, *Three Years in the Army of the Cumberland*, 257–58.

27. At the Battle of Jonesboro, Maj. Gen. Patrick Cleburne's division was commanded by Brig. Gen. Mark P. Lowrey, as Cleburne had temporarily assumed command of Gen. William Hardee's corps. Lowrey reported his division's losses in the two-day fight as 1,086, including 659 missing. *Official Records*, ser. 1, vol. 38, pt. 3, pp. 726–30. Gen. Absalom Baird initially reported that his Third Brigade captured 426 prisoners, only a fraction of whom were from Lowrey's division, but later revised the figure to 600. *Official Records*, ser. 1, vol. 38, pt. 1, pp. 753, 757.

28. Confederate brigadier general Daniel C. Govan of Arkansas was captured during the Battle of Jonesboro. *Official Records*, ser. 1, vol. 38, pt. 3, pp. 741–43.

29. The Seventeenth New York lost twenty-three men killed and seventy-four men wounded. The fact that the New Yorkers wore colorful Zouave uniforms may have led Miller to believe that their loss was heavier. *Official Records*, ser. 1, vol. 38, pt. 1, p. 678.

30. Morgan was killed in a skirmish with Federal troops at Greenville, Tennessee, on September 4, 1864. Basil W. Duke, *History of Morgan's Cavalry* (Cincinnati: Miami Printing and Publishing, 1867), 537–39.

31. E. W. Freeman of the Seventy-fifth agreed that the city was well fortified and could never have been taken by direct assault. *Howard Tribune* (Kokomo, Ind.), Oct. 6, 1864.

32. On September 19, 1864, Maj. Gen. Philip H. Sheridan defeated Lt. Gen. Jubal Early in the Third Battle of Winchester or Opequon Creek, Virginia. Faust, *Historical Times Illustrated Encyclopedia*, 835.

Chapter 9

1. The rumor was true. In late September 1864, General Hood moved his army north of Atlanta in order to cut the Western and Atlantic Railroad, the line that supplied Sherman's troops in the city. Hood hoped to draw the Union army north of Atlanta to fight a battle on ground of his own choosing. Although Sherman sent part of his forces in pursuit of Hood, a major battle failed to develop. After an unsuccessful assault on the Federal garrison at Allatoona on October 5, Hood withdrew into Alabama, while Sherman ended the pursuit and prepared his men for the March to the Sea. Faust, *Historical Times Illustrated Encyclopedia*, 7, 285.

2. Miller elaborates on his views regarding the treatment of Southern civilians in his November 12, 1864, entry. For similar sentiments by Miller's commander, William T. Sherman, and the limits on "hard war," see Grimsley, *Hard Hand of War*, 190–204.

3. In a surprise attack on Gen. Philip Sheridan's army at Cedar Creek, Virginia, on October 19, 1864, Confederate general Jubal Early initially forced the Union army to retreat. Sheridan personally rallied his troops, however, and a Union counterattack finally defeated the Confederates. Miller's estimates of Confederate prisoners is far too high (only 1,050 of Early's men were missing), but his report of lost Confederate artillery pieces is far too low (twenty-five guns). Faust, *Historical Times Illustrated Encyclopedia*, 121; Boatner, *Civil War Dictionary*, 132–34.

4. This is probably J. H. or J. M. Hendricks, "captain of the guerrillas by his own acknowledgement," also named as the commander of Company I, First Georgia Cavalry, who was captured by the Seventy-fourth Indiana Infantry a few days later. He was ordered to be confined in chains, if possible, or tied in such a manner as to prevent his escape. It is likely that this is the man executed by Sherman's troops. Also see Miller's entries for November 10 and 11, 1864. *Official Records*, ser. 1, vol. 39, pt. 1, 647–49; ser. 1, vol. 39, pt. 3, pp. 731, 744.

5. Gen. George B. McClellan and George Pendleton were the Democratic opponents of Lincoln and Andrew Johnson in the 1864 presidential election.

6. Men like Miller who had volunteered for service in 1861 and 1862 generally regarded Union army draftees with contempt. McPherson, *For Cause and Comrades*, 8–9, 116.

Chapter 10

1. Floyd, *History of the Seventy-Fifth Regiment*, 344–46.

2. Floyd, *History of the Seventy-Fifth Regiment*, 349.

3. *Official Records*, ser. 1, vol. 44:203–5.

4. John S. Shull of Warren, Indiana, a member of Company E. Terrell's *Report* incorrectly lists him as "died at Bowling Green, Ky., Nov. 12, '62," confusing him with William Y. Shull of the same company. Terrell, *Report of the Adjutant General* 6:223–24.

5. Maj. Gen. Howell Cobb was governor of Georgia 1851–53 and a congressman 1843–51 and again 1855–57. After fighting with Lee's army, Cobb returned to Georgia. During Sherman's March to the Sea, he commanded the District of Georgia and Florida and the Georgia reserve corps and was in Macon when the Federals

402 NOTES TO PAGES 280–87

arrived. His Hurricane Plantation was located just north of Milledgeville. Because of Cobb's Confederate service, Sherman ordered that the plantation be destroyed. Faust, *Historical Times Illustrated Encyclopedia*, 146–47; Boatner, *Civil War Dictionary*, 160; Anne J. Bailey, *War and Ruin: William T. Sherman and the Savannah Campaign* (Wilmington, Del.: Scholarly Resources, 2003), 62, 65–66.

6. Brig. Gen. Jefferson C. Davis fatally wounded Union Maj. Gen. William Nelson after an argument in a hotel in Louisville, Kentucky, on September 29, 1862. Davis was never tried for the offense. Faust, *Historical Times Illustrated Encyclopedia*, 207–8.

7. Brig. Gen. Judson Kilpatrick's Third Cavalry Division fought a serious skirmish with Maj. Gen. Joseph Wheeler's Confederates near Waynesboro on November 28, 1864. Kilpatrick's men were forced to withdraw. This is probably the action referred to by Miller. *Official Records*, ser. 1, vol. 44:55, 363–64, 408–9.

8. Miller refers to the town of Kingston, Georgia, which the Seventy-fifth passed through on October 11, 1864, on their way back to Atlanta following the pursuit of Hood's army into Alabama.

9. Miller was mistaken regarding the role of Maj. Gen. Wade Hampton. At this time Hampton was commanding the cavalry corps of Gen. Robert E. Lee's Army of Northern Virginia operating around Petersburg, Virginia. *Official Records*, ser. 1, vol. 42, pt. 3, p. 1191. Maj. Gen. Joseph Wheeler commanded the cavalry corps of the Department of South Carolina, Georgia and Florida during Sherman's march and ineffectively opposed the Federal advance. *Official Records*, ser. 1, vol. 44:406–12.

10. A reference to Camp Lawton, a forty-acre Confederate prison built in September 1864 at Millen, Georgia. After Atlanta fell to Federal forces, Union prisoners from Camp Sumter (Andersonville) were transferred to Millen. As Sherman approached Millen, ten thousand Union captives were evacuated from Camp Lawton to keep them from being liberated by their advancing comrades. Bailey, *War and Ruin*, 81.

11. A few days after he retreated from Wheeler near Waynesboro, Kilpatrick was charged by Sherman to make a strong reconnaissance back toward that town and to engage Wheeler's cavalry wherever they were encountered. On December 4, Kilpatrick gained his revenge when his troopers met a Rebel skirmish line near Waynesboro and drove them back upon their main line, which consisted of dismounted cavalry posted behind barricades. After a failed first charge on the barricades, the Yankees carried them with a second assault and drove Wheeler's men into Waynesboro. In town, Kilpatrick discovered a second line of barricades, which he also carried by direct assault, routing the Rebels. Baird's Third Division, including the Seventy-fifth Indiana, supported Kilpatrick. *Official Records*, ser. 1, vol. 44:55, 204, 364–65.

12. Brig. Gen. Jefferson C. Davis, commander of the Fourteenth Army Corps, ordered the army's pontoon bridge removed after his troops had crossed. Although some blacks were allowed to cross as well, most were left behind on the opposite bank of Ebenezer Creek. Panic ensued among the refugees when rumors spread that Rebel troops were approaching. Some blacks tried to cross the creek and drowned in the attempt. Davis defended his decision as a military necessity but was harshly criticized for this inhumane blunder by a number of Union officers, enlisted men, and

politicians. Hughes and Whitney, *Jefferson Davis in Blue,* 308–14; Bailey, *War and Ruin,* 93–94.

13. 1st Lt. Alonzo W. Coe of Joliet, Illinois, a member of Battery I, Second Illinois Light Artillery since 1862, was killed by a shell during an artillery duel with a Confederate battery on December 9, 1864. Reece, *Report of the Adjutant General of the State of Illinois* 8:701, 724. Further details on Coe's death may be found in Thaddeus C. S. Brown, Samuel J. Murphy, and William G. Putney, *Behind the Guns: The History of Battery I, 2nd Regiment, Illinois Light Artillery* (Carbondale: Southern Illinois Univ. Press, 1965), 127–28.

14. Miller was correct in that Union naval forces were near Sherman's army, although some distance from Fort Jackson. On December 13, Rear Adm. John A. Dahlgren of the South Atlantic Blockading Squadron sent word to Sherman that he had two ironclad ships at Wassaw Sound and a force of gunboats at Ossabaw Sound and the Savannah River, east and southeast of the city. Dahlgren believed that the best way to open communications with the army was from Ossabaw Sound into the Ogeechee River. Unfortunately for the Federals, the river was guarded several miles upstream by Confederate-held Fort McAllister, although Dahlgren thought that Sherman could successfully assault the fort. *Official Records,* ser. 1, vol. 44, p. 708. U.S. Naval War Records Office, *Official Records of the Union and Confederate Navies in the War of the Rebellion,* 30 vols. (Washington, D.C.: GPO, 1894–1922), ser. 1, vol. 16, pp. 140–41.

15. Fort McAllister was an earthen work located about twelve miles south of Savannah and seven miles from the Atlantic on the Great Ogeechee River. The fort was the key to the city's defenses and to the opening of a supply and communications link from the Union fleet to Sherman's forces. Although impervious to naval bombardment, the fort was vulnerable to land attack. Once McAllister was taken, communications were established with the coast and the Union fleet landed needed supplies for Sherman's army. Bailey, *War and Ruin,* 103; Faust, *Historical Times Illustrated Encyclopedia,* 275.

16. Maj. Gen. George H. Thomas, under siege in Nashville by Hood's Army of Tennessee, attacked the Confederates on December 15–16, 1864, and drove them from the field. *Official Records,* ser. 1, vol. 45, part 1, p. 40.

17. The rumor placing Gen. Joseph E. Johnston in command of Confederate troops in the region was premature. According to orders from Robert E. Lee dated February 22, 1865, Johnston was placed in command of two departments (Tennessee, Georgia and South Carolina, and Georgia-Florida) and then moved to oppose Sherman's army. *Official Records,* ser. 1 vol. 47, pt. 2, p. 1248. In December 1864, Lt. Gen. William J. Hardee technically commanded the Department of South Carolina, Georgia and Florida from Savannah, while Gen. P. G. T. Beauregard served as Hardee's superior in command of the Military Division of the West. *Official Records,* ser. 1, vol. 39, pt. 1, 4, 805; pt. 2, 880; ser. 1, vol. 44, 875.

18. Maj. Gen. Henry Warner Slocum (1827–1894), a veteran of the fighting at First Bull Run, Chancellorsville, Gettysburg, and several other battles, led the "Left Wing" of Sherman's army (the Fourteenth and Twentieth Army Corps) during the March to the Sea. Warner, *Generals in Blue,* 451–53.

19. Jefferson Davis, president of the Confederacy, died in 1889.

CHAPTER 11

1. Thomas reported that 4,462 soldiers and 53 artillery pieces were captured from Hood's army in the two-day Battle of Nashville. *Official Records*, ser. 1, vol. 45, pt. 1, p. 40.

2. Revolutionary War officer Count Casimir Pulaski was killed in the unsuccessful Franco-American assault on British-held Savannah on October 9, 1779. The monument to Pulaski still stands in the city.

3. Miller makes reference to a joint Union army-navy expedition in December 1864 to capture Wilmington, North Carolina, the last major port still in Confederate hands. Maj. Gen. Benjamin F. Butler commanded the land attack while Rear Adm. David D. Porter led the Union fleet. Beset by a number of problems, Butler and Porter ultimately failed in their attack on Fort Fisher, the key to Wilmington's defenses, and the Federal forces withdrew. Faust, *Historical Times Illustrated Encyclopedia*, 99–100.

4. Here Sgts. William Jasper and John Newton captured ten British soldiers who were taking American prisoners to Savannah to be executed. Miller is probably referring to one of the editions of Mason Locke Weems's *Life of General Francis Marion, a Celebrated Partisan Officer, in the Revolutionary War*, first published in 1809 but republished in the 1840s and 1850s.

5. Brig. Gen. Alfred Howe Terry (1827–1890), commander of the second Fort Fisher expedition, reported capturing 169 artillery pieces, 112 officers, and 1,971 enlisted men. Terry, a superior court clerk before the war, led a regiment at First Manassas and at the capture of Port Royal, South Carolina, and Fort Pulaski, Georgia. Promoted to brigadier general, Terry participated in Union efforts against Charleston, Richmond, and Petersburg. After service with Maj. Gen. Benjamin Butler during his failed attempt to capture Fort Fisher in December 1864, Terry commanded the joint army-navy force that took the stronghold on January 15, 1865. Terry was promoted to major general for his efforts and commanded a corps in the North Carolina campaign. Warner, *Generals in Blue*, 497–98; *Official Records*, ser. 1, vol. 46, pt. 1, p. 399.

6. Richmond was not evacuated until April 2–3, 1865.

7. Miller expressed a common sentiment in Sherman's army. Because South Carolina had been the first state to secede and its troops had fired the first shots of the war, many Federal soldiers believed the state deserved special punishment. Joseph T. Glatthaar, *The March to the Sea and Beyond: Sherman's Troops in the Savannah and Carolinas Campaign* (New York: New York Univ. Press, 1985), 79–80. In addition, historian Reid Mitchell argues that because the Carolinas did not "look, sound, or smell much like home," the plantations were built on the evil institution of slavery, and many soldiers had been gone from their homes for a long time, Federal troops were comfortable with treating the inhabitants more harshly. Mitchell, *Vacant Chair*, 36–37.

8. Probably Lt. Col. Frederick S. Lewie (1830–1877) of the Fifteenth South Carolina, who had been granted a furlough to visit his home, where smallpox had broken out, and was captured before reaching his destination. He was paroled in North Carolina. D. Augustus Dickert, *History of Kershaw's Brigade* (Newberry, N.C.: Elbert H. Aull, 1899; reprint, Dayton, Ohio: Press of Morningside Bookshop, 1973), 335.

9. John White Geary (1819–1873), a veteran of Chancellorsville, Gettysburg, and Chattanooga, served as military governor of Savannah, then as commander of the Second Division, Twentieth Army Corps in the Carolinas campaign. Warner, *Generals in Blue*, 169–70.

10. The Twentieth Corps of Sherman's army contained many troops who had seen service in the Eastern theater with the Army of the Potomac in the first two years of the war. Boatner, *Civil War Dictionary*, 193–94, 199.

11. A reference to the Revolutionary War battlefield of Camden, South Carolina, where the American Army of Gen. Horatio Gates was soundly defeated by British forces under Lord Charles Cornwallis on August 16, 1780.

CHAPTER 12

1. Floyd, *History of the Seventy-Fifth Regiment*, 379.

2. *Official Records*, ser. 1, vol. 47, pt. 1, pp. 561–63.

3. Floyd, *History of the Seventy-Fifth Regiment*, 384.

4. A common term in Sherman's army, referring to Union foragers who sought provisions. Its origin is obscure. Faust, *Historical Times Illustrated Encyclopedia*, 95.

5. On the morning of March 10, a Confederate cavalry force launched a surprise attack on Kilpatrick's headquarters camp at Monroe's Cross Roads. Although the Rebels quickly routed the Federals, they failed to follow up their advantage and Kilpatrick's men were able to recapture the camp. Miller is correct that a brigade of the Fourteenth Army Corps came to Kilpatrick's assistance. Kilpatrick claimed that he lost 103 men taken prisoner, while the Confederates boasted that 350–500 Union troops were captured. John G. Barrett, *Sherman's March through the Carolinas* (Chapel Hill: Univ. of North Carolina Press, 1956), 125–30; Mark L. Bradley, *This Astounding Close: The Road to Bennett Place* (Chapel Hill: Univ. of North Carolina Press, 2000), 14–15.

6. Major Steele, in command of a twenty-man foraging party looking for horses and mules, moved six miles ahead of the army, captured eleven Confederate pickets, and returned to camp without losing a man. *Official Records*, ser. 1, vol. 47, pt. 1, p. 562.

7. Technically the Hoosiers were not the first Federal troops to enter the city, although they would continue to claim that honor long after the war. Just as the men of the Seventy-fifth reached the center of town, Fayetteville's major surrendered to Lt. Col. William E. Strong and some of Maj. Gen. Giles Smith's forces from the Seventeenth Army Corps raised the United States flag over the market house. Mark L. Bradley, *Last Stand in the Carolinas: The Battle of Bentonville* (Campbell, Calif.: Savas Woodbury Publishers, 1996), 108–9. Also see J. G. Essington's March 11, 1865, diary entry, published in the *National Tribune* on March 7, 1889.

8. Miller was correct. Although General Baird's men maintained order in the town, and the Federals committed few acts of personal violence against Fayetteville's citizens, a good deal of personal property was destroyed. General Baird reported that his troops eliminated four of the city's cotton factories, two iron foundries, and the printing offices of three newspapers. *Official Records*, ser. 1, vol. 47, pt. 1, p. 551.

9. Union forces under Maj. Gen. Phil Sheridan routed Gen. Jubal Early's army at Waynesborough, Virginia, on March 2, 1865. Faust, *Historical Times Illustrated Encyclopedia*, 810–11. Maj. Gen. John M. Schofield (1831–1906) was commander of the Twenty-third Army Corps through the Atlanta and Franklin-Nashville campaigns. In February 1865, Schofield was named as head of the Department of North Carolina, including two army corps. Warner, *Generals in Blue*, 425–26. By this time, Schofield and one division of the Twenty-third Army Corps had moved from New Bern to Kingston to join the remainder of the corps marching up from Wilmington. They then continued on their way join Sherman's army at Goldsboro. Bradley, *Last Stand in the Carolinas*, 24.

10. Although Johnston's army enjoyed a great deal of initial success at Bentonville on March 19 by routing one division of the Fourteenth Army Corps, another division of the corps held fast as did a large portion of the Twentieth Army Corps.

11. The guns in question belonged to Lt. Samuel D. Webb's Nineteenth Indiana Battery, attached to the Fourteenth Army Corps. Bradley, *Last Stand in the Carolinas*, 337, 433. The Second Minnesota Infantry lost only two men wounded during the engagement, while the Seventy-fifth Indiana suffered no casualties. *Official Records*, ser. 1, vol. 47, pt. 1, p. 73.

12. Most likely the First South Carolina Heavy Artillery of Rhett's brigade, Taliaferro's division, Hardee's corps. Bradley, *Last Stand in the Carolinas*, 283–89.

13. Miller's remarkable ability to recall names and unit designations failed him here. No soldier with this name fought in the Fourth Georgia at Bentonville. Two possibilities are F. M. White of Company A, Thirty-ninth Georgia Infantry, who enlisted in March 1864 at Dalton, Georgia, or Francis M. White of Company A, First Georgia Regulars. Both regiments fought at the Battle of Bentonville, but no information could be found as to whether either soldier participated in the action. Compiled Service Records of Confederate Soldiers Who Served in Organizations from the State of Georgia, RG 109, Microcopy 266, Rolls 124, 446, NA.

14. Brig. Gen. Charles J. Paine's division of Maj. Gen. Alfred H. Terry's Provisional Corps consisted of nine regiments of United States Colored Troops. Terry's corps was made up of detachments from the Twenty-fourth and Twenty-fifth Army Corps. Bradley, *This Astounding Close*, 26–27.

15. Pvt. James Preble of Company K, Twelfth New York Cavalry was found guilty of the attempted rape of two women and the actual rape of a third and was shot to death as Miller describes. Robert I. Alotta, *Civil War Justice: Union Army Executions under Lincoln* (Shippensburg, Pa.: White Mane Publishing, 1989), 165; Bradley, *This Astounding Close*, 53–54.

16. Many soldiers apparently agreed with Miller regarding the disagreeable nature of military executions. For similar sentiments, see Linderman, *Embattled Courage*, 58–59.

17. This may have been either Lt. Gen. Wade Hampton or Col. John Logan Black, the last two mounted men to cross the Neuse River. Bradley, *This Astounding Close*, 97.

18. Company F's Lew Ginger recalled that General Baird told the Hoosiers they had done well and could consider themselves "privileged characters," urging them to

have fun but to respect private property. The men consumed at least part of three barrels of "applejack" then looted robes and masks from an Odd Fellows Lodge located on the top floor of a nearby three-story building. After parading around camp in the regalia, most of the men rested in the shadow of the building, singing songs, telling stories, and continuing to drink. Three or four men entered the lodge again, found a skeleton, and threw it through the window, glass, sash, and all. The men sitting below saw the flying skeleton approaching them with outstretched arms and fled the scene. *National Tribune*, May 2, 1889.

19. Sherman and Johnston met at the Bennett house near Durham's Station, North Carolina, on April 17 and 18 to discuss surrender terms. Sherman's proposals were rejected in Washington, but a peace agreement was finally signed on April 26. Faust, *Historical Times Illustrated Encyclopedia*, 683.

20. General Sherman's Special Field Order Number 58, issued at Raleigh, North Carolina, on April 19, 1865, noted that a suspension of hostilities had been established and that until the peace was arranged, a line would separate the two armies. The order further urged all officers to prevent "acts of vulgarity, rowdyism, or petty crime." *Official Records*, ser. 1, vol. 47, pt. 3, p. 250.

21. General Baird asked for permission to move his men to more open country, where they could be kept busy drilling. This would prevent them from foraging in the countryside and relieve the "poor inhabitants" of the area, who had been "stripped of almost everything they possessed." *Official Records*, ser. 1, vol. 47, pt. 3, p. 260.

Chapter 13

1. Floyd, *History of the Seventy-Fifth Regiment*, 387.
2. Ibid., 391–92.
3. *Howard Tribune* (Kokomo, Ind.), June 22, 1865.
4. Sherman and Johnston had signed a "Memorandum or Basis of Agreement" on April 18, 1865. In this document, Sherman overstepped his authority and dealt with political questions as well as military matters. The Union commander negotiated for the surrender of all remaining Confederate forces, not just Johnston's army. He allowed the Southerners to retain their arms and deliver them to their respective state arsenals, recognized Southern state governments, reestablished Federal courts in the Confederate states, guaranteed political and property rights for Southerners, and granted a general amnesty for those who had participated in the war. President Andrew Johnson and his Cabinet reviewed the document a few days later and unanimously rejected the agreement. Secretary of War Edwin Stanton's objections even appeared in the *New York Times* on April 23. The following day General Grant met with Sherman and advised him to offer Johnston the same terms proposed to Lee at Appomattox Court House. Sherman did so and signed the final surrender terms on April 26. Although many Northern newspapers condemned Sherman's actions, most of his soldiers stood behind their general. Bradley, *This Astounding Close*, 206–32, 268–69.
5. One Richmond newspaper labeled the march "the grandest military pageant of the day" and believed that "perhaps another such opportunity will not be presented the present generation." *Richmond Times*, May 12, 1865.
6. The scene of Federal defeats in July 1861 and August 1862.

7. Davis was captured near Irwinville, Georgia, on May 10, 1865. Contrary to popular belief at the time, Davis was not dressed as a woman but only used his wife's shawl to cover his head and shoulders in an attempt to escape. Faust, *Historical Times Illustrated Encyclopedia,* 208–9.

8. For some unknown reason, Miller's diary ends here and does not include his participation in the Grand Review or his journey back to Indiana.

BIBLIOGRAPHY

Books

Primary Sources

Angle, Paul M., ed. *Three Years in the Army of the Cumberland: The Letters and Diary of Major James A. Connolly*. Bloomington: Indiana University Press, 1959.

Basler, Roy P., ed. *The Collected Works of Abraham Lincoln*. 9 vols. New Brunswick, N.J.: Rutgers University Press, 1953.

Biberstine, Nora. *Wells County Marriages, 1838–1868*. Bluffton, Ind.: Wells County Historical Society, n.d.

Billings, John D. *Hardtack and Coffee: The Unwritten Story of Army Life*. Boston: George M. Smith, 1888. Reprint, Chicago: R. R. Donnelley & Sons, 1960.

Bowen, B. F. *Biographical Memoirs of Wells County, Indiana*. Logansport, Ind.: B. F. Bowen, 1903.

Chapman, Chandler P. *Roster of Wisconsin Volunteers, War of the Rebellion, 1861–1865*. 2 vols. Madison: Democrat Printing, 1886.

Dickert, D. Augustus. *History of Kershaw's Brigade*. Newberry, N.C.: Elbert H. Aull, 1899. Reprint, Dayton, Ohio: Press of Morningside Bookshop, 1973.

Duke, Basil W. *History of Morgan's Cavalry*. Cincinnati: Miami Printing and Publishing, 1867.

Evans, Clement A., ed. *Confederate Military History, Extended Edition*. 17 vols. Atlanta: Confederate Publishing, 1899. Reprint, Wilmington, N.C.: Broadfoot Publishing, 1987–89.

Fitch, John. *Annals of the Army of the Cumberland*. Philadelphia: J. B. Lippincott, 1864.

Floyd, David B. *History of the Seventy-Fifth Regiment of Indiana Infantry Volunteers, Its Organization, Campaigns and Battles, 1862–65*. Philadelphia: Lutheran Publication Society, 1893.

Heitman, Francis B. *Historical Register and Dictionary of the United States Army*. 2 vols. Washington, D.C.: GPO, 1903.

Hewett, Janet B., ed. *The Roster of Confederate Soldiers*. 16 vols. Wilmington, N.C.: Broadfoot Publishing, 1996.

Kautz, August V. *The Company Clerk*. Philadelphia: Lippincott, 1865.

Kennedy, Joseph C. G. *Population of the United States in 1860; Compiled from the Original Returns of the Eighth Census, under the Direction of the Secretary of the Interior*. Washington, D.C.: GPC, 1864.

Lewis Publishing. *Biographical and Historical Record of Adams and Wells Counties, Indiana*. Chicago: Lewis Publishing, 1887.

Minnesota Adjutant General. *Annual Report of the Adjutant General of the State of Minnesota*. St. Paul: Pioneer Printing, 1866.

Minnesota, State of. *Minnesota in the Civil and Indian Wars, 1861–1865.* St. Paul: Pioneer Press, 1890.

Nichols, George W. *The Story of the Great March.* New York: Harper & Brothers, 1865.

Ohio Adjutant General. *Official Roster of the Soldiers of the State of Ohio in the War of the Rebellion, 1861–1866.* 12 vols. Akron, Ohio: Werner, 1886–95.

Palmer, John M. *Personal Recollections of John M. Palmer: The Story of an Earnest Life.* Cincinnati: Robert Clarke, 1901.

Reece, J. N. *Report of the Adjutant General of the State of Illinois.* 9 vols. Springfield, Ill.: Phillips Brothers and the Journal Company, 1900–1902.

Reid, Whitelaw. *Ohio in the War.* 2 vols. Cincinnati: Moore, Wilstach & Baldwin, 1868.

Report of the Adjutant General of the State of Kentucky. 2 vols. Frankfort, Ky.: John H. Harney, 1866.

Scribner, Theodore T. *Indiana's Roll of Honor.* Vol. 2. Indianapolis: A. D. Streight, 1866.

Sherman, William T. *Memoirs of General William T. Sherman.* 2 vols. New York: D. Appleton, 1875.

Terrell, William H. H. *Report of the Adjutant General of the State of Indiana.* 8 vols. Indianapolis: Alexander H. Conner, W. R. Holloway and Samuel M. Douglass, 1865–69.

U.S. Adjutant General's Office. *Official Army Register of the Volunteer Force of the United States Army.* 8 vols. Washington, D.C.: Adjutant General's Office, 1865.

U.S. Naval War Records Office. *Official Records of the Union and Confederate Navies in the War of the Rebellion.* 30 vols. Washington, D.C.: GPO, 1894–1922.

U.S. Surgeon General's Office. *The Medical and Surgical History of the War of the Rebellion.* 6 vols. Washington, D.C.: GPO, 1870–88.

U.S. War Department. *Revised Regulations for the Army of the United States, 1861.* Philadelphia: J. G. L. Brown, 1861.

————. *Revised United States Army Regulations of 1861.* Washington, D.C.: GPO, 1863.

————. *The War of the Rebellion: A Compilation of the Official Records of the Union and Confederate Armies.* 128 vols. Washington, D.C.: GPO, 1880–1901.

SECONDARY SOURCES

Adams, George Worthington. *Doctors in Blue: The Medical History of the Union Army in the Civil War.* New York: Henry Schuman, 1952.

Alotta, Robert I. *Civil War Justice: Union Army Executions under Lincoln.* Shippensburg, Pa.: White Mane Publishing, 1989.

Bailey, Anne J. *War and Ruin: William T. Sherman and the Savannah Campaign.* Wilmington, Del.: Scholarly Resources, 2003.

Baird, John A., Jr. *Profile of a Hero: The Story of Absalom Baird, His Family, and the American Military Tradition.* Philadelphia: Dorrance, 1977.

Barrett, John G. *Sherman's March Through the Carolinas*. Chapel Hill: University of North Carolina Press, 1956.

Baumgartner, Richard A., and Larry M. Strayer. *Echoes of Battle: The Struggle for Chattanooga*. Huntington, W.Va.: Blue Acorn Press, 1996.

———. *Kennesaw Mountain, June 1864: Bitter Standoff at the Gibraltar of Georgia*. Huntington, W.Va.: Blue Acorn Press, 1998.

Boatner, Mark Mayo, III. *The Civil War Dictionary*. New York: David McKay, 1988.

Bradley, Mark L. *Last Stand in the Carolinas: The Battle of Bentonville*. Campbell, Calif.: Savas Woodbury, 1996.

Bradley, Mark L. *This Astounding Close: The Road to Bennett Place*. Chapel Hill: University of North Carolina Press, 2000.

Brown, Thaddeus C. S., Samuel J. Murphy, and William G. Putney. *Behind the Guns: The History of Battery I, 2nd Regiment, Illinois Light Artillery*. Carbondale: Southern Illinois University Press, 1965.

Castel, Albert. *Decision in the West: The Atlanta Campaign of 1864*. Lawrence: University Press of Kansas, 1992.

Cozzens, Peter. *No Better Place to Die: The Battle of Stones River*. Urbana: University of Illinois Press, 1990.

———. *The Shipwreck of Their Hopes: The Battles for Chattanooga*. Urbana: University of Illinois Press, 1994.

———. *This Terrible Sound: The Battle of Chickamauga*. Urbana: University of Illinois Press, 1992.

Downey, Fairfax. *The Guns at Gettysburg* New York: David McKay, 1958.

Duncan, Louis C. *The Medical Department of the United States Army in the Civil War*. N.p., n.d. Reprint, Gaithersburg, Md.: Olde Soldier Books, 1987.

Faust, Patricia L., ed. *Historical Times Illustrated Encyclopedia of the Civil War*. New York: Harper Collins, 1986.

Glatthaar, Joseph T. *The March to the Sea and Beyond: Sherman's Troops in the Savannah and Carolinas Campaign*. New York: New York University Press, 1985.

Grimsley, Mark. *The Hard Hand of War: Union Military Policy Toward Southern Civilians, 1861–1865*. Cambridge: Cambridge University Press, 1995.

Hess, Earl J. *Banners to the Breeze: The Kentucky Campaign, Corinth, and Stones River*. Lincoln: University of Nebraska Press, 2000.

———. *The Union Soldier in Battle: Enduring the Ordeal of Combat*. Lawrence: University Press of Kansas, 1997.

Hughes, Nathaniel Cheairs, Jr., and Gordon D. Whitney. *Jefferson Davis in Blue: The Life of Sherman's Relentless Warrior* Baton Rouge: Louisiana State University Press, 2002.

Johnson, Mark W. *That Body of Brave Men: The U.S. Regular Infantry and The Civil War in the West*. Cambridge, Mass.: Da Capo Press, 2003.

Kaser, David. *Books and Libraries in Camp and Battle: The Civil War Experience*. Westport, Conn.: Greenwood Press, 1984.

Lambert, D. Warren. *When the Ripe Pears Fell: The Battle of Richmond, Kentucky*. Richmond, Ky.: Madison County Historical Society, 1995.

Linderman, Gerald F. *Embattled Courage: The Experience of Combat in the American Civil War*. New York: Free Press, 1987.

Lord, Francis A. *They Fought for the Union*. Harrisburg, Pa.: Stackpole, 1960.

Marszalek, John F. *Sherman: A Soldier's Passion for Order*. New York: Free Press, 1993.

Martin, Samuel J. *Kill-Cavalry: The Life of Union General Hugh Judson Kilpatrick*. Mechanicsburg, Pa.: Stackpole Books, 2000.

McDonough, James Lee. *War in Kentucky: From Shiloh to Perryville*. Knoxville: University of Tennessee Press, 1994.

McPherson, James M. *For Cause and Comrades: Why Men Fought in the Civil War*. New York: Oxford University Press, 1997.

Mitchell, Reid. *Civil War Soldiers: Their Expectations and Their Experiences*. New York: Viking Penguin, 1988.

———. *The Vacant Chair: The Northern Soldier Leaves Home*. New York: Oxford University Press, 1993.

Noe, Kenneth W. *Perryville: This Grand Havoc of Battle*. Lexington: University Press of Kentucky, 2001.

Ramage, James A. *Rebel Raider: The Life of General John Hunt Morgan*. Lexington: University Press of Kentucky, 1986.

Schmidt, Alvin J. *Fraternal Organizations*. Westport, Conn.: Greenwood Press, 1980.

Sword, Wiley. *Mountains Touched with Fire: Chattanooga Besieged, 1863*. New York: St. Martin's Press, 1995.

Thornbrough, Emma Lou. *Indiana in the Civil War Era, 1850–1880*. Indianapolis: Indiana Historical Society, 1965.

Warner, Ezra J. *Generals in Blue: Lives of the Union Commanders*. Baton Rouge: Louisiana State University Press, 1964.

———. *Generals in Gray: Lives of the Confederate Commanders*. Baton Rouge: Louisiana State University Press, 1959.

Weitz, Mark A. *A Higher Duty: Desertion among Georgia Troops during the Civil War*. Lincoln: University of Nebraska Press, 2000.

NEWSPAPERS

Bluffton (Ind.) Banner
Bluffton (Ind.) Evening News
Charleston (Ill.) Daily Courier
Howard Tribune (Kokomo, Ind.)
Indianapolis Daily Journal
National Tribune (Washington, D.C.)

New York Times
Noblesville (Ind.) Republican Ledger
Portland (Ind.) Commercial Review
Richmond (Va.) Times
Wabash (Ind.) Plain-Dealer

CENSUS AND MILITARY RECORDS, NATIONAL ARCHIVES AND RECORDS ADMINISTRATION, WASHINGTON, D.C.

Compiled Service Records of Confederate Soldiers Who Served in Organizations from the State of Georgia. Microcopy 266, RG 109.

Compiled Service Records of Confederate Soldiers Who Served in Organizations from the State of Mississippi. Microcopy 269, RG 109.

Compiled Service Records of Volunteer Union Soldiers. RG 94.

Pension file of William Bluffton Miller. Pension Records of Volunteer Soldiers Who Served in Organizations from the State of Indiana. RG 15.

Registers of Enlistments in the United States Army, 1798–1914. Microcopy 233, RG 94.

Unbound Regimental Papers, 75th Indiana Volunteer Infantry. RG 94.

U.S. Bureau of the Census. *Eighth Census of the United States, 1860, Population Schedules for Wells County, Indiana.* Microcopy 653, Reel 309, RG 29.

INDEX

Fighting for Libery and Right was designed and typeset on a Macintosh computer system using QuarkXPress software. The body text is set in 11/13.5 Goudy and display type is set in Hadriano. This book was designed and typeset by Liz Lester and manufactured by Thomson-Shore, Inc.